NT Server: Management and Control

NT Server: Management and Control

Kenneth L. Spencer

For book and bookstore information

http://www.prenhall.com

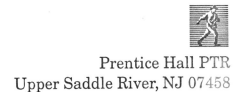

Prentice Hall PTR
Upper Saddle River, NJ 07458

Library of Congress Cataloging-in-Publication Data

```
Spencer, Kenneth L., 1951-
    NT server : management and control / Kenneth L. Spencer.
    p.  cm.
    Includes index.
    ISBN 0-13-107046-0 (paper)
    1. Client/server computing. 2. Microsoft Windows NT. I. Title.
    QA76.9.C55S75  1995
    005.4'4—dc20                                      95-34457
                                                         CIP
```

Editorial/production supervision: *BooksCraft, Inc., Indianapolis, IN*
Cover design director: *Jerry Votta*
Cover design: *Design Source*
Acquisitions editor: *Mike Meehan*
Manufacturing manager: *Alexis R. Heydt*

© 1996 by Prentice Hall PTR
Prentice-Hall, Inc.
A Simon & Schuster Company
Upper Saddle River, NJ 07458

Printed in the United States of America

10 9 8 7 6 5 4 3

ISBN: 0-13-107046-0

Prentice-Hall International (UK) Limited, *London*
Prentice-Hall of Australia Pty. Limited, *Sydney*
Prentice-Hall Canada Inc., *Toronto*
Prentice-Hall Hispanoamericana, S.A., *Mexico*
Prentice-Hall of India Private Limited, *New Delhi*
Prentice-Hall of Japan, Inc., *Tokyo*
Simon & Schuster Asia Pte. Ltd., *Singapore*
Editora Prentice-Hall do Brasil, Ltda., *Rio de Janeiro*

Table of Contents

Appendixes

Preface

INTRODUCTION

This book is the first in the series called Managing the Enterprise with Microsoft BackOffice from Prentice Hall. Each book in the series will focus on using a particular piece of BackOffice in a production environment but will also touch on other parts of BackOffice and other products as we find them useful.

My good friend Nick Gandhi joins me on the remaining books in the series as co-author. Nick is a very talented individual with lots of network experience with many platforms and will provide much insight into the other books.

My approach to this book has been to include anything that is relevant to managing an enterprise NT network, ranging from five clients to thousands of clients. The tools, tips, step-by-step lists, and notes were all designed to provide useful information on taming and managing an NT Server LAN.

TIPS ON USING THIS BOOK

Some commands and program lines in this book show a dash (-) at the end of a line and a second indented line under the first line. The dash indicates a continued command line or program line that should all be on one line. This syntax is also used on some Registry keys that are too long to fit on one line. A sample command follows,

```
WINNT32 /u:"This is my answer file name" -
   /b
```

Step-by-step lists are used extensively in this book due to a large number of requests from many different readers regarding magazine articles, books, and consulting engagements. Short how-to lists have been the primary request for my magazine columns and previous books. I have also heard from publishers that this type of information is frequently requested. FYI: I also use the material for this book as a handy reference tool when I am consulting or trying to solve a problem.

The book is designed as a reference tool for NT Server managers and administrators, as well as anyone who uses NT Server with more than a passing interest. The preface contains an overview of the NT Server architecture and mentions many of NT's features. Most items in the preface are covered in more detail later in the book. For instance, if you are interested in Network features, check out the notes in the preface and then refer to Chapter 3 on network configuration and management for more details.

There are also many cross references in the book to point you to related material. The page number in the reference should provide a starting point you can use to browse through the related material.

OPEN ARCHITECTURE

NT Server and all BackOffice products are members of Microsoft's open architecture that is defined by the WOSA (Windows Open Systems Architecture) specification. WOSA has long held the promise of a family of operating systems that were open and portable. 1993 was the year that this promise began to bear fruit with the introduction of NT 3.1.

NT Server currently sits at the high end of the WOSA architecture. Other members of the WOSA family include Pen Windows, Windows 3.x, Windows 95, Microsoft's At Work architecture, and Windows NT Workstation 3.5. Future members of the WOSA family include Windows NT 4.0 or Windows NT 96 (97?), which is now known as Cairo.

Evidence of the power of the WOSA architecture is available in many areas. Many of the application programs that ship with both Windows for Workgroups and the NT family are the same for both systems and interoperate in a network. These programs include Microsoft Mail, Schedule +, and many standard Windows utilities such as Write, Notepad, and File Manager. Other features such as the fax capabilities of Windows for Workgroups 3.11 are members of the At Work family. Windows 95 takes the integration one step farther as both it and NT are built on top of the Win32 API. Microsoft has taken a great step with the introduction of Windows NT 3.51 to standardized Win32 between both platforms.

SQL Server is another product that is designed to be part of WOSA. SQL Server for NT is a full Windows 32-bit database system that uses the full power and features of NT. SQL Server is a powerful database system that can run on a wide variety of NT systems and takes advantage of NT features such as multi-threading and multiple processors. SQL Server comes with tools for other 16-bit members of the WOSA family that allow them to administer SQL Server and serve as application front-ends in a true client–server environment. Other Microsoft and third-party tools such as Visual Basic, Access, and Microsoft Office can also access data stored in an SQL Server database.

The power of the WOSA architecture continues to move forward with the introduction of Windows 95. Windows 95 is a 32-bit operating system that shares many of the features of NT, including the ability to run NT programs. Windows 95 will also be the first Intel-specific version of Windows to run without DOS. This means that memory managers should be history (at least as we know them now) and you should not see any more EMM386 Exception errors or General Protection Faults. Other unhandled exceptions can occur with NT, but they are usually handled much more gracefully via the Event Log and do not affect other applications.

NT 3.1 OVERVIEW

NT 3.1 was the first version of NT introduced. The 3.1 version was used because the NT 3.1 interface was based on the Windows and Windows for Workgroups 3.1. The File Manager and other network features were comparable with Windows for Workgroups, making NT 3.1 feel like Windows' big brother, which is exactly the case.

NT 3.1 was the first operating system designed in WOSA as a high-end platform that would run on a wide variety of hardware platforms including Intel, MIPS, and Alpha processors. NT 3.1 was scaleable and easy to manage with its many similarities to Windows 3.1.

NT 3.1 introduced a number of utilities such as User Manager for Domains, Disk Administrator, Server Manager, Event Viewer, Performance Monitor, and others for managing the server, workstation, and network features of NT. Third-party vendors began to add to the NT utilities by porting well-known UNIX programs and creating others to NT.

NT's modular architecture provides the foundation for powerful systems such as SQL Server, Systems Management Server, Exchange Server, and others. Powerful solutions using these products and many others have been built on NT 3.1 that have provided many business solutions.

NEW FEATURES IN NT WORKSTATION 3.5 AND NT SERVER 3.51

NT Workstation 3.5 and NT Server 3.51 have several new features. The following list contains the major new features of 3.5, with each list entry followed by the chapter starting page number containing the main reference to the topic. N/A means that particular topic is specific to the NT Workstation version and is not covered in depth in this book.

- Improved performance (page 301)
- Runs with less stringent system requirements (memory speed, total memory, etc.) (page 23)
- Automatic restart with memory dump for server crashes (page 23)
- Integrated PCI bus support (N/A)
- Account lockout (page 337)
- TCP/IP performance and management improvements with DHCP and WINS (page 85)
- TCP/IP and IPX protocols can be routed over Remote Access Service (RAS) (page 85)
- Plotter support (N/A)
- OLE 2.01 (N/A)
- New kernel debugger for building device drivers (N/A)
- Windows 3.x programs run in multiple virtual DOS machines (VDM) (N/A)
- OpenGL interface 3D graphics API (N/A)

☞ Supports TrueType and Adobe Type 1 fonts (N/A)

☞ NetWare client software (page 85)

Most of the new features and improvements in the 3.51 versions are directly beneficial to NT Server-based networks. The 3.51 versions of NT are generally faster and easier to manage than the original 3.1 version.

NEW FEATURES IN NT 3.51

Just as I was wrapping up this book NT 3.51 was heading into a short beta program. You will find mention of some NT 3.51 features in the book, but only so far as I was able to test them during the beta program. The following list contains a short description of the major new features in NT 3.51.

☞ File and directory compression features added to NTFS File and Directory compression (page 201)

☞ Windows 95 common controls (several chapters)

☞ Windows 95 help system (N/A)

☞ New IPX stack for improved performance

☞ File input/output performance features (N/A)

☞ New command line utilities (PENTNT, NTBOOKS, and COMPACT) (several chapters)

☞ New licensing options (overview on page xxv and License Management applet on page 32)

☞ New Console applet in Control Panel for configuring DOS command prompt windows (N/A)

☞ Support for PCMCIA devices (N/A)

☞ New setup features for licensing and detection of the floating point problem in some Pentium processors

☞ New service API functions

☞ Replaceable security module for interactive logon

☞ All new Win32 API functions for Windows 95 are stubbed in NT 3.51

DIFFERENCES BETWEEN NT SERVER AND NT WORKSTATION

NT Server Is a Superset of NT Workstation

NT Server can do anything that NT Workstation can do. NT Server simply adds several new features and utilities to the basic NT system. NT Server also removes the 10-connection maximum that NT provides for network users, opens up the RAS connections to 256, and adds domains and many other network features.

NT Server is designed to perform as a network server and is tuned accordingly. NT Workstation is likewise tuned for higher graphics performance in its role as a high-performance workstation.

Domain Overview

NT Server uses domains for managing users and servers. The concept of domains is familiar to LAN Manager 2.2 managers but may take some getting used to for NetWare administrators.

Domains are groups of NT Server systems in a network. A domain shares the account and security database over the entire domain. A network user logs onto a domain, not an individual server. Administration of a domain is much easier because it can be managed as a single entity for most actions.

Domains can also have trust relationships with other domains. A trust relationship between two domains allows the users of one domain to be granted access to resources in another domain without creating additional user accounts for the users in the other domain.

Chapter 3 on the network configuration (page 85) has a more detailed discussion of domains and how to implement them.

Central User Profiles   User profiles allow users to log on to any NT system in the domain and have exactly the same configuration and preferences as when they use their own machine. This feature is also included in Windows 95, further enhancing the WOSA product line and its management capabilities.

Services for Macintosh   Services for Macintosh (SFM) allows NT Server to offer file and print services for Macintosh systems in addition to DOS, Windows, and NT clients. Users of these different systems can transparently share files from one system to another.

Extended Remote Access Service Support for up to 256 Ports Remote Access Service provides remote access capabilities for NT and NT Server. RAS supports both dial-up, ISDN, and X.25 connection methods. NT Server allows up to 256 RAS ports. This is a major enhancement over Windows NT desktop, which provides support for only one port.

NT SERVER SPECIFICATIONS

The following list identifies the general specifications for NT Server 3.51. All options shown are included with NT Server. Additional options such as the DECnet protocol can be purchased from other sources.

Maximum connections	Unlimited
Maximum RAM	4GB
Maximum hard-disk storage	408 million terabytes
Minimum hardware requirements	16MB of RAM, 90MB disk, 386/25

RAID support	0,1,2, and 5
Network topologies	asynchronous, Ethernet, FDDI, ISDN, Token Ring
Transport protocols	AppleTalk, DLC, NetBEUI, OSI, SPX/IPX, TCP/IP

OPEN ARCHITECTURE OF NT

WOSA is Microsoft's strategy for all the different components of the Windows architecture. WOSA includes not only NT, Windows 3.11, Windows for Workgroups 3.11, and Windows 95 but also other software platforms such as SQL Server and Systems Management Server (SMS).

NT interoperates with WOSA and all the WOSA components in one manner or another. Most WOSA specifications (such as MAPI and ODBC) are published, making it easy for third-party vendors to develop applications that also participate in WOSA.

Protocol Independence

NT provides support for TCP/IP, NetBEUI, IPX/SPX, AppleTalk (SFM), DLC, protocols, and additional protocols (such as DECnet) from third parties. This support allows NT to operate in a wide variety of networks as both a file and print server and an application server.

Standards

Distributed Computing Environment (DCE) compliant Remote Procedure Call (RPC) allows the development of NT programs that can communicate with other NT systems and systems running DCE-compatible systems. RPC is the mechanism that allows NT programs to actually split program tasks across multiple systems over a network.

Application Integration

Dynamic Data Exchange (DDE) and Network Dynamic Data Exchange (NetDDE) allow NT to integrate with any WOSA application that supports one or the other of these two standards. An NT Server can fully participate in both NetDDE and Object Linking and Embedding (OLE) sessions with other systems.

NT also supports Windows Sockets with the TCP/IP protocol. Windows for Workgroups 3.11 and Windows 95 also support Windows Sockets. Windows Sockets is API-compatible with Berkeley-style sockets found on many UNIX and other TCP/IP systems.

Client–Server Design

NT was designed as a client–server system from day one. It uses the client–server model internally and provides an enhanced client–server system for application development. SQL Server under both NT and NT Server has proven to be the easiest and fastest database for creating sophisticated applications.

NT provides many robust features that enhance the ability of SQL Server and other databases to run under NT. It is significant that in porting from OS/2 to NT the code shrank from 50,000+ lines to around 8000 lines and the product runs 10–20 times faster according to many customers.

If you combine NT, SQL Server, and a fast system like a multiprocessor Digital Equipment Corporation Alpha, you have a stable, high-performance system not available with other LAN architectures.

Common Support Structure

Advanced support features of NT include the system Registry, which tracks almost all system configuration information, the event logging system, and the performance monitoring system. These features combine to offer very effective problem tracking and a super support system for applications because each of these features is open to developers for recording application-specific information.

A good example of an application's use of these system features is SQL Server. During installation it installs its own counters in the performance monitoring system and installs an icon that loads Performance Monitor with SQL Server specific counters. This feature allows you to track things such as database performance against overall system utilization.

More and more applications should support these subsystems in the future because similar features are also included in Windows 95.

SYMMETRIC MULTIPROCESSING

NT Server supports up to four processors in its normal configuration. OEM implementations of NT Server can support up to 32 processors or more.

SMP support allows NT to use multiple processors actively to improve the performance of a system dramatically. Tests have shown from 60 to 80% improvement for each processor added, provided some other subsystem was not creating a bottleneck. I have several clients with Alpha systems and they really do live up to the speed claims. The Alpha 2100-500 with multiple processors is a joy to run with SQL Server.

SMP is most useful in environments where there is a heavy application load such as SQL Server. Servers that are providing only file and print services usually do not benefit much from adding an additional processor. If you think your system could use another processor, monitor the processor activity using Performance Monitor before making a decision.

FAULT TOLERANCE

NT Server adds several fault-tolerant features to the server environment over NT Workstation. The fault-tolerance options are discussed in more detail on page 39.

Disk Mirroring

Disk mirroring allows a system to automatically keep a second disk in sync with the master disk. Every disk write is completed to both disks. If a disk fails, the system keeps running using the other disk.

Disk Duplexing

Disk duplexing is essentially the same as disk mirroring except that in addition to the second disk the system uses a second controller for one of the disks. This configuration usually results in a faster system than one with disk mirroring only because the two controllers can read and write to the disks simultaneously and provide for failure of a controller in addition to disk failures.

RAID

Redundant Array of Inexpensive Disks (RAID) is a term used to describe several disks that are configured as a single drive. The levels of fault tolerance are rated from 0 to 5 with 5 providing the highest level of performance and fault tolerance. RAID 5 disks can drastically improve the performance of your system and provide complete fault tolerance at the disk level.

Many RAID systems allow you to hot-swap a bad disk without bringing the system down. The RAID packages usually have a fast RAID controller (like the Digital EISA or PCI controllers) that manage the RAID configuration in the controller. NT sees the entire RAID system as one drive. The physical disk drives usually plug into the RAID cabinet from the front and can be changed while the system is up and running.

NT Server 3.51 provides native support RAID level 0, 1, and 5. Other RAID levels may be used with NT Server if supported by the RAID controller and seen by NT Server as a normal disk. NT-compatible hardware controllers are available from HP, Digital Equipment Corporation, Dell, Compaq, and many other vendors.

FILE SYSTEMS

NT Server supports the NTFS, HPFS, FAT, and Macintosh file systems. Macintosh file system compatibility is provided only on NTFS volumes with SFM. NTFS is new with NT and supports many advanced features. HPFS and FAT are supported for compatibility with OS/2 and DOS, respectively. New file systems created with NT can only be NTFS or FAT. For more information on the NT file systems and using the file systems, consult Chapter 5.

NT SERVER AND MEMORY

Physical Memory

NT and NT Server both use the same memory model and support 4GB of physical memory per system with up to 2GB for applications and 2GB reserved for system storage. The NT memory system is a flat memory model and provides memory isolation between processes through its protected memory system.

Virtual Memory

NT uses a technique called paging to simulate more memory than may be physically resident in a system. Paging is the mechanism NT uses to address 4GB of memory when most systems that run NT have only between 16 and 512MB of physical memory—a long way from 4GB.

Paging creates "virtual" memory—memory that appears to be in the system but is actually not. In a paging system the operating system moves data from RAM to the hard disk to allow other data to move into RAM as it is needed. This feat is accomplished by dividing all the memory into pages of 4K each.

NT supports multiple page files, each of which may be on a separate disk. Spreading page files across multiple disks on a system with a sophisticated disk controller can improve performance. See the section on Virtual Memory in Chapter 10 (see page 328) for more information.

INTERPRETABILITY WITH LAN MANAGER AND OTHER SERVERS

NT works well with other LAN Manager systems including LAN Manager for OS/2, LAN Manager for UNIX, DEC Pathworks, and IBM LAN Server. It also interoperates well with NetWare servers and many other networks. Because NT is extensible due to its open architecture, it is likely to be enhanced by other vendors for their networks.

LICENSING

NT Server 3.5 changed the license policies and they have changed once again in version 3.51. NT Server 3.5 introduced the client license requirement where each client accessing an NT server had to have a license. This was a change from NT Advanced Server 3.1, but proved to be cost-effective in the long run, especially if you had several servers.

NT Server 3.51 has added a license wrinkle designed to lower the cost of network licenses and provide more flexibility to system managers. The Per Seat license option is the same as the license for NT Server 3.5, which required each client that accessed an NT Server to have a license.

The Per Seat option is best when your network clients all must access NT Server(s) at the same time. This license allows you to buy one license for each client and one license per server. You can add all the servers you want and pay only the cost for a server license.

The Per Server license is new and provides some flexibility for small networks or networks where only some users access NT Server and the specific users vary frequently. For instance, let's say you have a 500-user network with NetWare servers and you want to install an NT Server for use by up to 50 people. The trick is the 50 can be any 50 of the total 500 workstations on the network. With the Per Seat license, each workstation on the network would need a license. Using the Per Server license, you can license the server for 50 clients and save lots of money. According to Microsoft's documentation, you do not need client licenses for NT Server when a workstation accesses only an application such as SQL Server. You would, of course, need licenses for the product the clients are accessing.

The way licensing has been changing lately, make sure you read your license agreements and check out the latest options for the software you use. I expect to see more changes in the future as vendors such as Microsoft and others fine-tune their policies.

HARDWARE

One of the NT family's most talked about traits is its ability to run on many different hardware platforms. NT is currently running on everything from Intel PCs to many different RISC processors, including both MIPS, PowerPC, and the Digital Equipment Corporation Alpha. Each of these processors has its own strengths and weaknesses.

The portability of NT is accomplished primarily through a layer called HAL (Hardware Abstraction Layer). HAL sits between the rest of NT and the hardware and handles the software/hardware interface to interrupts, I/O, and so forth. The careful design of HAL allows programs to run on different hardware platforms without any changes, except for recompiling with a native mode compiler for the different architectures.

Intel

The Intel platform (286, 386, 486, and Pentium) is the first system that any version of Windows ran on and is still its most popular system. It is almost guaranteed that all future versions of NT will run on Intel processors. The Intel version of NT also finds itself with the widest number of native NT applications. This continues and in fact dramatically increases with the release of Windows 95 because all native Windows 95 applications are Win32 and should run on both Windows 95 and NT. Notice I said *should* and not *will* because there is the distinct possibility that some vendors will use specific features and idiosyncrasies of Windows 95 that will preclude them from running on NT.

RISC

MIPS   MIPS machines must have a CPU with an R4000 version 2.0 or later in order to run NT. Your hardware manufacturer will be able to supply the upgrade. After an upgrade your MIPS system must be reset before installing NT. Contact either your hardware manufacturer or Microsoft for specific instructions on the reset procedure.

Alpha   The Digital Equipment Corporation Alpha processor is or has been the fastest processor on the planet for running NT (and most other systems). Versions of the Alpha have been demonstrated running at up to 300-MHz. Systems using the Alpha range from PC-style desktop systems to the powerful Alpha workstation and server series. A particularly powerful series of servers code named Sable was introduced in late 1994. The Sable server 2100-500 can support up to four 275-MHz processors and supports up to seven front-mounted hot-swappable drives in a built-in StorageWorks shelf. One additional seven drive shelf can be installed internally. The 2100-500 is a real zinger in performance. The 1000 and 2000 series servers are also powerful and relatively affordable. To give you an idea, an AlphaServer 1000 with 2 or 3GB of disk is less than $20,000 at early 1995 prices.

Digital is constantly upgrading the entire Alpha line with both new models and faster processors for existing models.

Hardware Requirements for NT Server

NT Server can run on a wide variety of systems with many different configurations. Table P.1 shows the Microsoft recommendations and my own recommendations. Consider the Microsoft recommendations to be the absolute minimum and my recommendations as a realistic minimum. Note that RISC systems may have different minimum requirements than Intel systems.

The number of users for file and print sharing can be estimated based on average performance reported by some users and field experience. Table P.2 provides a rough starting point for most systems.

Table P.1 System Recommendations

System Feature	Microsoft Recommendation	Ken's Suggestion
Processor	386/25, MIPS or Alpha AXP	Pentium Intel, MIPS or Alpha AXP
Video system	VGA	VGA
Floppy disk	3.5- or 5.25-in. floppy disk	3.5-in floppy disk
Hard disk	90MB of free disk for Intel or 110MB of free disk for RISC systems	500MB of free disk on the system drive
Memory	16MB	32MB
CD-ROM disk	Supported SCSI drive (CD-ROM is required for RISC systems)	Supported double-speed or faster SCSI drive
Multiprocessors	1–4	1-Maximum supported by the system vendor. Some OEMs offer multiprocessor systems well beyond the four maximum with standard NT Server.

Table P.2 Minimum System Requirements

Number of Users	Memory	Processor
1–25	32MB	Pentium
26–100	64MB	Pentium
100–250	64MB	Pentium 90
> 250	64–128MB	Pentium 90/SMP or RISC

The same basic starting point can be used for client/server systems. Remember that a system such as SQL Server places much more demand upon the processor and possibly the memory system of a server than simple file and print services. You can use a rule of 1.5 times the base server requirements of a file and print server for a database server. For instance, a 90-user client/server system should start out with 96MB of RAM and a Pentium 90 or RISC processor.

NT RESOURCE KIT

You can obtain the NT Resource Kit directly from Microsoft and most Microsoft resellers. If you are running and supporting NT and do not have the kit, order it today.

The NT Resource Kit is the best investment you can make after your purchase of NT. It has low cost (street price of less than $200) and contains a wealth of information as well as many NT utilities for optimizing and troubleshooting your system.

TECHNET

TechNet is another tool available from Microsoft that is frequently referred to in this book. This resource is a monthly CD-ROM that is packed with good tips, solutions, and source code. It also includes numerous publications that relate to NT and Windows in general. The cost for the Resource Kit in 1994 was $195 per year. What a deal!

TIPS ON USING WINDOWS

I would like to include just a few tips for using Windows. These tips work for Windows 3.x and Windows 95. Windows 3.x includes all versions of Windows NT and Windows NT Server.

Selecting Items in Lists

1. Click on an item to select only that item.

2. Click the first item in a list, hold down the Shift key, and click the last item to select an all-inclusive list.

3. Click the first item in a list, hold down the Ctrl key, and click each item. This allows you to select items that are not contiguous.

Dragging and Dropping

1. Click an item and hold down the left mouse button.

2. Move the mouse to the drop location and release the left button. Watch for the mouse cursor to change shape indicating when it is OK or not to drop the item.

Starting Programs or Actions with Icons, Menus, and Buttons

☞ Icons—Double-click an icon in Program Manager or single-click an icon on a toolbar.

☞ Menus—Single-click a menu selection.

☞ Buttons—Single-click a button to trigger its action.

Many applications such as File Manager and Print Manager use toolbars with separate icons to represent different functions. NT 3.51 includes ToolTip help that was popularized by Microsoft Office and is built into Windows 95.

Displaying ToolTip Help

1. Place the mouse pointer over the icon and do not move it for several seconds (2).

Starting Help

1. Press the F1 key whenever you need help. If you have a question on a dialog box, then place the mouse in the field you need help on and press F1.

DISCLAIMER

All the information included in this book has appeared in print as common knowledge before this book was released from the publisher. Specifically, Windows 95 (Chicago) references pertain to information taken from publications such as *Microsoft TechNet, Windows Magazine, Windows Sources, PC Magazine, PC Week,* and *Information World.*

CHAPTER 1

Installation of NT Server

1.1 GENERAL INSTALLATION TIPS

NT and NT Server are both installed in the same manner. The traditional way to install NT is to use the boot floppy shipped with NT to start the Setup process from the CD. NT ships with several different methods of installation, and the resource kit adds other options. Table 1.1 includes the various options.

Setup normally presents you with the two standard operational methods of installation: Express and Custom. Express is almost always shown as recommended by setup. Nevertheless, choosing the Custom method provides much more control, and you can still take the default answers for any item by pressing the Enter key.

If you use Custom, you also have the option to install things like TCP/IP during the setup process. You must also use Custom if your network supports only TCP/IP (and not NetBEUI) and you are not installing NT Server as a Backup Domain Controller. If you plan to install a Backup Domain Controller, that system must communicate with the Primary Domain Controller during setup, thus requiring that both systems use the same protocol and be attached to the same network during setup.

1.1.1 Basic Information Before You Install

It is wise to collect several bits of information before you begin installing NT Server. You will use this information during the installation process or after the system is installed. It is always wise to have a complete picture of the compo-

Table 1.1 Installation Options

Method	Description
Setup	Setup is the traditional method of installing NT and uses the boot floppy shipped with NT for x86 (Intel) systems. RISC systems use the ARC menu to start the setup process.
WINNT	WINNT is used to install NT over a network or when your system has an unsupported CD-ROM. WINNT is used only on x86 (Intel) systems running DOS. The NT Resource Kit includes the SETUPMGR program, which can create automatic answer files for use with WINNT and WINNT32.
WINNT32	WINNT32 is used to upgrade a system already running NT. It performs the upgrade just like WINNT. The NT Resource Kit includes the SETUPMGR program, which can create automatic answer files for use with WINNT and WINNT32.
CPS	Computer Profile Setup (CPS) is included with the NT Resource Kit and is used to automate the installation of NT and NT Server on Intel platforms. The process is used to build a master copy of NT on a server and then to install the master system to target clients.

nents installed in your server and their configuration. This information will come in handy later when you must change the system's configuration or if you experience a problem.

You should also gather three or four blank formatted disks (depending upon your installation method and whether or not you will build an emergency disk), obtain the latest NT Server patches (download them or use Technet), and keep a notepad handy in case you need to take some notes. If you have a newer hardware device (such as a network card) or one that is not on the compatibility list, keep the setup disks and manuals for the device handy during the installation.

Before you start the installation of your first server, decide on the naming conventions (NT Server name, Domain name, TCP/IP address) to use for your system.

1.1.1.1 Hardware Configuration   You should keep a list of configurations for your system. This includes, but is not limited to, the items in Table 1.2.

This information will be very useful for maintaining and upgrading your servers. Make sure that you keep a hard copy and don't rely on a disk file for access to the information. Most managers skip this step because they are in a rush during installation or are very happy to just get the system installed and operational. Even though writing down configuration information may be the last thing on your mind, you should take a moment and record it.

WINMSD and other tools can provide most of the information listed in Table 1.2 and more. It's a good idea to run reports from one of these tools after you modify the configuration of a system or install new software. If you are running Windows 3.x before you install NT, you can run MSD, which is found in the Windows directory. Winsleuth Gold and other third-party tools can also provide this type of information.

Table 1.2 Hardware Configuration Notes

Item	Description
BIOS	BIOS (Basic Input Output System) information is normally shown when the system boots. Track the manufacturer (i.e., Phoenix), the version, and the date if shown.
CMOS	CMOS memory is used by Intel systems to keep configuration information such as the system time, memory, disk types and operation, and ROM shadowing methods. The information varies from one hardware vendor to another.
DMA	Many devices such as disk controllers or network cards may use DMA (Direct Memory Address). Record the address for each device in your system that uses DMA.
Memory address	Some network and SCSI controllers use a memory block to interface with the operating system. You should check your card settings to verify if the card uses a memory address and, if so, what the setting is.
I/O Port	Most network cards use input/output ports. Record any port addresses used.
Firmware	Some systems (RISC) use firmware to define features of the system. These systems may require updating to run NT or for enhancements to the hardware.
IRQ	Devices may also use IRQ (Interrupt Request) settings. Examples of devices that use IRQ values are disk controllers, network cards, and communications cards.
SCSI ID	Each device connected to a Small Computer Systems Interface (SCSI) controller must have a unique ID. Unless your system uses a storage system that automatically configures SCSI addresses, you should keep a record of all SCSI devices and their IDs. It is also a good idea to write down which devices have terminators and which ones do not.
Disk drives	It is a good idea to keep a record of all disk drives in your system. This information is very useful when a problem occurs or when you must plan for an upgrade to the system.
Devices	All cards in your system should be recorded. Note the IRQ and other parameters used by the card.
Network cards	The type of network card and its configuration are used in the installation. Specifically you need the IRQ, base I/O address, and possibly memory address range used. This information should be written in your system manual.
Misc.	Any items that are not explicitly mentioned in this list but that are part of your configuration should also be tracked. This information includes the type and speed of memory and modems.

Another tip is to use SMS (Systems Management Server) to collect and save the configuration information for each client and server on the network. SMS collects a tremendous amount of data during its inventory phase and places it in an

SQL Server database. You can easily print a copy periodically or even download a view of the data to a local Access database on a client. The next book in this series covers SMS in depth.

1.1.2 Potential Problems with SCSI Disks and Controllers

1.1.2.1 Drivers   If your system uses non-NT default drives such as those for the NCR chip set, or a nonsupported Ethernet controller, make sure that you have the miniport drivers for NT handy when you begin the installation. Select the Custom install and then use the miniport driver disk when NT complains about not finding your device bus and asks you to insert the disk with the drivers.

1.1.2.2 SCSI Drive ID   If your system has a problem detecting the CD-ROM drive, try setting the SCSI ID for the CD-ROM to anything besides 0 or 1. You should be able to use any ID not used by another device or the SCSI controller itself.

1.1.2.3 SCSI Hard Drives   All hard drives in your system should be on the NT compatibility list. You may still find an unexplained anomaly that can drive you nuts. For example, I ran into a situation while installing NT Server on an Alpha 2100-500 AXP from Digital Equipment Corporation. Time and again the setup process failed after the process started copying files to the hard disk. I also could not run ARCINST from the CD-ROM. If I copied ARCINST to a floppy, it ran fine. Strange?

The hard drive was located three connectors away from the CD-ROM on the SCSI cable. I moved the drive over to the connector next to the CD-ROM, and everything worked fine. The experience was very confusing.

The moral of this story is: make sure that all connectors are tight and that the SCSI bus is terminated correctly. If the problem still occurs, move the drive to another connector on the SCSI cable.

1.1.2.4 Network Controllers   Make sure that you know the configuration and type of network card in the system before you start the installation. If you start the installation and NT Server can't communicate with the network, unless you are installing the Primary Domain Controller or only a server, you are in trouble.

NT Server must be able to communicate with the domain to install a Backup Domain Controller or Server into an existing domain. You cannot change domains with an NT Server after it has been installed (see page 127). This means that you could install with a bad network card, but you would be forced to reinstall to join the existing domain. Test your network card before installing NT and note the configuration information. This information will be valuable in case there is a problem or NT can't detect the card.

1.1.2.5 Installing NT over a Previous OS or with Unformatted Disks
Replacing another operating system besides MS-DOS with NT should not be a problem. However, NT can fail during the installation procedure with a message stating that your system may have a virus. This message usually occurs during

the first phase of the installation when NT tries to boot and really gets your attention. This symptom can also occur when you install NT on a brand new system with new disk drives.

The virus message appears because NT sees the other operating system partition and can't recognize it. This message doesn't occur when the system runs MS-DOS or OS/2, but how about VMS or UNIX? NT is vulnerable during the installation phase, so instead of risking bringing up an infected system, it shuts down.

This problem is solved with a bizarre solution.

Replacing an OS (besides MS-DOS) with NT

1. Unplug all disk drives except for the system drive. If you use a hot-swappable system, simply pop the drives out half way.
2. Use ARCINST (RISC only) to partition the system disk. If your system is RISC-based, make sure that there is at least a 4MB FAT partition. I always create a 6MB system partition and leave the rest of the drive unpartitioned. NT will partition the drive during installation.
3. Install NT.
4. Reboot and test.
5. Plug the drives back in. You may need to shut down the system before plugging the drives back in.

I have tested this process on an Alpha 2100-500 and Alpha 2000, and it works fine.

1.1.3 What Type of Volume Do I Use for NT System Files?

NT Server can be installed on a brand new system or a system that is currently running another operating system. You can leave the existing file system in place if it uses the FAT or HPFS file system or rebuild the file systems during installation. The benefits and drawbacks to both approaches are listed in Table 1.3.

The first three options are available from the Setup menus during installation. Simply choose whether to leave the file system in place or to reformat the file system. The entire setup process can still be accomplished in less than 1 hour.

Installing on a Virgin Partition (Intel only)

1. Repartition the system drive using FDISK. You should make a bootable floppy disk and copy FDISK, FORMAT, EDIT, and any other programs you may need to the floppy. Make sure that you also save any startup files such as CONFIG.SYS and AUTOEXEC.BAT and any drivers or such that may be required by the SCSI systems or other devices. The partition size for the boot partition should be around 100–120 MB.
2. Install NT on the drive. Select the option to reformat the existing file system to NTFS during installation.

Table 1.3 Installation Considerations for File Systems

Replacing the file system	Replacing the file system when installing NT is the best option because it places NT on its own file system with no other operating systems.
Leaving the existing file system	Leaving the current file system in place leaves your system with the original files in place and NT installed on top of the existing file system. This may be a problem if your system was running Windows 3.x because NT will be installed in the Windows directory. I recommend this option only when you must upgrade Windows to NT Server, which is rarely the case. See installing on a virgin DOS system below.
Installing on a virgin DOS system	Installing NT on a FAT partition allows you to access the NT system files via DOS if the system becomes unbootable with NT. This approach creates a security problem because the NT system files can be accessed by booting with a DOS diskette.
Compressed drives	Never place NT system files on a compressed drive created within DOS or Windows 95. Make sure that the partition that is used for NT is not compressed and does not have the UNDELETE SENTRY enabled.

3. Format the other partitions and drives on your system for NTFS or FAT.
4. Run Control Panel and select the System applet. Make sure NT is the default operating system and change the time before it automatically boots to 5 seconds.

After NT is up and running, you can reboot the system using DOS at any time by restarting the system and selecting DOS within 5 seconds. If an NT file gets corrupted and NT will not boot, you can replace the file from DOS if the Repair Disk option does not repair the file.

Installing a clean copy of NT on a RISC system is similar to the process for Intel systems. You may need to run ARCINST in step 1 to delete any existing partitions on the system disk and create a new system partition.

Installing on a Virgin Partition (RISC Only)

1. Delete all partitions on the system disk using ARCINST.
2. Create a new system partition (6MB) on the system disk.
3. Install NT using the ARC menu options (Supplementary menu "Install NT from CD-ROM"). Select the remaining free space on the system disk for the NT system files and select the option to reformat to NTFS. An NTFS partition for the system files is created during the installation process.
4. Format the other partitions and drives on your system for HPFS, NTFS, or FAT.

1.1.4 How NT Handles Installation Media

NT can be installed from several different types of media including CD-ROM, floppy disks, and network resources. The major problem with installing NT is that it will always look for upgrades and new drivers from the original installation media, which is very inconvenient to say the least. This is a drastic change from Windows 3.x, but it takes off in the wrong direction!

There is a work-around for solving this problem. The solution originates in the November 1993 Microsoft TechNet database. NT looks for the setup media in two places: POINTER.INF in the SYSTEM32 directory and the SourcePath value in the Registry.

Changing the Installation Path for the NT Distribution

1. Expand the POINTER.IN_ file from the media you wish to use to the SYSTEM32 directory. The syntax for a pointer device is

```
EXPAND A:\POINTER.IN_ POINTER.INF
```

This command assumes that you are using a floppy disk as the new media. If you are switching to a CD-ROM or network, you must supply the correct drive and directory for that resource.

2. Use REGEDIT32 and change the SourcePath under the following key to point to the new source:

```
HKEY_LOCAL_MACHINE\SOFTWARE\Microsoft\Windows NT\CurrentVersion
```

After you make these changes, Setup looks for any updates on the correct device.

Table 1.4 includes the major INF files used by NT during installation. Each file has an INF extension when uncompressed. Additional information on modifying the setup files can be found in the NT Resource Kit Volume 1, Chapter 3.

1.2 INSTALLATION METHODS

1.2.1 Express Versus Custom

Microsoft recommends using the Express mode of setup unless you have any problems or peculiarities with your system. I heartily agree with this

Table 1.4 INF Files Used by NT During Installation

File Name	Description
DOSNET	Used by text-mode Windows NT Setup. Also used by WINNT and WINNT32 to determine which files are copied to the hard disk during installation. Used during all setup modes (Setup, WINNT, WINNT32).
INITIAL	Windows NT Setup script file for additional NT components. Used during all setup modes (Setup, WINNT, WINNT32).
PARTIAL	Windows NT Setup script file for optional NT components and to create Program Manager groups. Used during all setup modes (Setup, WINNT, WINNT32).
TXTSETUP	Text mode setup script for core NT components. Used during all setup modes (Setup, WINNT, WINNT32). Changes made to this file must be made on the first floppy disk or on the distribution share.

approach unless you have installed NT successfully before. Using Custom assumes that you have installed NT before or are planning to change a particular feature during setup.

During the Express mode, NT automates the process as much as possible, including asking the minimal number of questions during the installation and automatically detecting all the devices in your system.

If you try Express mode and have problems, you may have to use Custom mode and manually specify the location of device drivers that are not standard with NT. This may be the case if you have a new controller or other device that was produced after your NT kit was shipped. The manufacturer or another source may have the drivers available. You must use the Custom mode to tell NT to use the manufacturer's drivers.

Setup detects only one network adapter during installation if you are using Express mode. You can install other adapters after installation by using the Network applet in Control Panel. You can also install multiple network adapters during setup by choosing the Custom option.

1.2.2 Standard Installation

The normal procedure for installing NT is to run the setup program from either a CD-ROM or floppy installation media. Setup is similar to the installation program of the same name for most installation programs and makes the entire process very painless. Running WINNT or WINNT32 across a network is also very convenient, especially if you have created an automatic answer file that helps to automate the entire process.

1.2.2.1 Overview of the Installation Process

Completing a Standard Installation

1. Start setup (WINNT or WINNT32) or boot with the Setup disk.
2. Choose Custom or Express.
3. Select the partition, file system, and directory for NT Server system files.
4. Fill in your user name, computer name, and so on.
5. Enter the security role for the server.
6. Choose the local language for the system.
7. Verify or enter the parameters for the network card and choose the default network protocol.
8. Enter the domain name the server will participate in.
9. Set up a local printer.
10. Enter the password for the Administrator account if the system is the Primary Domain Controller.
11. Enter the local time.
12. Select video adapter settings.
13. Create the emergency disk.

Custom setup allows you to override a number of defaults for the installation process. Express setup automates the process by asking only a minimal number of questions and using defaults for everything else and is recommended for most users. One particular option you may need to override using Custom setup is the automatic hardware detection feature. This should only be turned off if setup fails on a system for some reason during or because of the hardware detection process.

In general, it is best to install NT with the suggested video display options because picking an incorrect mode or option may cause the installation to fail. Once NT has booted after installation, you can change the display settings. Any problems can be recovered gracefully by using the Last Known Good option during startup.

If you are installing NT Server into an existing domain, make sure that the network connection used for the new server is working and that the domain can be accessed from that connection. If you install the new server and it cannot reach the Primary Domain Controller, you must reinstall the server. This step is very important! Failure to heed it results in lots of lost time as you continue to reinstall the server.

1.2.2.2 Floppy Disk   Floppy disk installations are the most time-consuming option for NT Server and can be performed only on x86 architecture systems.

Setup automatically searches for a CD-ROM drive when it is started from the setup boot floppy. If it finds a CD-ROM, it offers you the opportunity to use the CD-ROM or floppy for the installation.

Installing from Floppy Disks

1. Insert the first Setup floppy disk in the drive.
2. Reboot the system.
3. Follow the general setup instructions to complete the installation.

1.2.2.3 CD-ROM (x86 Systems Only)   Installing from CD-ROM is one of the fastest and simplest method for installing NT Server. This process is simple and can be accomplished in 30 minutes to 1 hour, if you don't encounter any problems. Be sure to read the first sections of this chapter and follow all the steps.

Installing from CD-ROM

1. Insert the first Setup floppy disk in the drive.
2. Reboot the system.
3. Insert the Setup CD in the CD-ROM drive when prompted.
4. Follow the general setup instructions to complete the installation.

1.2.2.4 RISC Systems Only   RISC systems can install NT only from CD-ROM. Upgrades can be performed over the network using WINNT32 or the CD-ROM.

The first thing you must do to install NT on a RISC system is to determine the steps for starting a program from CD-ROM on your system. Use these instructions to start the Windows NT Setup program. Most RISC systems that can run NT use the ARC menu and have a menu option for installing NT under the Supplementary menu.

The system partition used for NT must have at least 2MB of free space, but I always use 6MB for a little free space. The hidden files OSLOADER.EXE and HAL.DLL must reside in the \OS\WINNT directory on this partition. The balance of NT Server can be placed on this partition or another partition formatted as FAT, NTFS, or HPFS. Use NTFS if at all possible because it provides the best performance and security.

Steps for Installing on RISC Systems

The following steps work on a Digital Equipment Corporation Alpha system. Systems used for testing this procedure were AlphaServer 2100 and Alpha-Server 2000 servers with varying configurations. If you have problems with these steps, consult your system manuals to determine the steps for installing on your particular model.

Creating a System Partition for NT

1. Load the NT Server CD-ROM.
2. Restart the system.
3. From the Boot menu, choose Run a Program.
4. Enter **cd:\alpha\arcinst** and press Enter.
5. Select Configure Partitions from the menu
6. Delete any existing partitions on the system disk.

Warning: This step deletes all files on the disk.

7. Choose Create Partition.
8. Select the disk to use for the system disk.
9. Enter the size for the partition (should be **6**) and press Enter.
10. Select Make Existing Partition into a System Partition.
11. Answer **Y** to the prompt to overwrite any existing system partition.

    If you receive a message that Boot Selections already exist, then return to step 5 and complete the procedure again. Make sure all partitions on the system disk are deleted before step 7.
12. Exit ARCINST.

After the system partition is created, you are ready to install NT. Make sure that the remaining space on the system drive is not partitioned.

Installing NT on a RISC system

1. Load the NT Server CD-ROM.
2. Restart the system.
3. From the ARC menu, choose Supplementary menu.

4. Select Install NT from CD-ROM.

5. If the last option is not available, choose Run a Program. Enter

```
cd:\system\setupldr
```

and press Enter. **cd:** is the device specification for the CD-ROM, which may vary on different systems. You may need to use the full ARC specification for your CD, such as scsi(0)cdrom(4)fdisk(0).

When the NT Setup screen appears, complete the installation in the normal manner.

Warning: During installation you may encounter a message that NT cannot continue with the installation because a possible virus has been detected. This message usually occurs when you have several unformatted drives on the system or when a disk is installed that has had another operating system installed that NT does not recognize (such as VMS). The workaround is to disconnect all disks except the system disk and finish the installation. When the installation is complete, reconnect and configure the other disks. For more information see page 4.

If you still encounter the error, make sure that the system has been powered down completely and restarted. Repowering will absolutely reset everything in the system and should allow you to continue.

1.2.2.5 Alpha AXP Examples This section covers several things you can do to configure an Alpha AXP RISC system for NT. These steps involve setting system parameters or upgrading firmware to work with newer versions of NT. Most of these steps should work with your RISC system because most RISC systems that work with NT use the ARC menu for system configuration. Commands issued at the >>> prompt are specific to certain versions of Alpha systems.

Some RISC systems that run NT come with NT installed so that these steps won't be necessary. If you have a system running another operating system like VMS, you may need to take some of or all these steps.

Note: If the system will be a Backup Domain Controller or Primary Domain Controller, you must reinstall NT. You cannot change an NT PDC or BDC from one domain to another (see page 130).

Setting the System to Boot NT and Starting the ARC Menu. Make sure that your RISC system is set to boot NT automatically if NT is the default operating system. The steps in this section work on the AlphaServer 2000 and 2100 systems, but vary on other Alpha versions.

If the system was running either VMS or OSF/1, you need to change the operating system mode to NT. At the boot prompt, enter

```
>>> Set os_type NT
```

After using this command, the system automatically starts the ARC menu system and boots NT when it boots. Enter the INIT command to change the setting permanently and reboot the system using

```
>>> Init
```

The ARC menu now displays as the default, and NT boots automatically using its BOOT menu.

You can also invoke the ARC menu at the boot prompt by entering

```
>>>ARC
```

When the ARC menu starts, you can access configuration commands by choosing options from the menu. Use the arrow keys to move up or down the menu and then press enter to select an option.

Device Definitions and Such.   The startup instructions for operating systems in the BOOT.INI file (Intel only) can give you a glimpse of the device descriptions for disk drives and other devices. This arcane format actually describes the type of bus and device and the actual device numbers.

The CD-ROM in an AXP system has a description like scsi(0)cdrom(4) fdisk(0), which describes the type of bus (SCSI), the bus number (0), and the SCSI number of the device (4). The description also shows that this device is a CD-ROM.

Devices on the system can be listed with the Show Hardware Configuration option on the Supplementary menu. Most systems will use CD: as a shorthand environment variable for the CD-ROM drive.

You may also need to configure EISA devices using the ECU (EISA Configuration Utility) program and RAID controllers using the SWXCRMGR or other vendor-supplied program. The documentation for your system should be consulted for the latest information on both of these programs.

1.2.2.6 DOS Systems with Unsupported CD-ROM   NT includes the WINNT and WINNT32 procedures for installing NT from a network or an unsupported CD-ROM drives. This process starts from DOS and copies the NT installation files to the local hard drive. This means that you must have an extra 70MB or so of storage to be used during the installation. The installation files are deleted automatically when the installation is complete. This process may take much longer than the normal installation from CD-ROM. The extended time is mainly because the files must be copied to the hard disk before the installation process starts.

Installing from an Unsupported CD-ROM (Intel Only)

1. Boot system from DOS.
2. Change to the drive and directory containing the NT installation files:

```
E:
CD \I386
```

3. Have at least four blank, formatted floppy disks handy.

4. Label the blank unformatted floppy disks—Disk 1, Disk 2, etc. See your NT manual for the exact number of disks for your version of NT.

5. Start the installation process by running WINNT.

6. Follow the normal NT setup directions.

7. Enter the name of the directory from which you started WINNT (e.g., **Z:\I386**) when prompted for the directory that contains the Windows NT Source.

8. Insert the blank disks when prompted (unless you use the /b parameter, in which case this step is skipped). Make sure you correctly label each disk as the files are copied to the disk.

9. Follow the instructions to complete the setup process.

If your CD is not supported under NT, you can get around some things by copying the installation images from the CD to the system's hard disk via DOS. Boot the system with a floppy disk that includes the CD drivers. Copy the directory structures to an NT hard disk that you can access. Note that this disk can only be a FAT disk. Then run the installation steps from the files on the hard disk using the WINNT command.

Even though this last procedure does work, you should get a CD that works with NT. Most NT software is available on CD, and many PC vendors are also moving most applications to CD.

1.2.2.7 Network-based Installation You can automate the installation process by placing the NT distribution on a network drive that is accessible to the new machines or sharing the CD-ROM drive from an available network system. The only restriction to this procedure is that the clients that install over the network must be DOS, Windows 95, or NT based and have access to the shared network hard disk or CD-ROM.

Loading NT Server Files on a Server

1. Connect to the shared directory that will contain the NT files.

2. Use XCOPY, or File Manager, or Explorer to copy the NT Server files from the CD-ROM to the server.

3. Disconnect the connection to the share.

Make sure to copy the files to the appropriate area on the share. For instance, the files for Alpha systems should be copied to a directory named the same as the Alpha files on the CD-ROM (typically \ALPHA).

I usually create a share called DistDisk$ that has subdirectories for all network installation files. DistDisk$ points to the Distribution Disks directory. The NT files are placed in the WINNT35 subdirectory with individual directories of ALPHA, MIPS, and I386. These directories should match the corresponding CD directories. With this structure you can add places for PowerPC or any other architecture files in the appropriate subdirectory. This structure will help when you are trying to remember which files are in what directory.

After you move the files to the server, modify any configuration files to your standards. For instance, you can specify the network protocols and the product ID in different INI files on the server. The easiest way to modify the setup files is to use the SETUPMGR.EXE program in the NT Resource Kit. SETUPMGR allows you to create or modify an answer file for installing NT. The answer file can be used with WINNT or WINNT32 to perform an unattended setup.

The answer file is one of the best approaches to installing multiple NT systems because it is easy to build and doesn't take up much space on the server. The answer file ensures that questions are answered the same each time it is used. See page 15 for more information on using an answer file.

The next step in the installation process is to install NT on the target machines. The target machine must be running DOS or NT and connected to the network drive that contains the NT distribution. You can use any compatible network (MSClient, Windows for Workgroups, or NT) that allows you to access the files. When you are connected to the network, change the current drive and directory containing the NT distribution.

Next start the DOS-based NT installation by executing the following command on a DOS system:

```
x:\WINNT35\i386\>WINNT
```

or the following command from an NT system:

```
x:\WINNT35\i386\>WINNT32
```

Use WINNT from a DOS system and WINNT32 from an NT system. The WINNT command will perform several steps during the installation process:

1. Create an NT Setup boot floppy disk plus several additional Setup floppy disks. The Setup boot floppy disk is used to start NT for the final stage of the installation process and the additional two floppy disks are used during that process. You can skip this step using the /b parameter.

2. Copy the entire NT distribution to the local hard disk. The directory on the local disk is WIN_NT.~LS.

3. Reboot when WINNT instructs you to reboot the PC with the Setup boot floppy disk still in the drive. NT boots from the floppy and completes the installation. The NT files are moved from the WIN_NT.~LS to the NT boot directory (usually either \WINNT35 or \WINDOWS).

This procedure works very well and can be used with either NT or NT Server. This process is very efficient because it allows you to copy the files from the network instead of either a floppy disk or a CD-ROM. You can start multiple installations at the same time from the same source.

Installing Without Floppy Disks (x86 Only).   You can cause WINNT or WINNT32 to complete the setup without building the floppy disks if you do not need to reformat the system partition during the installation process. This procedure simplifies and improves the performance of the installation process. The system partition can always be converted to NTFS after installation. The following command starts the installation process without building setup floppy disks:

```
WINNT /b
```

or the next command from an NT system:

```
WINNT32 /b
```

1.2.2.8 Using an Unattended Answer File for Network Setup NT 3.5x introduces a new method for installation with both WINNT and WINNT32, using an automated answer file to supply the setup answers. The answer file can be created and then used with WINNT or WINNT32 to install multiple systems quickly over the network. The command to run the automated setup is

```
WINNT /u:[answer_file_name]
```

or the next command from an NT system:

```
WINNT32 /u:[answer_file_name]
```

Running this command without specifying an answer file causes setup to run and use all default answers. The user name and/or organization name and license prompts (3.51 only) must be answered because there is no default for these options. You can create an answer file with defaults for these options, which can totally automate the process. This default file is valuable in organizations where a standard user name and company name are used.

The answer file is created with a neat little utility included with the NT Resource Kit called SETUPMGR.EXE. This program takes the pain out of building and managing existing answer files. The following steps show how to use the program.

Creating and Editing Setup Answer Files

1. Start the Setup Manager (SETUPMGR.EXE).
2. Click the Open button to edit an existing answer file or skip this step to create a new one.
3. Specify the settings for the file.
4. Specify the file name for the answer file.
5. Click OK.

Before using the file created in this process, you should add license information to the file if you are using 3.51. Edit the answer file and add information on the license options. The format for the license information for a PerSeat license follows:

```
[LicenseFilePrintData]
AutoMode = PerSeat
AutoUsers = 0
```

If you are using PerServer licensing, then use

```
[LicenseFilePrintData]
AutoMode = PerServer
;Change 100 in the following line to the number of licenses for
;your server.
AutoUsers = 100
```

If you make a mistake in the license information, WINNT displays the normal setup dialog box and stops the unattended mode of setup.

If your organization has slightly different configurations for different NT systems, you may need to create multiple answer files. The basic idea is to first create generic files that match the most popular configuration options (system, video, network, etc.) and then use these files to build the new configuration files.

Creating Generic Answer Files for Configurations

1. Start Setup Manager (SETUPMGR.EXE).
2. Create a new answer file. Specify the default values for the most-often-used options.
3. Specify settings for the nearest configuration that matches most systems.
4. Save the file.
5. Create a similar file for each major configuration.

Now that you have created generic files, you can use the following steps to create custom answer files.

Creating Specific Answer Files

1. Copy the generic files to the new answer file name.
2. Start Setup Manager.
3. Open the new answer file created in step 1.
4. Change the settings.
5. Save the file.

Don't forget that we can use our old friend the DOS prompt and its batch files to further automate this step.

1.2.2.9 Upgrading NT Server

NT Workstation.   You must consider carefully whether an NT system that will be upgraded to NT Server will be a stand-alone system or serve as a controller on a domain. You *must* perform a new installation if the server will be used as a Backup Domain Controller or Primary Domain Controller on an existing domain. A new installation is the only way to upgrade a system to a controller and have the domain tools installed on the system. Performing an upgrade switches only the tools on the workstation to the new version, but it does not upgrade the tools to NT Server tools.

Upgrading NT 3.1 to NT Server

1. Perform a new installation of NT Server.

NT Server.   There are several methods that can be used to upgrade NT Server. You can use any of the methods for installing NT Server that can be accessed by the server before the installation starts.

A special version of the installation program (WINNT32) is included for running from within NT Server. WINNT32 runs on both Intel and RISC systems.

The upgrades are usually painless because they use the information in the NT Registry to answer questions during the upgrade process. The only questions that must be answered relate to new features such as TCP/IP where Setup cannot find the information to perform the upgrade. Setup also asks you for a new disk for the emergency repair information.

Upgrading NT Server Versions with WINNT32

1. Connect to the network share or insert the NT Server CD.
2. Change to the appropriate directory on the installation share or CD (Alpha, MIPS, Intel, etc.).
3. Run the WINNT32 program in the appropriate directory.
4. Follow the instructions.

Upgrading NT Server Versions with Setup

1. Shut down the system.
2. Place the NT Server CD in the CD-ROM drive.
3. Insert the first Setup floppy disk.
4. Reboot the system.
5. Follow the instructions.

1.2.2.10 Computer Profile Setup Installation (NT Resource Kit)   The Computer Profile Setup (CPS) installation is another alternative to the WINNT-based setup. The CPS option is available as part of the NT Resource Kit from Microsoft.

Computer Profile Setup has two big caveats:

1. It can be used only for machines that are almost exactly the same. In other words, the same hardware drivers, program manager groups, etc., must be used on every system and the systems can only have Intel processors. The installation does allow for different size hard disks and larger memory, but that is about all. You can create several different profiles for different types of systems to work around this problem.
2. It works only on Intel systems.

The CPS files are located in the \I386\CPS directory on the NT Resource Kit CD. Copy the files to a directory on a server or to a directory on the system that will be used to create the master system. This system must be running NT or NT Server.

The Computer Profile Setup is composed of three parts:

1. Set up an NT System that will be used to build the profile for the master server.

2. Run Create Profile to create the .CPS template file or files that will be used for the installation. This step must be run from an NT machine with the configuration that you want to record.

3. Run Install Profile, which takes the information from the template file and installs NT with the correct settings.

The second part must be run from within NT. This means that NT must be able to connect to the network resource that contains the NT template file.

Creating the CPS Profile on a Server

1. Install and configure the NT Master system. This system must be configured exactly like the target systems to be installed. For instance, network functions, NT options, accessories, approximate disk space, and custom programs should be installed and working.

2. Create a directory to hold the profile on the distribution server and share the directory. This directory will hold the entire NT setup from the machine used to create the profile.

3. Upload the files from the master server to the distribution server by executing the uplodprf command with the following syntax:

```
uplodprf -s:x:\master\cpq1 -i:profile.ini [\dir1 dir2 ...]
```

-s   Directory where the master files will be stored.

-i   Name of the PROFILE.INI file to use.

dir1 dir2   Additional directories on the master system that you wish to preinstall on target systems.

After you have completed these steps, edit the DEFAULTS.INF file in the SYSTEM32 subdirectory of the new master installation on the server. You may want to change values in the [DefaultValues] section to automate the installation process completely.

Installing a New Machine Using the Master Installation

1. Create a bootable floppy disk that can access the network share or access the master installation files copied to a hard disk.

2. Execute the installation command WINNTP. This command is located in the Resource Kit directory and may be moved to another commonly accessible directory. The syntax is

```
WINNTP /S:\\server1\mastercpq1 /T: c: options
```

/S The \\server1\mastercpq1 specification points to the share name of the directory you used to install the profile to.

/T c:\nttmp specifies the temporary file location for the installation. Setup does this automatically if this option is left out.

/I:inf Can be used to specify another INF file besides DOSNET.INF.

/B Causes the installation to reboot automatically without pausing after the files have been copied to the temporary drive.

/U: Specifies the user name for the system.

/O: Specifies the organization name for the system. This name appears in the same dialog box as the user name during a normal setup.

/M: Specifies the machine name (computer name) for the system.

/N: Specifies the domain name for the system.

/Z: Specifies the time zone for the system. See the CPSREAD.TXT file included with the NT Resource Kit for details on this option.

/E: /E:NO causes the installation to not prompt to build a repair disk. The default is /E:YES.

All options except for /S, /T, and /I accept a trailing - (as in /B-) to override any default value or to negate the action of the original option (for instance /B reboots immediately while /B- cancels this action and pauses before rebooting, which is the default action).

CPS installations can be much more sophisticated than this illustration. For instance, you can create difference profiles that are the same except for certain items. Consult the end of Chapter 3 in the NT Resource Kit Volume 1.

1.2.3 Reinstalling NT

You can reinstall NT Server over an existing installation of NT or NT Server if you have at least 80MB of free disk space on the boot drive. The installation process requires a minimum of 80MB and does not consider whether or not you already have NT installed. This means that if your system has less than 80MB free on the boot drive you will have to remove part of or all your NT configuration before performing the reinstallation.

Before you take off and reinstall NT Server, let's take a look at several precautions. They are necessary because of the way NT manages security and files. The following list contains several things you should watch out for before starting the reinstallation process.

- ☞ You cannot move a computer to a new domain without reinstalling NT.
- ☞ The computer account for an NT system in a domain must be deleted before the reinstallation starts.
- ☞ Be sure to back up the NT Registry files before starting the reinstallation.

1.3 AUTOMATING THE CONFIGURATION OF A NEW SERVER

This is probably a good time to interject my opinion on automating things. I prefer to automate everything possible both to save time and to cut down on the possibility of errors entering the process.

Fortunately NT includes command-line options for most of its configuration commands. These commands allow us to build an automated script that will configure most of our options on new NT systems. You may want to build two different scripts—one for servers and one for workstations. You may also build logic into your script to have common setup options on all systems and only certain options on servers.

The code example in Figure 1.1 shows a simple batch command that can be tailored for your tasks.

This little command is very useful for configuring servers. In this example, insert your commands in one of the three locations: Common, Server, and NT Workstation. Common items for both servers and workstations go in the common area. Server only options go in the server area, while the workstation area gets only workstation commands.

There are many options you may want to place in this little **command.**

```
@echo off
Echo NT Configuration Script
rem kls 12/13/94
rem

rem ------------------- Common Area ----------------------------------
Echo Executing Common commands
rem Common Commands go here
rem ----------------------------------------------------------------
rem Check for Server or Workstation (default)
if "%1" == "SERVER" GoTo SERVER
if "%1" == "server" GoTo SERVER
GoTo WORKSTATION
rem ----------------------------------------------------------------
:SERVER
rem ------------------- Server Only Area --------------------------
Echo Executing Server Only commands
rem Server Commands go here
GoTo EXIT

rem ----------------------------------------------------------------
:WORKSTATION
rem ------------------- NT Workstation Only Area -------------------
Echo Executing Workstation Only commands
rem Workstation Commands go here
rem ----------------------------------------------------------------

:EXIT
```

Fig. 1.1 NTCONFIG.BAT example program.

Likely candidates are not only NET commands but also commands to build common directory structures, connect to a shared directory service and download certain files to the new system, enter user accounts that are standard for all systems, start or stop services, and so on.

Table 1.5 lists several options that you may want to include in this command.

The command is executed using the following syntax:

```
NTCONFIG [SERVER]
```

Specifying SERVER or server after the command will run only the common and server options, while executing only NTCONFIG will execute the common and workstation options.

1.4 UPGRADING AN EXISTING INSTALLATION OF NT

The normal upgrade process for a system already running NT Server is the same as a system running another operating system. You have the option of directly running WINNT32 instead of Setup or WINNT.

You should review the compatibility list for your hardware before you blast in and install any new major version. New versions usually support the same hardware as older versions, but this observation is not always true, especially in areas like network cards, video monitors, and SCSI controllers. If you are using a popular and standard model (say an EtherLink III) from 3Com, it will most likely be supported. Models such as ArcNet cards from an unheard of vendor may drop off the list. I have also heard of network cards from a large vendor (HP) that were supported in NT 3.1 but not in NT Server 3.5.

Table 1.5 Options for NTCONFIG.BAT Example

Command	Description
MD dirname	Creates a directory
NET USE x: \\server\share /y	Connects to a shared directory
COPY file file	Copies files from a network share to the local system
NET SHARE name=path /y	Shares a directory on the network

Server Configuration and Management

2.1 OVERVIEW OF MANAGING NT SERVERS

Windows NT Server contains several utilities for managing your NT Servers and other NT systems on the network.

Other sources of management utilities come with the NT Resource Kit from Microsoft, the Microsoft Systems Management Server system, third-party tools in general, and Simple Network Management Protocol (SNMP)-compliant systems from other vendors.

This chapter and others in the book cover the NT utilities, some of the NT Resource Kit utilities, and some other programs that were available when I wrote this book. I do not intend, nor would it be possible, to cover every possible management program thoroughly in this book without making it a giant tome. Use the management section of the book as a guide for tools and hints; then survey the market and see how the utilities mentioned in this book compare with others on the market.

2.2 INTRODUCTION TO THE NT RESOURCE KIT UTILITIES

The NT Resource Kit contains a number of programs that are extremely useful for any system manager. Some of the programs like the Animated Cursor Editor are useful for developers or bored managers, while many others such as the CTAPE program are critical tools for every system manager.

Table 2.1 lists the tools that I view as administrative-type programs in the 3.5 version of the NT Resource Kit. Not every program in the NT Resource Kit is covered in this book because not all the programs contribute to managing a system like NT Server. Also, some were considered to be outside the scope of the book. See the NT Resource Kit for more information on all programs.

You should obtain a copy of the new NT Resource Kit at your first opportunity.

Table 2.1 Administrative Programs in NT Resource Kit

Program Name	Description
ADDUSERS.EXE	Adds users to the system or dumps the user database to a text file
BROWMON.EXE	Monitors the status of the browser service
CAT.EXE	POSIX command to display or concatenate files
CHOICE.EXE	Provides input facility for batch files
CPS	Computer Profile Setup for automating NT installations
CTAPE.CPL	Control Panel applet to manage tape devices
DHCPCMD.EXE	DHCP Administrator's tool for NT Workstation
DHCPLOC.EXE	DHCP Locator Utility
DIRUSE.EXE	Displays the amount of disk space used per directory
DNS*	Domain Name Service for NT
DOMMON.EXE	Displays information on the status of the domain monitor
DOMPLAN.EXE*	Domain Planning utility for designing an NT network and configuring the domain(s)
DRIVERS.EXE	Displays a list of the current drivers on a system
DUMPEL.EXE	Dumps the Event Viewer log to a file
EMWAC	EMWAC Internet services for NT
ENUMPRN.EXE	Displays installed printer drivers
EXETYPE.EXE	Determines what type of operating system and processor is required to run a program
FINDGRP.EXE	Displays global and local groups that a user belongs to (works in the current domain or across domains)
FLOPLOCK.EXE*	Restricts access to the floppy disk drive on an NT system
GETSID.EXE	Displays and matches SIDs for two-user accounts
GRPTOREG.EXE	Loads Program Manager groups from *.GRP files created by REGTOGRP.EXE

Table 2.1 Administrative Programs in NT Resource Kit (Continued)

Program Name	Description
JETPACK.EXE	Packs a JET (Access) database used by WINS or DHCP
KILL.EXE	Terminates a task
LS.EXE	POSIX list utility similar to DIR
NETSVC.EXE	Controls services from the command line
NETWATCH.EXE	Shows which users are connected to resources
NTCARD.HLP	Network card help file
NTDETECT.COM[*]	Same as NTDETECT.COM shipped with NT but has debug switch turned on to display hardware detected during startup
PERFMTR.EXE	Displays performance statistics
PERMS.EXE	Shows what access a user has to specific files
PMON.EXE	Displays running tasks programs and some statistics
POSIX Utilities[*]	Miscellaneous utilities that run under the POSIX subsystem
PSTAT.EXE	Displays running programs and their tasks, along with the status of each task
PUTINGRP.EXE	Command-line utility to place program(s) into Program Manager groups
QSLICE.EXE	Displays the amount of CPU usage used by each running process
RASUSERS.EXE	Enumerates RAS users
RCMD.EXE	Remote Command Line Service for secure command-line operations with remote systems
REGBACK.EXE	Performs a backup of Registry files
REGENTRY.HLP	Help file with information on Registry entries
REGINI.EXE	Changes Registry via a script
REGKEY.EXE	Displays and changes certain Registry entries for Logon and FAT file system settings
REGREST.EXE	Restores the Registry files from the backup files created with REGBACK
REGTOGRP.EXE	Creates *.GRP files for Program Manager groups (These files are placed in the current directory and can be used only by GRPTOREG.EXE.)
REMOTE.EXE	Provides a remote command line to an NT system
RMTSHARE.EXE	Creates or deletes a remote share
SCOPY.EXE	Copies or moves NTFS files while preserving security

Table 2.1 Administrative Programs in NT Resource Kit (Continued)

Program Name	Description
SETUPMGR.EXE	Utility for assisting in automating the process of installing NT on multiple systems by creating an answer file for use with the WINNT and WINNT32 setup programs
SHUTDOWN.EXE	Allows remote or local shutdown of a system
SLEEP.EXE	Pauses execution of a batch file for a certain period of time
SMBTRACE.EXE	Traces SMB packets
SMI.MIB	MIB Source file for SNMP
SNMPUTIL.EXE	SNMP Browse utility
SNMPUTIL.EXE	Provides SNMP information from an SNMP host located on the network
SRVANY.EXE	Allows you to run your own application as a service
SRVMRG.EXE	Server Manager for Domains for NT Workstation
TAPE.EXE	Tape drive utility
TIMESERV.EXE	Service to synchronize the time on NT with a certified and/or nationally provided time service over either serial connections or the Internet
TROUBLE.HLP	Help file complete with troubleshooting flow charts
TZEDIT.EXE	Time Zone editor
UPEDIT.EXE	Allows you to change the system and default profiles on NT Workstation
UPTOMP.EXE	Upgrades a single processor NT system to a multiprocessor system
USMGR.EXE	User Manager for Domains for NT Workstation
USRTOGRP.EXE	Adds users to groups
WINAT.EXE	Graphical interface to the Command Scheduler (AT command)
WINCIM.EXE	WinCim utility for accessing CompuServe
WINDIFF.EXE	Displays the differences between two files or directories
WINEXIT.SCR	Screen saver that logs user out after time expires (shows up as Logoff Screen Saver in Control Panel)
WINVTP.EXE	Communications tool that works with Net2Com utility
WNBSTAT.EXE	Displays NetBIOS statistics
WNTIPCFG.EXE	Graphical version of the IPCONFIG utility for configuring TCP/IP

*This program or system requires an additional installation step beyond copying the files to the server or a workstation or running the NT Resource Kit installation program.

2.2.1 Using Programs from the NT Resource Kit

The NT Resource Kit contains versions of most of its programs for the Intel, MIPS, and the Digital Alpha processors. These programs are stored in subdirectories of the program that are named: I386 (Intel), MIPS (MIPS), and ALPHA (Digital Alpha). Make sure that you use the proper version for your system.

Running the install program in the root directory of the NT Resource Kit CD normally installs the correct version of the utilities for each system.

Most NT Resource Kit programs can be used by copying the program to a directory on the PATH or placing the programs directory on your PATH. The default directory is \RESKIT35, which is located on the WINNT boot drive, unless you selected a different drive and/or directory during installation. I normally place the programs in a utility directory located on the PATH if it is a program that I will use frequently. The NT Resource Kit installation program places the \RESKIT35 directory in the path.

Check the documentation for the commands to install the components of the Resource Kit. There are normally several setup commands to install all the utilities.

2.3 COMMAND PROMPT OPERATIONS

Many of the NT Command Prompt commands are useful for network environments where NT Server is used. Some of these commands perform tasks that the graphical commands can't (ever tried to list contents of a directory to a file in File Manager—use DIR), while others are somewhat quicker to use. This last point is especially true if you build batch programs that contain your commands.

The command prompt uses the command interpreter (CMD.EXE) to manage the command line, run programs, and so on. CMD.EXE is the NT equivalent of COMMAND.COM in MS-DOS. The command interpreter supports several internal command prompt commands such as DIR and COPY. Other features such as redirection (> and >>) and pipes (|) are also supported by the command interpreter.

Normally you won't be concerned with CMD.EXE because the command prompt and other features of NT that use DOS-type programs make its use transparent. You may find an occasion where you need to run a program explicitly using the command interpreter. You will usually notice this in NT Server 3.51 or greater with the AT command because it no longer loads the command interpreter by default. Batch files using DIR or COPY or the redirection or pipe features fail when they are run using the scheduler.

There is a simple fix for this problem with the command interpreter and AT. Simply prefix all your commands in the batch files with **cmd /c**. The /c causes the command interpreter to terminate at the completion of the command. This prefix tells the command interpreter to execute your command and then terminate. The following example shows how it works:

```
cmd /c dir c:\logfiles > c:\logfiles\errorlogs.txt
cmd /c copy c:\logfiles\errorlogs.txt n:\errorlogs\thisserver.log
```

2.3.1 Batch Programs

Let's look at how to build batch programs under NT. Except for a few differences, NT batch programs are similar to DOS batch programs. NT batch programs can end in a suffix of .BAT or .CMD. The program names must also conform to the file system that you are using (NTFS, FAT, or HPFS). For instance, if you are using NTFS or have long FAT names enabled, the following command name would be legal:

```
"Show Scheduled Accounting Jobs"
```

The quotes around the name allow you to use spaces in the name. Chapter 5 (page 189) contains more information on file systems used by NT and the allowable characters for the file system. Be aware that some programs such as EDIT or WINNT do not work with long file names, even on NTFSP.

2.3.1.1 Passing Parameters
Parameters can be used in NT batch commands just like those in DOS. The % character is used as the variable indicator both for parameters passed from the command line and for environment variables. Parameters passed from the command line start at %0 and go to %9; %0 contains the name of the batch program while %1 through %9 contain the options specified after the name. If you intend to specify more than nine parameters after the program name, check out the SHIFT command later in this chapter.

Accessing and using the parameters in your program are fairly easy. Simply substitute the name of the parameter each time you want to access its value. For instance, if you want to use the first variable, enter **%1**. The following batch program uses the ECHO command to display the first parameter:

```
ECHO %1
```

It is highly recommended that you check a variable before using it, especially if your program will be used by many people. You can check a variable with the IF command. I could expound on the previous example by using IF as follows:

```
IF NOT "%1" == "" ECHO %1
```

NT provides several default environment variables that are useful in NT batch file (see page 182). These variables are useful for certain tasks on NT such as determining which processor is used on a system. For instance, let's say you have several NT systems with a mix of Intel, Alpha, or MIPS processors. The following example determines which processor type is used and changes to a directory for that particular processor before executing a command. This type of logic is used by SMS and many other NT packages to determine which version of software to install or execute.

```
REM %PROCESSOR_ARCHITECTURE% test file
REM
if "%PROCESSOR_ARCHITECTURE%" == "x86" cd I386
if "%PROCESSOR_ARCHITECTURE%" == "X86" cd I386
if "%PROCESSOR_ARCHITECTURE%" == "mips" cd MIPS
```

```
if "%PROCESSOR_ARCHITECTURE%" == "MIPS" cd MIPS
if "%PROCESSOR_ARCHITECTURE%" == "alpha" cd Alpha
if "%PROCESSOR_ARCHITECTURE%" == "ALPHA" cd Alpha
INSTALL
```

An actual batch program typically has more logic to detect errors such as trying to run the program on Windows for Workgroups or Windows 95.

2.3.1.2 Displaying Choices (NT Resource Kit)   The Choice command that is included in the NT Resource Kit is useful for displaying choices and allowing users to choose a command. The syntax for Choice is

```
choice /C:12 /S /T:1,nn text
```

/C:12   The items after the /C: determine what options are displayed. The default is Y,N.

/S   Treats choices as case-sensitive.

/T:1,nn   Defaults to choice 1 after nn seconds.

The Choice command is very useful in batch commands for obtaining information from a user. The following example shows a command that is used to query the user for a yes or no choice:

```
Choice "Please enter Y or N for your choice"
if errorlevel 1 GoTo YES
:NO
Echo No was selected
GoTo Exit
:YES
Echo Yes was selected
:EXIT
```

2.3.1.3 Notes on Batch File If Commands   The DOS batch language has been around for a long time and has many little idiosyncrasies. The following notes provide some samples and insight into using this powerful command.

☞ Do not use *then* in an if statement:

```
if %1 == 5 GoTo to YES
```

☞ Use == when you wish to compare something:

```
if "%PROCESSOR_ARCHITECTURE%" == "x86" cd I386
```

☞ Check for both upper- and lowercase names:

```
if "%PROCESSOR_ARCHITECTURE%" == "alpha" cd I386
if "%PROCESSOR_ARCHITECTURE%" == "ALPHA" cd I386
```

☞ Use "" around both sides of the comparison operator to allow the command to work correctly when one side of the comparison is empty:

```
if "%PROCESSOR_ARCHITECTURE%" == "ALPHA" cd I386
```

☞ Use the Errorlevel option for checking return values from programs:

```
if errorlevel 1 GoTo YES
```

2.4 THE REGISTRY DATABASE

The Registry is the NT database where almost all configuration and performance information is stored. The database is broken up into major and minor keys. Each major key is called a *hive*. REGEDT32 displays the keys in an outline format, making traversing the keys easy. The four major keys are shown in Table 2.2.

Each hive is stored in the %SystemRoot%\SYSTEM32\CONFIG directory.

Each value in the Registry is tagged with the type of data it can contain. Each data type supported by the registry provides not only a certain type of value but also other attributes of the data such as whether the item is a multiple or single string. The registry data types are described in Table 2.3.

For more information on the structure of the Registry, consult the NT Resource Kit for version 3.5.

2.4.1 Editing the Registry Manually with REGEDT32

REGEDT32 is used for manually editing the NT Registry. Normally the registry is changed by management and administrative programs within NT or from application programs that automatically change entries relative to the program. These changes take place behind the scenes and are normally invisible to users and administrators.

Occasionally it may be necessary to change something in the Registry manually. This could be as simple as configuring NT to log on automatically at startup (see page 54) or to fix a device driver entry that cannot be fixed any

Table 2.2 Major Registry Keys

Registry Key	Description
HKEY_USERS	This key contains all the actively loaded user profiles. HKEY_CURRENT_USER is a subkey of this key.
HKEY_CURRENT_USER	This key is a subkey of HKEY_USERS and contains the current profile of the user currently logged on interactively.
HKEY_CLASSES_ROOT	This key contains Object Linking and Embedding (OLE) and other file-class-related information.
HKEY_LOCAL_MACHINE	This key is the most frequently accessed by administrators and contains information about the local system. It includes hardware and software information such as types of hardware devices, device drivers, and startup data.

Table 2.3 Registry Data Types

Data Type	Format	Description
REG_BINARY	Hexadecimal	Normally used for raw data. Most hardware information uses this format.
REG_DWORD	4-byte number: Hexadecimal, Decimal, or Binary	Represents a number that is 4 bytes long. Used for parameters for device drivers and services.
REG_EXPAND_SZ	Expandable string	Used for values that require a single string definition and allow for a variable to be expanded when called by an application. For instance, %SystemRoot% is an environment variable that is stored in the registry.
REG_MULTI_SZ	Multiple string	Used for values that require multiple strings. Most of these values are used for human-readable text. Each entry in the string is separated by NULL characters.
REG_SZ	String	Used for a single string in human readable form.

other way. When this type of manual change is required, REGEDT32 is the tool to use.

> *Note:* You can wreak havoc with your system by manually changing the Registry. At worst, your system will fail to boot. Please backup the Registry files before making any changes. Use RDISK to perform the backup.

REGEDT32 is actually easy to use and provides a nice front end into the Registry. Figure 2.1 shows REGEDT32 with the HKEY_LOCAL_MACHINE key expanded.

REGEDT32 works much like File Manager. Double-click a key to expand or collapse the subkeys, and then click an entry to select it. Various task menus appear across the top of the screen. The File and Edit menus contain the commands to actually change the database.

You can create an icon for REGEDT32.EXE in a personal program group to provide quick access to the program. Place the icon in a personal group to keep other users from seeing the program's icon.

2.4.2 Editing the Registry with RegKey (NT Resource Kit)

REGKEY.EXE provides another way to edit certain options in the Registry without having to slog through the different keys and such. This is another of those handy NT Resource Kit tools for performing a task quickly.

Figure 2.2 shows the REGKEY.EXE dialog box.

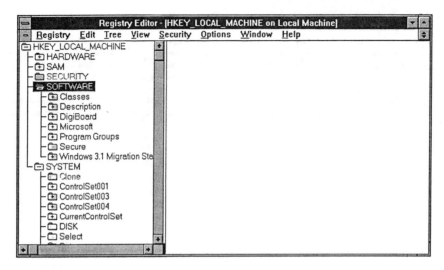

Fig. 2.1 REGEDT32 showing the HKEY_LOCAL_MACHINE key.

Fig. 2.2 RegKey allows you to set a number of configuration options quickly without having to use REGEDT32.

Table 2.4 explains the options available on the dialog box.

2.5 NT SERVER LICENSE MANAGEMENT

NT Server license options are maintained by the License applet in Control Panel. This simple application currently allows you to change only the following options:

☞   Change from a Per Server license to a Per Seat license (one time only). Per Server licensing basically forces you to purchase a server license for each

Table 2.4 REGKEY Settings Options

Option	Description
Display Shutdown button in Logon Dialog	This option displays the Shutdown button on the Logon dialog box, allowing you to stop the system without logging on. Use only when the system is secure such as in a computer room.
Display Last User in Logon Dialog	Turning off this option removes the last user name from the Logon dialog.
Parse Autoexec.bat for SET/PATH commands	Checking this option will cause NT to pick up SET and PATH commands from the AUTOEXEC.BAT file.
Number of User Profiles in Cache	Determines the number of User Profiles in Cache memory.
Default Background Wallpaper	Sets the default background wallpaper for the desktop.
Allow Long file names in FAT	Turning on this option allows long file names in FAT file systems.

NT Server you install. This is the mode pre 3.5 versions used. This option is best when you have only one server or a light load of users who frequently log on and off. Per Seat licensing requires a client license for every system connecting to the server as in NT Server 3.5. This license option is preferred for any networks with more than a few users and multiple NT servers.

☞ Change the number of licenses if you are using Per Server licensing. I leave the exploration of this application to you. It is extremely simple, and it is likely to change in a future version of NT Server. If you have questions about this applet, start it and select help (F1).

2.6 MANAGING DISK SYSTEMS

Disk Administrator is the primary tool for managing many aspects of the disk systems under NT. It is augmented by many of the standard commands such as FORMAT, DIR, DELETE, and File Manager. Most of these tools are used for user-type management chores and are not what are normally called management tools except perhaps for the FORMAT command.

Disk Administrator is used to

☞ Create and delete partitions, stripe sets (including Stripe Sets with Parity—RAID 5), volume sets, and mirrored drive arrangements;

☞ Format logical disk drives; and

☞ Assign drive letters.

Table 2.5 shows a number of other programs that are useful for managing disk or systems related to disks.

Table 2.5 Other Programs That Manage Disks

Program Name	Description
File Manager (WINFILE.EXE)	Can be used for many file-system-related tasks. It is also useful for formatting floppy disks, setting NTFS security, and setting audit parameters.
Performance Monitor (PERFMON.EXE)	Can display many useful statistics for both the physical and logical disks in a system or on other systems.
Event Viewer (EVENTVWR.EXE)	Displays system event messages that are generated regarding the disk system.
Format (FORMAT.COM)	Useful for formatting disks, both floppy and hard.
Label (LABEL.EXE)	Can be used for assigning or changing the label for a volume.
Convert (CONVERT.EXE)	Can convert a FAT or HPFS partition to an NTFS partition.

2.6.1 Disk Systems and NT

2.6.1.1 Physical Disk Drives, Partitions, and Volumes A physical disk is actually a device you can hold in your hand. Physical disks are known as disks, drives, and, for some systems managers who have been around a while, platters. The NT documentation simply calls any disk drive a physical disk.

The term *physical disk* is mainly used when installing disk drives into a system and when reviewing Performance Monitor counters. The Physical Disk object in Performance Monitor collects statistics related to the entire disk. When you use a hardware RAID controller, NT sees all drives in a single array as a single disk.

NT writes a unique signature on each physical disk that uniquely identifies the disk to NT. Disks may be moved on controllers or within an SCSI chain and will still show up correctly because of the signature used by NT. The signatures are stored in the Registry.

A disk partition is part of a physical disk that has been set aside for a logical drive. All application software treats a partition as a separate entity. A single disk will have at least one and possibly more partitions.

A primary partition is one that may be used by an operating system. A physical disk can have up to four primary partitions.

An extended partition can be created on a physical disk. Extended partitions can be subpartitioned to contain multiple logical drives. Only one of the partitions on a physical disk can be an extended partition.

Once you have partitioned a disk, you must format the partition and assign a drive letter to the formatted volume.

Drive letters are logical because they point to a formatted volume which represents a partition. If you do not assign drive letters, they may change as you add or remove disks to a system. The best way to look at logical drive letters is to think in terms of network shares. Remember how we can connect M: to one share today and another tomorrow? M: is a logical letter that may be used for different connections. Drive letters too may be useful for different connections for local volumes.

NT includes two special types of partitions:

☞ The system partition is the disk partition pointed to by the ROM BIOS and is used to boot NT. On RISC systems, this is the small (6MB or so) FAT partition that contains a few files.

☞ The boot partition is the disk partition that contains the NT system files.

The boot and system partitions can be duplexed or mirrored but may not be striped, parity striped, or put on a volume set.

2.6.2 Creating and Deleting Partitions

You can use Disk Administrator to create, remove, or change how a disk partition is used. Disk Administrator is an improvement over FDISK, which we became familiar with from MS-DOS. Disk Administrator graphically displays information about a partition and whether the partition is used. Partitions are color coded with keys showing the used space on a partition and the unused space.

The 3.5 version of Disk Administrator introduced a new wrinkle into its operation by forcing you to commit changes before they become final. The Commit Changes Now option is on the Partition menu.

Creating a Primary Partition

1. Run Disk Administrator.
2. Select an area of free space on a drive in the main window.
3. Choose Create from the Partition menu.
4. Enter the size of the primary partition that you are going to create.
5. Click OK.

Creating an Extended Partition

1. Run Disk Administrator.
2. Select an area of free space on a drive in the main window.
3. Choose Create Extended from the Partition menu.
4. Enter the size of the partition that you are going to create.
5. Click OK.
6. Select the Commit Changes Now option from the Partition menu. After the changes are committed, you can format the partition.

Deleting a Partition

Warning: This option deletes all data on a partition.

1. Run Disk Administrator.

2. Select the partition, volume, or logical drive to delete in the main window.

3. Choose Delete from the Partition menu.

4. Choose Yes in the confirmation box.

2.6.2.1 Volume Sets Volume sets are a collection of volumes that are referred to by a single logical drive letter. A volume set is a collection of more than one partition that is treated as a single unit. The entire volume set receives the drive letter. A user sees only the total space from a volume, not the individual partitions that make up the set.

Volume sets may be useful if you have many physical disk drives and would like to treat groups of them as one. I would recommend using one of the RAID implementations over volume sets unless you have fewer disks than required for a minimal RAID configuration.

2.6.3 Formatting a Partition

Before you can use a partition, it must be formatted. If you are installing NT on a DOS system, NT will use the existing FAT partitions. A new unformatted disk or a new partition created with Disk Administrator must be formatted before it can be used.

NT 3 adds a couple of new options to Disk Administrator that were sorely needed in the 3.1 version. The first option is Format, which now allows you to format a partition in Disk Administrator. For the first time, you can now create and format a partition and assign the label for the logical drive within the same tool. Format is located on the Tools menu.

Formatting a Partition with Disk Administrator

1. Run Disk Administrator.

2. Select the partition you wish to format in the main window.

3. Select the Format option from the Tools menu.

4. Choose the file system type from the drop-down list.

5. Enter a label.

6. Select Quick Format if the partition has been used before.

7. Click OK to start the format process.

You cannot use the Format option of Disk Administrator to format a volume that contains Windows NT system files.

The DOS Prompt FORMAT command can also be used to format disk volumes. This command is just like the old FORMAT command except that it now takes a switch for formatting different types of file systems. The following example shows how to format an NTFS drive using FORMAT.

Formatting a Volume or Diskette with FORMAT

```
FORMAT D: /fs:NTFS /v:LABEL
```

This command formats volume D: with the NTFS file system and assigns a volume label of LABEL to the new volume.

The FORMAT command is most useful for formatting floppy disks. Another useful option of FORMAT is for formatting NTFS partitions when you wish to override the allocation unit size that NT automatically sets. The allocation unit size default is based upon the size of the volume. The allocation unit size is set with the /a: switch and can be: 512, 1024, 2048, or 4096. The size of the allocation unit size value is the number of bytes per cluster.

You can also use File Manager to format floppy disks by choosing Format from the Disk menu. Make sure that the floppy disk is in the disk drive before selecting the command because Format goes out and retrieves information from the disk before it displays the Format dialog box.

2.6.4 Labeling a Volume

Volume labels show up in such places as File Manager and the DOS prompt. Many application programs also display volume labels when referring to a drive list box. I suggest using descriptive names for labels such as

☞ SYSTEM—volume containing the NT system files

☞ DATA—RAID volume used for data

☞ DB01—RAID volume used for a database

Disk Administrator allows you to modify the label of a volume using the Label option on the Tools menu.

Labeling a Drive with Disk Administrator

1. Run Disk Administrator.
2. Select the volume you wish to label in the main window.
3. Select the Label option from the Tools menu.
4. Enter the new label.
5. Click OK.

You can also use the Label command to perform this task at the DOS prompt.

Labeling a Volume with Label

```
LABEL D: LABEL
```

This command labels volume D: and assigns the name of LABEL to the volume.

2.6.5 Assigning Drive Letters to a Volume

Disk Administrator allows you to assign drive letters to a volume or volume set, change a drive letter, or specify that a volume does not have a letter assigned to it. The latter option is useful if you wish to create more than 24 volumes. Any partition or logical drive that does not have a drive letter cannot be accessed until a letter is assigned to it.

Disk Administrator is useful for assigning drive letters when moving a drive from one system to another. Simply run Disk Administrator after adding the drive and restarting the system; then select the new partition/logical drive and change the drive letter. This trick is especially useful when you move a drive that has references to its drive letter (such as in INI files, batch files, programs, or SQL scripts).

Assigning or Changing the Drive Letter for a Volume

1. Run Disk Administrator.
2. Select the volume or volume set you wish to change the letter for in the main window.
3. Select the Drive Letter option from the Tools menu.
4. Select the drive letter to assign to the current volume from the drop-down list.
5. Click OK.

Another new feature of Disk Administrator is the addition of "sticky" drive letters for CD-ROM drives. This feature allows you to assign a drive letter to a CD-ROM that will stay with the drive across boots of the system and changes to your other drive configurations. This feature is also accessed from the Tools menu.

Assigning Sticky CD-ROM Drive Letters

1. Run Disk Administrator.
2. Select the CD-ROM Drive Letters option from the Tools menu.
3. Select the CD-ROM you wish to change the driver letter for in the list on the left of the dialog box.
4. Select the Drive Letter from the drop-down list on the right.
5. Click Change.

Disk Administrator is used for manipulating most aspects of your disk systems.

2.6.6 Saving Disk Configuration Information

You should save the disk configuration information before and after you add or move a disk on an NT system. Saving the configuration information copies the disk information from the Registry to a diskette. The diskette can be used later to restore the configuration in the event that you must reinstall NT or upgrade to a new version of NT.

Saving the Disk Configuration to a Floppy Disk

1. Start Disk Administrator.
2. Choose the Configuration option under the Partition menu.
3. Choose the Save option under the Configuration submenu.
4. Place a formatted blank diskette in the first floppy disk drive (usually A:).
5. Create a label for the diskette. Make sure that it includes the date, a header such as Disk Configuration Backup, and your initials.
6. Click OK to start the save operation.

The Restore option allows you to load the disk configuration from the diskette and update the Registry. This step is dangerous because you must make sure that the diskette is current as of the last time you added or moved a disk. Performing a Restore from the wrong diskette could result in lost data.

Restoring the Disk Configuration from a Floppy Disk

1. Start Disk Administrator.
2. Choose the Configuration option under the Partition menu.
3. Choose the Restore option under the Configuration submenu.
4. Place diskette with the previously saved configuration in the first floppy disk drive (usually A:).
5. Click Yes to start the save operation.

Disk Administrator also includes the Migrate menu option on the Configuration menu. You can use Migrate if there is a previous version of NT on your system.

2.6.7 Disk Fault Tolerance

The disk fault tolerance features of NT Server are a big improvement over older network servers. NT Server provides support for mirrored disks, duplexed disks, and stripe sets with parity (RAID 5). These fault tolerance features are part of NT and are managed totally by NT. RAID (Redundant Array of Inexpensive Disks) consists of levels 0 through 5. Higher and more complex RAID levels will probably be added to NT in the future. NT does not support all RAID levels via software.

2.6.7.1 Disk Mirroring   Disk mirroring is the same as RAID 1. This technique uses a second disk to mirror the primary partition. Every write to the primary partition also goes to the mirror partition. Mirroring is a good technique to use for your system and boot partitions to make them fault-tolerant.

2.6.7.2 Disk Duplexing   Disk duplexing is disk mirroring on steroids! This technique is exactly like disk mirroring, except that a second disk controller is used for the mirror disk.

This configuration allows NT to improve performance because there are separate data paths to each drive. NT can read or write to each drive independently of the other, allowing NT to maximize system performance. This is especially true on reads where NT will read from the drive that can provide the data the fastest.

2.6.7.3 RAID in Detail RAID is a term used to define the method of combing several inexpensive disks into what appears to be a single large disk. RAID replaces the older method normally referred to as SLED (Single Large Expensive Disk) that we have traditionally been using for most systems. NT systems can mix both methods in one system.

RAID can be implemented in either a hardware or software configuration, and NT supports both methods. Hardware RAID implementations are usually the preferred method. See the section on Hardware RAID (page 79).

RAID is described in terms of levels from 0 to 5. Table 2.6 describes the RAID levels. RAID levels 0, 1, and 5 are supported in the NT Server software implementation, while hardware implementations may support all six or more levels.

Several RAID levels implement *disk striping,* which is a technique for performing disk performance, redundancy, or both. Striping basically creates one logical disk from a group of disks. Data are written across all disks in "stripes" instead of to one disk at a time. The performance improvements occur because reads and writes are split over multiple disks and can usually occur concurrently.

See the section in this chapter on hardware (page 79) for more information on using hardware RAID options with NT Server. Hardware options can dramatically improve the performance of your system by handling the management of the RAID system at the hardware controller and relieving NT of this management task.

Creating Mirror Sets. Mirror sets are created with Disk Administrator like other fault tolerance options.

Creating a Mirror Set

1. Click on the partition you wish to mirror.
2. Ctrl+Click on the second partition on a different disk with at least as much free space as the first partition.
3. Click on Establish Mirror from the Fault Tolerance menu. NT creates the mirror using a partition size on the mirror partition that matches the original partition.
4. Answer Yes to the confirmation prompt.

The size of member partitions may vary by up to 1MB when drives with different geometry are used in a mirror or stripe set because Disk Administrator rounds the size of the secondary members up to the next cylinder. Any extra space in a partition is not used. When building a mirror set, the second partition, which will become the mirror, should not be formatted.

Table 2.6 RAID Levels

Level	Advantages	Description
0	Performance only	RAID 0 is normally known as simply disk striping. Striping is used to improve performance of the drives but contains no fault tolerance. RAID 0 is actually less reliable than unstriped drives because the entire array will go down if a failure occurs and you must restore the entire array from a backup.
1	Fault tolerance only	RAID 1 is disk mirroring. Every time a write occurs to the primary disk, it is also written to the mirror disk.
2	Fault tolerance Improved performance	RAID 2 uses additional disks as check disks. Performance can be good if the system reads and writes large data blocks. Microsoft notes that RAID 2 is normally beneficial only in large systems.
3	Fault tolerance Improved performance	RAID 3 uses a single check disk for a drive array. The check disk receives the backup information for all drives in the array.
4	Fault tolerance Improved performance	RAID 4 uses a single check disk for a drive array like RAID 3. The check disk receives the backup information for all drives in the array. Data are written to the drives using block or sector striping instead of bit striping as used in RAID 3. Performance is improved over RAID 3 because data are transferred in larger blocks. Write operations are bottlenecked in both RAID 3 and 4 because all backup information must be written to the same drive.
5	Fault tolerance Improved performance	RAID 5 is the preferred fault tolerance method for NT systems because it provides fault tolerance and optimal performance (theoretically). RAID 5 dedicates the equivalent of one disk to storing backup information but splits the backup data over the entire array. Spreading the backup data over the entire array allows the RAID system to write to only two disk drives in any write operation. Multiple read operations can take place simultaneously, as can multiple write operations.

A mirror set can be disabled by breaking the set. Once the set is broken each volume becomes an independent member.

Breaking a Mirror Set

1. Click on the mirror set you wish to break.
2. Click on Break Mirror from the Fault Tolerance menu.

The original drive, or working drive if one drive is orphaned, retains the drive letter previously assigned to the mirror set. If both drives are working, the mirror drive will receive the next available drive letter.

Creating Stripe Sets. Stripe sets are created in the same manner as mirror sets. Disk Administrator is used to create the set and for other functions such as deleting a stripe set. A software implementation of striping can use from 2 to 32 drives in a stripe set. Stripe sets with parity (RAID 5) must use a minimum of three disks.

Creating Stripe Sets

1. Run Disk Administrator.
2. Click on first partition in the set.
3. Ctrl+Click on each additional partition.
4. Select Fault Tolerance and click on Create Stripe Set.
5. Enter the size of the new stripe set.
6. Click OK.

Creating Stripe Sets with Parity

1. Run Disk Administrator.
2. Click on first partition in the set.
3. Ctrl+Click on each additional partition.
4. Select Fault Tolerance and click on Create Stripe Set with Parity.
5. Enter the size of the new stripe set.
6. Click OK.

Deleting Stripe Sets of Either Type

Warning: This option deletes all data on the stripe set.

1. Run Disk Administrator.
2. Select the stripe set to delete.
3. Select the Partition menu and click on Delete.

When a Drive Fails.   When a disk failure occurs on a system using RAID 1 or RAID 5, the RAID system continues to operate. There is no fault tolerance on the array until the failed member is replaced. Disk failures show up in the System log in Event Viewer.

Disk Recovery using NT Software Solutions.   NT supports disk recovery with RAID 1 and 5. When a mirror or stripe member fails, it is called an *orphaned drive*. All new reads and writes are directed to the other disks in a set when a drive is orphaned.

Once a drive is orphaned, it must be replaced before the fault tolerance features are restored to the system. The procedures for recovering a drive are different between the two RAID fault tolerance levels. Hardware RAID systems also vary in how a bad member is replaced. A hardware RAID controller should ship with a monitor program that monitors the RAID system and feeds any problem reports to the NT Event Viewer System log when an error occurs.

Rebuilding a Damaged Mirror Disk.   RAID 1 is disk mirroring and has a separate "mirror" volume for each volume you mirror. When you install a new disk to replace the failed member, NT rebuilds the new volume to match the existing member.

Steps for Rebuilding a Mirrored Member

1. Run Disk Administrator.
2. Break the mirror set.
3. Replace the orphaned disk.
4. Reestablish a mirror set.

Rebuilding a Damaged Stripe Disk.   RAID 5 is slightly different because it uses disk striping. NT updates the new disk by rebuilding it from the backup information (Parity data) stored across the rest of the array.

Rebuilding a Stripe Set with Parity Member (Disk)

1. Replace the orphaned disk.
2. Run Disk Administrator.
3. Select the recoverable stripe set.
4. Select the replacement disk free space.
5. Select Fault Tolerance and click on the Regenerate command.
6. Quit Disk Administrator and restart the system.

This process uses the parity information to recreate the data that were stored on the disk that failed. The set will once again be fault tolerant.

You may experience a problem where a member is orphaned due to some problem outside of a physical disk problem. Examples are cable, controller, or power problems. When these problems occur, you should select the orphaned disk in step 4 and continue the process from there. NT will recreate the data on the member using the parity information and once again include the former member in the set.

Disk Recovery Using Hardware Solutions.   Most hardware implementations of RAID provide for quick disk recovery when a problem occurs. These systems normally use a *hot-swap* method, which allows you to pull a disk from the drive array and replace it while the system is running. This form of disk replacement is the coolest ever.

Many hardware systems automatically rebuild a failed member disk when it is replaced. You simply pull the bad disk and insert the new disk. The hardware controller takes care of the rest.

Some systems such as the Digital StorageWorks controllers take this procedure a step farther by providing capabilities for a *hot spare*. A hot spare is a disk inserted in the RAID array that is not used but is designated as the spare disk. When a failure occurs, the new disk is generated, the old disk is failed by the controller, and the system continues to run with complete fault tolerance. This is the ultimate in disaster preparation at the disk level.

Many hardware RAID solutions also provide software that can be used to determine the status of the RAID system and control certain aspects of the system. For instance, the Digital StorageWorks includes software that graphically displays each drive in the array. You can selectively touch each drive. One of the nice features of this software is the ability to select a drive and manually fail the drive. This feature effectively takes the drive out of the set. Using this technique, you can pull a drive and replace it gracefully without ever shutting down the system.

2.6.8 Converting a FAT or HPFS Partition to NTFS

The Convert utility can convert a FAT or HPFS partition to NTFS. The utility must run from the command prompt. The syntax is

```
CONVERT d: /FS:NTFS
```

This is a one-way process. You can't convert from NTFS to FAT or HPFS.

When you run this command on the boot volume, you receive a notice that NT can't run the command because the volume can't be locked. This notice occurs because the volume contains the NT system files that are in use. You will be asked if you wish to run the command the next time the system boots. Simply answer yes, and the Convert command is scheduled to run the next time the system boots.

2.6.9 Adding Disks

NT automatically determines when a new disk has been added, unless you are using a hardware RAID controller. The number of disks that a system may use is determined by the hardware configuration. For instance, some RAID systems may allow 32 disks while others may use only 8.

Adding a Disk Drive.

1. Install the new disk.
2. Run Disk Administrator.
3. Click OK when Disk Administrator notifies you that it needs to update its configuration.
4. Select the new disk and perform any operations necessary to put the disk in service (partition creation, formatting, etc.).
5. Choose the Configuration menu from the Partition menu; then choose the Save submenu option to save the disk configuration. Make sure to label the disk correctly (see page 37 for more information).

Hardware controllers typically require you to bring down the system, reconfigure the RAID system with a custom utility, and then restart the system.

2.6.10 Applications and Stripe Sets

Many applications can benefit from using stripe sets on your disk drives. Stripe sets usually outperform the same disks with traditional formatted volumes on each disk. This outperformance is especially true if you are using the new controllers that support striping in hardware. NT and applications see the entire stripe set as one huge disk, while the hardware handles the physical access to the disk drives.

The more drives you add, the better the performance should be—theoretically. This increase in performance occurs because each write to the stripe set is simultaneously split over the entire set of striped disks with the read or write operation happening simultaneously on multiple disks.

Stripe sets are particularly nice for systems running a large database program such as SQL Server. SQL Server and most major databases have for years provided the ability to split the database over different disks using a variety of methods to balance the Input/Output (I/O) load. None of the methods were easy and usually meant that someone spent a lot of time fiddling with device names and other fun things while continuously monitoring database performance. Make another change, monitor, make another change, monitor, and so on. You can't imagine what a pain this is until you have tried it.

Now the system administrator can simply take a fair-sized disk array, create a stripe set, and then place the entire database on the resulting volume. Microsoft engineers indicate that stripe sets almost always outperform traditional optimization methods for physical disk layout.

2.7 DEVICE DRIVERS

NT controls, and interfaces to, many different parts of a computer with device drivers. Device drivers normally provide the interface between NT and a hardware device such as a tape drive or disk controller.

Most device drivers are installed and configured automatically during the installation of NT or when a new device is added. For instance, adding a new adapter or tape device with Windows Setup will most likely install a new driver unless a compatible one is already on the system.

Devices can be manually started and stopped using the Devices applet in Control Panel. This applet is almost identical to the Services applet, which is also in Control Panel.

Starting a Stopped Device

1. Start Control Panel.
2. Select the Devices applet.
3. Select the device to start.
4. Click the Start button.

Stopping a Device

1. Start Control Panel.
2. Select the Devices applet.
3. Select the device to stop.
4. Click the Stop button.

Most devices are set up correctly when they are installed, and you never have to mess with the startup configuration. When the time comes to change these parameters, the Devices applet comes to the rescue.

Configuring Startup Options for a Device

1. Start Control Panel.
2. Select the Devices applet.
3. Select the device to setup.
4. Click the Startup button.
5. Select the desired startup option and close the dialog box.

2.8 SERVICES

NT uses services for a variety of tasks, ranging from operating system tasks such as NetLogon to network services like NetDDE or RPC (Remote Procedure Call) and numerous other tasks. Application and other add-on software can also install services for use with that particular application.

Services are similar to a device driver in the way they are managed and the tasks they perform. Most services can be considered part of the operating system or an operating system support feature for an application. For instance, SQL Server and Systems Management Server both install services that provide various functions for the particular application. Other services included things like the Scheduler service that provides the AT functionality for batch routines, the messenger service that provides messaging support, and the various network services such as NetLogon, Server, and Workstation.

Services provide an efficient behind-the-scenes mechanism for both NT and NT applications. Services don't show up in the task list and there is no icon for a service, but the services are running and performing their allotted tasks.

Services can be set to start up automatically when NT comes up. Services also do not terminate when a user logs out from the NT console. Most services for systems such as SQL Server and Systems Management Server are set to start automatically when NT boots. Services must be configured for automatic startup to provide continuous support for a particular function across logons at the console.

2.8.1 Managing Services

The Services applet in Control Panel is the primary interface for managing services. Server Manager and the Net command also provide access to managing services. Server Manager is particularly useful because you can use it to manage services on any NT system on the network or over RAS.

Server Manager provides direct access to the Services applet that is used in Control Panel. Once you have displayed the Services applet with Server Manager, managing services is the same as in Control Panel. One helpful feature of

Server Manager is that not only can you access lots of other server features but you can also access services on other systems and access services from a Windows 3.x client via the client tools edition of Server Manager.

Accessing the Services Applet from Server Manager

1. Start Server Manager.
2. Select the NT system to manage from the list of computers.
3. Choose the Services option from the Computer menu.

Either Net Start or the Services applet can be used to view the status of all running services quickly. These tools are frequently used to check on the status of currently running services.

Displaying Running Services with the Services Applet

1. Start Control Panel or Server Manager.
2. Start the Services Applet.

Displaying Running Services with Net Start

1. Access the DOS Command prompt.
2. Enter the following command:

```
net start
```

The best way to start a service that is used frequently is automatically at boot time. The following steps describe how to set this up.

Configuring a Service to Start Automatically

1. Run Control Panel and run the Services Applet or run Server Manager and select the Services command from the Computer menu.
2. Select the service.
3. Click Startup.
4. Click the Automatic button.
5. Click the System Account button or click This Account and select the user account for that service. If you select a user account, you must enter and confirm the password.

You may need to start a service manually from time to time. One occasion is when you set a service to start automatically but do not want to reboot the server to use the service. Simply set the startup options to start the service automatically the next time NT is booted and then manually start the service for the current session.

You will most likely run into another instance where a service fails to start at boot time. This failure is often caused by something like two systems trying to be the domain controller or an incorrect network setting. Simply use one of the following techniques to start the service after you have corrected the problem.

Starting a Service with Control Panel

1. Run Control Panel and run the Services Applet or run Server Manager and select the Services command from the Computer menu.
2. Select the service.
3. Click the Start button.

Starting a Service with Net Start

1. Access the DOS Command Prompt.
2. Enter the following command:

`net start SERVICE`

SERVICE is the name for the service.

For instance, to start the workstation service, enter

`net start workstation`

A service can start automatically or manually depending upon the settings in the Services applet. You can also disable a service and interactively start or stop a service. You may also Pause or Continue a service if there is a need to stop the service for a period of time.

Stopping a Service

1. Run Control Panel and start the Services applet or run Server Manager and select the Services command from the Computer menu.
2. Select the service.
3. Click the Stop button.

Pausing or Continuing a Service

1. Run Control Panel and start the Services applet or run Server Manager and select the Services command from the Computer menu.
2. Select the service.
3. Click Pause or Continue. The Pause button stops other users from connecting to the service until it is restarted or continued.

You may find odd times when you need to use these commands. Sometimes a service fails to start when NT boots for one reason or another and you must manually start it. Maybe you need to perform some type of maintenance and wish to stop the service manually, perform the task, and then restart the service.

Wouldn't it be great if we could create our own services? Imagine your own program starting automatically when the system boots and performing some magic in the background with no user intervention.

The NT Resource Kit provides a tool called SRVANY.EXE that performs this task. SRVANY.EXE allows you to run almost any application in the background as a service. Most programs behave properly in this manner, even as users log in and out. The documentation for SRVANY.EXE mentions that some 16-bit programs will not survive a logout, so test your program carefully by installing and configuring the service and then start the service, log out, then log back in, and make sure the service is still running. The best way to test an automatic starting service is to log out and reboot the system and then make sure that the service is running.

2.9 SYMMETRICAL MULTIPROCESSOR (SMP) CONFIGURATIONS

Symmetrical MultiProcessor (SMP) systems can add real bang to certain NT Servers. The biggest effect occurs when your system is processor-bound. A processor-bound system is typically performing lots of application tasks or working as a heavily used application server. File servers are rarely processor-bound but rather bottlenecked at the disk or network subsystems (I/O). Performance Monitor can provide lots of information on how heavily your system is taxing the processor subsystem.

NT schedules the highest priority thread first to ensure that the top-priority thread is always running. In an SMP system NT schedules the highest priority threads on all processors in the system. The low-priority threads always share a single processor. For instance, if your system has four processors, the three highest-priority threads run on three of the processors, while the remaining threads run on the fourth processor.

SMP systems such as the Compaq and Digital Equipment lines can add lots of power to file and application servers. I had the chance to install NT Server on a Digital 2100-500 AXP (Alpha) system. The particular system has 640MB of RAM, 18GB of disk, and a 190-MHz processor. As you can imagine, this system runs NT so fast that everything except for some disk activities seems to happen instantly. The 2100-500 design is elegant, because up to four processors can be installed in the same box. A few months later, another client purchased a 2100-500 with 128MB of RAM and two 275-MHz processors. Now this is a screamer. When processor performance becomes an issue on this type of system, it will scream again if you add a new processor. Imagine up to four 275-MHz processors in a system configuration like this.

Compaq and many other vendors have come out with high-performance SMP systems that are designed to run NT. As more and more systems come out, the price will drop for all of us. Watch the trends, and when the price is right, pull an SMP system into your network.

The NT Resource Kit has a utility to upgrade your system with an additional processor. This step must be performed before NT can use the additional processor.

Adding an Additional Processor to an SMP System

1. Run UpToMP.
2. Specify the drive that contains the NT distribution files.

3. Choose your processor (HAL) from the list box.

4. Click OK.

2.10 CONTROL PANEL

Control Panel is one of the key management tools for NT. Control Panel uses tool files for each major function or group of functions in Control Panel. Each tool file has a CPL extension. Table 2.7 lists the major tools included with NT Server.

Additional tools can be added to Control Panel by simply placing the tool file in the appropriate directory (%SystemRoot%\SYSTEM32). New tools are often provided by third-party vendors or with network applications that provide specific functions. Notice that all the program file names for control panel end in .CPL.

2.11 REMOVING NT COMPONENTS TO SAVE SPACE

Many NT components can be removed to conserve disk space and usage of system resources. Removing NT components also precludes users from accessing the programs and possibly causes problems.

The best way to remove NT components is with the NT Setup program. You can remove items such as readme files, games, and others. Removing a component deletes the files from the server and makes the services unavailable. Proceed with caution.

Table 2.7 Control Panel Support Files

File Name	Description
CURSORS.CPL	Allows you to customize the cursors used by NT.
DISPLAY.CPL	Manages the display settings for NT.
FTPMGR.CPL	Manages the FTP Server options.
MAIN.CPL	Provides functions for managing color, fonts, ports, mouse, desktop, keyboard, printers, international, system, and date/time.
MULTIMED.CPL	Manages multimedia options: Sound, MIDI Mapper, and Drivers.
NCPA.CPL	Manages the network settings for NT.
NWC.CPL	Manages the NetWare Services.
SFMMGR.CPL	Manages the Services for Macintosh.
SRVRMGR.CPL	Manages the following options: Server, Services, and Devices. Provides the same functions as Server Manager in the Administrative Tools group.
UPS.CPL	Manages the UPS service.

Removing NT Components

1. Start NT Setup.
2. Add/Remove Windows Components.
3. Select the components to remove.
4. Click Continue.
5. Click OK.

2.12 STARTING A SERVER

NT Server starts automatically, including the startup of services set to start automatically. Always check Event Viewer for details on any service that does not seem to be working. You may occasionally get a message on the Domain Controller or another server stating, "At Least One Service or Driver Failed During System Startup. Use Event Viewer to Examine the Event Log for Details." This message occurs when one or more services fail to start. When you consult Event Viewer, you should see an error at the top of the list if the list is sorted by Newest First (the default sort order). You can identify the event because the date and time should be close to the time the server started.

You may find a message in the Event Log noting that "Browser service forced an election on ...." This message occurs because the Domain Controller always comes up with a higher priority because it is the browsemaster for the network and therefore there is no other browsemaster available. This message is usually harmless. It simply indicates that there was no browsemaster available when the server started; it can be ignored. A *browsemaster* is the NT Server that maintains a list of browseable systems and services. You should consult the Event Log anytime there is a problem at startup either indicated by a message or when a service is not available.

2.13 STOPPING A SERVER

The normal procedure for stopping an NT system is to choose Shutdown from the File menu in Program Manager or select the Shutdown button on the Windows NT Security dialog box after pressing Ctrl+Alt+Del. Of course, to do this you must be an Administrator on NT Server or have explicit rights to shut down the server.

Another option for shutting down a system is to place a Shutdown button on the Welcome dialog box. This button allows anyone to shut down the system without logging on. This button can be useful in situations where the server or workstation is locked in a secure room or in a very low-risk environment.

The Shutdown button in the Welcome dialog box is enabled by making a small change to the Registry.

Adding a Shutdown Button to the Welcome Dialog Box

1. Run REGEDT32.

2. Change the value of ShutDownWithoutLogon value to a 1 for the following key:

```
HKEY_LOCAL_MACHINE\SOFTWARE\Microsoft\Windows -
NT\CurrentVersion\Winlogon
```

After this change is made, NT displays the Shutdown button on the Welcome dialog box. Remember this change before you move this system into a non-secure environment. You can remove the Shutdown button by changing the Winlogon value to 0.

You can add the Shutdown button to the dialog box using REGKEY.EXE from the NT Resource Kit (see page 31). This program provides one-click access to the change and is therefore much easier than using REGEDT32.

The NT Resource Kit provides another option for stopping a server with the Shutdown command. This command runs from the command prompt and works on both the current server and remote servers. The command can also be included in a batch program.

Stopping an NT System with Shutdown (NT Resource Kit)

1. Execute the following command:

```
shutdown \\computername /L /A /R /T:n /Y /C "Msg"
```

\\computername	Specifies the system to shut down. If not specified, the local system will be shut down if the /L switch is used.
/L	Specifies a local shutdown. This switch must be used to force a local shutdown.
/A	Aborts a shutdown in progress that has not reached time 0.
/R	Specifies an auto reboot after shutdown.
/T:n	Determines the amount of time (n) in seconds before the server shuts down. Default time is 20 seconds.
/Y	Automatically answers Yes to all questions.
/C	Automatically forces all applications to close without prompting to save any open files.
"Msg"	Specifies the shutdown message to display on the system going down.

The Shutdown command is extremely useful in production situations where you wish to perform several tasks before the system goes down. NT provides the standard DOS batch language to handle these types of tasks in conjunction with Shutdown. Systems managers from VMS installations will like this batch command called SHUTDOWN.BAT (remember SHUTDOWN.COM?).

```
@echo off
rem
```

```
rem ShutDown.bat
rem Ken Spencer
rem
Echo Do you wish to reboot after shutdown?
choice
echo .
if errorlevel == 1 set options=/R
echo Run site specific shutdown procedures?
choice
echo .
set RunSpec=n
if errorlevel == 1 set runspec=y
echo Select time in minutes until shutdown
choice /C02
if errorlevel == 2 set options=%options% /T:99
echo .
echo Force all applications to close?
choice
if errorlevel == 1 set options=%options% /C
echo .
echo Shutdown All Systems (N = only the local system) choice
set AllSystems=n
if errorlevel == 1 set AllSystems=y
if %runspec% == y GoTo RunSpec
GoTo SkipRun
:RunSpec
Rem
Rem Place site specific options here
Rem
Echo Executing Site Specific Shutdown options at this time
:SkipRun
Rem Place actual shutdown commands at this point
Rem -------------------------------------------
Rem
Rem Sample Local shutdown command
\reskit35\shutdown /L /Y %options% "System is Shutting Down" /Y
Rem
if %AllSystems% == y GoTo RunAll
GoTo SkipAll
Rem
Rem
:RunAll
Rem
Echo Shutting down all remote systems
Rem Sample Remote shutdown command
Rem \reskit35\shutdown \\Server /Y %options% "System is Shutting
    Down" /Y
:SkipAll
```

SHUTDOWN.BAT should be placed in a directory on the PATH that is located ahead of the RESKIT35 directory where SHUTDOWN.EXE is located. This position forces SHUTDOWN.BAT to execute first when you enter the command. The following example shows the correct way to set up the PATH if SHUTDOWN.BAT is in the C:\U directory.

```
PATH=C:\WINNT\system32;C:\WINNT;D:\SQL\BINN; -
    D:\SQL\DLL;C:\u;E:\RESKIT35\;m:\sql\bin;C:\WINNT; -
    C:\DOS;E:\MDIABLTZ;e:\CONTROLS;
```

The next example shows the prompts and output from SHUTDOWN.BAT.

```
Do you wish to reboot after shutdown?
[Y,N]?Y
.
Run site specific shutdown procedures?
[Y,N]?Y
.
Select time in minutes until shutdown
[0,2]?2
.
Force all applications to close?
[Y,N]?N
.
Shutdown All Systems (N = only the local system) [Y,N]?N
```

Specific programs that should run each time you shut down the system can be placed in the section under the ":RunAll" label. These commands are executed each time you run SHUTDOWN.BAT and answer **Y** to the prompt "Run site specific shutdown procedures?"

Multiple NT systems can be shut down with one command. Simply add the other systems in the section of SHUTDOWN.BAT labeled "Sample Remote shutdown command." Copy the sample command, remove REM at the start of the line, and edit the computer name.

Answering **Y** to the "Force all applications to close?" prompt immediately closes all running applications. Any unsaved data are lost. Answering **N** allows each application to prompt to save any open files.

The handiest way to run this program is to create an icon in Program Manager that points to it.

2.14 CONFIGURING AUTOMATIC LOGON FOR NT SERVER

You may find it useful to have a server automatically log on to a user account when it boots. Reasons for this may be to start Performance Monitor or Event Viewer or some other program at startup. The automatic logon process is fairly simple to set up using REGEDT32.

Setting up an Automatic Logon at Startup

1. Run REGEDT32.
2. Enter values for DefaultDomainName, DefaultUserName, and Default-Password under the key:

```
HKEY_LOCAL_MACHINE\SOFTWARE\Microsoft\Windows-
NT\CurrentVersion\Winlogon
```

3. If the password entry does not exist, make an entry for DefaultPassword with a type of REG_SZ and the value equal to the password for the Default-UserName.

4. Add an entry for AutoAdminLogon = 1 with a type of REG_SZ.

5. Restart the system after you have changed the values and exited REGEDT32.

You may encounter one problem with automating the logon process. This problem exists because the logon may finish before some services have had time to start. For instance, NT may try to connect to network services before the required network services have started or an application in the Startup group may try to start before a required service it depends on starts.

I ran across this problem when trying to load both the OS/2 External and Dispatch utilities for Microsoft Mail during the automatic logon process when NT Server started. The batch file I created to run the programs from the Startup group started before the OS/2 subsystem started. I solved the problem by creating a small Visual Basic (VB) program that runs in place of the original logon batch file.

This VB program works by asking the system for the time when it starts. The time is reformatted and has 10 minutes added to it. This time is then fed to the AT scheduler for each command in a small batch file. At the conclusion of the process, the batch file is executed by the Shell command.

I also developed another way to solve the same problem also using VB. This time I just created a small application with a form, one text box, and a timer control. I set the timer interval to 60,000 (1 minute), tracked the total number of minutes with a global counter, and then started the correct program using the Shell command when 10 minutes was up. This program takes about 10 minutes to write and debug. You can add any number of programs to start or even use an INI file to list programs to start. I also placed a loop in the timer event that beeps the number of minutes remaining as the program counts down. This way I have an audible and visual indicator of when programs will start after NT boots and logs on. The following code sample shows the entire Visual Basic code for the application.

```
Dim MinuteCounter As Integer

Sub Form_Load ()
    MinuteCounter = 0
    Text1.Text = MinuteCounter
End Sub
Sub Timer1_Timer ()
Dim x As Integer
    If MinuteCounter = 9 Then
        x = Shell("E:\WGPO\EXTEROS2.BAT")
    Else
        MinuteCounter = MinuteCounter + 1
        Text1.Text = MinuteCounter
        For x = 1 To MinuteCounter
            Beep
```

```
        Next x
    End If
End Sub
```

The "Dim MinuteCounter As Integer" statement should be placed in the global declarations statement of the form. To add more programs to the startup list, copy the SHELL line in the TIMER1_TIMER subroutine and change the program name between the double quotes (" ").

2.15 CHANGING THE LOGON WALLPAPER FOR NT SERVER (AND WHY?)

You are probably wondering why we would want to change the wallpaper used during the logon process for an NT Server. This task is usually reserved for work-station users who spend much of their time tweaking the colors and other appearance items of their systems.

Changing the wallpaper actually has one good use: Identifying the name and purpose of the server. Displaying the name and purpose (File Server, DB Server, etc.) makes it easy to see which server is which or which server you have connected to via a switch such as those marketed by Black Box, Network Technologies, and other vendors that allow you to set up several servers that use the same monitor, keyboard, and mouse.

The secret in setting up different wallpaper for the logon screen is using REGEDT32 to change the default setting.

Changing the Default Wallpaper for the Logon Screen

1. Create the new BMP file.
2. Copy the file to the Windows NT system directory (WINNT32 by default).
3. Start REGEDT32 (see page 30).
4. Find the key:

```
HKEY_USERS\DEFAULT\Control Panel\Desktop\Wallpaper
```

5. Change the string from LANMANNT.BMP to your new BMP file.

You can also use REGKEY from the NT Resource Kit to perform this change quickly.

2.16 CONNECTING TO ANOTHER SYSTEM USING IPC$

Sometimes you may want to manage a system remotely but do not have an account on that system with the same user name and password or the machine is in another domain that does not have a trust relationship with your domain. Simply execute the following command:

```
NET USE \\servername\IPC$ /USER: domainname\username *
```

Replace servername with the server you wish to connect to. Replace domainname\username with the domain and user name where the system you are connecting to is located. The * causes NET USE to prompt you for your password. Once the command completes, you can access the system from the Administrative tools by entering the server name in the Select Computer dialog boxes.

When you create a trust relationship using the IPC$ connection, NT will not confirm the creation of a trust relationship as long as the IPC$ connection exists. This is most likely because a computer cannot be logged in to a domain from two sources such as RAS and a network connection at the same time. The trust relationship works as soon as the IPC$ share is disconnected.

2.17 MANAGEMENT FROM AN NT WORKSTATION

You can manage most features of your NT Server from any NT Workstation. This includes running most of the NT Server administrative tools from the client workstation. The utilities for NT Server are also included with the NT Resource Kit. The Resource Kit includes a license allowing you to use the utilities from NT Workstations.

This license can be slightly confusing because many of the NT Server tools look and/or sound like an NT Workstation tool. Examples of these tools are NT's User Manager (MUSRMGR.EXE), NT Server User Manager for Domains (USRMGR.EXE), and the NT Server "Server Manager" program (SRVMGR. EXE). The NT Server Server Manager program adds a new front end and a few features to the standard NT "Server" applet in Control Panel (SRVMGR.CPL), which is also included with NT Server.

Other NT Server tools such as Performance Monitor (PERFMON.EXE), Disk Administrator (WINDISK.EXE), and Event Viewer (EVENTVWR.EXE) are the same on both NT and NT Server. Performance Monitor and other standard NT tools can access the same features on an NT Server as on a regular NT machine. You do not need to do anything special other than select the server name when using the tool.

Using NT Server-specific tools from an NT workstation is slightly more interesting because you must access the tools over the network or move the tools to your local machine. The easiest way to access these tools is to create a share of the SYSTEM32 directory on the NT Server and access this share from your workstation. I set up a connection from drive Z: to this directory on my system to provide permanent access to the resources in NT Server and then created a Pro gram Manager icon for each of the NT Server tools I needed.

The easiest way to place a program icon in Program Manager is to connect to your shared connection in File Manager and move the File Manager window until you can see both the File Manager window with the new drive and Program Manager at the same time. Then click on the file you wish to set up in Program Manager, drag it over the Program Manager group, and release the mouse button. Program Manager warns you that this file may not be available later because it is on a network drive. Select OK and you are through. Repeat this process for each application you wish to set up.

Setting up Program Manager icons with Drag and Drop from File Manager is much quicker than using the File New method from Program Manager.

There is one caveat to setting up the tools this way. The NT Server license allows you to use the Administrative tools from only one machine at a time. Microsoft has solved this by placing the NT Server tools in the NT Resource Kit. You can install the programs on any NT or NT Server system. The Resource Kit comes with a site license for all the programs, making it necessary to buy only one copy of the kit per site.

2.18 MANAGEMENT FROM WINDOWS 3.X AND WINDOWS 95 SYSTEMS

Many of the NT management tools have been ported to Windows 3.x via the WIN32s API. These tools (User Manager for Domains, Server Manager, etc.) allow a Windows for Workgroups 3.x , or Windows 3.x client to be used to manage the NT desktop and NT Server machines on the network.

Several programs for 16-bit versions of Windows ship with NT Server. These programs include

☞ User Manager for Domains,

☞ Server Manager,

☞ Event Viewer,

☞ Print Manager for Windows NT Server, and

☞ Tools for File Manager that add the Security menu allowing you to change security settings on an NTFS volume.

You must install a new redirector (VREDIR.386) for Windows for Workgroups 3.11 or LAN Manager systems before using these tools. Check the readme file contained with the server tools to determine if this applies to your system and the procedure for installing the redirector. This file and others for Windows for Workgroups are located in the \Clients directory on the NT Server CD.

Each of the Win16 tools works just about like its counterpart under NT Server. The most notable difference occurs during startup when you must select a server. This prompt doesn't occur when running the tools on NT Server because they default to the current system. The exceptions are Server Manager because it focuses on the current domain and File Manager because its focus is on whatever drive you are using.

Installing NT Server Tools for Windows 3.11

1. Share the CD-ROM or hard disk that contains the distribution files. The files are stored in the directory tree (\Clients\SrvTools\Windows) on the distribution CD.

2. Connect to the share from the Windows for Workgroups system you wish to install on.

3. Run the Setup program under the \Clients\SrvTools\Windows directory on the share.

You should be able to run these tools or possibly the full NT version of the tools on Windows 95. Check the TechNet CD and with Microsoft to determine which ones to use. You can also experiment by trying to run the NT version of the tool on Windows 95. If that doesn't work, then try the 16-bit tools. Remember that even though Windows 95 uses WIN32, it doesn't support some security aspects of NT, making it likely that, even on the shipping Windows 95 product, some tools won't run.

2.19 SYSTEM ALERTS

NT generates a number of different alerts for system events. These alerts are separate from the alerts that can be set on counters in Performance Monitor. Alerts are generated by various subsystems of NT as events occur. Alerts are generated for security problems, access problems, server problems, potential power outages reported by the UPS subsystem, and printer problems.

Alerts can be triggered by any NT Workstation and NT Server system. Any system that generates alerts must be running the Alerter and Messenger services. Systems that receive the alert message must be running the Messenger service. Figure 2.3 shows the Services applet with the Alerter and Messenger services started. Note that the Startup parameter is set to Automatic. For more information on configuring services, see the section in this chapter on services (page 46).

Checking the Services Required for Alerts

1. Make sure the Alerter and Messenger services are running on the server.

Fig. 2.3 The Services dialog box shows the services running on a particular system. This dialog box is accessed from Control Panel/Services or from using Server Manager and selecting Services from the Computer menu.

2. Start Control Panel/Services or Server Manager and select Services from the Computer menu.
3. Verify that the correct services are running. Figure 2.3 shows both the Alerter and Messenger services running with the Startup option set to Automatic.

You can determine the user and systems that receive alerts by using the Server applet in Control Panel. This applet provides a way for you to enter either a user name or system name to receive alerts. Multiple alert targets can be entered on one system.

Assigning Systems and Users to Receive Alerts

1. Start Server Manager.
2. Click the Alerts button.
3. Enter the user names and computer names that you wish to be notified when alerts occur.
4. Click the Add button or press Enter.
5. Repeat steps 3 and 4 until you have entered all the names.
6. Close the dialog box.

For more information on other alerts, check the section in Chapter 10 on performance monitor alerts (page 306).

2.20 EVENT LOGGING

2.20.1 Overview

NT includes a superb event-logging system that is similar to the performance-monitoring system. Both the event-logging and performance-monitoring systems serve as a central place for recording events and performance counters for applications, security systems, and the operating system. The event-logging system allows third-party systems to plug into the central system instead of each application implementing its own log files.

This centralized event tracking makes it much easier for a systems manager to review any type of occurrence on the system: start Event Viewer and review each of the logs. Event Viewer is in fact the primary place to look for information on almost any type of event in the system. You will be amazed at the wealth and detail of information included in the various event logs. Everything from a notification (print job completion), security event (logon attempt fails), potential problem (server disk is nearing capacity), to startup problems (a service fails to start) is recorded.

NT supports three types of event logs:

☞ System records events from the operating system.

☞ Application records events from application programs.

☞ Security records security and audit events.

2.20.2 Event Viewer

Event Viewer is the central tool for manipulating event logs. Event Viewer's interface is clean and straightforward, as shown in Figure 2.4.

Event Viewer is a powerful and simple tool to use. Simply start Event Viewer and you are in the network management business. You can perform a number of other tasks using Event Viewer.

Displaying Details on a Log Event

1. Start Event Viewer.
2. Double-click the event or select the event and press Enter.

Filtering the Event Viewer Display

1. Start Event Viewer.
2. Select Filter from the View menu.
3. Select the options for the filter and click OK. Multiple options can be set at one time to make a complex filter. Figure 2.5 shows the Filter dialog box.

Setting Event Log Options

1. Start Event Viewer.
2. Select the Log Options menu option from the Log menu.
3. Select the log to change settings for in the top list box.

Date	Time	Source	Category	Event	User	Computer
3/15/95	9:31:37 PM	DhcpServer	None	1011	N/A	NTAS-TRI-STAR
3/14/95	8:13:43 AM	Srv	None	2000	N/A	NTAS-TRI-STAR
3/14/95	8:13:43 AM	Srv	None	2000	N/A	NTAS-TRI-STAR
3/14/95	8:07:52 AM	Srv	None	2000	N/A	NTAS-TRI-STAR
3/14/95	8:07:51 AM	Srv	None	2000	N/A	NTAS-TRI-STAR
3/13/95	9:01:30 AM	Srv	None	2000	N/A	NTAS-TRI-STAR
3/13/95	9:01:30 AM	Srv	None	2000	N/A	NTAS-TRI-STAR
3/12/95	10:24:52 PM	Rdr	None	3012	N/A	NTAS-TRI-STAR
3/12/95	8:57:20 PM	Rdr	None	3012	N/A	NTAS-TRI-STAR
3/12/95	8:45:10 PM	Srv	None	2000	N/A	NTAS-TRI-STAR
3/12/95	8:45:10 PM	Srv	None	2000	N/A	NTAS-TRI-STAR
3/12/95	5:36:55 PM	Service Control Mar	None	7000	N/A	NTAS-TRI-STAR
3/11/95	10:47:01 PM	Service Control Mar	None	7026	N/A	NTAS-TRI-STAR
3/11/95	10:46:46 PM	BROWSER	None	8015	N/A	NTAS-TRI-STAR
3/11/95	10:46:45 PM	BROWSER	None	8015	N/A	NTAS-TRI-STAR
3/11/95	10:45:29 PM	ntxall	None	4103	N/A	NTAS-TRI-STAR
3/11/95	10:45:29 PM	Serial	None	3	N/A	NTAS-TRI-STAR
3/11/95	10:45:29 PM	Serial	None	25	N/A	NTAS-TRI-STAR
3/11/95	10:45:29 PM	Serial	None	25	N/A	NTAS-TRI-STAR

Fig. 2.4 Event Viewer lists the events from most recent to oldest. The sort order can be changed using the View menu.

Fig. 2.5 This filter is set for only the TCP/IP source. You can quickly select many other options to fine-tune the display to only the events you are interested in.

4. Change the desired settings.

5. Click OK.

Make sure you have set the log options to limit the event logs to a reasonable size. "Reasonable" in this case must be small enough not to choke your system but large enough to display adequate event information. You should also use care when performing operations that may quickly load up the log. For instance, running CACLS from a batch file to reset permissions on a bunch of user directories is one command that may fill up the security log in a hurry.

2.20.3 DumpEL (NT Resource Kit)

DumpEL is a tool from the NT Resource Kit for dumping Event Logs. DumpEL dumps an event log from one system and log at a time into a delimited text file. Once the data is in the delimited file, you can manipulate it easily with many different tools. The nice thing about DumpEL is that it can be easily automated with a batch program.

DumpEL can be used to dump the log on the local system or on a remote system. Selection filters can be used to limit the information extracted. The syntax is

```
dumpel -s ServerName -f OutPutFile -l LogName -m -r
```

-s   Server name, not including leading backslashes (\\). Defaults to the current server.

-f   Output file name. Defaults to the screen (stdout). This option overwrites any file existing with the same name.

-l   Log file name.

-m   Source of the records to dump (e.g., Serial, TCP/IP). Only one source at a time can be used.

-e   Event id to filter for. The format is -e n1 n2 n3 ... n10, with up to 10 event ids specified at once. Can be used only with the -m switch. The -r switch can be used to reverse the action of -e, in which case all events specified by -e will be ignored and everything else will be dumped.

-r   Reverses the filter action. When -r is used, it excludes any events selected with the -m and -e options.

-t   Separates strings in the output with tabs. Spaces are the default.

The ability to dump by event id is neat because you can filter the event log for certain problems. Every event logged has some type of event id such as 2000 or 2010. Determining the suspect event ID can be as easy as finding a few suspect events in the event log using Event Viewer and writing down the event ID numbers. Then use DUMPEL to pull all suspect events out of the log.

Some examples of how to use this command are in order. To dump the SYSTEM log on the current system to the event.out file:

```
dumpel -l system -f event.out
```

To dump the APPLICATION log on the current system:

```
dumpel -l application -f event.out
```

To dump the SECURITY log on the current system:

```
dumpel -l security -f event.out
```

To dump the SYSTEM log on the server FS01:

```
dumpel -s FS01 -l system -f event.out
```

To dump the SYSTEM log on the current system for only TCP/IP events:

```
dumpel -l system -f event.out -m tcpip
```

To dump the SYSTEM log on the current system for everything but TCP/IP events:

```
dumpel -l system -f event.out -m tcpip -r
```

2.21 CONFIGURING AUTOMATIC RESTART OF A SERVER

A useful feature of the 3.5 version of NT Server is System Recovery, which provides the ability to configure automatic reboot of the server when a fatal error occurs and the option of reporting the failure. The System applet in Control Panel is used to configure the System Recovery feature.

The standard configuration for error recovery is for the server to write event log data to the system log, send an alert to Administrators, dump system memory to a file, and then automatically reboot the server. This recovery happens when a fatal error occurs and NT cannot recover gracefully.

You can change the following items using the System applet:

☞ write an event to the system log,

☞ send administrative alerts,

☞ insert options for the log file, and

☞ automatically reboot or shut down and wait to be rebooted

Setting System Recovery Options

1. Start Control Panel.
2. Run the System applet.
3. Choose the Recovery button on the System dialog box.
4. Change the appropriate options.
5. Click OK.

The server may need to be rebooted for some of these changes to take effect. If rebooting is required, NT will prompt you.

Notice that the default log file is MEMORY.DMP and is in the system root directory (WINNT by default).

Why should you use any of these features? NT Advanced Server 3.1 automatically stops when it hits certain errors. This reaction is similar to many systems when they are hit with a "fatal" error. Have you ever seen a parity error on a PC or a PC lockup for another hardware problem such as a General Protection Fault (GPF) or the dreaded "black screen" when Windows 3.x goes away? It's the same thing. This reaction can be aggravating under certain circumstances, such as when you have lots of users on a system and can't afford extended downtime. It is much better to have the system reboot after writing the exception data to a log file.

This type of behavior is exactly what the new shutdown features are designed for. Simply set NT Server to auto reboot, write an entry to the event log, and write the memory dump to the log file. If the system ever hits a "fatal" STOP error, it will recover and you can use the memory dump to debug the problem.

2.22 REPAIRING DAMAGED SYSTEM FILES

NT stores information to repair the system on the Emergency Repair disk created during the installation and in the \SystemRoot\REPAIR directory.

The REPAIR information can be used when your system files become corrupted for some reason. It can also be useful when you have toasted your system files and need to quickly replace them. Make sure that the Repair disk is up to date before starting the repair process to avoid losing information added since installation. (See Chapter 9 on tips for the Registry.)

Using the Repair Process

1. Start the NT Server Setup program in the same manner used to install the system.

2. Press **R** during the DOS part of Setup when Setup asks if you want to install NT or repair files.

3. Follow the instructions, inserting the Repair disk when prompted.

4. Restart your system at the completion of the process by following the instructions given by Setup.

The Repair process can replace a number of files and perform verification checks on the system. Table 2.8 lists the items that NT Server can check and repair.

See the section on using Rdisk in Chapter 9 for information on updating the Repair disk. This step should be performed on a regular basis.

Table 2.8 Options That Repair Process Checks and Repairs

Option Checked	Description
System files	All NT Server files on the system partition and the \SystemRoot tree are checked to verify that all files are present and that none are corrupt. Any corrupt or missing files are updated. Setup automatically removes and restores permissions during the repair process if the files are on an NTFS partition.
Default system configuration	All Registry files are checked for errors. If any are corrupt, they are replaced. Setup prompts you to replace them with files from the installation media. *Note: Unless you have updated the Emergency Disk recently, you will lose all user accounts and file security plus other Registry changes.*
Boot variables	Boot variables are checked and replaced from the Repair disk if necessary.
Boot sector for x86 systems	Setup checks the boot sector and repairs it by updating any files and writing a new boot sector on the partition.

2.23 BOOT.INI OPTIONS

BOOT.INI is stored in the root directory of the boot drive for Intel systems and in memory for RISC systems. The boot loader reads BOOT.INI during the startup process to determine the options displayed in the startup list. BOOT.INI is maintained by the System applet in Control Panel.

You may find it useful to add or change the options in BOOT.INI (Intel only) manually in certain instances. Options that are useful are multiple boot options for NT, special debug options for NT, setting the startup options for NT, and, if you are running NT on an Intel processor, an MS-DOS boot option.

```
[boot loader]
timeout=30
default=multi(0)disk(0)rdisk(0)partition(1)\WINNT35
[operating systems]
multi(0)disk(0)rdisk(0)partition(1)\WINNT35="Windows NT Server -
    Version 3.51"
multi(0)disk(0)rdisk(0)partition(1)\WINNT35="Windows NT Server -
    Version 3.51 - [VGA mode]" /basevideo
C:\ = "MS-DOS"
```

Options for NT are specified on the same line as the desired NT boot option, after the description, and are preceded by a /. Table 2.9 contains the boot.ini options. Notice the /basevideo option in the last example for a boot.ini file.

2.23.1 Adding a Second Boot Option for NT

One of the options you should consider for management purposes is adding a second entry for NT to BOOT.INI. This entry should include the /DEBUG and /BAUDATE=9600 switches to the end of the line. This setting turns on the DEBUG option for NT and sets the speed to 9600. The debug option allows Microsoft support engineers to dial into your NT system if it dies due to a hardware exception error. Note that I said *if it dies*. This means that when the sys-

Table 2.9 BOOT.INI Options

Option	Description
/NODEBUG	Default: No debugging information is collected or transmitted during startup.
/DEBUG	Enables debugging information to be sent and collected during startup. The COM port used is the last one detected during startup unless a port is specified with the DEBUGPORT option.
/DEBUGPORT=COMx	Specifies the specific COM port to use for debugging. Specify the one used for your modem connection.
/BAUDRATE=xxxx	Specifies the speed at which data are sent through the debug COM port. Default is 19200.
/CRASHDEBUG	Enables an amount of stack pages to be accessible via the debugger. These stack pages are made available only after the system encounters a FATAL error. The default amount is 9600 for debugging via a modem.
/SOS	Turns on the display of drivers as they are loaded during NT startup.
/NoSerialMice=x	Turns off serial mouse detection during startup. If x is specified, checking is turned off only on that COM port. If no port is specified, then checking is turned off on all COM ports. Multiple ports can be specified as: /NoSerialMice=COM1,COM3....

tem dies with the big blue screen, they can still dial in and debug the memory dump. Pretty cool!

Adding a Second Boot Option for NT

1. Change the attribute for BOOT.INI from "Read Only," to allow editing the file, using the ATTRIB -R command:

```
ATTRIB -R C:\BOOT.INI
```

2. Edit BOOT.INI:

```
EDIT BOOT.INI
```

3. Copy the boot entry for NT and add the following to the end of the line:

```
/DEBUG /BAUDRATE=9600
```

4. Change the attribute for BOOT.INI back to "Read Only," using the ATTRIB + command:

```
ATTRIB +R C:\BOOT.INI
```

2.23.2 BOOT.INI Options for UPS and Other Hardware Devices

UPS and some other devices may require turning off mouse detection on the COM port used for the UPS signal line. Each time NT starts it tries to detect all devices attached to the system, including any mice attached to a COM port. This detection has the possibility to turn the UPS off during the detection process when the UPS picks up the signal and thinks it should shut down. Of course, this situation is undesirable.

Turning off Mouse Detection (Intel Only)

1. Change the attribute for BOOT.INI from "Read Only," to allow editing the file, using the ATTRIB -R command:

```
ATTRIB -R C:\BOOT.INI
```

2. Edit BOOT.INI:

```
EDIT BOOT.INI
```

3. Edit the boot entry for NT and add the following to the end of the line:

```
/NoSerialMice=COMx
```

where x equals the COM port used for the UPS device

4. Change the attribute for BOOT.INI back to "Read Only" using the ATTRIB + command:

```
ATTRIB +R C:\BOOT.INI
```

2.24 STOPPING AN APPLICATION ON THE SERVER

You can normally use the task list to kill a program that is executing on the server. Simply press Ctrl+Esc to display the task list, select the program by clicking on the name, and then click Terminate.

KILL (NT Resource Kit) is another way to stop a program. KILL is a utility that allows you to stop a program by specifying the name of the application or the name of its executable or by its Process ID.

You can determine the Process ID from TLIST or PVIEW or Performance Monitor. If you specify the name of the executable and more than one instance of the application is running, all instances are killed.

As you can guess, this is one of those extremely useful applications that must be carefully guarded. A user with access to a privileged account could create some interesting problems with KILL.

```
KILL { PID | programname } /f
```

PID   PID Indicates either the process ID for a process or the task ID for a task.

programname   You can optionally specify the program's name or its window title.

/f   Causes the process to terminate immediately without waiting for the process to kill itself.

TLIST is another NT Resource Kit utility useful when you need to kill a process. If you don't know the name of a process or want to specify its process ID, simply type **TLIST** and press Enter. You will be presented with a nice list of all the running processes and tasks on the system.

2.25 NT ERROR AND INFORMATIONAL MESSAGES

NT Server 3.51 comes with the Messages database. This handy tool provides information on the many messages that NT displays. The Messages database is built using Microsoft Access and can be a ready reference once it is installed. It is not installed during the NT Server installation.

Installing the Messages Database

1. Obtain access to the installation media (only on the CD-ROM).
2. Run the following command:

   cd_rom:\SUPPORT\WINNTMSG\SETUP

3. Enter your name and organization.
4. Click Continue.
5. Answer Yes to the Multiuser Installation.
6. Enter the directory to install the messages.

Double-click the Windows NT Messages icon to start the application.

After the Microsoft Windows NT Messages program starts, click the Find button to search the messages database. The program allows you to search the database on message ID, message text, and Notes.

2.26 MICROSOFT DIAGNOSTICS (WINMSD)

The WINMSD utility is the NT counterpart of the MSD utility that shipped with Windows 3.x. WINMSD is useful for determining a variety of configuration information concerning an NT system without having to resort to digging through the Registry.

WINMSD provides a GUI interface into many configuration parameters and gives you access to several other tools as well. You can use WINMSD to view any file (including EXE files) and display many configuration settings for your system. These include settings for Network, IRQs, memory, operating system version, processor, and ports among others. As you can gather from this list, WINMSD is a very powerful tool for determining system settings and for diagnosing problems. It is also useful for determining the current settings before you install any new hardware in your system.

The first step in using WINMSD is to create an icon for the program in a Program Manager group. The executable for the program is WINMSD.EXE and is located in the SYSTEM32 directory.

WINMSD uses another program called WINMSDP.EXE when you use the Tools menu and request a report. The WINMSDP program can be called independently of WINMSD with command-line options to specify the program's action. The options are listed in Table 2.10.

Two of the options are what I call wildcard options. The /A switch reports on all settings, while /N reports on only those settings that affect network activities.

The report is always saved in the file MSDRPT.TXT. If a previous report file exists, it will be saved as MSDRPT00.TXT. The 00 will be incremented depending upon how many preexisting files exist.

You may want to set the WINMSDP.EXE program up as a batch job to automatically dump all settings for your systems at regular intervals. The batch pro-

Table 2.10 WINMSD Command-Line Options

Option	Description	Option	Description
/A	All Settings	/Y	Memory resources
/D	Drives	/P	Port resources
/S	Services	/U	DMA resources
/R	Drivers	/W	Hardware
/M	Memory	/E	Environment
/I	Interrupts resources	/N	Network-related settings

gram could also copy the report file to a shared directory making the file accessible to the system managers over the network. This would be especially useful if you create a program that picks up all changes from all NT machines and updates a management database on the network. This program will ensure that you have up-to-date information on all your systems as of the last time the batch jobs ran.

2.27 USING MULTIPLE SERVERS WITH A SINGLE KEYBOARD/MOUSE/MONITOR

You will most likely end up with several NT servers in your computer room if your system is of any size and/or performs many tasks such as File and Print servers plus a Database server, plus a Systems Management Server (SMS), and so forth. Several servers soon create a mess of cables, monitors, and keyboards (not to mention mice) that must be managed. The easiest solution is to use an automated switch that handles all three devices and shares them among multiple servers.

A number of vendors make suitable switches for servers. Some vendors also build cabinets with switches included. There are potential problems with implementing a switch that may preclude choosing the most cost-effective switch from a catalog. The following list includes several potential problems:

☞ *System uses workstation-style monitors with coax connectors.* Systems such as Alpha and other RISC systems may use coax connectors that have specific cable-length requirements and that do not work with standard VGA switches. Network Technologies (800-RGB-TECH) provides standard cables, custom cables, and switches that work with either coax-style connectors or standard VGA monitors.

☞ *Keyboard fun and games.* You may encounter keyboard problems with a fast system (such as a Pentium 60 or faster) and some switches. Call the switch vendor and request updated firmware to resolve the problem.

☞ *Fuzzy monitor.* This is the same type problem as the keyboard, except the monitor just looks "fuzzy." The problem may be with either switch firmware or the type of cables used to connect the monitor and switch.

2.28 DESIGNING A SYSTEM FOR PERFORMANCE

There are many parameters to choose when designing the hardware platform for NT Server. This section is not meant to be an all-inclusive guide to hardware but rather to provide suggestions on major issues for your server.

One important factor in deciding upon your choice of hardware is the service provided by the hardware vendor. Make sure that your vendor can support not only the hardware but also NT. Their support for NT should include knowledge of possible failure codes for NT and how they relate to the particular platform you will use as a server. I have seen problems occur with NT that Microsoft could not solve but that the hardware vendor technical support could resolve in less than 5 minutes. The vendor could break down the error code to point to a specific problem on the machine. Make sure that your choice of server is not from a company that is experiencing customer support problems or that has a poor track record in the industry.

2.28.1 Server Types

NT supports many different types of general-purpose and specialty servers. The common nature operations performed on certain types of server leads to general conclusions about the loading of different types of servers. This information can be extremely valuable in designing the servers and choosing the hardware for each server. Table 2.11 lists some general parameters to consider as you plan new servers and upgrades for existing servers. Table 2.11 can also be used as a guideline on items to monitor for particular servers.

2.28.2 Fast Processor with 256K or Greater CACHE

Viable processors for NT systems range from Pentium systems to MIPS and Alpha-based RISC systems. NT has leveled the playing field for computer hardware, turning most systems into commodity items. It has also given users a distinct advantage because you can protect your investment in software and freely upgrade hardware to more powerful platforms without being locked into a single vendor's solutions.

Table 2.11 General Server Parameters

Primary Server Function	Most Important Subsystems	Notes
File and print	Disk, disk controllers, network cards	Most activity on File and Print servers takes place on the disk subsystems and the network interface.
Application (DB)	CPU, memory	Application servers typically run systems such as SQL Server, Systems Management Server, SNA Server, and Exchange Server.
		The stress points of an application server typically involve CPU and memory. Database servers also place high demands on the disk and network systems and thus may also experience a heavy load depending upon the particular application and data requirements.
Communications (RAS)	Communications, network cards, memory, CPU	Communications servers typically stress the communications subsystems (serial, X.25, etc.) and network. Memory and CPU are increasingly important as the load on the server increases.

2.28.2.1 Intel   Intel servers for NT Server should have a Pentium or faster processor. Given mid-1995 prices, I would suggest buying a high-end Pentium system as the server. Some of the new systems from Digital, Dell, and Compaq (not to mention others) are sporting multiple processors that make an ideal server for NT. Remember that the faster the processor(s), the better.

2.28.2.2 RISC   The Alpha and MIPS systems provide outstanding price/performance benefits for most organizations. These systems are usually better built than most of the PC clones on the market. In particular, the new 2100 server from Digital is a screamer. It can house from one to four 275-MHz processors with up to 2GB of memory (1GB with four processors) and 200GB of disk. If the PCI disk controllers are used, the disk throughput is 132MB/sec. The 2100 also has sophisticated fault management software and a built-in maintenance processor and diagnostics control bus. It is an outstanding system for NT Server. Digital has also added the AlphaServer 1000 and 2000 to its line of servers. These systems follow the same architecture as the 2100.

2.28.3 Lots of Memory

NT is very sensitive to the amount of memory in a system. Memory is used by applications and the operating system, for caching the disk drives, and for other functions. The more memory your system has, the better NT is able to use the available memory dynamically.

There are no set bench marks for servers and the amount of memory they should have, but I would make the following suggestions:

Number of File/Print Server Clients	Server Memory
25 or less	32MB or more
26–50	64MB or more
51–100	128MB or more
101 and up	Over 128MB

I suggest adding more memory than you think will be required. If you need 32MB, start with 64MB. This built-in expansion factor provides good performance and allows usage of your system to grow over time with no system changes.

Database servers do not fall into the same general categories as file and print servers because of the varied nature of the application and database design for these systems. The database software itself varies greatly in efficiency depending upon the overhead it places on the server operating system and the degree to which it integrates with and uses features of the server.

Database servers should typically start out with more memory than a file and print server for the same number of users. For instance, a database server for 40 clients should start with 64MB of memory or more. A 100-user system should probably start at 256MB. These RAM sizes are extremely reasonable in the mid-1990s due to current prices. You should also consider a platform that can handle multiple processors (SMP) for your database server. SMP systems can usually handle more physical memory and have higher capacity I/O systems, providing a much nicer incremental growth path for your system.

Make sure that any NT system can support adding memory without throwing away the existing memory. For instance, purchase a 32MB system with 16MB SIMMS instead of 8MB SIMMS to save open memory banks for future expansion; 32MB using 8MB SIMMS requires four banks while using 16MB SIMMS requires only two.

2.28.4 Network Cards

Use the fastest network cards you can get. This usually means a 16-bit smart card such as a 3C509 (EtherLink III) from 3Com. Network cards are available now for the high-speed PCI bus, EISA bus, and ISA bus.

Adding additional network cards can also improve the performance of your system. Multiple cards can segment the network and reduce the traffic on each segment while allowing each network card to process half as many packets. This type of configuration must be carefully established and balanced with the needs of users to access resources on each segment.

2.28.5 Video Systems

Servers may or may not need a high-speed video system depending upon the amount of time you use the monitor attached to the server and the type of applications you run on the server. The price of video systems has come down so that it makes sense to put a high-priced video system on the server because most standard components supply adequate power.

2.28.6 Disk Drives and Controllers

2.28.6.1 Controllers NT supports many different types and styles of disk controllers. Some of the most popular controllers in recent systems are the local bus variety that are built onto the motherboard. These controllers are usually very fast and provide different levels of functionality depending upon the vendor. Check out the speeds and features for your particular system. For instance, the Alpha 2100 from Digital comes with a built-in controller and RAID system with hot-swap drives. Other systems may have similar features that include controllers or controllers and disk systems. Systems with built-in components are normally easier to set up and manage and are more reliable.

2.28.6.2 Caching Drives and Controllers Caching drives and controllers are a great way to add performance to a system. The controller or drive usually carries a large memory cache, which drastically enhances the performance of the drive.

There is one large caveat to these types of drives: Do not use them for storing a SQL Server database unless the drive has write-through assurance. The reason for this caveat is that SQL Server guarantees that data were written to the physical disk and cannot do so when using a caching drive unless write caching on the drive is turned off.

You should carefully weigh the use of caching controllers or any other device that uses memory. NT does a good job using its memory to the maximum extent possible, so spending your money on more RAM for NT may make more sense than using a high-priced caching controller. This decision must be made based on a particular controller, the BUS architecture of the system you are using for your server, and other factors such as the amount of RAM your system can handle. For instance, older systems that use the ISA bus may benefit from a caching controller because less data must be moved over the bus into RAM. A server using a fast disk controller on a PCI bus may make better use of system RAM than a caching controller. Caveat Emptor! Don't believe everything you hear from a vendor or read in the press. Evaluate carefully and then make a decision.

2.28.6.3 RAID Systems Are Usually Fast   RAID systems can usually improve the performance of your system because they can write to more than one disk at a time. NT supports both a software solution (set up with Disk Administrator) and hardware implementations.

Using a hardware implementation of RAID 5 provides the best possible performance and gives you the highest level of fault tolerance.

Hardware implementations of RAID handle the entire striping process in the controllers and drives and do not cause any overhead on the server because NT sees the entire RAID system as one drive. This allows NT to function at an optimal level.

Choose carefully when picking a hardware implementation because these drives are usually very expensive and can vary in performance levels from one vendor to another. See page 189 for more information on setting up RAID systems.

One caveat for RAID systems: Make sure that you have good tape backups of all RAID drives. I have seen a RAID controller die and take the entire array with it. There is no substitute for good backups!

2.28.6.4 Bus Architecture   Bus architecture is a prime concern for any system that will be used as a server. The bus is the primary channel that all I/O flows through to the disk drives and network. The PCI (Peripheral Component Interconnect) local bus standard is my favorite of the PC buses circa 1995. The PCI bus is fast (80MB/sec of sustainable throughput), processor independent (PCI is used in PC, PowerPC, Alpha, and other systems), and autoconfiguring.

The next bus I would use would be EISA (Extended Industry Standard Architecture). EISA is sort of fast (33MB/sec) and is software-configurable through a special setup program (normally called ECU–EISA Configuration Utility). An ECU cannot run unless the system is shut down and restarted.

2.28.7 Configuration Issues

2.28.7.1 Multiple Paging Files   NT uses page files to simulate memory using the hard disk system by moving data and programs from physical memory to the page file(s) when memory demand is high. NT does this by using a sophisticated algorithm to determine what to move. If your demands on memory outgrow the physical memory available, NT begins using the page files. Remember that page files are slow compared to physical memory. High usage of page files drastically slows down your system.

You can spread the page files over multiple disks and controllers to allow NT to access multiple-page files at the same time. This is especially good for fast drives and smart controllers that handle disks very efficiently. The System applet in Control Panel is the tool for managing page files. Click on the Virtual Memory button to make changes or to review current settings. Look for newer industry standard controllers from leading vendors and check their features.

2.28.7.2 Correctly Size the Paging Files   Paging files automatically grow up to the maximum allowed in the Virtual Memory dialog box. This maximum allows NT to adjust the size of the file as needed due to demands of the system. Any time a page file is extended, it usually slows down the system during the extension process and results in a more fragmented disk, which will adversely affect performance.

You can monitor page file fragmentation by setting a large maximum page file size and watching the actual size of the page file(s). If the file(s) grows beyond the initial setting, defragment the disk and create a larger page file. Continue to monitor the page file(s) until it does not grow.

Use some common sense when planning your page file size and configuration. If your system has lots of RAM (256MB or more) and is never using the page file, you don't need a very large page file. However, the cost of disk is relatively low these days, so using a good-sized page file to account for future growth should not be a high-cost item.

2.28.7.3 Disable Unused Network Cards   Disabling unused cards reduces the amount of overhead on the server because every network card that is enabled processes packets from the network even when the server is not using anything on that particular segment.

2.28.7.4 Carefully Choose Your Protocol   NetBEUI is a small fast protocol but cannot be used for WAN connections. TCP/IP is much more robust because of its routing features and management tools, but until recently (circa mid-1994) it was significantly slower than NetBEUI. NT 3.51, Windows for Workgroups 3.11, and Windows 95 include an updated TCP/IP stack that performs almost as well as or better than NetBEUI on a LAN. This is very good news because now we can use only TCP/IP and still have the best performance on LAN and a WAN.

You can also install multiple protocols such as TCP/IP and NetBEUI. This is often the optimal situation for certain networks when you need both protocols for some reason. For instance, I was working with a development tool in mid-1995 that relied on a network protocol (TCP/IP or NetBEUI) for its communications. There was supposed to be no difference in using either protocol, but the package would not perform one particular function using TCP/IP (the default). After many hours of work, I changed the protocol used by the package to Net-BEUI and it worked. This was an easy step because both the server and the client were running NetBEUI and TCP/IP.

2.29 HARDWARE NOTES

2.29.1 Typical Hardware Problems

Sooner or later your server will crash. It is almost inevitable with the sophistication we have today that eventually a system will go down. This is especially true of some clones or other name-brand systems that use cheaper parts such as memory, I/O cards, controllers, and disks.

Microsoft and other support groups can remotely diagnose your NT system if you have a modem. This is very important to remember because not all Microsoft Product Support technicians offer this information. If you have a machine down and other solutions to the problem don't work, they can transfer the problem to another team that can remotely dial in and diagnose the system.

You should also keep a copy of tools like the NT Resource Kit, Microsoft TechNet, the messages database, and others around to use for research when an error occurs. You may also find I have covered the error, although that is not guaranteed.

Another good source of information is the TechNet CD from Microsoft. This gem ships each month and contains the Microsoft Knowledgebase and all kinds of useful information on NT and almost every other Microsoft product. Microsoft also publishes another CD with this disk that includes driver updates and patches for NT as well as many other Microsoft products. You can obtain TechNet directly from Microsoft for a nominal fee ($195 U.S.—circa 1995).

2.29.2 Preventing Hardware Nightmares

Many hardware problems can be prevented by buying the right kind of hardware for your server and keeping spare parts. I strongly recommend that all servers use hardware that is on the Microsoft NT compatibility list.

Using compatible hardware ensures that at least the system has been tested with NT and that the support engineers for the component should have some NT knowledge. They may even know what the hardware-specific error codes mean. The sophistication of NT and current hardware trends means that choosing a vendor like Digital or Dell over some other manufacturers makes sense. I mention these two because I have had great success with the support staffs of both. I also like the new Compaq machines but have had disappointing luck with their support staffs on DOS and Windows systems much less NT.

NT is a very robust operating system and places a great deal of stress on its hardware components, which includes all components in the system. Other operating systems such as DOS may run fine on a system using RAM of a different speed while NT may fail on that same box. NT may also fail on systems that use inexpensive components that usually have marginal performance and quality standards. I have seen a cheap monochrome card cause a NetWare network to go crazy. The hardware used for a server must be of top quality, as NT puts as much or more strain on a server as NetWare. Network clients running Windows for Workgroups or Windows 95 should also be first class to prevent raising your support requirements.

Another good tip for saving yourself some headaches is to keep spare parts around. When I managed a large NetWare LAN, I kept a spare server in running condition and several other spare parts. When a server died I would move the disks (unless it was a disk problem) over to the spare system and fire it up. The network was usually back up in 10–15 minutes. Then I could take my time to debug the problem system. Hot-swap drives and storage systems make this solution even easier to accomplish than older systems using internal drives and cables.

2.29.3 General Hardware Notes

I have included the phone numbers for the various vendors mentioned in this book as a reference (see the Listing of Products and Companies Mentioned appendix), although you should be able to get most of the devices from mail order houses or a local store.

2.29.3.1 Standard Hardware Recommendations I strongly recommend that NT Server systems have the following minimum configuration:

☞ Pentium 60-MHz or faster processor for Intel systems; RISC systems should be based on a processor equivalent to a MIPS R4400 or DEC Alpha.

☞ A multiprocessor machine with two or more CPUs. More process-intensive systems such as Application and Database servers will benefit more from multiple processors than a traditional File and Print server. NT Server supports up to 4 CPUs out of the box, while OEM systems can support a much greater number of CPUs such as 8, 16, or 32.

2.29.4 Digital Equipment Corporation

The newest Alpha systems from Digital (circa mid-1995) are the AlphaStation and AlphaServer line. These systems are powerhouses. They come with a built-in StorageWorks cabinet with hot-swappable drives.

Two of the most cost-effective systems are the AlphaServer 1000 and 2000 lines. The 1000 uses one processor while the 2000 can use two. Both systems use 275-MHz or faster processors promised for the near future.

The 2100-500 AXP has a 275-MHz processor (as of mid-1995) and can use up to four processors in the same box. Imagine four 275-MHz screamers! New systems have been announced with faster processors. These systems can also contain vast amounts of RAM, disk, and peripherals. The system contains EISA, PCI, and ISA buses.

Digital also has two lines of Pentium servers that are first class. The DECpc XL and Prioris lines are both top performers with a very good design. These systems not only perform well but are easy to work on and provide state of the art features. The Prioris XL and the DECpc XL are both traditional PC tower systems, but with significantly better construction than most vendors.

The Prioris HX line is a step up from other traditional tower network servers. This system has an internal StorageWorks bay for seven hot-swappable drives and is built from the ground up as a big server. It is a great system that supports dual processors and dual power supplies.

Digital also has a remote management package for most of their servers called Remote Server Manager. This package works over standard phone lines and can even dial into a dead system. The client software runs on NT and can manage multiple systems at once.

2.29.5 Compaq Proliant

The Compaq Proliant series offers a powerful option for servers. They have very good hardware components, lots of horsepower due to the multiprocessor options, and many other options for peripherals. Compaq systems have first-rate quality and support and are usually rated as fast as anything else.

The COMPAQ INSIGHT Manager links in to the low-level hardware of the Proliant server to provide diagnostics, configuration, firmware updates, and reboots. The system can be managed both locally and remotely.

The package is SNMP-compliant and supports NT and NT Server.

2.29.6 Dell and HP

The other vendors I would consider using to run NT are Dell and HP. Both vendors have a long track record of quality in both production and design. They also have good support groups that understand NT.

New servers in 1995 from both vendors promise to be both powerful and solid. Both vendors are proactive in providing management software for their products to ease the support crunch. Check with the vendors for information on specific models and features.

2.29.7 Disk Drives

2.29.7.1 Storage Arrays and Other Custom Disk Systems   One of the most interesting things to come along for network managers is the new breed of storage systems coming from a number of vendors. Most of these systems support multiple disk drives, tape drives, and power supplies in one cabinet.

Typically the cabinets are modular and allow you to plug the drives and devices in via a front panel. Most of these systems are hot-swappable, which means you can pull a drive or power supply from the system and replace it without turning off the system.

Some of these systems have also simplified the problem of installing SCSI devices and trying to get the correct match of device numbers for your system. Simply plug the drives into the storage cabinet and it sets the correct SCSI number. In reality, the SCSI number is set for the cabinet slot and passed to the drive.

Hardware RAID Solutions. RAID systems implemented in hardware provide the best performance. Hardware RAID systems off-load NT from managing the RAID system, removing any overhead associated with managing RAID from the operating system. NT sees the entire RAID volume as one volume, regardless of the number of disks.

Another benefit of hardware solutions is the hot-swap capability provided by most top-line systems. Because hot-swap systems allow you to remove or insert a drive in the array without stopping the system, you may never need to shut down your system to swap a disk if you keep an extra drive on hand!

Hardware RAID systems use the controller to handle creation and regeneration of the RAID methodology. Hardware implementations are normally the preferred method of implementing RAID because the hardware handles control of the entire RAID device.

Some hardware implementations can mix two or more levels of RAID at the same time. For instance, some systems can combine both 0 (striping) and 1 (mirroring) to obtain maximum performance and reliability.

Performance and functionality can vary greatly with RAID systems from different vendors. For instance, as shown in Figure 2.6, one of the Digital Equipment storage works controllers has three channels on the controller. This allows you to have three separate RAID arrays from this one controller or spread the three channels across one RAID array. Imagine a RAID system with eight disks, with a separate channel for each with three disks except the last two. This is high-performance RAID at its best.

2.29.8 SCSI Devices

2.29.8.1 Overview Small Computer Systems Interface (SCSI) devices have been around for many years and have proven to be one of the most reliable disk architectures available. SCSI devices are also very flexible because many different drives work with a variety of manufacturers' controllers and vice versa. SCSI devices are ideal for NT because of their robust architecture and the common availability of different·drives and controllers. SCSI drives in particular are also available in many different sizes ranging from less than 100MB to 4GB or greater. NT uses the disk drives in a much more aggressive manner than DOS and many other systems, placing much more stress on the entire disk system. NT transfers larger blocks of data and uses faster disk transfer modes than DOS.

Cabling. SCSI cables vary in quality from supplier to supplier. The SCSI-II standard defines the following characteristics for cables:

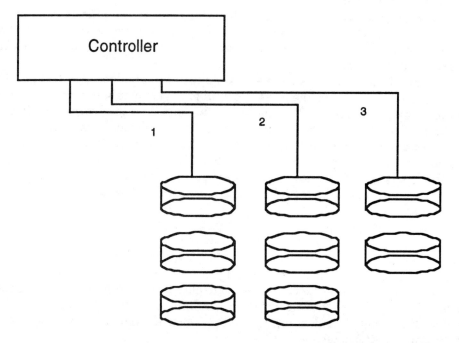

Fig. 2.6 The controller card is an EISA StorageWorks card produced by Digital Equipment Corporation. Each of the three channels can control its own array or combine across one array.

☞ 100% shielded round cables with 25 twisted pairs of wires,

☞ impedance between 90 and 110 ohms for each pair, and

☞ Wire gauge of 26 or 28.

Systems with only one or two devices may work fine with a cable that does not meet these specifications, but when another drive is added the devices fail. You may also have SCSI devices that worked fine with another operating system and no longer work with NT. Either of these situations can be caused by an improper cable.

The following vendors make SCSI cables available to end users:

☞ Digital Equipment Corporation—800-DIGITAL

☞ Amphenol Interconnect Products (better known as AMP)—607-786-4221

☞ Icontec—408-945-7766

☞ Black Box—412-746-5500

Also contact your system vendor.

The Microsoft Technet CD lists the following publications for those of you who would like to explore SCSI more fully:

Title: *Building Fast SCSI Subsystems*
Available from: Technology Focus
                 Distributed Processing Technology
                 140 Candace Drive
                 Maitland, FL 32571
                 Phone: 407-830-5522

Title: *The SCSI Bench Reference* (copyright 1989)
Author: Jeffrey D. Stai
Available from: ENDL Publications
                 14426 Black Walnut Court
                 Saratoga, CA 95070
                 Phone: 408-867-6642

Title: *SCSI: Understanding the Small Computer System Interface*
Author: John B. Lohmeyer (Chairman, X3T9.2) NCR Corporation
Publisher: Prentice-Hall, New Jersey
ISBN: 0-13-796855-8

Title: *Fast Track to SCSI: A Product Guide* (copyright 1991)
Author: Fujitsu Microelectronics, Inc.
Publisher: Prentice-Hall, New Jersey
ISBN: 0-13-307018-2

Connecting SCSI Devices. SCSI devices that are not part of a storage system are typically connected on a daisy-chain cable. The cable runs from the SCSI controller to each device, continuing on to the next device. Each SCSI controller supports up to seven devices.

SCSI devices use a terminator to prevent signal reflections. Proper use of terminators ensures faster and more reliable operation from your system. A SCSI system requires that only the devices on the ends of the SCSI bus have terminators. Terminators come in several types. External terminators look like an external SCSI cable connector with no cable attached. They are used on external SCSI devices that have two cable ports. The terminator goes on the unused port when the device is the last one on the SCSI bus.

Internal terminators usually consist of two or three resistor SIPs (single in-line packages) that look like a small circuit board with connectors along the side. Internal terminators are normally located on or at the end of the circuit board that attaches to the device. Switched or jumped terminators use a switch or jumper setting to enable or disable the termination.

Automatic termination is found on many of the new disk subsystems that are sold by different vendors. For instance, the Digital StorageWorks system can automatically set the correct termination for the bus.

SCSI devices each have a unique ID for all devices on the system. The ID numbers range from 0 to 6. Internal SCSI devices require you to set the SCSI ID of the device manually. The difficulty of performing this task varies with your device. Automatic configuration is found on many of the new disk subsystems.

For instance, the Digital StorageWorks system can automatically set the correct SCSI ID for a drive when it is plugged into the subsystem. You can actually move devices around in the subsystem, and their ID will change with the slot they are plugged into. You should consult your device documentation for instructions on setting the ID for the device.

Do not configure your CD-ROM with a SCSI ID of 0 or 1. Doing so may cause problems with NT and its ability to detect the CD-ROM drive because ID 0 and 1 are normally used for hard disks.

2.29.9 Serial Communications

NT supports many different types of serial interfaces ranging from the standard COM1 and COM2 capabilities of most PCs to add-in boards that have powerful processors and provide a number of enhancements for your serial communications. Up to 256 serial ports are supported by NT.

The Control Panel Ports applet is normally used for configuring serial port parameters. This applet can be used for ports from 3 through 256 but not for ports 1 and 2. If you wish to change the IRQ, I/O Address, COM port number, and FIFO-enabled parameters, you must use REGEDT32.EXE.

2.29.10 Changing Hardware

2.29.10.1 Adding a CD-ROM Drive   When you add a CD-ROM drive to a system running NT, you must make sure that the SCSICDRM service is set to start automatically when NT starts.

Automatically Starting the SCSICDRM Service

1. Run Control Panel.
2. Select the Services applet.
3. Select the SCSICDRM service.
4. Click Startup.
5. Check the Automatic button.
6. Click the System Account button.

This procedure forces it to start when the system starts.

2.29.10.2 Adding a Video Display   Video cards are simple to install if you follow a few basic steps. If you don't, you will have to choose a VGA boot option and reset the card. It is much simpler to do it right from the start.

Installing a New Video Card

1. Choose the Display option in Control Panel and configure the system for the new card.
2. Shut down the system.

3. Install the new card.

4. Restart the system.

If the system fails to start, select the VGA boot option to allow the system to restart. Change the settings with the Display option in Control Panel and check it out with the Test button. You must always use the Test button when making a video change to ensure that the change is correct or Control Panel will not let you make the change. Incorrect changes can also damage your monitor, so proceed with caution when making changes to refresh rates or things other than resolution.

2.29.11 Hardware Issues on Performance

Some Intel systems may experience a performance loss when you upgrade from 8 to 16MB of RAM. This loss could be because the hardware cache is specifically designed for a certain amount of memory and is not capable of managing larger amounts. If this occurs, try disabling the hardware cache. Be sure to measure the performance before and after the changes using Performance Monitor or another tool. You should also check with your hardware manufacturer for more information on improving performance and possibly upgrading the cache.

2.30 TECHNICAL SUPPORT FOR YOUR SYSTEM

The best plans and preparations sometimes go awry and require that you use some type of technical support. This support may be in the form of a phone call or access to an information source such as CompuServe, the Internet, or the Microsoft Network. There are a variety of other sources that you may choose from. Table 2.12 lists several sources and the access method for each source.

Table 2.12 Sources of NT Technical Support

Source	Description	Access/Contact
Microsoft Fast Tips	Fast tips over phone—recorded information	206-635-7245.
CompuServe	On-line service	GO WINNT or GO MSKB. Lots of other useful sources and support areas. (800) 848-8199 for introductory kit.
Microsoft Down Load Service	BBS with latest patches and stuff from Microsoft	206-936-6735 (1200,2400,9600, no parity, 8 data bits , 1 stop bit). Also available on CompuServe (GO MSL), Internet ftp.microsoft.com with anonymous login.
Internet	The Information Super-Highway.	Lots of stuff related to NT and NT networks. Look under BUSSYS on ftp. microsoft.com. Microsoft also supports a World Web server: www.microsoft.com.

Table 2.12 Sources of NT Technical Support (Continued)

Source	Description	Access/Contact
Microsoft Solution providers	Third-party vendors with direct links to Microsoft. Provide support, training, consulting, and development.	Computer Technologies Inc. 910-547-1407 ask for Ken Spencer. Microsoft can provide names of other solution providers at 800-227-4679 and on the TechNet CD. All Solution Providers charge for support services.
Microsoft	Microsoft Technical Support	900-555-2100 @ $150 per call added to your phone bill. 206-635-7022 @ $150 per call on your credit card. A faxback service is also available. Check the MS documentation for the current number or call one of the numbers above. Annual support plans are also available from MS or Solution Providers.
Technet	Monthly CD from Microsoft	Contact Microsoft.
Developers Network	Quarterly CD for developers	Contact Microsoft.
NT Resource Kit	Books and CD packed with useful stuff and utilities	Order from your NT vendor.

Network Configuration and Management

Network management takes on many different forms for a powerful system such as NT. You may be looking at client problems today, network planning tomorrow, and client/server situations the next day. Another scenario happens when all these problems or opportunities occur on the same day.

NT and the various client operating systems and utilities provide many of the tools we need to manage our systems from day to day and to solve problems when they occur. Many problems can be solved by proper planning and implementation on the front-end, which turns out to be the best approach almost every time. This chapter focuses on some of the typical tasks, tools, and techniques you can use to both plan and manage your network.

The first thing you must consider is that a network should not be viewed as a network with servers and clients but as a single system or entity. I like to refer to a network as "the system" and view it as a single entity made up of modular components such as servers, clients, bridges, routers, and network cards.

Viewing the entire network as a system creates a managerial mind-set that allows you to understand fully the power that we have available. This approach also provides us with a good understanding of the different components and how they fit together because we must develop this knowledge in order to manage the system.

3.1 NETWORK ADMINISTRATION GROUP (IN PROGRAM MANAGER)

The Network Administration group has several utilities that are useful for managing various components of a network. Each of these tools is discussed at one time or another in this book as they relate to certain tasks. This chapter mentions them for completeness and discusses several things that you should consider about the tools from a management perspective.

There is one thing to keep in mind about almost all NT management tools: they can be used to remotely manage other servers and/or clients. Remote management can make the manager's life much easier. Always look on the leftmost menu in each application for the Connect or Select Computer or Domain option. Many of the command-line utilities with the NT Resource Kit also support remote management.

3.1.1 Network Client Administrator

The Network Client Administrator is used to install and update client workstation components (such as network drivers and components like the redirector). Check the client directory on the NT Server CD and review the readme files to determine which updates are on your CD. Remember that, based on the date you purchase NT Server, you may get additional updated components and clients from the current CD. With the Network Client Administrator you can build installation disks, copy client network administration tools, and view Remoteboot Client information.

3.1.2 DHCP Manager

DHCP Manager is used to manage the DHCP system within NT Server (see page 107). It is used to initialize the DHCP system and for management once the system is in use. DHCP fortunately does not require very much in the way of management if it is set up correctly.

3.1.3 WINS Manager

WINS Manager manages the Windows Internet Naming System (see page 95) for NT Server 3.51. WINS Manager is similar to DHCP manager in that it is used both to configure the WINS system and to manage the system. WINS may be used on an on-going basis to add and manage static TCP/IP nodes that do not participate in DHCP.

3.1.4 Telnet and Terminal

What are Telnet and Terminal doing in a network management section? They are satisfactory tools for managing some TCP/IP devices such as network print servers and hubs. Many of these devices have a character mode setup feature that is accessible via the Telnet service over TCP/IP. Telnet and Terminal great choices because they are included with NT.

3.2 NETWORK TOPOLOGIES SUPPORTED

NT supports different types of network architectures for connecting your NT system to the network. The most popular options by far are Ethernet and Token

Ring. I do not intend to try to solve the war between all the fans of either; instead, I cover how they play with NT Server environments. Both work with NT Server depending upon the environment that you are using. I personally prefer Ethernet because of the diversity and ease of use it offers. Ethernet is generally more cost-effective than Token Ring especially with the explosion at the low end of the component market in recent years.

3.3 PROTOCOLS AND RELATED STUFF

NT supports several major protocols out of the box: TCP/IP, NWLINK IPX/SPX, DLC, and NetBEUI. IPX/SPX is the default protocol installed by NT. Your choice of protocol depends upon your background and what you plan to accomplish with your network. Most users with a UNIX or minicomputer background will probably choose TCP/IP. New network managers will probably opt for NetBEUI because it installs with virtually no interaction with the system, while users with NetWare networks will use IPX/SPX.

NetBEUI is useful for LANs with from 1 to 200 workstations that don't need to communicate over a Wide Area Network (WAN). The new TCP/IP drivers for both Windows and Windows NT are about as fast as NetBEUI and can be used in larger systems and over a WAN. TCP/IP requires more expert knowledge of the protocol and the LAN but provides many benefits over the other protocols because of its ability to connect to the Internet, to provide SNMP (Simple Network Management Protocol) support for NT and other SNMP-compliant systems, and to support the wide availability of tools and programming tool kits.

If you are planning on using your NT system in a WAN, you should choose TCP/IP or another protocol that is routable. NetBEUI cannot be routed and is not useful for a WAN. Other protocols such as DECnet can be used on NT and are routable, which makes them valuable on a WAN. The problems with choosing a protocol is making sure that the protocol is usable by all systems on your network that need access over the LAN or WAN.

Let's look at a network that has 20 Windows for Workgroups workstations and an NT Server. This LAN must communicate with another LAN that consists of 150 Windows for Workgroups, an NT Server, and a VAX. If you choose to run DECnet on the local NT Server, you will be able to communicate with the VAX over the WAN, but the Windows for Workgroups workstations will not be able to communicate over the WAN. NT supports multiple simultaneous protocols that allow the NT systems to communicate over both NetBEUI (for the LAN Windows for Workgroups workstations) and DECnet (for the WAN access to the VAX).

Another option is to run TCP/IP on both the NT Server and all other systems on both sides of the WAN. This allows all workstations to communicate over the WAN as well as the LAN. Installing TCP/IP in this manner can be effective but may also raise the cost of your systems. TCP/IP comes with NT and you have a free TCP/IP driver for Windows for Workgroups on the NT Server CD, but you usually must pay for TCP/IP on systems like VMS. You must carefully choose a protocol when your system will be part of a larger system or when there is potential for your system to grow beyond a LAN.

You also need a protocol such as IPX/SPX or DECnet if your NT Server must participate in a NetWare or other network that uses only a particular protocol.

It is beyond the scope of this books to present an exhaustive discussion of which protocol to use, but it is my goal to emphasize that you should choose with care. While choosing wrong is a minor pain, it is multiplied greatly when you must update a vast number of workstations and servers after they have been running only a few months. Let's look at TCP/IP and NetBEUI in a little more detail.

3.3.1 NetBEUI

NetBIOS Extended User Interface (NetBEUI) is a transport protocol used by Microsoft and other networks. NetBEUI is small and fast, making it ideal for small networks. It is also easy to configure because it requires only a computer name. NetBEUI is also self-tuning, which makes it ideal for small networks without a support staff.

NetBEUI is best used for small to medium networks up to 200 nodes.

Table 3.5 in the Choosing a Protocol section (see page 104) provides a quick list of which protocol to use when.

3.3.2 NBF

NetBEUI Frame (NBF) is the protocol driver used by NT to implement Net-BEUI. NBF provides support for other systems running NetBIOS or NetBEUI. For instance, Windows for Workgroups works with NT systems using the Net-BEUI protocol.

The biggest problem with NBF and any other version of NetBIOS is its inability to be routed. This means that you can't use NBF across a WAN, as noted earlier.

This section on NetBEUI is much shorter than the section on TCP/IP because NBF is very easy to set up. It is automatic when you install NT. You simply give your system a unique computer name, and, voila, your system is part of the network. TCP/IP and other protocols such as DECnet are much more difficult because you must manage a node address and node name for each workstation.

3.3.3 TCP/IP

NT includes the TCP/IP protocol and a number of TCP/IP utilities. NT also supports SNMP, which allows an NT system to participate in an SNMP management system. This feature is very important because, with SNMP, you can monitor NT systems along with hardware devices such as routers and bridges using the same tools. NT also supports other standards or pseudostandards such as the Dynamic Host Configuration Protocol (DHCP) and the Windows Internet Name Service (WINS), both of which automate most of the management of TCP/IP (more on this later in this chapter). Other features such as FTP (File Transfer Protocol) are also included in the standard NT kit. NT also includes the TCP/IP stack for Windows for Workgroups. TCP/IP is not a standard but is guided by approved RFCs (Request For Comments) that define the many different elements of the protocol and its utilities.

TCP/IP is a much more complex protocol than NetBEUI, but it is also more powerful. NT includes a number of tools that may actually make it easier for you to manage your system. All the standard NT utilities work over TCP/IP as well as NetBEUI. The TCP/IP-specific utilities allow you to run a number of connection-type tests over the network as well as perform traditional TCP/IP services over the network.

This book is not intended to be a tome on TCP/IP, so I refer you to other sources of information for a more in-depth discussion of TCP/IP: *Internetworking with TCP/IP* (Prentice Hall) and *TCP/IP Illustrated* (Addison Wesley). The Windows NT Resource Guide from the NT Resource Kit also has an excellent section on TCP/IP. The NT documentation also has a good description of TCP/IP, terms, concepts, and overall operations.

Now let's take a brief TCP/IP primer before we look at NT's version of TCP/IP. The TCP/IP protocol is composed of two major parts:

☞ TCP is the Transmission Control Protocol, which is the high-level part of TCP/IP.

☞ IP is the Internet Protocol and is the low-level part that actually delivers the network packets.

3.3.3.1 TCP/IP Node Addresses   Now for the fun part! Remember when I said that TCP/IP was more complex than NetBEUI? Welcome to the concept of IP addressing. Every node (host in TCP/IP parlance) on your network must have a unique IP address. Hosts include every device that attaches to the network and uses TCP/IP. Examples of different types of hosts are computers (both clients and servers), routers, gateways, 10Base T hubs, and network print servers that use TCP/IP.

If your network plugs into the Internet, it must be assigned a unique network address from the Defense Data Network—Network Information Center (DDN—NIC) or an Internet access provider. It is not a bad idea to obtain a unique network number any time you build a new network to ensure that your network is unique.

The IP address is a long string (32-bits) of numbers separated by periods. The IP address consists of three parts: a class descriptor, a network ID, and a host ID. The network ID uniquely identifies the network class, the unique network ID, and a particular host (workstation or server). Let's look at a sample IP address:

```
145.201.102.33
```

IP addresses are currently broken into three different classes. Each class describes the number of possible addresses by specifying a range for the class number. For instance, class A starts with 1 and goes through 126. In addition to determining a range for the first number of IP addresses, the class defines the default subnet mask. Table 3.1 describes these basic elements of the current three classes.

Table 3.1 IP Address Classes

Class Descriptor	Address Range	Default Subnet Mask
A	1–126	255.0.0.0
B	128–191	255.255.0.0
C	192–223	255.255.255.0

Using Table 3.1 for an example, a typical class A IP network might have the first part of its address as 123. Notice that in the world of valid IP addresses there are only 126 class A networks. A typical class B address might be **133.128.** IP addresses are handed out by the sanctioning body of the IP world for those who want to participate in the Internet. The easiest way to obtain a block of addresses is to work with your Internet provider.

If your network is not going to be part of the Internet, you can pick any address range you want as long as the subnet mask you use matches the range from the table. For instance, a network address of **201.123.3.1** cannot have a subnet mask of **255.255.0.0** because our IP address in this example can be used only on a class C network. Take care in choosing your network numbers because you can start out easily and end up with a mess. For instance, let's say that you start with an address range of **201.123.3.x** for your first systems. Choosing this range means that you can't have more than 254 hosts on a given subnet! Why? Because 201 is a class C network and can't use a subnet mask other than **255.255.255.0**. If you change the network range to **132.x.x.x**, you can use different subnet masks to split up your network.

Subnets can be useful for splitting up a network into smaller logical networks. Typically, all nodes physically connected on a LAN should have the same network and subnet ID. The exception to this is when you intentionally use subnet masks to subdivide your network and manage the traffic.

Our example assumes that the subnet mask for this network is **255.255.0.0**. The subnet mask is used to break the IP address into its network and host ID. The subnet mask works by converting the subnet mask to binary (ouch!) and using it with the full IP address to determine which parts to use for the network and which to use for the host. The actual operation performs a bitwise AND with the IP address, and the subnet mask splits out the host and network components.

Notice from Table 3.1 that the default subnet masks always use 255 in the first one, two, or three positions of the mask. This cleanly breaks the network and host portions of the IP address into two components separated at one of the decimal points. There is no need for any binary mess here.

If you wish to delve beyond the normal subnet masks (**255.255.255.0** and the like), the Microsoft Technet CD has a good description of the process in article PSS ID Number: Q96683, title: Subnet Masks in TCP/IP.

The values 0 and 255 are used for broadcast purposes by all nodes and must not be used for a any part of a host IP address.

The NT documentation has reasonably good coverage of TCP/IP concepts and addressing. I suggest reading this section of the documentation thoroughly.

3.3.3.2 IP Routers and Gateways

IP gateways or IP routers are used to connect multiple subnets, which are connected to an internet. Notice the lowercase *i* for *internet* this time? Any time multiple subnets are connected, they constitute an internet. The IP gateway (I am using the term gateway generically to indicate either a router or gateway in this TCP/IP section) handles all packets that move from one subnet to another.

Every router or gateway must have an IP address. If it has more than one channel (such as two WAN ports), then each channel must have its own address.

IP routers can be devices that perform only routing services, or they may be more general-purpose systems that have routing capabilities such as NT or UNIX systems. NT can be used as a router by installing two or more network cards that create subnets and using NT as a router between the two subnets. When NT is configured with more than one network adapter, each adapter that will use TCP/IP must have its own IP address.

3.3.3.3 How TCP/IP Management Works with NT 3.51

NT 3.5's most notable improvement besides performance improvements centers around TCP/IP. Microsoft has developed technology that is compliant with the RFC for the DHCP. This specification calls for management tools that handle both the client and server administration of TCP/IP. The new tools provide for easy administration of the entire process when clients that are compliant with DHCP are used on an NT network. Windows for Workgroups 3.11 clients are compliant with DHCP when using the new TCP/IP stack that Microsoft has included with NT Server 3.51.

Microsoft has also developed a service called the Windows Internet Name Service. WINS maintains an Access database of TCP/IP addresses and computer names on the WINS server. WINS can run on any NT server on the network and also supports backup WINS servers. WINS is an invaluable service because it provides name resolution for TCP/IP hosts. Name resolution occurs when a request is made to access a TCP/IP host using its name instead of the TCP/IP address. For instance, entering **PING MySystem** (see page 110 for more information on using PING) triggers a WINS name resolution to provide the TCP/IP address for MySystem. See page 95 for more information on WINS.

The DHCP and WINS specifications are implemented by a number of tools that are still evolving from different vendors. What is important about these tools is the functionality they provide. A system manager can use the management tools to specify the parameters for the network. These parameters include the allowable IP address range, the network subnet number, and other global parameters that affect the entire network. You can also specify excluded addresses that are used by routers or other devices. Another feature is used to specify static address numbers for non-DHCP workstations and servers.

DHCP and WINS automate almost the entire TCP/IP management process for administrators. Each DHCP client system checks with the DHCP server each time the system boots. If the system does not have a valid TCP/IP address, it requests one from the DHCP server. The DHCP server sends down a potential set of configurations that works for the client. The client chooses one set and the DHCP server then provides all the configuration information for the client. A DHCP client also communicates with a DHCP server from time to time when it needs an updated lease on its address.

When the client obtains the IP address, it actually gets a lease for the address from the DHCP server. This lease runs for the time specified by the system administrator on the DHCP server. Just as a normal lease on a house or car, the IP address lease must be renewed on a set schedule. The lease schedule is set by the administrator and is suggested to vary according to the dynamics of your network. Setting the lease renewal time to less than a week means that you can make drastic changes to your network structure, reboot all the machines, and the network will come back up. The only problem with this approach to a very short lease is that the DHCP server must be up just about every time a client boots. A backup DHCP server is a necessity here. If your network configuration is less dynamic and does not have computers moving around from segment to segment, you can get by with a longer lease time such as 30 days. Long leases of a month or longer work well in this type of network where changes are rare.

In planning your DHCP strategy, also consider notebooks and laptops that connect to the network and how many users you have per segment. Lots of notebooks and laptops indicate that a shorter lease be used. Short lease times are also useful when a network segment has a high percentage of users to IP addresses. For instance, if you have 254 available addresses and 240 active users, then use a short lease time. For the same network, 40 active users could get by with a long lease time because the demand for the IP addresses is low.

By supplying the IP address with a lease, the DHCP server can actually give the same IP number to another system. For instance, a system gets turned off for a week while the user is on vacation. During the same time, 10 new systems are added to the network. It's very possible that the lease expires on the system that is off for a week, thereby freeing the address for use by one of the new machines. Now one of the new machines has the address that the machine that is off had when it was turned off. What happens when the machine that was turned off for a week comes back up? The machine asks the DHCP server if the IP address is OK, receives a reply back that it is not, and is then supplied with a new IP address. The WINS server is notified, and the system continues its boot process without any problems. This is a simplified version of what happens during the boot process but basically explains the functionality that DHCP and WINS provide. The two services work together to maintain the address list (of TCP/IP address and computer name) on the WINS server.

3.3.3.4 Name Resolution Name resolution denotes what happens when one system tries to access a service or send information to another system on the network using the target system's name. The original method for talking to another system was to use only the TCP/IP address to target the other system. For instance a user could use the PING command to test for the existence of another system by entering the following command to find out if Joe's system was alive and well:

```
PING 198.84.8.10
```

This example tries to determine if the system with address 198.84.8.10 is actually running on the network. This method was fine when there were two or three systems and you had memorized the addresses. What happens when there are hundreds or thousands or more hosts on the network and all you know is the system's name? This dilemma long ago led to the concept of name resolution. For example, I want to access the other system by name and have my system automatically determine and use the TCP/IP address. Using some type of name resolution, I should be able to enter the following PING command if Joe's computer is known by the name JOEMKTG:

```
PING JOEMKTG
```

This command works if my system can successfully determine the address for JOEMKTG and reach the other system. How does this name resolution happen? NT and most other Microsoft systems support several different methods of name resolution. Each of these methods is fully described in the Windows NT Networking Guide in the NT Resource Kit, Chapter 12. The following list provides a brief overview of each method used by NT:

- ☞ *Windows Internet Name Service.* The WINS server maintains a list of the hosts TCP/IP addresses on the network and the respective name for each host. Whenever a request is made for a host from a WINS-compliant client, the WINS server supplies the IP address for the server. WINS provides the preferred method for network hosts (clients, servers, and other devices) to obtain the address of another system. It is typically faster and more reliable than other methods of address resolution. See page 95 for more information on WINS. The method used by WINS is also known as p-node name resolution and is defined in RFC 1001/1002. WINS provides support for NetBIOS over TCP/IP (NBT) systems.

- ☞ *Broadcast Name Resolution.* Broadcast name resolution requires each host to broadcast its name over the network for resolution. All systems on the network area targeted by the host must interact to challenge duplicate name registrations. Each system must also respond to a name query for its registered name. Broadcast name resolution is defined in RFC 1001/1002 as b-node.

- ☞ *Domain Name System (DNS).* DNS is a name resolution system that is similar to WINS. DNS is available on many different systems including UNIX, VMS, and NT (in the NT Resource Kit). DNS provides support for NetBIOS over TCP/IP (NBT) and Windows Sockets applications. DNS traditionally maps domain names to TCP/IP addresses. Many systems use the Windows for Workgroups or NT computer name for the host part of the domain name. DNS also does not provide automatic name registration where WINS does for DHCP systems.

☞ *HOSTS and LMHOSTS files.* HOSTS files provide support for name resolution requests using the domain name used by Windows Sockets applications. LMHOSTS provides support for NetBIOS over TCP/IP (NBT) systems. Both HOSTS and LMHOSTS files are simple text files that map TCP/IP addresses to computer names (see below).

☞ *Combination Modes.* NetBIOS over TCP/IP (NBT) is defined in RFC 1001 and 1002. NBT provides support for several of the preceding methods (b-node and p-node). NBT also has two combination modes that use more than one method of name resolution:

> m-node uses b-node first and then, if name resolution fails, p-node.

> h-node uses p-node first and then, if name resolution fails, b-node.

NT defaults to h-node name resolution when WINS servers are specified (see page 95); b-node name resolution is the default mode if there are no WINS servers specified. You can enable DNS and LMHOSTS lookups using the Network applet in Control Panel and configuring the TCP/IP protocol.

3.3.3.5 TCP/IP Name Resolution and the HOSTS Files   TCP/IP has traditionally used a HOSTS file to define the name of each host on the network and its TCP/IP address. This file is a simple ASCII file that lists both the address and the name for each host. I consider the HOSTS file simple until it's time to maintain one with names and addresses for every host on the network, then the HOSTS file becomes a nightmare.

Windows Sockets applications on a Microsoft network uses the HOSTS file for name resolution. A HOSTS file is roughly equivalent to having a DNS server on the network. When a system using a HOSTS file must resolve a TCP/IP name request, it looks up the name in the HOSTS file and determines the corresponding TCP/IP address. Other software such as terminal emulators or any TCP/IP application may also use the HOSTS file to look up the TCP/IP addresses of target systems.

You may want to consider augmenting WINS with a HOSTS file to provide these types of lookups (see page 95). If you have legacy hosts (such as a VMS or UNIX system) that do not use DHCP or any other kind of host that you must supply addresses for, it makes sense to maintain the addresses in a central HOSTS file. This file can be maintained with the addition of each static system (this does not happen often) and used to load the addressees for WINS, because WINS can import static addresses from a HOSTS file.

The biggest restriction in the format of a HOSTS file is that white space (space or tab) must be included between the address and the name. NT includes a sample HOSTS file (HOSTS.SAM) in the \WINNT35\SYSTEM32\DRIVERS\ETC directory.

Creating a HOSTS file

1. Copy the HOSTS.SAM file to HOSTS.
2. Edit HOSTS and replace the sample entries with your own.

An example of a working HOSTS file follows:

```
199.10.5.1      MyServer     #Master Server
199.10.5.2      NewServer    #Last Server purchased
199.10.5.88     Joe          #Joe's PC
```

NT reads the HOSTS file when it cannot resolve the name any other way. If you must use a HOSTS file, create an icon for the file in the Administrative Tools group (File/New/Program Item) in Program Manager to provide double-click access to the file for editing/reviewing.

Another HOSTS file that was added by Microsoft for LAN Manager systems is LMHOSTS. This file provides name resolution for NetBIOS over TCP/IP in a similar manner to WINS. LMHOSTS is still used for small networks that do not use WINS and in large networks to specify hosts that are beyond the local subnet.

LMHOSTS is also a simple ASCII file and NT includes a sample in the \WINNT35\SYSTEM32\DRIVERS\ETC (LMHOSTS.SAM) directory. This file can be modified for your network.

Creating a LMHOSTS file

1. Copy the LMHOSTS.SAM file to LMHOSTS.
2. Edit LMHOSTS and replace the sample entries with your own.

An example of a working LMHOSTS file follows:

```
199.10.5.1      MyServer     #DOM:MasterDOM              #PDC
199.10.5.2      NewServer    #Last Server purchased
199.10.5.88     Joe          #Joe's PC
#source server
#
#BEGIN_INCLUDE
#INCLUDE \\localsrv\public\lmhosts
#INCLUDE \\rhino\public\lmhosts
#END_INCLUDE
```

The # indicates a comment in this file and is also used as the prefix for special keywords like #DOM and #BEGIN_INCLUDE. LMHOSTS is much more sophisticated than HOSTS and has many options. Consult the Windows NT Networking Guide from the NT Resource Kit (Chapter 12) for more information.

If you use either HOSTS or LMHOSTS, it is handy to keep a master on a server and simply update the master; then copy it to other systems when changes occur. This procedure also reduces inaccuracies and potential problems from occurring.

3.3.3.6 WINS WINS servers provide many benefits to a network, including

☞ replacing the need for HOSTS and LMHOSTS files,

☞ replacing the need for DNS servers,

☞ reducing IP broadcast traffic by replacing b-node name resolution,

☞ increasing browsing capabilities for NT, Windows for Workgroups, and LAN Manager 2.x clients in large networks,

☞ providing built-in scalability and redundancy, and

☞ providing automatic name registration for DHCP clients and servers.

Installing WINS removes the need for having a HOSTS or LMHOSTS file on every system in the network (except in certain instances, see page 94). Installing WINS on an NT server and enabling WINS name resolution on your clients allows your systems to perform name resolution automatically using WINS. WINS is used automatically after it is configured and resolves the need for each client to have a HOSTS or LMHOSTS file. The WINS database is updated automatically via DHCP when a DHCP client obtains a new address. Performing name resolution on DHCP client systems would be an almost impossible task without using WINS because of the dynamic changes in TCP/IP addresses with DHCP clients over time.

WINS is also the desired choice for name resolution in large networks. WINS uses a distributed database that can support multiple WINS servers. Each server can be a partner with another server. The partner relationship supports both pull (server1 requests an update from server2) and push (server 1 sends an update to server2) relationships. Microsoft suggests that all partners support both a push and pull relationship with other partners. You can have more than one partner for a server. Using multiple servers spreads the WINS load across multiple systems and provides redundancy when one WINS server goes down.

Another concept supported by WINS is using a proxy system to listen for UDP name queries from non-WINS systems. A WINS proxy can be any NT system that is not running WINS server but has enabled WINS for name resolution.

WINS can also work with DNS servers by using the DNS server shipped with the NT Resource Kit. See Chapter 21 of the Windows NT Networking Guide from the NT Resource Kit.

You may not need to install the WINS server if you installed it along with the TCP/IP protocol earlier. Check the Services applet and Control Panel and look for the Windows Internet Name Service. If it is installed, then WINS is already installed and may require configuration only.

Installing a WINS Server

1. Start the Network applet in Control Panel.
2. Click the Add Software button.
3. Select the TCP/IP Protocol and Related Components in the Network Software box.
4. Select the options to install the WINS Server Service.
5. Optionally select the option to install the SNMP Service.
6. Click OK.
7. Enter the path to the distribution files and click Continue.
8. Configure the TCP/IP service.
9. Click the Close button and allow the system to reboot.

Make sure the Windows Internet Name Service is started before continuing. Use the Services applet in Control Panel or Server Manager to verify the status of the service.

Network clients must be configured to use WINS before they can use it for name resolution. The following steps show how to configure WINS on both Windows for Workgroups and Windows 95 clients. You can make sure WINS is working by performing the test following the client configuration options.

Configuring a Windows for Workgroups Client to Use WINS

1. Start the Network applet in Control Panel.
2. Click the Drivers button.
3. Select the TCP/IP protocol and click the Setup button or double-click the TCP/IP protocol.
4. Enter the TCP/IP address of the preferred WINS server in the Primary WINS Server box.
5. Enter the TCP/IP address of the secondary (optional) WINS server in the Secondary WINS Server box.
6. Click OK.
7. Close the Network applet and reboot the system.

Configuring a Windows 95 Client to Use WINS

1. Select Network from Control Panel.
2. Select Microsoft TCP/IP.
3. Click the Properties button.
4. Click the WINS Configuration tab.
5. Select Enable WINS Resolution.
6. Enter the TCP/IP address of the preferred WINS server in the Primary WINS Server box.
7. Enter the TCP/IP address of the secondary (optional) WINS server in the Secondary WINS Server box.
8. If a DHCP server is available, select Use DHCP for WINS Resolution instead of entering the addresses for the WINS server. Selecting the DHCP option enables automatic detection of a WINS server over DHCP, removing the need to maintain a specific IP address on each client for a WINS server.
9. Click OK to close the TCP/IP Properties form.
10. Close the Network form.
11. Reboot the system if prompted.

As with any network options, it is a good idea to test any configuration changes, especially when it is an action that may affect a large portion of your network. The following steps provide a quick check of the operation of WINS. You should also get to know PING well because it is a powerful tool for troubleshooting.

Testing WINS from a Client

1. Start a DOS prompt session.
2. Make sure that there is not a HOSTS or LMHOSTS file present in the Windows directory or the PATH.
3. Execute a PING (see page 110) command using the name of a host on your network that is defined in the WINS database.

PING should receive a reply from the host almost instantly. If you do not receive a reply, try using PING with the IP address of the host. If using the IP address works, make sure WINS is enabled and running on the server and that the system you are trying to PING is in the WINS database. You should also verify that the WINS settings of the client system are pointing to the correct WINS server or using automatic detection with DHCP (Windows 95).

3.3.3.7 Planning WINS Servers   The NT Resource Kit contains a great deal of information on configuring and planning for WINS servers in the Windows NT Networking Guide. The book also has detailed suggestions on implementing systems to optimize performance. The information on planning and performance is summarized in Table 3.2.

Table 3.2 WINS Server Planning Summary

Topic	Description
Number of systems per WINS server	Plan for one WINS server and at least one backup WINS server for every 10,000 systems on the network. This figure is based on a performance ratio of 1500 name registrations per minute and 760 name queries per minute. You should include at least one WINS server on each LAN segment.
File system for WINS database	Use NTFS for the system drive and any WINS files. This software improves performance because NTFS is much more robust and faster than the other available file systems.
Processors	WINS runs about 25% faster on a system with two processors.
Renewal time	Adjust the renewal time of the WINS server after the system is up and running. Lengthening the renewal time decreases the name registration traffic.
WINS proxy systems	Limit the number of WINS proxy systems on the network to limit the resources used for name query responses.
Replication time	Change the replication time between WINS partners to match your needs. WINS servers across a WAN should have a longer replication time than servers on a LAN.
Logging	Setting the Logging Enabled and Log Detailed Events options on the WINS Server Configuration dialog box turns on logging of changes to the WINS database. The Log Detailed Events option should be turned off unless you are troubleshooting to conserve system resources.

3.3.3.8 Configuring a WINS Server

A number of tasks must be considered for managing and configuring a WINS server. This section does not provide exhaustive coverage of each option but touches on the main parameters necessary for efficient operation of WINS. For a more detailed look at any option of WINS, consult

- ☞ Windows NT Networking Guide from the NT Resource Kit,
- ☞ NT System Documentation and help files, or
- ☞ Microsoft TechNet.

Static Addresses. Static addresses are TCP/IP addresses that are manually entered on a given host system, in other words, non-DHCP systems. Typical systems that have manual addresses are DHCP servers, non-DHCP-compliant systems such as many hubs, print servers, older systems (UNIX, VMS), and anything else attached to your network that requires a manually entered TCP/IP address. DHCP servers are the exception to the rule because, even though you must enter the address for the server manually, DHCP will send its name and address to the WINS server.

Before you can use WINS to resolve a static address, you must add the mappings manually to WINS. Page 95 has more information on combining the HOSTS and LMHOSTS files with WINS to address this issue. You can also enter the static mappings in WINS manually.

Adding a Static Mapping to WINS Manually

1. Start the WINS Administrator program.
2. Select the WINS server to modify.
3. Select Static Mappings from the Mappings menu.
4. Click the Add Mappings button.
5. Enter the host name.
6. Enter the host TCP/IP address.
7. Click the Add button.
8. Continue steps 5–7 for all static mappings.
9. Click the Close button.
10. Close the WINS Administrator.

Adding a Static Mapping to WINS by Importing a File (HOSTS or LMHOSTS)

1. Start the WINS Administrator program.
2. Select the WINS server to modify.
3. Select Static Mappings from the Mappings menu.
4. Click the Import Mappings button.
5. Select the import file.
6. Click OK.

7. Click the Close button.

8. Close the WINS Administrator.

Miscellaneous Options for WINS. The WINS Server Configuration dialog box provides quick access to many of the WINS options.

Setting WINS Options (General)

1. Start the WINS Administrator program.

2. Select the WINS server to modify.

3. Select Configuration from the Server menu.

4. Change the desired options.

5. Click OK to close the configuration dialog box.

One of the options that should be set on every WINS system is the backup database path. Setting this option triggers WINS to perform a backup of the WINS database every 24 hours. If the WINS database becomes corrupted, WINS restores the database automatically from the backup.

Setting WINS Backup Options

1. Start the WINS Administrator program.

2. Select the WINS server to modify.

3. Select Configuration from the Server menu.

4. Click the Advanced >> button.

5. Enter the path for the backup database or click the Browse button and select the directory.

6. Click OK to close the configuration dialog box.

3.3.3.9 TCP/IP on Windows Clients The new Microsoft TCP/IP stack for Windows and Windows for Workgroups is included with Windows NT. The stack is also available from CompuServe and the Internet. This new stack sets the standard for TCP/IP pricing—free if you are running Windows.

New features of the various TCP/IP projects from Microsoft drastically reduce the pain of using TCP/IP. The new Windows 3.11 TCP/IP stack is a protected mode stack and thus takes no conventional memory. The performance was quoted as being within 10–15% of the NetBEUI protocol during the beta project. NetBEUI and IPX/SPX have traditionally outperformed TCP/IP because they were designed for LAN use only and did not include routing information.

According to Microsoft, the goal for the released TCP/IP product was to make it as fast as NetBEUI. This is truly amazing for a protocol that provides both LAN and WAN support. Check with Microsoft (206-882-8080) and on the Microsoft CompuServe forums for more information on the new TCP/IP stack for Windows 3.11. The stack is included in the client tools on the NT Server 3.51 CD.

Performance improvements made in the Windows 3.1 TCP/IP stack also appear in the 3.51 version of NT and NT Server.

The other new feature of these TCP/IP products (Windows 3.11, Windows 95, and NT) is support for the DHCP and WINS. These two features provide automatic TCP/IP address maintenance on a network when an NT server is running DHCP and WINS. These features were discussed in more detail earlier in this chapter.

3.3.3.10 TCP/IP Utilities Overview   NT Server comes with several utilities that are useful for TCP/IP management. These programs range from utilities providing access to other systems to others that are useful for managing TCP/IP systems and networks. Table 3.3 lists several of the programs and provides a short description of their use. The TCP-32 column indicates which programs have comparable versions in the MSTCP-32 driver set for Windows for Workgroups and Windows.

3.3.3.11 TCP/IP Options   The TCP/IP options for NT have many different components. You do not need to install all TCP/IP components to use TCP/IP or some of its options. Table 3.4 lists the TCP/IP options available during the installation process or when configuring TCP/IP.

3.3.4 SMB

Server Message Block (SMB) is a high-level protocol used by Microsoft systems to make file and print service requests over a network. SMB commands are imbedded in transport protocols such as TCP/IP or NetBEUI.

3.3.5 DLC

The Data Link Control (DLC) protocol is another built-in protocol that allows NT to communicate with IBM systems or any other device that uses the DLC protocol. Because of the complexity of communicating with the various IBM systems, I do not cover it in-depth here. If you are using NT in such an environment, you should purchase the NT Resource Kit from Microsoft and take a hard look at SNA Server from Microsoft. There are also many third-party tools for use in an IBM environment.

3.3.6 NWLINK, IPX/SPX, and Other NetWare Stuff

NWLINK is a NetWare-compatible transport used by NT to allow NetWare workstations to communicate with NT application servers.

NWLINK is a 32-bit implementation of IPX/SPX and supports full SMB networking. It supports sockets, RPC, Novell NetBIOS, and the NetWare IPX/SPX API. NWLINK supports a wide variety of network cards through the NDIS 3.x interface. NWLINK is supported on all NT platforms including both Intel and RISC systems. It also supports SMP systems.

Several different frame types are supported to allow you to configure your system for different types of networks. You must set the frame type using the

Table 3.3 MT Server Programs for TCP/IP Management

Program	TCP-32	Description
ARP	✓	Used to display or modify the IP-to-Ethernet or Token Ring address translations tables used by the Address Resolution Protocol (ARP).
DHCP Manager		Used to configure and manage the DHCP server. An icon for this program (DHCPADMN.EXE) is in the Network Administration group.
FINGER		Displays information about a user or users on another system.
FTP	✓	Used to transfer files to and from another system. The other system must be running an FTP service. FTP has a complete command set, which is covered in the NT documentation.
HOSTNAME		Displays the name of the current host.
IPCONFIG	✓	Used to display information about the TCP/IP configuration of the current system. Can also be used to disable TCP/IP on the current system and release the DHCP configuration for that system.
NBTSTAT	✓	Displays protocol statistics and current TCP/IP connections. It uses the NBT (NetBIOS over TCP/IP) protocol.
NETSTAT	✓	Displays protocol statistics and current TCP/IP connections.
PING	✓	Used to check the TCP/IP connection between two systems. It is one of the most-used utilities for TCP/IP.
RCP		The Remote Copy command, used to copy information between systems. The remote system must be running rshd (remote shell daemon), which is available on UNIX systems.
REXEC		The remote execution utility, used to run commands on remote systems. The REXEC service must be running on the remote system.
ROUTE	✓	Used to display and change routing tables on an NT system.
RSH		Used to run commands on remote systems running the RSH service.
TELNET	✓	A terminal emulator that runs over TCP/IP. TELNET uses the Telnet service.
TFTP		Transfers files with systems running the Trivial File Transfer Protocol (TFTP).
TRACERT	✓	Traces the route to a destination system through each router on the network.
WINS Manager		Used to configure and manage the DHCP server. An icon for this program (WINSADMN.EXE) is found in the Network Administration group.

Table 3.4 Windows NT TCP/IP Services

Option	Description of Facilities Installed
TCP/IP internetworking	TCP/IP protocols, NetBIOS, Windows Sockets, and diagnostic utilities for TCP/IP.
Connectivity utilities	Connectivity utilities: finger, ftp, rcp, rexec, rsh, telnet, and tftp.
SNMP service	SNMP agent and other support utilities.
TCP/IP network printing	Support for TCP/IP printers directly connected to the network (such as the NetQue from Emulex) or UNIX systems.
FTP server service	Allows sharing files on an NT system with other systems that support FTP. This option is not required if you share files only with systems running Windows for Workgroups or DOS.
Simple TCP/IP services	Provides the TCP/IP Character Generator, Daytime, Discard, Echo, and Quote of the Day.
DHCP server service	Software to support DHCP for TCP/IP management.
WINS server service	Software to support WINS.
Automatic DHCP configuration	Enables automatic configuration of TCP/IP parameters from a DHCP server. Not available if this computer will be a DHCP or WINS server.

Network Control Panel applet to configure the NWLINK frame type to match that of your NetWare Server.

NWLINK is used as the protocol for both application servers in a NetWare environment and for supporting NetWare Core Protocol (NCP) for NT and Windows clients accessing a NetWare Server.

NT systems can also run the Microsoft Compatible Workstation Service (MCWS) that allows NT systems to access file and print services on a NetWare Server.

The NetWare Compatible Gateway is also included with NT Server and allows NT Server clients to access file and print services on NetWare servers. The gateway translates between the SMB protocol used by Microsoft networks and the Novell NetWare Core Protocol.

What all this means is that using NWLINK and NWCS an NT system can function both as an application server and client and as a file and print system client in a mixed network using both NT and NetWare systems.

You should need only the NWLINK protocol in the following situations:

☞ Your NetWare client/server applications work only with IPX/SPX.

☞ Routers in your network work only with IPX/SPX.

☞ Network clients that must talk to NT are running only IPX/SPX.

Microsoft also began testing a new product/feature called File and Print Services for NetWare as this book was winding down. File and Print Services for NetWare adds to the feature set of the standard NT NetWare tools, making NT look and feel like a NetWare server to clients running the NetWare protocol.

3.3.7 AppleTalk and EtherTalk

NT Server can use AppleTalk as a protocol with Services for Macintosh (SFM). This capability enables Macintosh clients to participate in an NT Server network using either the standard AppleTalk network included with Macintosh systems or Ethernet. AppleTalk is slow and should be used only as a last resort.

EtherTalk can also be used with SFM. EtherTalk runs over Ethernet and is much faster than AppleTalk. EtherTalk also takes advantage of the wide variety of standard devices in the Ethernet market. Using EtherTalk can also simplify your life as a network manager because you can standardize on Ethernet for all your network clients. Maintaining two network protocols that use different network topologies and devices is expensive and a real pain.

3.4 CHOOSING A PROTOCOL

Choosing a protocol is similar to choosing a network architecture like Ethernet—everyone has his or her own idea. The choices are becoming easier now because of the move toward the Information SuperHighway and the spread of TCP/IP in the networking field. TCP/IP is the one protocol that is moving toward a de facto standard.

More networks are moving from proprietary networks such as SNA or DECnet to TCP/IP. Reasons for this movement are varied, but several important factors should influence your decision. Table 3.5 covers TCP/IP, IPX/SPX, and NetBEUI and offers suggestions on which to use.

Table 3.5 Protocol Summary

Protocol	Notes
TCP/IP	TCP/IP is widely used and connects to most systems via standard or third-party protocol stacks. Microsoft includes an NT TCP/IP stack with NT and NT Server. NT Server also includes DHCP, WINS, and MSTCP-32 for Windows and Windows for Workgroups 3.x. TCP/IP can be used on small, medium, and large networks.
NetBEUI	NetBEUI is a small and fast protocol that is best used on small to medium networks up to 200 clients. It is the easiest protocol to install, configure, and manage, but it is not routable.
IPX/SPX	IPX/SPX is useful for networks that include a NetWare server or applications that require this protocol. Microsoft is recommending IPX/SPX as the default protocol on Microsoft networks.
Other	Vendors such as Digital Equipment offer protocol stacks that allow NT and NT Server to access systems with proprietary protocols (i.e., DECnet).

3.5 INSTALLING OR CHANGING PROTOCOLS AND OTHER NETWORK ITEMS

Protocols are installed and managed using the Network applet in Control Panel, which is shown in Figure 3.1. Using the Network applet, you can change settings for a protocol and add or remove a protocol, among other things. Other sections of this book contain information on changing other options.

Notice how you choose which components to work on from the list and then click the corresponding button to perform an action.

Adding a Protocol or Other Network Software

1. Start the Network applet in Control Panel.
2. Click the Add Software button.
3. Select the new protocol from the list in the Add Network Software dialog box.
4. Choose configuration options and close the Network applet.
5. Reboot the system if requested.

You may need to change parameters for a protocol or other network software option such as TCP/IP. The configuration dialog box functions exactly as it does during installation in most cases.

Changing a Protocol or Other Network Software

1. Start the Network applet in Control Panel.
2. Select the protocol from the list.
3. Click the Configure button.

Fig. 3.1 The Network applet in Control Panel provides an interface for changing most network parameters.

4. Choose your configuration options and click OK.

5. Close the Network applet.

6. Reboot the system if requested.

The Network applet also provides a way to remove a protocol or other network software.

Warning: Be careful with this step because you may lose network functions or other abilities if you delete the wrong software.

Removing a Protocol or Other Network Software

1. Start the Network applet in Control Panel.

2. Select the protocol or software from the list.

3. Click the Remove button.

4. Answer Yes to the confirmation question.

5. Reboot the system if requested.

If problems occur after one of these steps, see the instructions on recovering a system configuration at boot time using the last known good system configuration.

3.5.1 General Overview

3.5.1.1 Configuring TCP/IP   TCP/IP provides lots of utilities for managing and configuring the protocol and its related components. Many of the utilities are needed only when a problem occurs on the network or you must change a TCP/IP parameter manually. Both DHCP and WINS have removed much of the management load from using TCP/IP.

TCP/IP can be configured using the Network applet in Control Panel. You can use this process to turn on DHCP or manually enter the IP address and subnet mask. Using manual entry of the IP address means that you must track the IP addresses for each system on your network. This is a real pain in the neck and requires detailed records for each system. If you miss or incorrectly list one address, you are set for future (maybe quite soon) problems with duplicate addresses. Most systems such as Windows for Workgroups, Windows 95, and Windows NT provide a duplicate address error message, but it can still be a pain to debug.

The dialog box in Figure 3.2 is used for TCP/IP configuration, including manually setting the IP address and enabling DHCP.

Configuring TCP/IP

1. Start the Network applet in Control Panel.

2. Select the TCP/IP protocol.

Fig. 3.2 The TCP/IP Configuration dialog box is used for accessing the numerous TCP/IP options.

3. Click the Configure button.
4. Enter the parameters for TCP/IP.
5. Click OK.
6. Restart the system if prompted.

3.5.1.2 Multiple Network Adapters and TCP/IP

Systems using multiple network adapters with TCP/IP are termed multihomed systems. Each network adapter in this type of system actually creates its own network segment and requires a separate IP address.

Configuring Multiple Adapters for TCP/IP

1. Start the Network applet in Control Panel.
2. Select the TCP/IP protocol.
3. Click the Configure button.
4. Select the adapter to configure from the list at the top of the dialog box.
5. Enter the parameters for the adapter.
6. Repeat steps 4 and 5 for each adapter that will use TCP/IP.
7. Click OK.
8. Restart the system if prompted.

3.5.1.3 DHCP

Enabling DHCP.   DHCP services must be enabled before you can access a DHCP server from other systems. This process is actually very simple and involves one step on the server and one on each client. Control Panel contains most of the tools for installing and configuring services. Other tools for administering DHCP and WINS are located in the Network Administrative Tools groups.

Enabling DHCP Servers and Clients Overview

1. Configure DHCP on the Server(s).
2. Enable DHCP on the client.

The first step must be taken on each system that will be a DHCP server using DHCP Manager.

Enabling DHCP on NT Server

1. Run the DHCP Manager.
2. Click on Local Machine.
3. Select Create from the Scope menu.
4. Enter the address range for the scope.
5. Enter the subnet mask for the scope.
6. Enter the scope name.
7. Enter a description for the scope in the comment field.
8. Click OK.

You can enter any excluded address ranges for the scope on the same form. Fill in the Start Address and End Address under the Exclusion range and click the Add button. This procedure excludes that range of addresses from use by DHCP. Most likely, you will exclude the same addresses as those listed as static addresses in WIN5.

Enabling DHCP Client Services on Windows for Workgroups Clients

1. Run the Network Setup program in the Network group.
2. Click the Drivers button.
3. Select the TCP/IP protocol and click the Setup button.
4. Click the check box to enable DHCP.
5. Close all the Network Setup dialog boxes and reboot.

Enabling DHCP Client Services on Windows NT and NT Server

1. Run Control Panel and start the Network applet.
2. Select the TCP/IP protocol.
3. Click the Configure button.
4. Click the check box to enable DHCP.
5. Click OK.
6. Restart the system if prompted.

Enabling DHCP Client Services on Windows 95

1. Start the Network applet in Control Panel.

2. Select TCP/IP from the list. Make sure it is the correct TCP/IP item as you may see one bound to a dial-up adapter, whereas another is bound to a network adapter.

3. Double-click the TCP/IP item in the list or click the Properties button.

4. Click the Obtain an Address from a DHCP Server option.

5. Click OK.

Figure 3.3 shows the properties dialog box for the TCP/IP settings.

3.6 THE OPTIMAL PROTOCOL CHOICE—MULTIPLE PROTOCOLS

NT supports using more than one protocol at a time. Because NT is a 32-bit protected mode operating system, using multiple protocols doesn't present much of a negative impact on NT. The same is true for Windows for Workgroups and Windows 95 using the new TCP/IP driver from Microsoft and NetBEUI.

Using both NetBEUI and TCP/IP usually gives you the most bang for the buck in a WAN environment. Most WAN environments have a number of users on a LAN at different locations, which are connected via a router and communications line.

The secret to using both protocols is to use NetBEUI or IPX/SPX for the LAN protocol and TCP/IP for the WAN protocol. The process is easy to set up

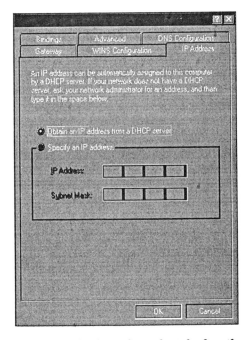

Fig. 3.3 The TCP/IP Properties dialog box where the tabs for other options provide one-click access to major settings options.

and works because NT uses the proper protocol for both WAN and LAN communications. For this process to work correctly, you must set NetBEUI as the first protocol in the provider search order. NT then uses NetBEUI for all the systems on a LAN because NetBEUI will be used first in a connection attempt. When NT tries to connect to a system over the WAN, NT uses TCP/IP because NetBEUI will not go over the WAN and the first connection attempt using NetBEUI will fail.

3.7 TROUBLESHOOTING PROGRAMS FOR TCP/IP

NT Server TCP/IP provides by far the most tools for troubleshooting your network of any of the standard NT protocols. This is partly because of the long history of TCP/IP and the outgrowth of tools for troubleshooting the protocol and the implementation of some new tools such as DHCP and WINS support by Microsoft. You will find many of these tools by the same name or a slightly different name on other Microsoft systems such as Windows for Workgroups, Windows 95, and the DOS network products. Some tools such as PING are also standard on almost all TCP/IP network systems.

3.7.1 Verifying Connections with PING

PING is the simplest and best known of the TCP/IP utilities. It is also possibly the most useful when you can't communicate from or to a particular system.

The first step I use is in diagnosing a communication problem with a server or workstation is to fire up PING and see if the problem system is alive. It is also a good idea to run PING from the problem system and see if it can talk to any other systems.

The syntax for PING is

```
PING name | address
```

name   The name of the target system.

address   The address of the target system.

The following example uses PING to try to connect to a system called JOHNS:

```
PING JOHNS
```

If you receive a reply from the other system, you know the connection is OK. If the other system does not answer, there is a problem somewhere between the two systems. Try using PING against several systems to determine the source of the problem.

Hint: You may experience problems with accessing a shared print or file resource on a host system such as VMS (Pathworks) or UNIX. Sometimes when this occurs PING returns a reply indicating that the target system is alive and well. The problem may be in the security the TCP/IP vendor uses for TCP/IP. TGV's MultiNet product can restrict access by IP address. I have seen a problem where an NT system could not access a file service but PING worked fine. If this problem occurs, try using another system to connect to the resource. If the other system works, look at the security settings for your IP address or DHCP range on the server. If you can't access the system from another system, then check the security settings for all addresses on the system.

Instead of specifying the name of the other system you can also use the TCP/IP address. This is very useful when there may be a problem with name resolution (see page 92) such as an error in a HOSTS or LMHOSTS file or a problem with the WINS server or database. Let's assume that our PING test to JOHNS failed and we are curious about the next step. Try this PING command where 198.84.8.10 is the TCP/IP address for JOHNS.

```
PING 198.84.8.10
```

A reply from this command would indicate that JOHNS is alive and well and that a problem exists in resolving the name JOHNS with the TCP/IP address 198.84.8.10. The next step is to check your name resolution setup. You should also try using PING from more than one system when you can't contact a target system. For instance, in our test if PING JOHNS worked from another system and failed on ours, then the problem must be in name resolution for our system. Check the WINS configuration, HOSTS or LMHOSTS files, or DNS, depending upon your network configuration.

3.7.2 Checking Your DHCP Configuration with IPCONFIG

IPCONFIG is useful for checking the TCP/IP configuration of a system. The following command and output uses the default IPCONFIG options and displays only addressing information for a client workstation:

```
IPCONFIG

    Windows IP Configuration Version 1.0

    Ethernet adapter EtherLink III:

        IP Address. . . . . . . : 199.199.199.110
        Subnet Mask . . . . . . : 255.255.255.0
        Default Gateway . . . . :
```

This is convenient because if the system is using DHCP, how else do you find out its IP address?

What happens if we want a full breakdown of configuration information? Use the /ALL switch on IPCONFIG.

```
IPCONFIG /ALL

    Windows IP Configuration Version 1.0

        Host Name . . . . . . . : DEC-P5-KENS
        DNS Servers . . . . . . :
        Node Type . . . . . . . : Hybrid
```

```
        NetBIOS Scope ID. . . . :
        IP Routing Enabled. . . : No
        WINS Proxy Enabled. . . : No
        DNS Resolution For Windows Networking Applications
    Enabled: No

Ethernet adapter EtherLink III:

        Physical Address. . . . : 00-60-8C-CC-F1-1F
        DHCP Enabled. . . . . . : Yes
        IP Address. . . . . . . : 199.199.199.110
        Subnet Mask . . . . . . : 255.255.255.0
        Default Gateway . . . . :
        DHCP Server . . . . . . : 199.199.199.101
        Primary WINS Server . . : 199.199.199.101
        Secondary WINS Server . :
        Lease Obtained. . . . . : Wed 2nd. Nov 1994 10:38:18 pm
        Lease Expires . . . . . : Sat 26th. Nov 1994 10:38:18 pm
```

This option provides some useful information. We have the physical address of the workstation, the IP address, and even lease information for DHCP. This information is useful if you are having trouble with a workstation and need to verify that it has a valid lease. It is also useful for verifying routing information for the workstation or server.

IPCONFIG can also release the current DHCP lease, effectively shutting down TCP/IP. The following command shows the syntax:

```
IPCONFIG /Release
```

You can also use this command to renew the DHCP lease. This command is useful when you need to make sure the lease is updated or want to verify whether a system is connecting with the DHCP server.

```
IPCONFIG /Renew
```

3.8 CONFIGURING BROWSING ON YOUR NETWORK

3.8.1 Browsemasters and Such

Windows for Workgroups systems must have the new redirector (VREDIR.386), which ships with NT Server 3.5x installed to participate in browsing with an NT server across a router. Windows 95 includes the features of this redirector by default.

Windows for Workgroups systems should be set up in different workgroups of 25 or so workstations. Each workgroup should have a name that is different from the domain. This organization breaks up browsing among the different workgroups and provides the optimal performance.

You can improve performance of specific Windows for Workgroups workstations by making the workstation ineligible to be a browsemaster. Set the value of MaintainServerList to no in the SYSTEM.INI Network section.

```
[Network]
MaintainServerList=no
```

3.8.2 Browsing Other Domains

NT Server must be told in certain instances to show other domains when a user browses the network. This instruction usually occurs for LAN Manager 2.2 domains (such as Digital Equipment's Pathworks 5.x). You may also need to issue this instruction when you have domains separated by a router and you have not set up WINS.

You can add and remove domains from the browse list using the Network applet in Control Panel. Figure 3.4 shows the Computer Browser from the NT Control Panel Network applet.

Adding a Domain to the Browser

1. Run Control Panel.
2. Start the Network applet.
3. Click Computer Browser.
4. Enter the domain name in the box and click Add.
5. Click OK.

Removing a Domain from the Browser

1. Run Control Panel.
2. Start the Network applet.
3. Click Computer Browser.
4. Click on the domain name to remove.
5. Click the Remove button.
6. Click OK.

It may take up to 15 minutes or more for the browse lists to be updated after you make a change due to the time lag between updates to the browse list.

Fig. 3.4 The Browser Configuration dialog box is used to alter the browse list for the current domain.

3.8.3 Monitoring Browsers

Two tools that come with the NT Resource Kit are handy for monitoring and troubleshooting browser services: Browser Monitor and BrowStat. Browser Monitor is a GUI tool while BrowStat is character-based.

Browser Monitor displays a lot of information on browsers and their status. You can tell at a glance which system is the browsemaster for a domain or workgroup and whether there is a problem. Figure 3.5 shows a simple network (one domain and one workgroup) viewed from the Browser Monitor main window.

You can double-click an entry for any transport to display the Browser Status window for that system, as shown in Figure 3.6. The details window provides useful information such as the number of servers currently in the domain or

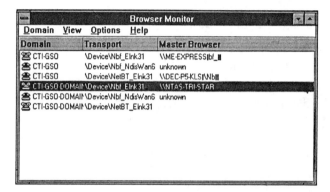

Fig. 3.5 Notice the different shapes of the icons to the left of the domain name. The top, fourth, and sixth icons are actually blue and indicate a well system. The second, third, and fifth icons show systems that indicate some type of problem. A separate entry is shown for each transport used by a system.

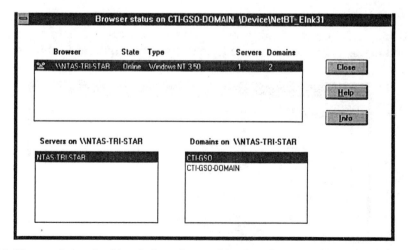

Fig. 3.6 The top frame in this window shows a blue icon for \\NTAS-TRI-STAR indicating that the system is currently on-line. You can see at a glance the type of software on the system, number of servers, and domains.

workgroup, the domains and workgroups visible to the browsemaster you are viewing, and several summary statistics and details in the top frame.

The Info button provides access to detailed statistics on the browser. Systems such as NT may provide more detailed statistics than Windows 95 or Windows for Workgroups 3.11.

Browser Monitor is a good tool for troubleshooting browsing services. The details provided by the tool do not necessarily give you an instant solution to a problem, but they do point you in the right direction. The Browser Status window provides a helpful summary for a quick check on a server. The main Browser Monitor window is also a good place to check because of the graphical overview.

The status on all systems is updated every 900 seconds (15 minutes) by default. The default refresh rate can be changed using the Intervals option on the Options menu.

You can also set Browser Monitor to alert you when an error condition occurs. Click the Alarm on Error option on the Options menu.

3.9 SHARED RESOURCES

NT resources that can be connected to over the network consist of printers and directories that have been explicitly shared or are special shares that are automatically created by NT. The ClipBook and applications can also share resources, but they are not covered in detail in this book. Shared resources can be used by any supported client or server on the network as if they are local resources. Shared resources are subject to the NT security established on both the share and any directories and files in the shared directory path.

All NT shares are referred to using the UNC (Universal Naming Convention). UNC names are specified by using the server name and the resource name:

`\\SERVER \RESOURCE`

SERVER   Name of server with the resource.

RESOURCE Name of the shared resource.

Any system can connect to the device by using the UNC name directly or by using a browse dialog box to build the UNC name by selecting first the server and then the shared resource name. Many systems can use the UNC name to point to a shared resource without explicitly mapping a drive letter to the share. For instance, Microsoft Word can use the following command line in its icon to specify the location of Word:

`\\Server1\WINWORD\WINWORD.EXE`

This example uses a server named SERVER1 and a share named WINWORD. Using the UNC name allows the client to find the Word files even if the shared resource containing the files is not currently mapped to a drive letter. Also notice that direct connect network printers show up in Print Browse dialog boxes using UNC. UNC names are also used by the NET USE command and many network API functions.

3.9.1 Special Shares

NT creates several special shares for specific purposes. As shown in Table 3.6, these shares are automatically created and managed by the system and should not be deleted or modified.

Adding a $ to the end of any share name turns that share into a hidden share that does not display in any browse list. This is a handy trick to use on those shares that you don't want anyone to mess with (such as the MSMAIL share or all users' home directories). I use this on all shares that users do not need to browse. This trick works in NT, Windows for Workgroups, and Windows 95.

Creating a Shared Directory with File Manager

1. Start File Manager.
2. Select the directory to share in the file window.
3. Select the Share As command from the menu or toolbar.
4. Enter the share name.
5. Enter permissions for the share.
6. Click OK.

Figure 3.7 shows the New Share dialog box creating a share named BOOKS.

Creating a Shared Directory with Server Manager

1. Start Server Manager.

Table 3.6 Special NT Shares

Share Name	Description
driveletter$	All drives on an NT system are shared with a share name of the drive letter and a $. The shares are considered administrative shares and can be accessed by only administrators, server operators, and backup operator accounts.
ADMIN$	The ADMIN$ share points to the Windows NT root directory (usually C:\WINNT) and can be accessed only by administrators, server operators, and backup operator accounts. This share is used during remote administration of NT.
IPC$	The IPC$ share is used to communicate between systems. It is used by named pipes.
PRINT$	This resource is used to support shared printers.
REPL$	This share is required for export replication servers and is created by the system.
NETLOGON	The NETLOGON share is used by other NT servers when processing logon requests.
ShareName$	Any directory shared with a $ after the share name will not be listed in any browse list on the network.

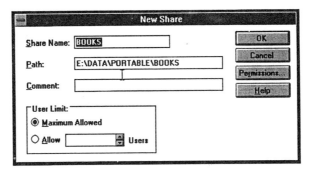

Fig. 3.7 The New Share dialog box in File Manager can be used to create a new shared directory.

2. Select the server you want to manage.
3. Select Shared Directories from the Computer menu.
4. Click the New Share button.
5. Enter the share name, path, and optionally comments.
6. Enter permissions for the share.
7. Click OK.

The Shared Directories dialog box in Figure 3.8 is handy for resolving share problems or reviewing all shares on a server.

One advantage of using Server Manager is its ability to create new shares on remote servers. This is convenient because it allows you to manage shares from any remote computer running Server Manager. Remember that you can do this in the Windows 3.1 client version of Server Manager also.

You can also create new directories with the NetShare command:

```
NET SHARE sharename=path
```

sharename   The name for the new share.

path   Description of the complete path of the share (C:\MDIR).

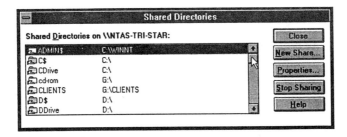

Fig. 3.8 The Shared Directories dialog box from Server Manager provides quick access to a number of options for shares.

After you have created a share, users can connect to the share with File Manager or the Net Use command.

Connecting to a Shared Directory with File Manager

1. Start File Manager.
2. Select the Connect Network Drive command from the menu or toolbar.
3. Select the drive letter to use for the resource.
4. Enter the UNC name or select the resource from the browse box.
5. Click OK.

The Connect Network Drive dialog box shows up in many places. As shown in Figure 3.9, it is a common dialog box within Windows and can be used by virtually any application. When you click the Network button in a file open or save dialog box, you get this dialog box.

Click the Reconnect at Logon box if you want to connect to this share automatically each time you logon.

Turning off the Expand by Default check box speeds the display of this dialog box because it does not automatically expand the workgroups and domains when the dialog box opens. This action allows you to immediately enter the path manually or select it from the history list without waiting on the browse list to return.

3.9.2 Monitoring Shared Resources

There are several ways to monitor shared resources in NT Server using both standard server tools and NT Resource Kit tools. Server Manager is the most obvious tool to use and is located in the Administrative Tools group in Pro-

Fig. 3.9 This is the Connect Network Drive dialog box from File Manager in Windows for Workgroups. This dialog box works basically the same way in both Windows for Workgroups and NT.

gram Manager. Net Watch is another useful tool and comes with the NT Resource Kit.

Figure 3.10 shows Net Watch running on NT Server.

Double-clicking a share connection displays details on the connection including the number of files that are currently open on the connection. Double-clicking a share displays information on the share itself and the number of connections to the share. You can stop sharing a resource by clicking on the share name and pressing Delete or selecting Stop Sharing from the connection menu.

Using NetWatch to Monitor Shared Resources

1. Double-click Net Watch in the NT Resource Kit group to start NetWatch.
2. Select the server to monitor.
3. Double-click any share to see the details of the current usage.

I personally like NetWatch because it presents a nice graphical interface showing the shares and any users of a share. Because it monitors only shares, it is designed with great efficiency in mind for performing that task. Any task can be performed with only a few clicks of the mouse.

Server Manager is another tool that is useful for managing shared resources. Server Manager is useful because it not only shows the shares but also provides quick access to other information on current users, files in use, and other server-related options.

Monitoring Shares in Use with Server Manager

1. Start Server Manager.
2. Click the Shares button.
3. Select the resource in question.
4. Review the bottom window, which shows all users connected to the resource. Pay attention to the In Use column. In Use indicates when a user has a file open on the resource by displaying a value of Yes by the file. A No value indicates that the user has a connection to the resource but is not actively using the resource. A quick look down this list should show what users are placing the load on the resource.

Fig. 3.10 Net Watch monitors the shares on the PDC in this sample.

3.10 DOMAIN OVERVIEW

A domain is a domain is a domain. A domain in this sense is Microsoft's terminology for a grouping of NT servers and other LAN manager servers. The key thing to remember about a domain is that you can treat a domain of servers as a single unit for management and security purposes. Systems are added to a domain by assigning the domain name to a new system during installation or from an NT Server, which is a Backup Domain Controller (BDC) or a Primary Domain Controller (PDC) in the domain (more on this later).

Domains are really neat because all the servers in the domain share the same user account and security database. Users log in to the domain one time and have access to resources throughout the domain. This access makes using and managing a domain much simpler than a network that has several individual servers (such as NetWare 3.x). There are no multiple servers to manage account and security databases for and no myriad of server names for users to remember. What a dream!

Domains also segregate the workstations in a network when a user browses the network for file or print resources. All servers and workstations in a domain appear indented under the domain in a browse list. You also see workstations in a workgroup listed under the workgroup name in the list. Both workgroups and domain workstations can appear in a browse list at the same time.

3.10.1 Primary Domain Controller

The key to the successful implementation of the domain concept is the organization of the servers in the domain. NT Server uses one server in each domain to serve as the PDC.

The PDC maintains the master copy of the account and security database. Currently only NT servers can serve as PDCs because they are the only servers that fully support trusted domains and other features of the NT Server network.

The PDC is the system that makes all changes to the account and security database. NT Server allows you to manage the account and security database easily with User Manager for Domains. User Manager for Domains allows you to choose which domain to manage by selecting the domain from a list. User Manager for Domains automatically updates the database on the PDC as changes are made.

The user account and security database is copied from the PDC every 5 minutes to all BDCs in the domain. All other NT Server BDCs in the network ask the PDC if any changes to the database have been made. Changes are then sent to each NT Server BDC in the network. The entire database is not sent, only the changes are sent.

Microsoft uses the term *Replication* to indicate the copying of anything from one system to another system. See the section on Replication (see page 154) for more information on copying files to other systems.

The PDC is a very busy system because of all the tasks that it performs. The larger the network, the busier the PDC. The PDC validates most of the network logon requests, performing replication of the SAM database, maintaining the browse list for domain resources, and attending to other tasks related to the domain.

3.10.1.1 Tips for a PDC The following list contains several tips on successful use of a PDC.

☞ For networks larger than a few workstations (say 100), install a separate NT Server as the PDC. This server doesn't need much disk (500MB) or RAM (32MB).

☞ Don't share any printers or file resources on the PDC.

☞ Don't run SQL Server or any other intensive software on the PDC.

☞ If you do run SQL Server on the PDC, don't check the Boost SQL Server Priority box in the SQL Server Setup program.

☞ Run the latest version of NT Server on the PDC. If you run higher versions of NT Server on a BDC than on the PDC, newer features (such as account lockout in 3.5) are disabled. If you run the new version on the PDC, NT Server usually enables the features for the entire network.

3.10.2 Backup Domain Controllers

Every NT Server BDC in a domain can serve as a backup to the PDC by maintaining a copy of the domain database. Any NT Server BDC can be promoted to the PDC with the assurance that the domain database is no more than 5 minutes out of date.

The NT Server BDC in a domain also improves the performance of the network. Each NT Server BDC can process a logon request by any workstation in the domain. This capability drastically improves the performance of the domain when a large number of users log on to the domain at one time, such as first thing in the morning after they get to work.

This discussion of other NT servers in a domain becomes more important in our discussion on tips for managing your domain later in this chapter (see page 127).

3.11 DOMAIN MODELS

The Microsoft NT Server documentation (Concepts and Planning Guide) lists four different domain models. I have added my own to the end of the list.

☞ *Single Domain Model.* This type of domain consists of a single domain for all servers. This model is best for organizations that have small networks (with only a few servers in one location) or do not need to split their network into multiple domains for organizational purposes.

☞ *Master Domain Model.* This model uses a single Master domain that is trusted by all other domains. The master domain contains all user accounts and global groups that are recognized by the other domains.

☞ *Multiple Master Domain Model.* This model is built on the master domain model and primarily adds scalability to the concept. A small number of master domains are used as the account domains, which are trusted by all other domains. This model is very flexible and works well with large organizations and large networks.

☞ *Complete Trust Model.* This model is well suited to organizations that are decentralized and want local departments to manage their own domains. Each domain in this model trusts every other domain in order for each user account to be available on every system. This model is very flexible but requires managing lots of trust relationships [no of servers * (no of servers − 1)]. This task may not be too monumental because a trust relationship is usually established once and left alone.

☞ *Roll Your Own.* The best model to use may be your own variation of one of these models. Most networks do not require all users to have access to all domains in a network. This is especially true for typical organizations in industries such as manufacturing, banking, insurance, or any other organization where people are locally based and do not travel extensively.

The documentation mentions briefly the concept of an account domain. This is a domain that contains the accounts for other domains that do not have their own accounts. The master domain models use account domains for the master domains.

3.11.1 Single Domain Model

The single domain model consists of one or more NT servers in a single domain. The domain is very easy to manage and establish. The single domain model can consist of any number of workstations and servers but has only one domain. This model is easy to manage because there are no trust relationships or multiple domains, but it will suffer in performance if the domain grows too large.

3.11.2 Master Domain Model

The master domain model has one domain that contains all user accounts and groups. All other domains in the network trust this domain and use the accounts and groups from the master domain. A network based on this model is still very easy to manage because all user accounts and groups are located in the master domain.

The ease of management of the master domain model is one reason that this model is used in Microsoft's own networks. Networks based on this model have one domain that contains all user accounts for the company while each office typically has its own domain. The local domains in each office have groups that reference the user accounts in the master domain. Using this model, which is shown in Figure 3.11, a user can move to any office in the company while keeping the same user account.

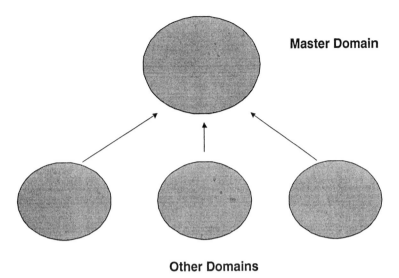

Fig. 3.11 Organization of a master domain model. Notice how all the other domains trust the master domain, which allows them to use the account database from the master domain.

3.11.3 Multiple Master Domain Model

The multiple master domain model uses several master domains to manage the domain databases for the network. Each domain trusts all the master domains, and the master domains trust each other. This relationship makes all user accounts in the master domain available to all other domains.

In Microsoft's multiple master domain model, domains other than the master domains are not trusted by any other domains, as shown in Figure 3.12. You may want to establish a trust relationship between other domains if you have added users to those domains that are not in the master domains. This would also apply to the master domain model.

Microsoft uses the master domain model for its own networks. According to an internal Microsoft NT product manager, Microsoft has over 9000 user accounts on the master domain. It has trust relationships with all other domains in the different offices and locations around the world. Personnel can move from one location to another within the entire organization and simply log on and go to work.

3.11.4 Complete Trust Model

The complete trust model (see Figure 3.13) is the most flexible of all the domain models and also the most difficult to set up. This model is built by establishing a trust relationship with every other domain in the network. This means that an account can be added to any domain in the system and instantly used on any other domain.

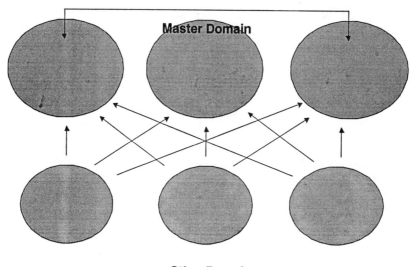

Other Domains

Fig. 3.12 Organization of a multiple master domain model. Notice how all the other domains trust all the master domains, allowing the user accounts from the master domains to be used on all other domains.

The only problem with this model is the overhead of creating the trust relationships. The number of trust relationships is [no of servers * (no of servers − 1)]. As mentioned earlier, this number does not seem so bad when you consider that once the relationships are created you do not have to manage them further except when you add a new domain.

The complete trust model may add to your management chores because of the number of security databases that must be backed up or restored and managed. You should be backing up all servers in your network anyway, but this model means that a lost connection to the servers in a domain or the loss of a domain with no BDC disables all accounts that are in that domain.

3.11.5 Roll Your Own Model

The flexibility of the domain architecture makes it easy to design your own model. You may need a network that has only two domains with some type of trust relationship between them. This type of architecture would be ideal for local management by the department that owns the domain.

On the other hand, you may have a large organization that requires several diverse networks each with its own domain and domain database. A Wide Area Network could be used to link the domains and allow both local and remote administration of each domain.

Another organization may have part of a network that works on the complete trust model with other parts of the network based on the master model or a combination of one or the other. The key thing to remember for your network is

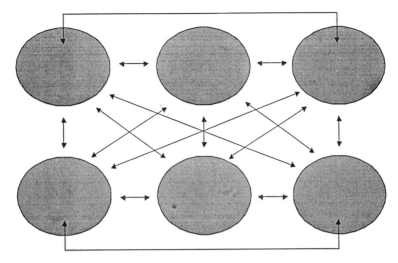

Fig. 3.13 Organization of a complete trust model. Notice how all domains trust all other domains.

to spend the time to plan its architecture and maintenance. You should include your cable plants, network components, backup plans, and common sense in your plans. Remember that, if it can fail, it will fail.

3.11.6 Domains and Systems Management Server

Systems Management Server depends upon the domain structure for many of its operations and power. The SMS site model consists of one or more domains for managing systems. The logical ordering of sites and domains can make life much easier if the domains and sites are built carefully.

The master domain model fits nicely with the site model when the master domain is the central site. This grouping is a natural because, with this model, all information collected by SMS will roll up to the central site.

Networks using SMS should install multiple servers for the best performance. SQL Server runs best when it is running on a dedicated or lightly loaded server. You can install SMS on any system running NT Server. You can also set up other NT Servers as helper servers. The only requirement is that every site must have its own SMS server.

More information on SMS and other Back Office products can be found in other books in this series from Prentice Hall.

3.12 DOMAIN, SERVER, USER ACCOUNT, AND GROUP NAMES AND TIPS

Naming conventions are a very important part of your planning process for the system design. Domain, server, and user account and group names are used in every NT Server network. Many users in the past have not placed much significance on naming conventions as their systems have grown over time. Ignoring these conventions often leads to problems with confusing names as more and more users are added to the system. I have seen many networks where servers are named after comic strip characters, TV shows, and the like. Even worse, some systems have servers named SERVER1, SERVER2, etc. The same problem occurs with domain, server, and group names as system managers become more familiar with the concepts.

I prefer to use a more formal system that makes creating the names easy and prevents (to some extent) problems with duplicate names. Every name should be meaningful and related to the operations it supports. For instance, a server that provides file and print services may have a prefix of FSPS or FP. The entire name could be FPSHIPPING. A file server might be FSHIPPING. Likewise domain and group names should relate to what they are used for. You may have a domain called Manufacturing or Shipping. This is much better than DOMAIN1 or DOMAIN. I also like to add _DM as a suffix to domain names to distinguish them from workgroup names.

Table 3.7 includes several items to consider.

The major point of all the naming conventions is to decide on a format and stick to it. Avoid using names that are cute but meaningless because this practice can lead to confusion when users browse the network.

3.12.1 Domain Names

Domain names can be from 1 to 15 characters in length and must be unique from all other domains. A domain name is only a descriptive name as in the case

Table 3.7 Domain Naming Conventions

Name	Description
Domains	Domain names should describe the function of the domain. If you have only one domain and it will never grow, you may choose to call it the name of your company. If you have a much larger system, the domain names may be the location or function of the domain. The major point is to establish a format and stick to it.
Users	User names are required for people to access the network. User names may be very simple (users' initials) or very complex (5+2+1 format—first 5 characters of last name + first two characters of the first name + a single digit starting at 1).
Shares	Share names for servers should be descriptive and simple. Share names are used for both file and print services.
Computers	Computer names should describe the function of the server. You may want to prefix server names if your servers are used for different functions. For instance, the application server in shipping would be APSHIPPING while the file server in shipping would be FSSHIPPING. Naming systems this way sorts the servers by type in any browse list they appear in. Other conventions can be used depending upon your needs.

of a user name. The domain name is linked to a security ID that is never visible and is used by NT as the internal ID for the domain name.

Changing a Domain Name

1. Start the Network applet in Control Panel.
2. Click the Change button beside the current domain name.
3. Enter the new domain name.
4. Close the Network applet.
5. Reboot the system if requested.

3.12.2 Computer Names

Computer names can be from 1 to 15 characters in length and must be unique from all other computers on the domain. Each NT computer must also have an account on the domain server.

Computer names must be entered during the installation of NT Server but may be changed later. The Network applet in Control Panel is used to make the change.

Changing a Computer Name

1. Start the Network applet in Control Panel.
2. Click the Change button beside the current computer name.
3. Enter the new computer name.
4. Close the Network applet.
5. Reboot the system when requested.

Use care when changing the computer name of a production server, as workstations, servers, and many applications may have the computer name stored in password lists, program INI files, and so on. Even though the system ID for the server does not change, the simple name change can be trouble. This can create havoc when you change a computer name and users can't access the system.

3.13 HINTS FOR MANAGING YOUR DOMAIN

Domains are both the easiest and most difficult to maintain network features of NT Server. Properly managed domains are easy to set up and manage as long as you follow the rules. Where have we heard that before? What constitutes a good domain practice from a bad practice. Here's the list.

☞ Make sure that a backup server can communicate with the domain controller during the installation process. If it complains when you supply the domain name, then check out the network connections (cable, card, repeater, etc.) before continuing. If you install a backup server with the same domain name as a new domain, you must reinstall NT Server before you can use the server on the original domain!

☞ Plan your domain strategy before installing the servers and creating domains.

☞ Don't duplicate user names within different domains.

☞ Plan the naming architecture for domains, user accounts, and groups.

☞ Plan the network topologies and protocol(s) to be used for your network.

3.14 REGISTRY SIZE AND DOMAINS

The Registry can grow as needed as your system changes and grows. There is one possible scenario that you may run into if you have a large network. The Registry has a default size limit of 15MB for the SAM database, which can be exceeded if you have many user accounts. Fortunately, it is easy to change the size limit.

The size limit for the SAM database is controlled by the Registry key

```
HKEY_LOCAL_MACHINE\SYSTEM\CurrentControlSet\Control\RegistrySize
   Limit
```

This key controls the overall size of the Registry, which is 25% of the default Paged Pool Size default 32MB. The smallest size the Registry Size Limit can be is 4MB and the maximum size is 102MB. The other trick is that the size of the Registry Size Limit value can't be greater than 80% of the Paged Pool Size, which can be a maximum of 128MB. The value for Paged Pool Size is under the key

```
HKEY_LOCAL_MACHINE\SYSTEM\CurrentControlSet\Control\SessionManager -
\Memory Management\PagedPoolSize
```

A Registry Size Limit of 8MB can support a user accounts database of 5000 users. The maximum size of 128MB can support 80,000 users, but Microsoft does not recommend using this value. If you change the Registry Size Limit on the PDC to allow for more user accounts, you must also update all BDCs to use the same size limit.

Changing the Registry Size Limit and the Paged Pool Size

1. Calculate the size of the new Registry Size Limit. Total the value of the Registry Hives in the \WINNT\SYSTEM32\CONFIG directory and multiply by at least 1.3 to provide a 30% buffer. You can set the Registry Size Limit to 0xffffffff to force the size limit to 80% of the current Paged Pool Size.

2. Calculate the new size of the Paged Pool. Multiply the new Registry Size Limit by 1.2.

3. Start REGEDT32.

4. Edit the value for the Registry Size Limit key and replace it with your new entry.

5. Edit the value for the Paged Pool Size key and replace it with your new entry.
6. Exit REGEDT32.
7. Restart the system.

NT Server 3.51 introduced a change to the System applet in Control Panel that allows you to change the maximum Registry size quickly. The bottom of the Virtual Memory dialog box now contains a frame titled Registry Size. The Maximum Registry Size (MB) box contains the new size, while the current size is displayed just above the maximum.

Changing the Registry Size Limit with Control Panel

1. Start the System applet in Control Panel.
2. Click the Virtual Memory button.
3. Enter the new Registry size in the Maximum Registry Size (MB) box.
4. Click OK.
5. Close the System applet.
6. Restart the system when prompted.

3.15 ADDING OR REMOVING AN NT WORKSTATION OR NT SERVER IN A DOMAIN

An NT system must be added to a domain before it can use any resources on the domain. During the process a user account is created for the new system on the domain. The user account is used by the system each time it logs on to the domain and is transparent to the user of the NT system.

There are several ways for an Administrator to add a system to a domain.

Adding an NT System During Installation

1. Choose to join an existing domain and enter the domain name when prompted.

Adding an NT System Using Server Manager

1. Start Server Manager.
2. Choose Add to Domain from the Computer menu.
3. Click the button for NT Workstation or NT Server.
4. Enter the system's name in the Computer Name box.
5. Click Add.
6. Click the Close button when you are finished adding systems.

You can also remove an NT workstation or server from a domain. Removing an NT system from the domain does not allow that system to participate in domain security. There are two ways to remove an NT system.

Removing an NT System Using Server Manager

1. Start Server Manager.
2. Select the system to remove.
3. Choose Remove from Domain from the Computer menu or press Del.
4. Click the Yes button on the confirmation box.
5. Click OK on the information box.

Removing an NT System Using Net Computer

1. From the command prompt, enter the following command:

```
NET COMPUTER \\computername /DEL
```

You may find that you must remove a computer account if you are reinstalling NT Server or another server on the domain. I have seen the installation fail because the account for the system already existed on the domain. This problem usually occurs when you do a reinstall, not an upgrade. If it occurs, just follow the steps for removing the account from a domain and then perform the reinstall.

3.16 CHANGING DOMAINS WITH A SERVER—NOT!

An NT Server, which is a PDC or a BDC, cannot be moved from one domain to another without reinstalling the NT Server software. This limitation makes NT Server servers as secure as possible.

The only way to bring up the server on the new domain is to do a complete reinstall on the server after it is connected to the new domain. All security information on the system is replaced. This is actually not too bad when you consider that the security information will be updated within 5 minutes or so from the PDC.

3.17 SYNCHRONIZING DOMAIN CONTROLLERS

All servers on a domain are automatically synchronized every few minutes (5 minutes is the default). There is usually no need for any intervention by a system manager except for special circumstances. One such circumstance could be when you need to down the domain controller for maintenance or some other reason. You may want to do an immediate synchronization to make sure that the backup server you use to replace the PDC is in synch with the current PDC. Immediate synchronization may also be required when you change a user parameter (say the logon script name) and then try to test the change. If the logon server that processes your logon is the PDC, you are okay. However, if a BDC processes the logon, it probably will not have received the replicated change when you perform your logon. The solution is to perform an immediate synchronization with the PDC.

The normal synchronizing process updates the security database of all BDCs with the PDC. Once the process takes place, the security database on all backup servers should be the same as the PDC until a change is made to it. Any backup server can be promoted to the domain controller with no problems immediately after the synchronization is completed.

What happens when you need to make absolutely sure that a backup server is synchronized with the domain controller? You can take one of the following steps, depending upon whether or not you want to update only one system or all the backup servers on the network.

Synchronizing All Backup Servers (Server Manager)

1. Start Server Manager.
2. Select the Primary Domain Controller from the computer list.
3. Choose Synchronize Entire Domain from the Computer menu.

Synchronizing One Particular Backup Domain Controller (Server Manager)

1. Start Server Manager.
2. Select the server to be updated from the computer list.
3. Choose Synchronize with Domain Controller from the Computer menu.

Synchronizing One Particular Backup Domain Controller (Net Accounts)

1. Enter the following command on the BDC to synchronize:

```
NET ACCOUNTS /sync
```

Synchronizing All Backup Domain Controllers (Net Accounts)

1. Enter the following command on the PDC:

```
NET ACCOUNTS /sync
```

The more servers and users you have in a domain, the longer the synchronization takes. For several hundred users and less than five servers, the process normally occurs in seconds. Just be aware that it can vary with your particular configuration.

3.18 PROMOTING A BACKUP DOMAIN CONTROLLER TO A PRIMARY DOMAIN CONTROLLER

There will come a number of times in each network where it is desirable to switch the role of PDC to another system. Shutting down the PDC, performing maintenance on the PDC, and testing a BDC are just a few possible reasons. Fortunately the process is simple using Server Manager.

Promoting a Backup Domain Controller to a Primary Domain Controller

1. Start Server Manager.
2. Synchronize the server to be the new PDC with the current PDC (see page 130) if possible.

3. Select the Server to be the new domain controller from the computer list.

4. Choose Promote to Domain Controller from the Computer menu.

You normally will not need to demote a PDC to a server unless the domain controller is off-line for some reason when the new PDC is promoted. When this situation occurs, the old domain controller must be demoted before it can be placed back on-line. If it is not demoted, the Net Logon service will not start on the original domain controller.

This situation is actually not too rare because it can easily occur when the PDC goes down, after which a BDC is promoted to PDC. When the old PDC is rebooted, it still thinks it is the PDC.

Demoting a Primary Domain Controller to a Backup Domain Controller

1. Boot the original domain controller without connecting it to the network.

2. Log on as Administrator.

3. Start Server Manager.

4. Select the server to be demoted from domain controller.

5. Choose Demote to Server from the Computer menu.

3.19 STOPPING THE PRIMARY DOMAIN CONTROLLER

Whenever the domain controller must be taken off-line for any reason, you should promote another BDC to be the PDC to ensure that the network still functions correctly (see page 131 for the steps required). During the promotion process the security database of the new server will be synchronized with the PDC, then the BDC can be safely promoted to PDC.

The only time you should take down the PDC without promoting another BDC first is if the PDC is unstable and the promotion cannot be performed.

3.20 LOGGING ON TO A BACKUP DOMAIN CONTROLLER

You should not log on immediately after reboot to a system that has just been set up as a BDC because attempting to log on immediately may cause the logon process to complete before the account database has been replicated to that system. Because the replication of the database occurs every 5 minutes, you should have to wait no longer than 5 minutes to log on. You can be sure that this is the case if you cannot log on with a valid account but can successfully log on with the default Administrator account with no password.

3.21 TRUST RELATIONSHIPS

Computers trusting computers is a scary thought! A *trust relationship* is a term Microsoft came up with to describe how one domain interacts with another domain. Most networks require a user on one area of the network to have an account on another server in order to access resources on the other system. The trust relationship between any two NT Server domains removes this restriction by allowing user accounts and global groups in one domain to be granted privileges in another domain.

The trust relationship is implemented by treating the two domains that will have the trust relationship as different entities. One domain becomes the trusting domain, which recognizes the user accounts and global groups of the trusted domain. The split trust distinction allows one domain to access another domain while users in the second domain cannot access the first domain. This split trust relationship can allow you to build a hierarchy of domains with different types of access between each domain.

Every trust relationship is between two domains only and represents a one-way relationship between them. You must implement a two-way trust relationship as two separate trust relationships.

The trust concept brings a tremendous flexibility to managing your network, but it also adds a lot of responsibility. When you give permission to a global group or add a global group to a local group in a domain, the administrator of the other domain can add other users to your domain automatically by adding them to the global group. See Chapter 11 (page 337) for more on security issues in domains.

The Concepts and Planning Guide has a good discussion of trust relationships and their inner workings with other domains.

3.21.1 Using Trust Relationships

3.21.1.1 How They Work   A trust relationship is created between two domains with User Manager for Domains.

Creating a Trust Relationship

1. The trusted domain administrator chooses the trusting domain with User Manager and enters the trust password.
2. The trusting domain administrator establishes the other side of the relationship with User Manager.

Trust relationships are secured by the servers in a domain by an automatically changing password that is hidden by NT Server. Whenever a new trust relationship is added, the server immediately changes the password. This password is then changed regularly by NT Server to further secure the trust relationship. When a trust relationship is broken, it cannot be reestablished by simply adding one end of the relationship back because there is no way to know the trust password. The relationship must be removed completely from both ends and reestablished.

The Microsoft Knowledge Base mentions a caveat that can occur when you create a domain. After the relationship is set up on the trusted domain, the administrator of the trusting domain has only one chance to enter the password correctly. As soon as the password is entered on the trusting domain, the NT Server changes it. If the password was entered incorrectly, it will not match. The only resolution to this problem is to totally remove the trust relationship on the trusted domain and add it again. The administrator of the trusting domain can then complete the trust relationship.

3.21.1.2 Creating Trust Relationships   Trust relationships are managed with User Manager for Domains. The process is simple and usually takes only a few minutes.

Creating Trust Relationships

1. Start User Manager for Domains.
2. Select Trust Relationships on the Policies menu.
3. Click the Add button for the appropriate relationship.
4. Enter the domain name and password.
5. Close the dialog box.

You must go through this procedure once for each relationship. For instance, if you want to have a trusted and trusting relationship with another domain, you must run the procedure twice on each system. Figure 3.14 shows the Trust Relationships dialog box used for this process.

Notes.   You may encounter a message that the trust relationship cannot be confirmed on the domain. This error usually occurs when your domains are separated over a WAN. After you have set up the trust relationship, test it by trying to access a public service with an account on your domain. If it works, the relationship should be okay.

Duplicate user accounts on different domains can cause problems when the two domains trust each other. Make sure that users have an account on only one domain and that they use that account for assigning permissions. This assignment will clear up any problem because only one account with that user name will exist.

Fig. 3.14 The Trust Relationships dialog box allows you to establish a trust relationship with other systems.

3.22 DESIGNING NETWORK SERVERS

NT was designed for distributed computing environments. Many traditional mainframe and network systems embraced distributed environments only when they had to, resulting in patches to existing systems to facilitate the new requirements. Because of the modular design in NT and the support for client/server architecture in the NT internals, NT is most at home when used in a distributed environment.

Table 3.8 lists several types of suggested servers and describes why each should be used.

Don't be constrained by the suggestions in Table 3.8. You may find that you need one or more dedicated or shared servers for specific tasks such as controlling factory machines or managing specific application functions. It is not unusual to have several dedicated database servers on one network, each handling a particular application or set of applications.

3.23 COMPUTER NAMES AND NT SERVER

Every NT Workstation or NT Server on the network must have an account name for the system. The account entry is normally generated automatically when a system is added to a domain. Users and system managers do not have to be concerned with the account name unless the computer name is changed.

Table 3.8 Types of Common Servers

Server Type	Description
Primary Domain Controller	The PDC handles most logon requests, plus lots of other overhead. For systems other than small networks, this server should be a separate system (see page 120).
Backup Domain Controller	Normally every NT Server should be a BDC. A BDC provides assistance during answering logon requests and takes over as PDC only if the PDC goes down.
Database server	A system such as SQL Server or Oracle running on NT should be on its own server. A dedicated database server can be tuned for performance and will not be bogged down by other requests.
File and print server	Heavy demand for file and print servers often suggests a dedicated server or at least a combination file and print server.
Systems Management Server	Large sites should have a dedicated server for SMS if there are frequent logon/logout occurrences and many packages being distributed. Remember that SMS must have access to SQL server.
Communications Server	A dedicated communications server is a good idea when there will be sizable numbers of frequent RAS users and possibly heavy demand for fax services.

Changing a Computer Name

1. Log on with an Administrator account to the machine you are going to change the name on.
2. Start the Network applet in Control Panel.
3. Click the Change button beside the computer name.
4. Enter the new name and click OK.
5. Log on to the domain as a Domain Admin user and start Server Manager from the Administrator Tools group.
6. Select the system you changed the name on.
7. Select Remove from Domain from the Computer menu or press Del.
8. Resynchronize the domain with all BDCs.
9. Select Add to Domain from the Computer menu.
10. Select Windows NT Workstation or Windows NT Server for Computer Type.
11. Enter the computer's name.
12. Click the Add button.
13. Resynchronize the domain with all BDCs.
14. Click Close.
15. Reboot the system that you changed the name on.
16. Change any user specifications that referenced the old server name, including any UNC names in the command line of icons, startup files, INI files, and so on.
17. Change any user specifications that referenced the old server name, including any UNC names in the command line of icons, startup files, INI files, and so on.

3.24 MULTIPLE NETWORK INTERFACE CARDS IN ONE SERVER

NT Server allows you to install multiple Network Interface Cards (NICs) in one server to improve the performance of the network. Each card must be installed on a different network segment (Ethernet) or ring (Token Ring or FDDI). Figure 3.15 illustrates a sample of how not to hook up multiple network cards. The problem with this figure is that NIC 1 and NIC 2 are both connected to the same logical network through the router. In this example, the router routes all traffic on the network segments to all other segments. This setup can cause a variety of problems from duplicate name found messages to machines that won't boot.

One resolution to this situation is to disconnect one or the other NIC from the network. In our example either NIC 1 or NIC 2 would be disconnected. Another option is to use the router to filter traffic where the two segments do not see the same packets.

The best approach is to separate the two networks and make the only place they come together at the server via NIC 1 and NIC 2. This last approach is actually how a system with multiple network cards is designed to work. Network

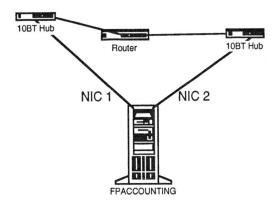

Fig. 3.15 How not to configure multiple NICs in one server.

traffic is segregated across the two networks improving performance and there are two paths in and out of the server, again improving performance.

3.25 MIXED LANGUAGE NETWORKS

NT Server works well in networks that use foreign languages because of its support for UNICODE and other features supporting multiple languages. One instance you should be aware of is using domains with mixed languages. When an NT server is added to a domain with another language, the Administrator account on the new server changes its spelling to match the Administrator account from the domain. This change occurs because the domain account database is replicated to the new server shortly after it is added to the domain.

The Knowledge Base suggests two possible resolutions to the problem:

☞ Creating accounts on the domain for all possible spellings of Administrator that could be applicable on your network.

☞ Adding separate accounts for user management and placing them in the Administrators group for the domain.

3.26 COEXISTENCE OF WINDOWS NT SERVER WITH OTHER NETWORKS

3.26.1 LAN Manager 2.x Servers

LAN Manager 2.x Servers can validate logons for LAN Manager 2.x, Windows for Workgroups, and other clients but cannot validate logons for any Windows NT workstations or servers. For this reason, I recommend that LAN Manager 2.x servers not be used to validate logons in your network. Intel servers running LAN Manager 2.x should be upgraded to NT Servers so that they can be full members in the domain.

Users cannot access LAN Manager resources on a remote domain with both NT servers and LAN Manager servers unless the user has an account on the domain controlled by the NT server. This is because LAN Manager Servers do not recognize global groups or trust relationships between domains. To gain access to LAN Manager resources, the user must explicitly log on to the domain containing the LAN Manager server resources.

3.26.2 Pathworks 5.x

Pathworks 5.x from Digital Equipment Corporation is a LAN Manager 2.2 server and includes support for LAN Manager 2.2-style domains. A Pathworks server can participate in a domain managed by NT Server but cannot be promoted to the PDC.

The easiest way to use NT Server with Pathworks 5.x is to install NT Server before installing Pathworks. If you have already installed Pathworks, continue the steps in this paragraph. Install NT Server in the normal manner, and make the NT Server the domain controller during the installation. Once NT Server is installed, make sure that you can connect to resources on the new server from somewhere on the network. The first connection should be to a shared directory that has permissions set for the share. Log on to the domain with the user name with permission to access the share, then try to connect to the share. Once you can log on successfully and connect to a share, you can proceed to the next step. If you cannot log on or access the share, do not try to install other servers (either NT or Pathworks) until you have resolved the problems.

Now that NT Server is up and running, you can integrate Pathworks with NT Server. This process is actually fairly simple, but it must be performed in the right sequence.

Integrating Pathworks 5.x and NT Server from the NT Server

1. Make sure that both NT Server and Pathworks are using the same protocol (NetBEUI and/or TCP/IP).
2. Make sure that an NT Server is the PDC.
   Run Server Manager.
   Select the NT server.
   Select Promote to Domain Controller from the Computer menu.
3. Enable the Guest account on the NT Server and make sure that the password is null. The password should also be set to never expire.
4. Enable browsing of LAN Manager 2.x clients on NT.
   Run Network applet in Control Panel.
   Choose Computer Browser in the Installed Network Software box.
   Click the Configure button.
   Add LANMAN domains.
5. Enable browsing of NT servers by LAN Manager 2.x servers
   Run Network applet in Control Panel

Choose Server in the Installed Network Software box.

Click the Configure button.

Check the Make Browser Broadcasts to LAN Manager 2.x Clients check box.

6. Synchronize the time between the two servers (NT Server and Pathworks).

Integrating Pathworks 5.x and NT Server from the Pathworks Server

1. Log on to an administration account.

2. Edit the LANMAIN.INI file and change the following lines:

```
applyhostmapcomment = yes
hostmapmode = if_exist_else_default
hostpaswordsync = yes
```

3. Set the server's role to stand alone:

```
$ NET ACCOUNTS /ROLE:STANDALONE
```

4. Create an Administrator account that exactly matches the Administrator account on the NT server

5. Log on to the Pathworks server using the new Administrator account.

6. Change the server's role to member or backup:

```
$ NET ACCOUNTS /ROLE:BACKUP
```

7. Synchronize the time between the two servers again.

Integrating Pathworks 5.x and NT Server—Final steps from the NT Server

1. Make sure the Administrator accounts use the same password on both NT and Pathworks.

2. Start Server Manager.

3. Select the NT server.

4. Select Synchronize with Primary Domain Controller from the Computer menu.

Moving Pathworks 5.x Users to NT Server

1. Log on to an administrator account on the Pathworks server.

2. Run @SYS$UPDATE:PWRK$CONFIG.

3. Answer **Yes** to the question: Is this server joining an existing domain?

4. Enter the NT Server domain name when prompted for the name of the existing domain.

5 Select the Additional Utilities option and select the Merge UAS option. This option merges the Pathworks Users with the NT Server security database. You have the option of doing a complete merge or using the Upgrade Reports option. For more information on using Upgrade Reports, see your

Pathworks documentation. The upgrade process should provide you with status information as it updates the NT Server database.

6. Start the Pathworks server.

The Merge UAS option should have populated the NT Server domain security database with the Pathworks users and groups. Log on to the NT Server domain and run User Manager to check the security database. If the Pathworks users are not in the database, you may need to rerun the upgrade process on the Pathworks server.

After the upgrade process, the Pathworks server should restart. Run the Admin utility and make the Pathworks server a Member Server using the Accounts menu—Security option. Make sure that the time on both the domain controller (NT Server) and Pathworks server have the time set within 5 minutes of each other. The domain controller updates the Pathworks server account database every 5 minutes (default time).

Once the Pathworks server is a member of the domain, clients can access both Pathworks and NT Server resources with a single logon. The logon will be processed and validated by the NT Server(s).

3.26.3 Gateway Services for NetWare

The overview of the NWLINK transport and other NetWare utilities are covered in the protocol section of this chapter (see page 87). Overviews are great, but how do we make this stuff work?

The NWLINK protocol is installed by default along with NetBEUI during the NT Server installation process.

Preparing for Installing (GSNW) Gateway Services for NetWare on NT Server

1. Create an account to use as the gateway account on the NetWare server.
2. Create a group with the name NTGATEWAY on the NetWare server.
3. Add the gateway account created in step 1 to the NTGATEWAY group.
4. Add the proper file permissions to the NTGATEWAY group.

Installing GSNW

1. Start the Network applet in Control Panel.
2. Click the Add Software button.
3. Select the Gate Service for NetWare from the list.
4. Click the Continue button.
5. Click OK.
6. Reboot the system when prompted.

Configuring GSNW

1. Start the GSNW applet in Control Panel.

2. Select the preferred NetWare server from the drop-down list.
3. Configure the required print options.
4. Click the Gateway button to access the configuration dialog box.
5. Check the Enable Gateway button.
6. Enter the NetWare account to use for access by NT Server.
7. Add or remove NT shares to NetWare services in the lower box. Use the Add and Remove buttons to manage the shares. The Permissions button allows you to set NT permissions on the shares.

GSNW creates and maps NetWare server shares and printers to make them accessible to NT clients such as Windows for Workgroups and Windows 95. User can access the NetWare services and have no idea that they are connected to anything but NT resources.

Sharing NetWare Print Resources to NT Server Clients

1. Start Print Manager.
2. Click on the Connect to Printer button.
3. Select the NetWare printer to use in the browse list.
4. Follow the prompts to complete the installation. NT will most likely prompt to load a driver for the printer.
5. Choose the Properties option on the Printer menu.
6. Click the Share this Printer on the Network check box.
7. Enter a share name.
8. Enter the printer's location.
9. Close the Properties dialog box.

Users from any client of the NT server will now see this printer as an NT printer.

Sharing NetWare Print Resources to NT Server Clients

1. Start the GSNW Control Panel applet.
2. Click the Gateway button.
3. Enter the user account.
4. Click the Add button to select the NetWare volumes to share as NT shares.
5. Enter the network path to the NetWare volume (i.e., \\Server-Name\VOL1).
6. Enter the NT share name.
7. Enter a comment for the share.
8. Close the GSNW dialog boxes.

Once these steps are complete, users can access the NetWare volumes as if they are NT shares. The performance will be slightly slower because all file requests are going through NT to get to the NetWare server.

3.26.4 Setting the Search Order for Multiple Network Providers

Installing multiple networks on an NT system can cause performance problems if the network used the most frequently is not specified first in the search order. NT uses a specific search order based on the settings in the Network applet.

The current search order can be displayed by selecting the Network button in the Network applet. The search order is displayed in the list box starting at the top. You can change the order by clicking on the network you wish to change and then clicking the up or down button to change its order in the list. Move the network that is used most frequently to the top of the list.

3.26.5 Binding Network Components

The Network applet in Control Panel is used to configure network services such as protocols, the workstation and server services, and others related to the network. The normal process for configuring a network service is to select a service (i.e., TCP/IP) and then click the Configure button.

All network components perform specific tasks related to the network. Each component must be "bound" to other system components to form a working group before it can be used. For instance, NetBEUI must be bound to a network adapter before you can use the NetBEUI protocol.

Normally you will find groups of two or more components bound together. For instance, you will normally find the Workstation service bound to a protocol such as NetBEUI, and NetBEUI will in turn be bound to a network adapter. This component packaging allows a system manager total flexibility in configuring the components and how they are used.

The Network Bindings dialog box can be used for several tasks such as determining how the network components are bound together, removing a component from other components, and specifying the order that the system uses the transports bound to an adapter.

The Network Bindings dialog box is especially useful in the latter two cases. For instance, if you have both Token Ring and Ethernet cards in a system, you can use this dialog box to bind certain protocols to each adapter, improving the performance of your system. The default is to bind all protocols to all adapters.

You should change the order of network bindings to reflect the real world your systems are used in. If you use TCP/IP for most connections, move TCP/IP to first in the bindings order. Taking this small step can make network connections much faster.

To Change a Binding

1. Start Control Panel.
2. Start the Network applet.
3. Select the Bindings button.
4. Select the Binding to Change.
5. Click the Enable or Disable button to change a binding.

You can change which bindings are shown in the list by clicking on the drop-down list at the top of the dialog box and selecting the object to display.

3.27 OPTIMIZING MEMORY UTILIZATION ON A SERVER

The Network applet allows you to control how much memory to use for network operations. This option can be used to tailor NT for the manner in which your system is used. You have the option of selecting only four settings. Table 3.9 shows the settings suggested by Microsoft in the NT documentation.

The steps for changing the memory usage settings are simple.

Changing the Server Memory Settings

1. Start Control Panel.
2. Start the Network applet.
3. Select the Network Settings button.
4. Select the Server button.
5. Select the desired setting.

If you design your network using distributed servers for different tasks, it will be easy to determine which setting to use. Dedicated file and print servers are usually set to Maximize Throughput for File Sharing. Dedicated database servers use Maximize Throughput for Network Applications. Both Minimize Memory Used and Balance are adequate for small networks only and are not suitable for NT Server as a server should never be used for much interactive work.

Table 3.9 Suggested Settings for Server Memory Utilization

Option	Normal System Loading or Usage
Minimize Memory Used	Places the minimum memory load on the server and is usually adequate for up to 10 network connections.
Balance	Attempts to balance the memory used for network operations and server operations. This option is adequate for approximately 64 connections. Default setting.
Maximize Throughput for File Sharing	Provides the best performance for network servers, especially systems with over 64 simultaneous connections. Network File Sharing operations are given priority in using system memory.
Maximize Throughput for Network Applications	Maximizes memory for network applications that perform their own memory caching. The System Guide mentions SQL server as an example of these types of programs. I recommend checking with your application manuals for the settings suggested for specific applications and then testing the application to make sure it performs in the manner desired.

3.28 REMOTE ACCESS SERVICE

Remote access is a very powerful and important tool that is included with both NT and NT Server. The difference in the NT Server version of Remote Access Service (RAS) is the support for up to 256 connections instead of the single connection in NT Workstation.

RAS is composed of two services and several applications for administering and using RAS. Table 3.10 lists the major components.

NT Server RAS supports the following features:

☞ Open access to all file and print services on the RAS server and systems accessible over the RAS server's network. This is the most important feature of RAS and allows access to any server accessible with a protocol common to the NT server running RAS.

☞ RAS clients can access remote network services using any combination of NetBEUI, TCP/IP, and IPX.

☞ Point-To-Point (PPP) and Serial Line Internet Protocol (SLIP) have been added to RAS. PPP also supports IPX for NetWare support. PPP is the newest and preferred of the two protocols for accessing the Internet (SLIP and PPP).

☞ Automatic modem detection during installation of RAS.

☞ Access to resources such as SNA Server for Windows NT, SQL Server, and numerous others.

☞ Numerous RAS access methods: ISDN, X.25, serial (modem and with a NULL-modem cable).

☞ Integration with NT security system.

Table 3.10 Major Components of RAS

Name	Description
Remote Access Server	RAS service
Remote Access Connection Manager	RAS service
Remote Access	User program for connecting to a RAS system. This program includes the phone book and dialing tools for RAS.
Remote Access Monitor	Monitor program for RAS. This program monitors the communications line used for RAS and contains four indicators that show the status of each modem signal.
Remote Access Admin	Administrator's program for RAS. Remote Access Admin is used to set up permissions for RAS users and start and stop the RAS Server. It can also be used to view users who are currently accessing the system via RAS and view the status of the RAS system.

☞ IP (for TCP/IP protocols) and IPX (for NetWare protocols) routing on the NT server.

☞ Modem pools.

3.28.1 Design and Configuration

3.28.1.1 Hardware   RAS systems perform much better with a faster serial interface than a standard serial port can provide. Intelligent adapters are the best choice for RAS because they off-load the processing of serial services to the adapter. Off-loading frees the NT system from handling the details of the serial system. Check the NT hardware compatibility list under the heading Multiport Serial Adapters for the latest versions. The NT HCL in included with Windows NT Server and an up-to-date copy can be found in the Microsoft Software Library. I have used the 2Port adapter from DigiBoard and can certify that it works fine. The ChiliPorts product from Consensys also looks like a great product.

The ISDN Adapters heading contains a list of certified ISDN adapters for use with RAS. ISDN is usually much faster than a standard line but is not as widely available. You should check with your local telephone suppliers for availability in both areas that will be used in an ISDN connection. Some devices do provide ISDN support for dialing in from a standard phone connection. ISDN configuration is not covered in this book due to the wide variation in availability and the disparity in supporting ISDN at local phone companies. I view ISDN as an emerging technology (in mid-1995) that is starting to take off. Consult the various NT news letters and magazine articles, plus TechNet for more information on ISDN.

Your choice of modems and other RAS support equipment is also critical but has less impact on the server than the serial adapter to use for RAS. One point to keep in mind is the new series of high-speed modems. All the current crop require a high-speed serial interface such as a DigiBoard, ChiliPort, or some other adapter. The standard RS-232 interfaces in a PC do not provide a fast enough throughput for these high-speed modems, except for some late 1994 and after systems that have high-speed modem support built in.

Another issue regarding modems is compatibility between an RAS client and an RAS server. I recommend using modems from the same manufacturer on both ends of the connection if possible. Using the same model modem on each end of the connection is also a good idea. The faster the modem the more likely you will experience problems if the modems are not from the same manufacturer. This is especially true if the modems are V.35 or V.42 compatible or even more so if the modems are one of the new fast modems.

This suggestion is not just a repeat of the Microsoft documentation. I have experienced the problems with both RAS and mail servers. We have also had problems using PC Anywhere with some modems, so choose your vendors carefully. Remember that having both modems from the same vendor is easier to manage and replace when a modem fails. This also includes having to learn the peculiarities of only one set of modem commands.

3.28.1.2 Fitting in with Domains   What does RAS have to do with domains? The overall configuration of your network is important for users and administrators of RAS for several reasons. The Security Account database is used by RAS when a user attempts to connect. RAS checks the local domain for the RAS user's account, and, if it is not found, it simultaneously checks all trusted domains for the account. The first response for that username from a domain is used by RAS for the authentication. This response seems to do the job, but that depends.

If the user has more than one account in the domain and any of the trusted domains, all the passwords must be the same. If the user has an account on a trusted domain and the user does not have an account on the local domain, the user may or may not be able to log on with RAS. The best policy is to create only one account for a user on all domains and make sure that there are no duplicate user accounts. Considering the implications of the user account issues, think about using the master domain model for your network.

Using the master domain model does not mean that the RAS servers should all be in the master domain. You should locate the RAS servers in a domain that is local to a logon server. In other words, don't place an RAS server in a domain where the logon server is accessed over a low-speed connection such as a modem.

3.28.2 Installing RAS

The installation of RAS is a simple process and can be accomplished in a short period of time, if done correctly. The entire process should take somewhere between 15 minutes to 1 hour, depending upon your hardware setup. ISDN may require a little longer to set up (it will take quite a bit longer until the phone and equipment vendors get their act together).

Installing RAS for Serial Communications

1. Install the hardware to be used with RAS.
2. Restart the Server if necessary.
3. Start the Network applet in Control Panel.
4. Click the Add Software button.
5. Select the Remote Access Service from the list.
6. Click continue.
7. Enter the path to the NT distribution files if asked, then click Continue.
8. Select the COM port to use for RAS.
9. Allow Setup to detect your modem or click Cancel to select the modem from a list.
10. Click Network to access the Network Configuration dialog box.
11. Check the box for each protocol to use over RAS. Make sure to check both dial-out and dial-in boxes. Check the box for either dial-in or dial-out or both depending upon how you are planning to use RAS.

12. Click the Configure button beside each protocol in the Server Settings section to set the parameters for that protocol such as whether to use DHCP to assign addresses or to use static addresses for TCP/IP.

13. Click OK when you are finished with the Network Configuration dialog box.

14. Choose whether to allow remote users to access only the current computer or the entire network, then click OK. This setting is by protocol.

15. Click OK after reading the note on the Remote Access Service Setup dialog box.

16. Click OK in the Network dialog box to complete the installation. This step takes a few minutes because it involves configuration programs for all the network software including RAS.

17. Reboot the system by clicking Restart Now when prompted. RAS will not work until the system has been rebooted.

3.28.3 Assigning RAS Permissions to Users

The Remote Access Service Administrator program is used for managing many features of RAS, including assigning permissions to users. Before a user can access the system using RAS, he or she must be granted permission to do so.

Assigning RAS Permissions

1. Start Remote Access Service Administrator.

2. Select the Users menu.

3. Select Permissions.

4. Set the desired options from this dialog box. Table 3.11 outlines the options available.

5. Click OK on the Permissions dialog box.

Table 3.11 RAS Permission Options

Option	Description
Revoke All	Revokes RAS permission for all users in the user account database.
Grant All	Grants RAS permission to all users in the user account database.
Grant Dial-in Permission to User	Grants permission to the user or selected users. If you grant permission to all users, make sure you revoke permission for the GUEST account or add a password for this account.
Call Back	Button group to determine call-back options for the selected user.
No Call Back	Does not enable call-back for the user.
Set By Caller	Allows the user to enter the number for the return call.
Preset To	Presets the call-back number. Enter the number to call back for this user in the box below this button.

Remember that a user must have both RAS permissions to access RAS and NT permissions to do anything on the network or server. Just because a user has permission from RAS to access the server doesn't imply that they can do anything.

3.28.4 Managing the RAS System

RAS is managed in a number of ways, including using the standard administrative tools for NT such as Event Viewer, Control Panel, User Manager, and so forth. One of the primary tools is Remote Access Service Administrator. This tool can be used for a number of different tasks:

☞ control permissions for RAS users,

☞ start, stop, and pause RAS,

☞ view and manage RAS activity by user and server, and

☞ Perform all the preceding activities on other servers.

RAS Administrator is located in the Remote Access Service group as are all the other RAS tools. The other RAS specific tools are the RAS Monitor and the Remote Access programs. Table 3.10 provides an overview to each of the RAS components.

3.28.4.1 Configuring RAS Hardware

Modems.   RAS supports a number of different modems, which are listed on the NT hardware compatibility list, and provides a mechanism for configuring unsupported modems. The following steps outline the process for setting up your modem to use with RAS.

Configuring a Modem

1. Start the Network applet in Control Panel.
2. Select Remote Access Service from the list.
3. Click Configure.
4. Select the port you wish to configure on the Remote Access Service dialog box. If the port you wish to configure is not listed, click the Add button and choose the new port from the list.
5. Click Configure.
6. Select your modem from the list or select a modem that is close to yours.

Warning: If your modem is not on the list and you do not have a driver from the vendor, you may be in for bigger problems.

7. Choose the port usage option for the port to determine its allowable actions for dial-in.
8. Click OK.
9. Click Continue.

10. Click OK on the Network dialog box.

11. Reboot your system if you configured a port that was not in use.

You may need to use the Ports applet in Control Panel to configure a port for RAS to use. RAS can use only ports that are defined in the Ports applet. If your port is not shown, you can select the Add option and define the port. Make sure the IRQ and memory options are set correctly.

I like to test the ports in a clean manner before configuring RAS or if RAS has a problem. The easiest way to do this is to make sure that the port is defined correctly, attach a modem to the port, access the MS-DOS prompt, and run the following command:

```
echo ATDT12213 > COM2:
```

This example is testing COM2:. The command tells the modem to dial (ATDT) the phone number 12212. If the command works, the modem dials and the lights flash. If this does not happen, the port is probably not defined correctly or some other problem is preventing the modem from receiving the command. There is no sense in fooling with RAS until this step works.

Hardware devices such as DigiBoard adapters may need other types of configuration. For instance, the DigiBoard adapter is installed and configured using the Network applet in Control Panel. The hardware vendor should provide the documentation for installation and configuration of any devices not supported directly from the NT distribution.

3.28.4.2 Starting, Stopping, and Pausing RAS   RAS can be started, stopped, and paused in several different ways. The RAS Admin utility has options for all three options on the Server menu.

One way to start RAS is to use the Services applet in Control Panel or from Server Manager. The Services applet allows you to start and stop RAS and to configure RAS to start automatically when NT starts.

Automatically Starting the RAS Service

1. Start the Services applet in Control Panel.

2. Select the RAS service.

3. Click the Startup button.

4. Select the Automatic button for Startup Type.

5. Select System Account for the Log On As option.

6. Click OK.

7. Click Close.

When you must start and stop the RAS service for maintenance, the Remote Access Administrator is the most convenient method. It not only provides access to start and stop the service but also provides management services for most of the RAS features as well.

Starting the RAS Service (Remote Access Administrator)

1. Start the RAS Admin program in the Administrative Tools group.
2. Select the Start Remote Access Service command from the Server menu.
3. Enter the name of the Server that you wish to start RAS on.
4. Click OK.

Stopping the RAS Service (Remote Access Administrator)

1. Start the RAS Admin program in the Administrative Tools group.
2. Select the Stop Remote Access Service command from the Server menu.
3. Click Yes.

Pausing the RAS Service (Remote Access Administrator)

1. Start the RAS Admin program in the Administrative Tools group.
2. Select the Pause Remote Access Service command from the Server menu.

Occasionally you need to stop or start a service at the command prompt or in a batch program. The NET commands are normally the best resource for accessing services. The following steps show you how to start the Remote Access Service using Net Start.

Continuing and Starting the RAS Service (Net Command)

1. Start the RAS Admin program in the Administrative Tools group.
2. Select the Continue Remote Access Service command from the Server menu.

You can also use Net Start to start the Remote Access Service:

```
Net Start Remote Access Server
```

3.28.4.3 Managing the RAS Phonebook   Rasphone is the utility used to manage the phonebook for RAS. This utility is straightforward and has several useful options in addition to entering phone numbers and dialing RAS servers. You can configure each phone number for a different port and type of service such as ISDN, X.25, Modem, or switched.

The following outlines cover the steps for entering entries in the phonebook and configuring them to use a certain type of service.

Entering New Phonebook Entries

1. Start Remote Access.
2. Click the Add button.
3. Enter the following fields for this phone book entry.
   Entry Name
   Phone Number
   Description

4. If you wish to use the user's current user name and password to authenticate them on the remote system, make sure that the Authenticate Using Current User Name and Password box is checked.

Assigning Modem Parameters to Entries

1. Start Remote Access.
2. Select the entry to change.
3. Click the Edit button.
4. Click the Advanced button.
5. Click OK.

Connecting to an RAS Server

Just as there are several options for starting RAS, there are also several options for dialing.

☞ Start RASPHONE and double-click the entry to call.

☞ Start RASPHONE, select the entry to call, and click DIAL.

☞ Enter the following command at the DOS prompt or as the command line for an icon:

`RASDIAL entryname`

Windows for Workgroups supports RAS connections to NT systems. The procedure is the same as using NT because the RASPHONE utility is included with Windows for Workgroups.

You must be logged on to a domain to use any resources on the NT system once you are connected with RAS. This step is not necessary if you are connected to a network that has a trust relationship with the NT domain you wish to access. When you connect to the domain, you will be prompted if you must log in. Answering **Yes** will display the logon dialog box asking you for user name and password.

There is a potential problem when you are logged in to one domain and use RAS to connect to another domain with which the current domain does not have a trust relationship. You must log out of the first domain and then log on to the new domain before you can use any services on the domain.

3.28.5 Miscellaneous Notes

You should always close the Network applet in Control Panel before you try to start RAS or any other network service. If the Network applet is open when you attempt to start the service you may receive an error.

Remote Access Service supports 256 simultaneous connections on an NT server. This limit was raised in NT Server 3.5x from 64 in NT Advanced Server 3.1.

The DSR (Data Set Ready) and DCD (Data Carrier Detect) signals should be set to function normally on your modem. RAS requires these signals to be operating to function properly. These signals are used to determine when the phone line has been hung up. When a hangup occurs RAS resets the modem by sending the modem initialization string.

If your system is remaining connected until the time-out occurs (default is 20 minutes) you should check the cable to your modem and the switch settings for DCD and DSR. You can tell if RAS has not hung up because RAS Admin shows a port status of "Connected, user authenticated" after the line has been hung up.

You can change the time-out value by editing the Registry. The key is

```
\\HKEY_LOCAL_MACHINE\SYSTEM\CurrentControlSet\Services -
\RemoteAccess\Parameters\AutoDisconnect
```

Change the value from 20 (hex 0x14) to whatever you like. A value of 0 disables the automatic time-out.

3.28.6 Accessing an RAS Server and Guest Accounts

NT does not automatically use a guest account when someone tries to connect to the server with an unknown account. The user is denied access to the network, even though a valid Guest account exists on the server. If a user does not have an account on the server or domain, they must specify **GUEST** as their logon name in order to connect to the system.

You will notice an anomaly if you check out the Event Log after a user has tried to access the network with an unknown account. The log shows a successful logon for the user followed by a logout because NT actually logs the user in through RAS, checks the user's logon name and password, and then logs the user out. During the time the user is logged on for this check, NT does not allow any access to system resources.

3.28.6.1 IRQ and Add-On Cards   Some cards may cause problems if they require an IRQ for each port configured on the card. The DigiBoard series is nice because the IRQs are usually turned off when using NT. This configuration allows you to use a card and set the ports for COM3 and COM4 with no conflicts with COM1 and COM2.

3.28.6.2 Limiting Access to System Resources   You can set NT to limit access to selected network protocols or the entire network except for the RAS server. This setting is useful when you wish to restrict access to the entire network for remote users or want to supply only selected information to remote users via the RAS server. For instance, you can disable all access to the network for RAS clients and routinely import the information the RAS clients should access to the RAS server. NT server is ideally suited to this task by using its replication feature. You could of course perform this manually on an NT Workstation system with a simple program.

Access to the LAN can be restricted by setting the NETBIOSGATEWAY-ENABLED parameter to **0**. It is normally enabled with a setting of 1. This value is located under the key

`SYSTEM\CurrentControlSet\Services\RemoteAccess\Parameters`

3.28.7 RAS with Windows for Workgroups 3.11 and Windows 95

Windows for Workgroups 3.11 includes RAS client software that works with both the Windows for Workgroups Point-to-Point RAS software and RAS for NT. The Windows for Workgroups RAS client is similar to the NT RAS client software.

Before trying to install RAS, check out the CompuServe or Internet conferences or Microsoft Technical Support for any updates to the software. You should always run the latest copy of RAS because it contains enhancements to the software.

The RAS software is simple to install, depending upon your system configuration and types of modems that you are using. Check out the system documentation for Windows for Workgroups for more information on installing the software.

Windows 95 uses dial-up networking to connect to NT over RAS. Simply start the dial-up networking application and follow the prompts.

3.28.8 OS/2 RAS Servers

When an NT server is added to a network with an OS/2 RAS server, it can no longer be administered from any OS/2 server on the network, including the RAS server. All administration must be done from an NT system using RAS Administrator.

3.29 NET2COM

Net2Com is a utility that provides network support for NT modems, allowing Windows 3.x, Windows for Workgroups 3.11, and MS-DOS clients to use the modems for out-bound calls. NT clients can also use Net2Com to access modems via Windows or MS-DOS-based terminal programs. NT clients may also use the WINVTP.EXE terminal program that comes with the NT Resource Kit.

Net2Com can be downloaded from CompuServe. The file name is TECHNE.ZIP and is located in the WINNT forum, library 1. I have not tested this program, but for completeness I have included the installation steps from the release notes.

Installing Net2Com

1. Copy the files to a directory.
2. Extract the files using a PKZIP-compatible tool. Use the -d switch to retain the directories. The file contains files for Intel, Alpha, and MIPS, each in its own directory.
3. Run the Net2Set program from the appropriate directory.

Starting Net2Com

1. Start the Services applet in Control Panel.
2. Select Net2Com and click the Start button. You should use the Startup button at this point to have the service automatically start each time.

The only configuration options available for Net2Com are the COM port and the name of the NetBIOS service. The default COM port for the service is COM2. These values are stored under the Registry key

```
HKEY_LOCAL_MACHINE\SYSTEM\CurrentControlSet\Services\ -
Net2Com\ComMechDLL
```

This key has two entries: The fifth line under the first entry is normally blank and defaults the COM port to COM2. The fifth line under the second entry is set to LIONHEART by default.

3.30 REPLICATION OF FILES TO OTHER SYSTEMS

NT supports replication of files to synchronize files from one system to another. NT uses a system called the *export server* that contains the files to replicate, whereas an *import server* is any NT or LAN Manager system that receives the files. The export server must always be an NT server. NT server supports both import and export replication of files. The Workstation version of NT supports only import replication.

The replication process works by the following process:

1. The import server establishes a connection to the export server at regular intervals.
2. Any files or directories subject to replication that have changed on the export server are replicated to the import server, and the directories of the import server are synchronized with the export server.

The default directories are shown in Table 3.12.

Replication can work between computers in a domain and across domains. If an export server exports to a domain, all import servers in the domain receive the export data. If an import server is configured without specifying an export server, the import server automatically replicates files from the export server in its domain. Replication can also take place between two computers in different domains if the domains have a trust relationship.

Table 3.12 NT Replication Default Directories

Directory	Description
C\WINNT\SYSTEM32\REPL\EXPORT	The default export directory tree. Up to 32 subdirectories with 1000 files each can be exported.
C\WINNT\SYSTEM32\REPL\IMPORT	The default import directory tree.

Configuring an Export Server

1. Start User Manager.

2. Create an account for the replication process. It is a good idea to name the account ReplicatorAccount or something similar to identify the account. Remove the check mark from the User Must Change Password at Next Logon check box. Make sure that the account has the right Log On As a Service by placing it in the Replicator group.

3. Run the Services applet in Control Panel.

4. Select the Directory Replicator service and click Startup. Make the Startup Type Automatic.

5. Click the button for This Account in the Log On As box and select the account you created in step 2 for replication from the account list. You can access the account list by clicking the ... button beside the account box. Be sure to enter the password if you entered one for the account (recommended).

6. Run Server Manager.

7. Select the system you have chosen as the export replicator and choose Properties from the Computer menu.

8. Click the Replication button.

9. Click the Manage button to configure the directories you wish to export. The default directory path is \WINNT\SYSTEM32\REPL\EXPORT. The Manage button allows you to configure the subdirectories under the tree that you wish to export. The default directory to replicate is SCRIPTS. Checking the Entire Subtree box causes the selected directory and all of its subdirectories to be exported. The Add Lock button locks a directory from replication until all the locks have been removed. This button is useful when you wish to make some changes to a directory and you need to make sure that the directory is not exported until you are finished. The Wait Until Stabilized box is also useful because it forces NT to wait for 2 minutes after the last file has changed before it replicates the directory again.

10. Close the Manage dialog box.

11. Click the Add button to add systems that you wish to export to. You can enter the name of a computer or domain when prompted. If you specify a domain, the replication is to any system in the domain that is configured as an import server.

12. Close the Directory Replication dialog box. NT attempts to start the Replicator service if it is not already started. If it does not start, use Event Viewer to review the error log for details.

Configuring an Import Server

1. Run the Services applet in Control Panel.

2. Select the Directory Replicator service and click Startup. Make the Startup Type Automatic.

3. Click the button for This Account in the Log On As box and select the account you created for replication on the domain from the account list. You can access the account list by clicking the ... button beside the account box. Be sure to enter the password if you entered one for the account (recommended).

4. Run Server Manager.

5. Select the system you have chosen as the Import Replicator and choose Properties from the Computer menu.

6. Click the Replication button.

7. Select Import Directories. The default path is \WINNT\SYSTEM32 \REPL\IMPORT.

8. If you wish to restrict replication to a specific system, click Add and add the system that will be exporting to your system. By default the list of export servers is blank and the system imports from the local domain. Adding any entries to the list of export servers overrides the default operation and causes NT to replicate files only from the systems on the list.

9. Click Manage to display the directory management dialog box. The Add Lock button can be used on an import server to temporarily stop a directory from receiving updates. The Status field can contain any one of the following indicators:

OK	The subdirectory receives regular updates from an export server.
No Master	The subdirectory is not receiving regular updates.
No Sync	The subdirectory has received updates, but its data are not up to date.
Blank	The subdirectory has never been updated.

3.30.1 Miscellaneous Notes on Replication

Some additional notes on Replication are timely at this point:

☞ NT supports replication across domains with trust relationships. You should make sure that the same Replication account and password are used in all domains. Microsoft strongly recommends using the default import and export paths due to the complex permissions that are established on both paths.

☞ You can make an NT Server both an import and export replicator while NT Workstation can be only an import server.

☞ An import replicator that uses a FAT drive for its import drive and receives files from an NTFS system receives only the 8.3 file names.

☞ NT adds the Replicator account to the Backup Operators and Domain Users groups.

3.30.2 Replication Between NT Server and OS/2 Servers

NT Server can import and export files from and to an OS/2 LAN manager server. Files that are exported to an OS/2 LAN manager server must meet the criteria for the OS/2 server file system. In other words, if the OS/2 Server is using a FAT system, then the exported files must meet the requirements for a FAT system. If the OS/2 server is using HPFS, then the exported files must meet the requirements for an HPFS file system. For exact details on the naming requirements for each system see Chapter 5.

3.30.3 Software Metering and Inventory

System Management Server can perform software metering to some extent. SMS basically performs metering by checking for the installed software on a client workstation with the SMS inventory agent.

If you want to perform actual software metering as applications are running, then you need a product that works with SMS or provides stand-alone software metering.

SMS includes help desk support for remote control and inspection of a client system, automated software delivery, running programs on client systems, performing tests on clients, and all kinds of other interesting things. Also included is a killer sniffer called Network Monitor.

3.31 NET PROGRAMS

The NET programs are a set of commands that run from the NT command prompt. The programs are all prefixed with the word NET when the command is executed. NET is actually the program (NET.EXE) that executes each of the 60 or so separate commands. The following example shows a simple execution of the NET CONFIG command:

```
NET CONFIG
```

Most NET commands are similar in usage to the NET commands from LAN Manager, Windows for Workgroups, Windows 95, and the Microsoft MS-DOS clients. The following sections cover some of the more useful NET commands for managing servers. Other chapters have similar information on NET commands for other tasks.

3.31.1 NET CONFIG

NET CONFIG is a useful command for several tasks. You can add a comment to a server name using the following syntax:

```
NET CONFIG SERVER /SRVCOMMENT:"Master Server"
```

This comment is displayed in most applications that display information about the server such as NET VIEW and File Manager. You can also enter and edit the comment via the Server applet in Control Panel. The comment works identically to the one that you set up with the Network applet in Windows for Workgroups.

Another useful NET CONFIG option is its ability to display information about the NT server or workstation. The syntax for displaying information about a server is

`NET CONFIG SERVER`

This command displays the following information:

```
Server Name \\CTI-MEXP-NTAS
Server Comment CTI Master Server
Software version Windows NT 3.51
Server is active on Nbf_Elnk301 (00608ce98f1b)
Server hidden No
Maximum Logged On Users Unlimited
Maximum open files per session 2048
Idle session time (min) 15
The command completed successfully.
```

As you can see this information is valuable for a quick look at the status of the server. Among other things, this view shows you the number of users the system supports, the current server version, the protocols and network card the server is running on, the maximum files that may be open per session, and the idle time that can expire before the user session is disconnected.

The syntax for displaying information about a workstation is

`NET CONFIG WORKSTATION`

```
Computer name \\CTI-MEXP-NTAS
User name ken
Workstation active on Nbf_Elnk301 (00608CE98F1B)
Software version Windows NT 3.51
Workstation domain DOM-KEN
Logon domain DOM-KEN
COM Open Timeout (sec) 3600
COM Send Count (byte) 16
COM Send Timeout (msec) 250
The command completed successfully.
```

3.31.2 NET ACCOUNTS

Entering NET ACCOUNTS with no options displays several bits of policy information for a domain.

`NET ACCOUNTS`

```
Force user logoff how long after time expires? 0
Minimum password age (days) 0
Maximum password age (days) Unlimited
Minimum password length 0
```

```
Length of password history maintained None
Lockout threshold Never
Lockout duration (minutes) 30
Lockout observation window (minutes) 30
Computer role BACKUP
Primary Domain controller for workstation domain \\MyServer
The command completed successfully.
```

3.32 SYNCHRONIZING TIME ACROSS A NETWORK WITH NET TIME

NET TIME is available with both Windows NT, Windows 95, and Windows for Workgroups. It can be used to display the time from another system on the network and set the system clock on the current system with that of another system. It can be used to obtain the time from Windows for Workgroups, NT, NT Server, or LAN Manager systems.

NET TIME is useful in logon scripts and by itself.

The format is

NET TIME [\\computer | /WORKGROUP:wgname] [/SET] [/YES]

computer	The name of the computer (time server) whose time you want to check or synchronize your computer's clock with.
/WORKGROUP	Specifies that you want to use the clock on a computer (time server) in another workgroup.
wgname	The name of the workgroup containing a computer whose clock you want to check or synchronize your computer's clock with. If there are multiple time servers in that workgroup, NET TIME uses the first one it finds.
/SET	Synchronizes your computer's clock with the clock on the computer or workgroup you specify.
/YES	Carries out the NET TIME command without first prompting you to provide information or confirm actions.

3.33 SYNCHRONIZING TIME ACROSS A NETWORK WITH VISUAL BASIC

Another way to synchronize the time is to use a small Visual Basic (VB) program that runs at startup or during the logon process. The NTLogon (see page 180) has this routine built in to synchronize the time on the client at each logon. Another way to run this routine is to use a timer and fire it every 1 or 2 hours depending upon how close your requirement is to keep the time consistent across workstations.

The VB code for this program follows. You can place this code in a module, and it should run with no problems. Replace the Default_Server entry in the Sub Main procedure with the name of your LAN Manager server.

```
Option Explicit
Type TOD_Info
    TOD_elapsedt  As Long       ' time from 1-1-1970 in seconds
    TOD_msecs     As Long       ' milliseconds
    TOD_hours     As String * 1 ' hours
    TOD_mins      As String * 1 ' minutes
    TOD_secs      As String * 1 ' seconds
    TOD_hunds     As String * 1 ' hundredths
    TOD_timezone  As Integer    ' time zone in minutes from GMT
    TOD_tinterval As Integer    ' timer interval (units=0.0001 sec)
    TOD_day       As String * 1 ' day
    TOD_month     As String * 1 ' month
    TOD_year      As Integer    ' year
    TOD_weekday   As String * 1 ' day of week
End Type

Declare Function NetRemoteTOD Lib "NETAPI.DLL" (ByVal pszServer
As-String, pbBuffer As Any, ByVal cbBuffer As Integer) As Integer

Function UT_ByteToInteger (tChar As String) As Integer
    UT_ByteToInteger = Asc(Left$(tChar, 1))
End Function

Sub SetTimeFromNetwork (txtServer As String)

    Dim TOD_Network As TOD_Info
    Dim nResult As Integer
    Dim tTempStr As String

    nResult = NetRemoteTOD((txtServer),
     TOD_Network,Len(TOD_Network))
    tTempStr =
     Trim$(Str$(UT_ByteToInteger(TOD_Network.TOD_month)))
    tTempStr = tTempStr & "/" & -
     Trim$(Str$(UT_ByteToInteger(TOD_Network.TOD_day)))
    tTempStr = tTempStr & "/" & Trim$(Str$(TOD_Network.TOD_year))
    Date$ = tTempStr
    tTempStr =
     Trim$(Str$(UT_ByteToInteger(TOD_Network.TOD_hours)))
    tTempStr = tTempStr & ":" & -
     Trim$(Str$(UT_ByteToInteger(TOD_Network.TOD_mins)))
    tTempStr = tTempStr & ":" & -
     Trim$(Str$(UT_ByteToInteger(TOD_Network.TOD_secs)))
    Time$ = tTempStr
End Sub

Sub Main
    SetTimeFromNetwork Default_Server
End Sub
```

3.34 SYNCHRONIZING NT TIME WITH TIMESERV (NT RESOURCE KIT)

You can further automate this program and make it much more accurate by using one of your NT servers to run the TimeServ application included in the NT Resource Kit. TimeServ can use a dial-up line via modem or the Internet to access a host of time services around the world. This application is documented in the NT Resource Kit, which provides both tips on setup and configuration and the time services available.

Using an application like TimeServ makes synchronizing workstation times easy with our little VB program. Just have the program fire every 0.5 or 1 hour (depending upon your requirements) and reset the time from the updated time server. It is simple but elegant.

3.35 SENDING MESSAGES TO USERS ON A SERVER

Before you take a server down for maintenance or begin an upgrade, it is often useful to send a message to the users connected to the server. This process is very easy using Server Manager.

Sending Messages to All Users on a Server

1. Start Server Manager.
2. Select the server from the list.
3. Select the Send Message command from the Computer menu.
4. Enter the message and click OK.

You may also find other times that you would like to communicate with specific users via a message instead of using mail. Messages are processed immediately and displayed immediately instead of arriving in a queue and sitting until the user takes action to read the message.

The NET SEND command provides a quick way to send a message to one user or all users on a server. This command must be run from the DOS prompt because there is not a GUI equivalent yet. The syntax is

```
NET SEND name | /domain:name | /users "message"
```

name	User, message name, or computer name to receive the message. If a user name is used, the user must be logged in.
/domain:name	User name in another domain to receive the message.
/users	Send the message to all users on this system.
"message"	Text of message to send.

NET SEND is useful by itself and in a batch file. The following command shows an example of a message sent to Administrator:

```
NET SEND administrator "Lets take the system down at 5:00pm"
```

This command also works nicely in various batch files. For instance, in a shutdown batch file (see page 52) you could include a NET SEND command to notify users that the system is going down in a certain period of time. Other batch files could be maintained to send messages to certain groups of users. For example, if you have a stored procedure in SQL Server, use NET SEND to notify a user that the procedure is completed. There are many uses for this command.

You should be aware of several points when sending messages:

☞ Windows for Workgroups and Windows users must have WinPopUp running to detect and display messages.

☞ NT and NT Server must have the messenger service running to send and receive messages.

☞ Windows 95 must use WinPopUp just like Windows and Windows for Workgroups. Place WINPOPUP.EXE in the Startup folder to start messaging services at startup. Because Windows 95 allows you to run Windows programs from the DOS prompt, you can execute WinPopUp when a user logs on in the logon script for the user. Starting WinPopUp a second time simply places the focus on the currently running copy.

User Management

4.1 DOMAIN USER ACCOUNTS

4.1.1 What Is a Domain User Account?

A domain user account is the magic account by which anyone gains access to resources on an NT Server network. Domain user accounts are exactly the same as an NT workstation user account but are valid across the domain the account is created in. Domain accounts may be used to access other domains via a trust relationship to the domain.

A user account consists of an account name and the full name for the account. Many other properties are tied to the account (such as logon times and groups).

An account can be from 1 to 20 characters in length and may consist of all the characters except for

```
" / \ [ ] : ; | = , + * ? < >
```

User accounts may be both uppercase and lowercase and must be unique for the domain. User accounts are not case-sensitive. For example, if you created an account named Smith, you could log on using either SMITH or smith.

Each account also has a password that can be up to 14 characters in length. Passwords can also use either lower- or upper-case characters, but passwords are case-sensitive! This means that the password JoeBlow is different from the password joeblow.

Chapter 11 (see page 337) has more information on passwords.

4.1.1.1 Guest Accounts Guest accounts should not be disabled on domains that have Windows for Workgroups clients. If security is a concern, you should remove the access rights and privileges for the guest account.

4.1.1.2 Account Duplication User accounts should not be duplicated on different domains that have trust relationships with each other. This can cause problems when a logon is attempted using an account name from a Windows for Workgroups workstation on a domain with a duplicate account name.

4.1.2 Modifying, Creating, Deleting, and Copying User Accounts

User Manager for Domains is the primary tool used for managing accounts, groups, and policies. You can also perform many of these tasks from the DOS prompt using various NET commands. Figure 4.1 shows User Manager.

This section covers the basics on performing actions on user accounts.

Creating a User Account

1. Start User Manager for Domains.
2. Choose the New User command from the User menu.
3. Fill in the New User dialog box.
4. Click Add to add the new user.
5. Click the Close button to close the dialog box.

Figure 4.2 shows the User Properties dialog box from User Manager.

Fig. 4.1 The accounts are listed in the top pane, and groups are listed in the bottom. The two panes are not linked. Clicking on a user account does not show the groups the user belongs to in the bottom pane.

Fig. 4.2 The User Properties dialog box contains user information and access to most user properties.

Deleting a User Account

1. Start User Manager for Domains.
2. Select the user accounts to delete.
3. Choose Delete from the User menu.
4. Confirm the deletion when prompted.

Copying a User Account

1. Start User Manager for Domains.
2. Select the user account to copy from.
3. Choose Copy from the User menu.
4. Modify the properties of the account.
5. Click the Add button to add the account.
6. Modify the properties and click Add for all additional new accounts from the original.
7. Click Close when you finish with the copy process.

4.1.2.1 Adding Many Users at a Time   What happens when you have many user accounts to add at one time? This is a good place to use the NET commands for performing the operations. The following code example shows a batch file that uses NET USER to add many users at once.

```
NET USER ADAMS     password /ADD    /FullName:"Joe Adams"
NET USER ADAMSD    password /ADD    /FullName:"David Adams"
NET USER GRAND     password /ADD    /FullName:"Jack Grand"
NET USER JONES     password /ADD    /FullName:"Nancy Jones"
NET USER SMITHJ    password /ADD    /FullName:"Joe R. Smith"
NET USER AMAB      password /ADD    /FullName:"Tom Amab"
```

This example adds each user, sets the initial password to "password," and enters the user's full name in the FullName field. This short example is part of a file created by a Visual Basic program that converts a VMS user list into NT users. The actual file contains about 300 account names. We also split out users for different sites into separate files, generate files for adding users to groups, add shares for each user, and so on. This organization takes the pain out of upgrading to NT from systems such as Pathworks 4.x or VMS that don't have conversion tools on the market. Computer Technologies, Inc., uses this tool and many others during conversions for many of their clients.

Another option for loading many users at one time is ADDUSERS from the NT Resource Kit. ADDUSERS is also useful for dumping the user list from NT. ADDUSERS either writes the user list to a comma-delimited file (CSV) or loads new users from a file with the same format.

ADDUSERS is preferred for many environments because it can add users to a group and specify their home directory and logon script at the same time the users are added. This is a convenience. There is one caveat: A group must exist before the group is referenced with this command.

The format for ADDUSERS is

```
addusers [\\computername] /C | /D filename
```

\\computername   Specifies the system to perform the operation on.

/C   Create accounts.

/D   Dump accounts.

Creating an ADDUSERS Template File

1. Dump users to a file:

```
addusers /D filename
```

2. Edit the file and delete all accounts but leave the header.

This process generates a file with only a header. The file is easily used for creating new users at any point in the future. The format of the template file is

```
User Name, Full Name, Password, Comment, Home drive, Home Path,
    Profile, Script
```

Adding Accounts with ADDUSERS and a Template File

1. Copy the template file to a new name.
2. Edit the file and add the new users to the file under the header.
3. Add users with

```
addusers /C filename
```

4.1.2.2 Performing Operations on Multiple Existing Accounts

Performing Operations on Multiple Accounts

1. Select the accounts by clicking the first account; then hold down the Control key and click each additional account. You can also select a range of accounts by clicking on the first account and then holding down the Shift key while clicking the last account in the range.
2. Press Enter or Select Properties from the User menu and make your changes. Changes made affect all user accounts.

4.1.3 Account Templates

Account templates are a handy trick for managing different types of user accounts where the accounts have certain types of properties for different users.

For instance, manufacturing users may have different logon times by shift or department. This schedule can be managed very easily by creating a template account for each type of user. Creating a new user account is simply a matter of copying the template account and changing the User Name and Full Name fields.

Another handy trick for account templates is to create a short prefix for the User Name or Full Name fields. A good prefix might be PS01 for Plant Shift 01. With the prefix in place, you can sort the accounts by either field to provide quick access to the group of accounts. For instance, if you need to change the logon hours for all PS01 accounts, simply sort the accounts by the field you use the prefix in, select all the accounts with the PS01 prefix, select Properties from the User menu, and make your changes. The total time is 4 minutes or less.

Creating a Template Account

1. Start User Manager for Domains.
2. Create a new user account.
3. Name the account with a generic name for the type of user it represents. For instance, a special account for the Marketing Department might be called TEMP_Marketing.
4. Modify the properties for the template account.
5. Click Add to add the account.
6. Click OK to close the New Account Properties dialog box.

Creating an Account from a Template Account

1. Start User Manager for Domains.
2. Select the template account from the account list.
3. Press F8 or select Copy from the User menu.
4. Name the account with a specific name for the user it represents.

5. Modify the properties for the new account.
6. Click Add to add the account.
7. Click OK to close the New Account Properties dialog box.

4.1.4 Sorting User Accounts

User Accounts can be sorted by user name or full name. The View menu commands Sort by Full Name and Sort by User Name will switch the User Manager for Domains display to the new order.

Sorting the User Accounts display

1. Start User Manager for Domains.
2. Select Sort by User Name or Sort by Full Name from the View menu.

4.1.5 Controlling Which Workstations a User May Use to Log On

Controlling which workstations and servers a user can log on from is useful in environments where a high level of security is required or where a selected group of users needs to be restricted to only certain workstations. For instance, you can restrict secretaries to only the workstations located at secretaries' desks.

A Windows for Workgroups workstation generates a Network Error 2240 when a user attempts to log on and the workstation is not a valid logon workstation for that user.

Restricting Workstations Users Can Use to Log On

1. Start User Manager for Domains.
2. Select the accounts to modify.
3. Select Properties from the User menu or press Enter.
4. Click the Logon To button.
5. Click the Users May Log On To These Workstations button.
6. Enter computer names for each system the user can log on to in boxes 1 to 8.
7. Click OK to close the dialog box.

The Logon Workstations dialog box is shown in Figure 4.3.

4.1.6 Controlling Logon Times

The Logon Hours in Users Rights control when a user can access the domain. The user is allowed to log on only during the allowable times and can optionally be forcefully logged off when the time expires and he or she is logged on. Forced logoff is set in the Account Policy dialog box.

Restricting hours a user can log on to a system is a useful technique for two purposes. One, you can prevent people from logging on at times when no one

Fig. 4.3 Boxes 1 through 3 have computer names. Clicking OK at this point allows only the user KLS to log on to these workstations.

should be using the system. This is useful if you have an 8–5 type operation and are certain that users or at least certain users do not need access to the system after hours or on weekends. Simply set their logon times to 8–5 or 7–6 during normal working days (M–F). You can do this selectively by user or for several accounts at once. I usually set the logon times for users to exclude the period when the backup runs. Most backups are run at 2 or 3 A.M. when there should be no users on the system unless your system is in an environment where users work 24-hour days or is used by people in many time zones.

4.1.6.1 Controlling Logon Times and Forcing Users Off When Logon Time Expires   Logon times are set with the Logon Hours dialog box. This dialog box is very graphical allowing you to select logon hours by highlighting a block of hours across several days. This makes setting logon times very easy. I also like to set the logon hours on a dummy account and copy the account so that the logon hours are established correctly by default.

Restricting Hours of Access

1. Start User Manager for Domains.
2. Select the accounts to modify.
3. Select Properties from the User menu or press Enter.
4. Click the Hours button.
5. Using the mouse, select the hours the user can log on or the hours he or she cannot log on.
6. Click the Allow or Disallow button.
7. Click OK to close the dialog box.

Figure 4.4 shows the graphical design of the Logon Hours dialog box.

Setting the Forcibly Disconnect Remote Users from Servers When Logon Time Expires option on the account policy dialog box does exactly what the name implies. When the user's logon time expires, any open files the user has open will

Fig. 4.4 The Logon Hours dialog box from User Manager. Notice that only one user (KLS) is selected.

be closed and the user will be logged off. This feature is very useful along with the Logon Hours dialog box to control when users can access the server.

Before the logon times can be used to force users off, you must set the account policy option to force users off. This setting needs to be made only once on a domain because it affects the entire domain account database.

Changing the Policy for Forcing Users to Log Off When Time Expires (User Manager)

1. Start User Manager for Domains.
2. Select Account from the Policies menu.
3. Click the Forcibly Disconnect Remote Users from Server when Logon Hours Expire box.
4. Click OK on the Account Policy dialog box.

The Net Accounts command can also be used to change the Account Policy for forcing users off.

Forcing Users to Log Off When Time Expires (Net Accounts)

1. Enter the following command at the command prompt:

NET ACCOUNTS /forcelogoff:minutes /DOMAIN

minutes   The number of minutes to notify the user before forcing the logoff to occur.

Turning Off Forcing Users to Log Off when Time Expires (Net Accounts)

1. Enter the following command at the command prompt:

```
NET ACCOUNTS /forcelogoff:NO /DOMAIN
```

The /DOMAIN option is needed only if you execute this command from an NT Workstation. NT servers automatically update only the domain security database.

4.1.7 Locking Out an Account

4.1.7.1 Lockout Period   Accounts can be set to lock out automatically when a certain number of failed logon attempts occur for that account. This option is set on the Account Policy form.

Setting Account Lockout Policies

1. Select Account from the Policies menu.
2. Click the Account Lockout button.
3. Change the defaults as needed.

Figure 4.5 shows the Account Policy dialog box.

This is a key part of your security system because it controls what happens when an intruder is trying to guess a password. Many intruders are smart enough to know the default accounts for NT and NT Server and will try to log on when they suspect that the system is running NT. Setting the Account Lockout

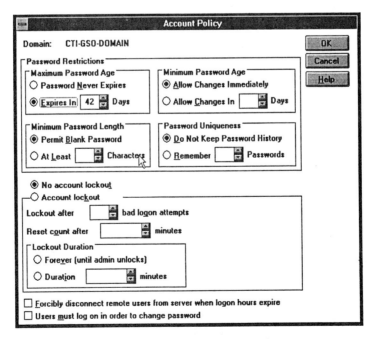

Fig. 4.5 This account policy has been set to automatically lock out an account when five bad logon attempts occur. Notice that you can force an account to be totally locked out until it is cleared using the Forever button.

parameters can force an account to stay locked out for a period of time or until it is reset. Locking out accounts until they are manually reset may be a reasonable approach to take on the default accounts.

4.1.8 Disabling the Default User Name in the Logon Dialog Box

Another trick is to disable the display of the default user name displayed in the logon dialog box. A simple Registry key change makes it disappear. You can also disable the display in Windows for Workgroups by using a small program to periodically wipe out the UserName= value in SYSTEM.INI. Good times to wipe this out are just after a logon (when it gets set) and when the system boots.

The user name can be removed from the NT logon dialog box much more easily. Simply create the following entry with a value of 1:

```
HKEY_LOCAL_MACHINE\SOFTWARE\Microsoft\WindowsNT\ -
CurrentVersion\WinLogon\DontDisplayLastUserName
```

4.1.9 Disabling and Renaming User Accounts

You can disable a user account in order to prevent anyone from using the account. This method is preferred for handling accounts for users who have left the company or are out of the office and have sensitive accounts. Disabling the account allows you to reactivate the account and all its privileges simply by unchecking the Account Disabled box.

If you remove the account, it will be impossible to recreate the account and its associated permissions without manually performing each step. An account cannot be recreated and have the same access privileges and group membership because the Security ID (SID) is used to link the user account to all items in the Security database. Recreating an account with the same name will have a different SID. Disabling an account leaves the SID for the account intact where it can be restored to full status very easily.

Disabling an Account

1. Start User Manager for Domains.
2. Double-click the account to modify or select multiple accounts and choose Properties from the User menu.
3. Check the Accounts Disabled box.
4. Click the OK button to close the dialog box.

Reenabling a Disabled Account

1. Start User Manager for Domains.
2. Double-click the account to modify or select multiple accounts and choose Properties from the User menu.
3. Uncheck the Accounts Disabled box.
4. Click the OK button to close the dialog box.

You can also rename an account, retaining all the account's properties for the new user. This is very useful for a user who assumes the position of the former owner of the account because it immediately gives the new user access to everything the former account owner had access to.

Renaming a User Account

1. Start User Manager for Domains.
2. Double-click the account to modify.
3. Enter the new user name.
4. Click the OK button to close the dialog box.

4.1.10 Restricting an Account for Local Use

You can restrict an account for local use in User Manager for Domains. This setting is on the Account Information dialog box. Selecting the Local Account button restricts the account for use on the local NT system only and does not allow the user to participate in a domain. The default is set to Global Account, which allows domain access as shown in Figure 4.6.

4.1.11 Tips

Don't start User Manager for Domains in the Startup group of an NT workstation or NT server. Doing so may cause User Manager for Domains to focus on the machine name instead of the current domain name. This shift in focus occurs because User Manager for Domains can start before the NetLogon service is completely up and running. You can start User Manager and other programs in this manner if you create a program to start the programs in a specific group after a certain delay.

4.1.12 Special User Accounts

Every access to an NT system must take place via a user account, as discussed in Chapter 11 (see page 337). Even programs that are started by the NT

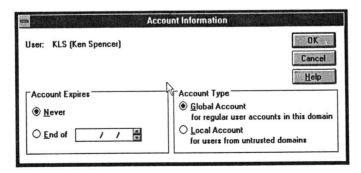

Fig. 4.6 The Account Information dialog box for setting an expiration date an account or for forcing the account to be used locally on the current domain.

Scheduler (AT Command) must run using a user account to log on to the NT system.

Several services require special consideration for the user account assigned to the service. Table 4.1 lists several services that may require special user accounts.

Services use the default system account as the logon account unless you change it. The change can be made using the Services applet in Control Panel.

Changing the Logon Account for a Service

1. Start the Services applet in Control Panel or run Server Manager, select a server, and then select the Services command from the Computer menu.
2. Select the service you wish to change the account for.
3. Click the Startup button.
4. Click the This Account button.
5. Enter the account name or click the button beside the text box to select the account name from a list.
6. Enter and confirm the password for the account.

Note: If you later change the password for the account, you must change the password for the service on every server that uses the account for the service.

Accounts that are used for services should be set up for passwords that never expire.

4.2 USER PROFILES

4.2.1 Overview of User Profiles

User profiles store information about a user's desktop environment in a separate file for each user or a group of users. The types of information stored are Program Manager groups, program items in groups, printer connections, and window characteristics and colors. Profiles provide system managers with a

Table 4.1 Services That Require Special User Accounts

Service	Description
Scheduler	The Scheduler service may need a special account if it is used to run the backup command, in which case the account must be in the Backup Operators group.
Replicator	The Replicator service needs a domain account that is in the Backup Operators group.
Systems Management Server	SMS requires its own account for the SMS Service.

great deal of control by allowing the manager to restrict users from modifying the information in the profiles. Profiles can be created for a specific user, and other profiles can be created and shared for multiple users. The User Profile Editor provides complete control over creating and managing profiles. User Manager for Domains is used to assign a profile to a user or group of users.

User profiles perform the same functions as logon scripts but are much more powerful than logon scripts because of their ability to store information about preferences, control a user's configuration capabilities, and specify which Program Manager group is used as the startup group.

NT maintains a default profile for each user who has logged on to an NT workstation except for guest accounts.

Settings made in the User Profile Editor have no effect on Administrator accounts except for the Startup group setting.

4.2.2 Potential Problems with Profiles

The biggest problem with user profiles is that they work only on NT systems, which limits their usefulness on a network that is using NT Server as a server and has many MS-DOS, Windows for Workgroups, and Windows 95 clients. The MS-DOS and Windows for Workgroups clients must use logon scripts. Windows 95 supports user profiles, but the Windows 95 profiles are not compatible with NT profiles.

Profiles are device-dependent regarding screen resolution and possibly other settings. Profiles should be created on the lowest resolution device for users who share the profile. Ideally you should create separate profiles for users with high-resolution monitors so that they can take full advantage of the screen resolution.

Profile changes may not appear to take effect immediately after the change is made on domains with more than one server. This change takes some time because the profile must be replicated to all the servers in the domain before it is totally effective. You can force this to happen by using Server Manager, selecting the PDC from the servers list, and then selecting Synchronize Entire Domain from the Computer menu. This selection causes all the servers in the domain to be immediately updated with all replication changes.

4.2.3 Types of Profiles

4.2.3.1 Individual or Group   The individual or group profile is created by logging on as the user and selecting File/Save To Current Profile. You can also create an Individual or Group profile by selecting File/Save As File. This choice will save the profile settings as a file, which can then be specified for a user or group of users.

4.2.3.2 User Default   A User Default profile is the one used when a new user is created. You can create this type of profile by selecting File/Save As User Default.

4.2.3.3 System Default   The System Default profile is used by a system when there is no user logged on to the system. This type of profile is created by selecting File/Save As System Default.

4.2.3.4 Mandatory   Mandatory profiles allow you to control a user's ability to change their environment. A Mandatory profile can also be edited to allow users to have access to new applications.

4.2.4 Creating and Assigning Profiles

Profiles are created and modified with the User Profile Editor, which is usually located in the Administrative Tools group. See Figure 4.7.

When you enter the location for the User Profile, make sure that you use the UNC definition for the file location. Using the UNC definition causes NT to connect to the designated server and service to find the profile. If you use a typical FAT designation such as C:\USERS\PROFILE, NT always looks on C: for the location of the profile. The UNC designation is always the preferred method for specifying a file location because it forces NT to connect to the correct server even if no connection exists.

4.2.5 Controlling Network Connections with Profiles

User profiles store information about current printer and file connections. The user profile causes the connections to be reestablished at logon time. These new connections take the place of persistent connections in both Print Manager

Fig. 4.7 The User Profile Editor is used to create profiles for different users. A profile automatically configures an NT workstation or server when the user logs on.

and File Manager because these two programs are available only on a local machine when a person logs on again on the same machine. Server-based user profiles make persistent connections available to a user at any workstation they use to log in to the network.

4.2.6 Storage of Profiles

Profiles that are stored on a server should be stored on a high-availability server. This server should be up all the time to make sure that profiles are available to users.

You can store a master copy of the profile on the server and use directory replication to move a copy of the profiles to each individual system. This structuring probably works fine for department-level or group-level profiles. The overhead in replicating a large number of individual profiles to all the workstations on the LAN might be too high in larger networks.

Replicated files should be located in the IMPORT/SCRIPTS directory of the import server. These files are automatically shared as NETLOGON and are accessed during logon to find logon scripts and profiles.

4.3 Logon Script

In the simple days of NetWare 2.0a and all-DOS clients, Logon scripts were very simple. You simply used NetWare's famous (re: infamous) SysCon to create the script and you were in business. NT Server brings a tremendous amount of flexibility to the good old logon script while at the same time adding complexity to the process (flexibility and complexity always seem to go together).

Windows for Workgroups, Workgroup Add-On for MS-DOS, MSClient, Windows 95, NT, and NT Server all inherit the same basic logon script capabilities. The only problem with NT and logon scripts is determining which logon script to run on which machine. This problem occurs because NT downloads the logon script to the client workstation for processing. If you specify a batch file using NT batch commands for a user and then log on to that account from a DOS machine, the logon script fails. If you log onto the account from an NT workstation the logon script works fine.

Special environment variables are provided for logon scripts under NT or NT Server systems at logon time. These variables are documented on page 182 of this book, in the NT documentation, and in my NT book from CBM.

NT restores persistent connections before running your logon script.

Logon scripts and their associated files should be stored in the \WINNT35 \SYSTEM32\REPL\IMPORT\SCRIPTS directory. This directory automatically shares as NETLOGON.

Computer Technologies, Inc., has developed a tool called NTLOGON that works with Windows for Workgroups clients logging in to an NT Domain. This program uses the standard Windows for Workgroups logon routines and allows you to have customizable toolbars based on the user (using another CTI product called FloatBar), connect to specific services for each user during logon, and numerous other tasks. See page 180 for more information.

4.3.1 Client Participation with Logon and Startup Scripts

Another part of client configuration is what happens on your client workstations when they boot or when the user interface comes up, such as when Program Manager starts with Windows for Workgroups. You can accomplish a lot with these small VB programs and pave the way for further interaction with your server via the logon script. These programs can also save the user time when they are run as the workstation boots. Users seem to be more patient when a workstation takes awhile to boot versus a workstation that boots quickly and then takes forever to log on after logon IDs have been entered.

The following list contains some of the more interesting things you can do with these programs.

- *Client Configuration Data.* With a little ingenuity you can create a program to collect information on your clients with little effort. Your NT and Windows for Workgroups clients in particular can benefit from Visual Basic programs that execute when Windows starts. A neat little VB program can grab the configuration data for your machine and stuff it on a server drive. Then it's easy for NT to pick up the data and update your configuration database. The types of data you can collect include memory configuration, processor type, math coprocessor, and applications listed in the WIN.INI file or Registry. You can tweak your CONFIG.SYS or AUTOEXEC.BAT files to include SET statements for other important pieces of data such as the number for the workstations network cable.

- *Starting Other Programs.* You may have certain programs that must be started when a user logs in. Examples of these programs are Schedule+ and a mail-monitoring program. You might ask: "Why not start these programs in the Startup group of the user's workstation?" Starting the programs in the logon script allows the user to have access to them wherever they log on and not just from their normal workstation. You must check with individual programs to determine their idiosyncrasies for running from different locations for a single user. For instance, Microsoft Mail requires that the mail files be kept on the Post Office if the user accesses mail from different places or if more than one user logs on to mail from a workstation.

- *Connecting to Network Resources.* Another useful trick is using the logon program to connect to standard services during the logon process. This process removes the need to rely on the system to reconnect to all services that were connected when the user shut down the client or logged out. You can use the NET commands such as NET USE to connect or disconnect any network resources during the logon process.

4.3.1.1 Logon Script Examples

Sample DOS/Windows/Windows for Workgroups Logon Script. I needed to solve a problem involving SMS.INI when developing a procedure to install new PC workstations at a client site. SMS.INI is installed automatically using several defaults for users to fill in regarding whether the PC can be remotely monitored and controlled. This client as is the case with many others did not want to give the users the option but force the user to allow remote control. I solved this problem using a small batch program and a little VB-DOS program. The following code sample shows the batch program.

```
Echo Logon Script for NewPCs
Echo.
Echo Execute standard SMS logon script
net use x: \\server1\netlogon
net use w: \\server1\sms_shr
set oldpath=%path%
path=%path%;x:\;
w:
call smsls
Echo
Echo Reset SMS.INI variables
x:SETSMS
c:
net use x: /d /y
net use w: /d /y
path=%oldpath%
```

This routine performs the following tasks:

1. Connect to the NetLogon and SMS_SHR shared resources.
2. Save the current Path in the variable old path.
3. Change to the W: drive (SMS_SHR).
4. Run the SMSLS.BAT logon script.
5. Run the SETSMS.EXE program on drive X: (NetLogon).
6. Change to the C: drive.
7. Disconnect both shared resources.
8. Restore the path.

SETSMS.EXE is actually a small VB-DOS program that edits the SMS.INI file and changes several settings.

This little routine saves lots of time by

☞ Logging on to the new system using the NEWPC account and
☞ installing and reconfiguring SMS on the fly.

You should be able to take this example and configure it for your needs. Here is one word of caution: if a logon script does not terminate normally, it will hang the logon process. If you experience a logon script that is hanging, try using a simple script that does nothing to verify that the PC can log on successfully. More complex logon scripts such as those used by SMS can run into this problem frequently if there is a logic or other problem that hangs the logon script.

SMS Logon Script.   SMSLS.BAT is the standard LOGON script for Systems Management Server and runs the standard SMS items for inventory and the like.

The following files must be on the NetLogon share for SMS to find them during a normal logon:

CHOICE.COM

CLRLEVEL.COM

DOSVER.COM

NETSPEED.COM

NETSPEED.DAT

SETLS16.EXE

SETLS32I.EXE

SMSLS.BAT

You can also use NET USE in a logon script to connect to the SMS_SHR and then run SMSLS. This procedure removes the need to copy the files to the NetLogon share and also resolves a problem that occurs when SMSLS.BAT runs on the NetLogon share and finds itself there. It then tries to run as if it were running from the SMS_SHR.

Most of these files can be found in the SMS\LOGON.SRV directory. The SETLS16.EXE file can be found in the X86.BIN subdirectory of LOGON.SRV, while versions of SETLS321.EXE are found in the appropriate subdirectory for the server (ALPHA.BIN or X86.BIN). A SETLSOS2.EXE program is in the X86.BIN directory for OS/2 clients.

There are also two other SMSLS programs: an SMSLS.CMD for OS/2 and a SMSLS.SCR for NetWare. The NetWare version should be included in the system login script.

4.3.1.2 NTLogon and FloatBar   NTLogon from Computer Technologies was designed specifically to work with NT clients such as Windows for Workgroups. It will be enhanced to work with Windows 95 shortly after Windows 95 ships.

NTLogon disconnects users if they are connected when the program runs. Before the disconnection takes place, File Manager and MSMail are disconnected if they are running.

NTLogon allows a system manager to have more control during the logon process. A user file (USER.INI) that is located in the user's home directory controls the shares connected during logon. Shared directories and printers are simply listed in USER.INI, and the connections take place automatically. All other shares are disconnected regardless of whether or not the shares are persistent.

The default server is listed in NTLOGON.INI in the U: directory on the SiteSys$ share, along with any shared resources that all users should connect to. A sample NTLOGON.INI is shown in the following code sample:

```
[SERVER]
ServerName1
[FILEPUBLIC]
z:\\ ServerName1\distdsk$
[PRINT]
```

Both NTLOGON.INI and USER.INI share the same format.

The next to the last thing NTLogon does is set the workstation time from the default server listed in NTLOGON.INI in the U: directory on the SiteSys$ share. If you simply keep the server time set correctly, every workstation follows as long as they log on each day. If you set the Force Users Off When Logon Time Expires option, each user must log on if you limit their logon time to every 23.75 hours per day.

NTLogon also calls FloatBar if the FloatBar option is installed. FloatBar is a toolbar from the same vendor that provides the standard toolbar features and adds network functionality. When used with NTLOGON, FloatBar is reinitialized each time a user logs on. After the logon occurs, FloatBar reconfigures its icons and options to match those of the new user. This new configuration allows a user to move to different systems and have the same functions available.

Another interesting feature of FloatBar is its ability to hide both Program Manager and Print Manager. It does not terminate either program, it just makes the program inaccessible to the user. FloatBar also can be set to autominimize when a user clicks an icon. This option leaves only a small bar visible on the screen. Simply moving the cursor over the bar displays the icon strip again. It works very much like the roll-ups in CorelDRAW.

4.3.1.3 Windows NTLogon Scripts   Windows NT and NT Server both use a flexible format for logon scripts. You can call any executable program as a logon script from either system. This flexibility allows you to use a mixture of batch programs and executable programs depending upon the requirements of your network. This flexibility also means that you don't have to learn a new logon script language to take advantage of this powerful tool.

I like using a tool like Visual Basic or Visual C++ for logon scripts because they provide speed. They also are compiled to EXE files and the source code is hidden from the user. Maintaining source code versions is easier with these tools because I can be sure that no one has tweaked a file at a remote server and forgotten to update the master copy on the server.

The only problem with using Visual Basic for a logon script is that NT does not support it. A logon script must be a batch file (BAT or CMD) or a true executable such as those created by C++ or Visual C++. You can get around this restriction with a little ingenuity, such as calling the logon functions from a VB logon utility like NTLogon.

Default Variables.   Table 4.2 defines special variables that may be used within logon script programs but only when logging on from an NT system. A similar table can be found in the Concepts and Planning Guide manual.

These parameters are useful for determining special options at logon time depending upon the user's operating system, machine type, domain, and so forth. You access these parameters by specifying its name in a command. The method of access is slightly different for each language you may use for a logon script.

Logon Script Tips.   Some useful tips for logon scripts follow:

☞ Connect to specific resources.

☞ Most networks require that certain file and print resources are available when a user logs in to the network.

☞ Make sure that specific resources are not connected.

☞ Run specific application programs

☞ Run update programs

Table 4.2 Special Environment Variables for Logon Script Programs

Parameter	Description
%HOMEDRIVE%	Specifies the drive letter that points to the drive containing the user's home directory. When no home directory is used, the default is the drive NT is installed on.
%HOMEPATH%	Specifies the full path name for the user's home directory. When no home directory is used, the default is \Users\Default.
%HOMESHARE%	Specifies the share name for the service containing the user's home directory. When no home directory is used, the default is the blank.
%OS%	Specifies the operating system for the user's workstation.
%PROCESSOR_ARCHITECTURE%	Indicates the processor architecture for the system. It is used with the %PROCESSOR_LEVEL% variable to identify the exact type of processor. This option returns ALPHA, MIPS, or X86 depending upon the system.
%PROCESSOR_LEVEL%	Specifies the processor level for the user's workstation. Examples for this variable are 21064 for Alpha systems and 5 for an Intel Pentium system.
%USERDOMAIN%	Specifies the domain containing the user's account.
%USERNAME%	The user name for the user running the logon script.

Preferences and last-shared connections are set and reconnected before logon scripts are executed.

The path to a logon script is built by adding the NetLogon path to the logon script name.

4.3.1.4 Home Directories Home directories are typically a location on a server where a user stores personnel files. Every user should have a default home directory that is connected each time they log on. Every user's connection to the home directory should also use the same letter.

For instance, say every user has an account under the USERS directory. This account should be shared with the user name followed by a $ (to make it a hidden share). When each user logs on, each user should connect the same drive letter to its own share. If my user name is KENS, I should connect to the KENS$ share. I normally use the drive letter specified on most Pathworks networks— M:. This is a good choice because users think of M: as MY drive.

You can specify a home directory for users using User Manager. Select the Properties for a user and then click the Profile button. Include either a local path or a UNC name. The UNC name is my favorite because it works for both interactive and network logons over the LAN.

One problem with home directories is that Windows for Workgroups and DOS clients do not see their home directories unless you connect them in the logon script. You should either use a logon script to connect to the user's home directory or use the NTLOGON program or one similar. This setup makes sure that a user is always connected to his or her own home directory with the same drive letter. It cuts down on a lot of confusion.

The NET USE command supports an option for attaching to home directories (/HOME); the only thing is that it does not work. I tried several approaches to get the command to work but to no avail. I proved the command would not work on Windows for Workgroups by using an NT system to test and ran the same tests with the same user accounts on both systems. NT is fine, and Windows for Workgroups does not work—period.

4.4 GROUPS

4.4.1 Local Groups

NT and NT Server include several default local groups. Table 4.3 lists the default groups and indicates whether the group is for NT or NT Server only.

Local groups are represented by an icon with two faces superimposed over a computer:

A local group is useful only on the NT workstation or NT Server domain on which it was created. Local groups can contain user accounts from the workstations, user accounts, and global groups from the domain and trusted domains.

Table 4.3 Default User Groups

Group	Description
Administrators	Members have more control over managing systems than any other group.
Backup Operators	Members of this group can back up and restore files on primary and backup domain controllers. They also have the ability to log on to the servers interactively and shut them down.
Server Operators	Members of this group can manage the domain's PDC and BDC for tasks such as backup, printer management, share management, backup chores, formatting the server's disk, miscellaneous tasks, and shutting down the servers.
Account Operators	The Account Operators local group is designed for managers that need to manage user accounts. Account Operators can use User Manager for Domains for most tasks but cannot modify or delete the following groups, users, or policies: groups (Administrators, Domain Admins, Account Operators, Backup Operators, Print Operators, or Server Operators), users (administrators), and policies (security).
Print Operators	The Print Operators group is designed for users who must have full management over printers.
Users	The Users local group lists all users of an NT system. Users normally contains the Domain Users group.
Guests	The Guests local group is for users who require minimal access to the network. Guests usually contains the Domain Guests global group.
Replicator	The Replicator group is designed to provide support for Replicator functions. The only account that should be in this group is the domain user account used to log on to the Replicator services.

Local groups are useful for maintaining security permissions on a domain because a local group can contain global groups and users from trusted domains. For instance, you can create a group on a domain that contains both users on the current domain and users on trusted domains, as well as global groups.

Local groups with the same name can be created in different servers and/or domains, but can cause confusion.

4.4.2 Special Groups

NT Server also includes other default groups that contain no members. These groups are used only to specify how a particular user is using the NT system at a certain point in time. These groups are listed in Table 4.4.

The special groups are useful when NT Server presents a list of users for tasks such as setting permissions. These generic groups allow you to assign permissions by type of user instead of only by the local or global groups or user account. For instance, if you want to prevent access to a particular directory or file over the network, simply assign no access permission to the Network Users group.

Table 4.4 Default Groups That Contain No Members

Group	Description
Interactive	Users who log on interactively to the system.
Everyone	Every user who accesses the system in any manner.
Creator/Owner	The user who creates or takes ownership of a resource.
Network Users	Users who access a resource through the network.
System	The operating system.

4.4.3 Global Groups

Global groups are represented by an icon with two faces superimposed over a globe:

They are used only on NT Server domains. A global group can contain only user accounts from the domain and global groups from trusted domains.

Global groups can pass through trust relationships, while local groups cannot. In other words, a global group can be accessed anywhere you can see groups and users such as in the Permissions dialog box in File Manager. NT Server creates three global groups at installation: Domain Admins, Domain Users, and Domain Guests.

If a global group is created with the same name as a local group, they will be treated as two separate entities. Any permissions assigned to one group will not carry over to the other group because both groups have separate security identifiers.

It is a good idea to add a special identifier to the front of a global group name to make it readily identifiable even though the icon for global groups is different from the icon for local groups. A prefix such as Domain at the front of a global group name provides instant recognition for your global groups wherever they are used or viewed. Notice that this prefix is the same prefix used by Microsoft for the built-in global groups.

Table 4.5 includes the built-in global groups with NT Server.

4.4.4 Managing Groups

Global and local groups are managed in the same manner. The main difference in creating a new group is whether you choose New Local Group or New Global Group from the User menu in User Manager.

Creating a New Group

1. Start User Manager for Domains.
2. Select the initial users for the group.
3. Choose New Local Group or New Global Group from the User menu.

Table 4.5 NT Server Built-in Global Groups

Group	Description
Domain Admins	Members have more control over managing systems than any other group.
Domain Users	The Domain Users group is (by default) a member of all NT and NT Server local users groups, extending membership in the users group to all domain users. New domain users are automatically added to Domain Users.
Domain Guests	The Domain Guests group contains the built-in guest account on NT Servers. Domain Guests is a member of the Guests local group on the domain.

4. Enter the name of the group in the Group Name box.

5. Enter an optional description for the group (recommended) in the Description box.

6. Add any new members not selected to the group by clicking the Add button and selecting the users.

7. Choose the OK button to close the dialog box.

Copying a Group

1. Start User Manager for Domains.

2. Select the group to copy.

3. Choose the Copy command from the User menu.

4. Enter the name of the group in the Group Name box.

5. Change the description for the group (recommended) in the Description box.

6. Add any new members not selected to the group by clicking the Add button and selecting the users.

7. Remove any users not desired in the new group

8. Choose the OK button to close the dialog box.

Groups can be deleted quickly with User Manager.

Deleting a Group

1. Start User Manager for Domains.

2. Select the group to delete.

3. Choose the Delete command from the User menu or press Del.

4. Confirm the deletion by choosing OK and then Yes.

Removing Users from a Group

1. Start User Manager for Domains.

2. Double-click the group to modify.

3. Select the user(s) to remove.
4. Drag the users to the Not Members box or click the Remove button.
5. Click the OK button to close the dialog box.

Users gain access to all permissions and rights given to a group when they become a member of the group.

Adding Users to a Local Group

1. Start User Manager for Domains.
2. Double-click the local group to modify.
3. Click the Add button to display the Add Users and Groups dialog box.
4. Select the users.
5. Click the Add button.
6. Click the OK button to close the dialog box.

Adding Users to a Global Group

1. Start User Manager for Domains.
2. Double-click the global group to modify.
3. Select the users.
4. Click the Add button.
5. Click the OK button to close the dialog box.

Modifying Properties of a Group

1. Start User Manager for Domains.
2. Double-click the group to modify.
3. Modify the desired properties (description and users).
4. Click the OK button to close the dialog box.

A neat future that can be obscured in the steps to create a group is the ability to automatically add users to a new group.

Creating a New Group and Automatically Adding Users

1. Start User Manager.
2. Select the users from the user list.
3. Choose New Local Group or New Global Group from the User menu.
4. Enter the name of the group in the Group Name box.
5. Enter an optional description for the group (recommended) in the Description box.
6. Add any new members not selected to the group by clicking the Add button and selecting the users.
7. Choose the OK button to close the dialog box.

The NT Resource Kit includes a utility that is useful for managing groups. USRTOGRP.EXE can add many users to a group at one time. The specifications for the users to add are supplied from a text file. This command is especially useful because a group will be created, if it does not exist. User accounts must exist before they are referenced in this command.

The command also works well in a trusted domain environment because it searches all trusted domains for users that are added to local groups. USRTOGRP checks only the current domain for user accounts added to a global group.

The format for the input file is

```
domain: domainname
localgroup(or globalgroup): groupname
Username1
Username2
...
```

Adding Many Users to Groups with USRTOGRP.EXE (NT Resource Kit)

1. Edit or create the input file.
2. Execute the command:

   usrtogrp filename

4.5 LOGGING IN FROM MULTIPLE WORKSTATIONS

A user may not receive pop-up messages correctly when they are logged on to multiple machines simultaneously with the same user name. This message occurs when the user has logged in to several machines with the same user name and a network pop-up message is sent to the user account and not a machine name. The message is sent to the user account because the first workstation the user logs in to registers the user name and subsequently captures the pop-up message when it is sent.

4.6 CHANGING PASSWORDS FROM AN OS/2 SERVER

Administrators should not change their passwords from an OS/2 server because doing so will lose the rights associated with the account.

File Systems

5.1 OVERVIEW

Like any good operating system, NT must support some type of file system. NT goes beyond this simple requirement by containing native support for several different file systems:

- ☞ NTFS is the NT File System and contains the most advanced features of any file system supported by NT.
- ☞ FAT is the File Allocation Table file system that is carried over from DOS.
- ☞ HPFS is the High-Performance File System first introduced with OS/2. HPFS has support for extended file names and other features that the FAT system does not support.
- ☞ The CDFS file system supports the industry standard CD-ROM devices that are typically used in PCs today.
- ☞ MAC-NT supports the Macintosh via the Services for Macintosh subsystem. SFM must be installed as an option and only works with NTFS.

Each of these file systems is designed for a specific purpose and may be mixed and matched in NT to support your particular environment. For instance, many Intel systems run a small FAT partition (200MB) to hold the NT operating system and then use NTFS on the remaining disk space. Other users may use NTFS, FAT, and HPFS on the same system if they are supporting DOS and OS/2 users.

5.2 NT FILE TYPES

NT has quite a number of files that are used as part of the system or by different applications. Table 5.1 contains a useful list of most of the file types used on NT sorted by file extension and includes short descriptions.

Table 5.1 NT File Types (Extensions)

Extension	Description
	Some Registry files and others have no extension
ALT	Registry files for alternate configuration
ANI	Animated cursors
BAS	Basic programs
BAT	Batch programs
BMP	Bit-mapped picture—graphic file
CMD	Batch programs for OS/2
COM	Executable programs
CPI	Font files
CPL	Control Panel tool files
CUR	Cursor files
DLL	Dynamic Link Library
DRV	Drivers
EVT	Event Viewer files
EXE	Executable programs
FNT	Font files
FON	Font files
FOT	Font files
HLP	Help files
IND	Full text search index for help files
INF	Setup files
LEX	Spelling lexicon files
LOG	Log files for Registry and other applications
NLS	National language files
PCD	Plotter Driver files
PMA	Performance Monitor Alert settings file
PMC	Performance Monitor Chart settings file
PML	Performance Monitor Log settings file
PMR	Performance Monitor Report settings file

Table 5.1 NT File Types (Extensions) (Continued)

Extension	Description
PMW	Performance Monitor Workspace settings file
PPD	Adobe PostScript printer description files
SCR	Screen savers
SEP	Separator page files
SEQ	Introduction to NT sequence files
SYS	Drivers
TIF	Tagged Image Format graphic file
TTF	Font files
TXT	Text files
WAV	Sound WAV files
WRI	Windows Write file
Other	Miscellaneous files

This is not a complete list of every NT file type, but it covers most programs, applications, and support files.

5.3 NT FILE SYSTEMS IN GENERAL

NT supports huge file systems up to 408 million terabytes in size. For many people that number is beyond comprehension. The importance of the number is that it will be a long time before your NT system runs out of disk space capability. In fact, you will probably bump up against the physical limit of disk space on your server before the NT limit comes into play.

NT also supports large volume sizes for your disks, allowing you to have a partition that uses the entire disk instead of having to split the disk across several partitions as was the case in some versions of DOS. I have installed NT Server on systems with as little as 1GB of total space to 20GB systems using mirrored volumes for the system disks and RAID 5 storage for data. NT scales beautifully with its wide support of file systems and storage types.

5.3.1 NTFS

NT File System (NTFS) is a new file system designed explicitly for NT. It has extended features such as transaction processing for file system meta data, advanced security, and long file names. It also supports short file names for any program or system that does not support long file names. The following list covers the main features of NTFS:

☞ NTFS supports cluster sizes of 512, 1024, 2048, and 4096 bytes.

☞ Names can be up to 256 characters.

☞ Paths can be up to 259 characters.

☞ Blanks and periods can occur anywhere in a file or directory name.

☞ The following characters cannot be used in a file or directory name: < > : " /
\ | * ?.

☞ Case can be upper, lower, or mixed in a file or directory name.

☞ It is fast, very fast.

You must use quotes (" ") around a file name that contains spaces to force NT
to parse the file name properly. Luckily you can access most files from File Manager and programs that use directory list boxes to provide access to the file system. This type of graphical interface makes accessing files with long file names
easy and removes the need to remember or to type a 200-character file name.

Tip: When creating an association for a file in File Manager, be sure to
use quotes around the file name parameter to enable the application
to open a file with spaces in the name.

Creating File Associations for File with Spaces in the Name (File Manager)

1. Start File Manager.
2. Select the Associate option from the File menu.
3. Select the file type to change from the list.
4. Click the Change Type button.
5. Click in the Command box and press the End key to move the cursor to the
end of the command.
6. Change the parameter from %1 to "%1".
7. If the file type has more than one Action property (Open, Print, etc.), make
the changes in steps 5 and 6 for each action in the Action list.

Using spaces in names is a common approach once you get used to NT, so
this step is very useful, especially for programs like Performance Monitor or
Microsoft Word. Any time you have a problem accessing a file name with spaces,
check out the syntax and make sure that you have included the quotes.

NT automatically creates short file names for all NTFS files, unless the
short file name feature is turned off. NT uses the following rules for creating
DOS file names from NTFS names:

☞ All spaces and UNICODE characters are removed.

☞ Periods are removed except for the last period that precedes a character.

☞ The first three characters after the period become the DOS extension.

☞ All NTFS characters that are illegal in the FAT system (. " / \ [ ] : ; = ,) are
converted to underscores (_).

☞ The prefix for the DOS file becomes the first six characters of the NTFS file
name plus a tilde (~) and a single digit number from 1 to 4. NT increments
the number until the short file name is unique. If the resulting name is not

unique after the number reaches 4, then the first characters of the name are used followed by 4 characters generated from the long file name. A ~5 or other number is appended to the resulting 6 character name to guarantee uniqueness.

☞ All characters in the file name are translated to uppercase.

The exception to these rules is when the NTFS file name is less than eight characters and contains a space. To work around this problem anytime you have an NTFS name that is less than eight characters use another character (such as _ or -) to replace the space.

You should plan on disabling short-file-name generation at some point in the future when all users have upgraded to NT, Windows 95, and use only programs that can handle long file names. Turning off short-file-name generation will improve file system performance.

Disabling Short-File-Name Generation

1. Start REGEDT32.
2. Change the DWORD value for the following entry to 1:

```
HKEY_LOCAL_MACHINE\SYSTEM\CurrentControlSet\Control\ -
Filesystem\NtfsDisable8dot3NameCreation
```

5.3.2 FAT

The File Allocation Table (FAT) system has been around for years on systems using MS-DOS. NTFS continues support for FAT to maintain compatibility with the many millions of systems still using DOS.

The FAT file system generally uses more space to store files than HPFS or NTFS. Files require more storage space because FAT uses fixed 4K clusters to allocate disk space for files. For instance, when a file is created to hold 256 bytes of data and the cluster size for the partition is 4K, the file requires 4K of disk for the 256 bytes. The more files you store that are smaller than the cluster size, the more wasted space will occur.

The following list shows the parameters for FAT file systems on NT:

☞ Names up to 8.3 characters. Version 3.5x or higher NT workstations and NT servers can both handle FAT names up to 255 characters. This limit is also true for Windows 95.

☞ Full path names can be up to 64 characters.

☞ Blanks cannot occur anywhere in the file or directory name.

☞ A period can be used only to separate the name from the extension.

☞ The following special characters can be used in a file or directory name: - ( ) ! @ # $ % ^ & _ ~ '.

☞ All other special characters cannot be used in a file or directory name.

☞ Case of file or directory names will always be upper, except on version 3.5x or higher NT workstations and NT servers, which can use mixed-case file names. This is also true of Windows 95.

☞ NT 3.5x automatically generates short file names in the 8.3 format using the same short-file-name generation method as NTFS.

5.3.3 HPFS

The High Performance File System (HPFS) is a carryover from OS/2 and is included primarily for compatibility with OS/2 systems that share a network with NT. NT 3.51 and later allows you to use an existing HPFS volume but does not provide support for creating one. The following list covers the parameters for HPFS:

☞ HPFS supports cluster sizes of 1024 bytes.

☞ Names can be up to 254 characters.

☞ Paths can be up to 259 characters.

☞ Blanks and periods can occur anywhere in the file or directory name.

☞ The following characters can be used in a file or directory name: [ ] , + = ;.

☞ The following characters cannot be used in a file or directory name: < > : " / \ | * ? &.

☞ Case can be upper, lower, or mixed in a file or directory name.

5.4 SUGGESTED DIRECTORY STRUCTURES

NT's default directory structure is laid out with the systems manager in mind. The structure supports the NT system and provides an initial directory tree for user directories. Table 5.2 shows the directories installed by NT and a short description of the directories contents and/or purpose.

5.4.1 USERS Directory

The USERS directory is the default directory for user directories. This directory should be on an NTFS partition and should have restrictions placed on it as to who can do what. This setup stops prying users who have access to the server from getting into other people's files.

Another benefit of hanging all users directories from the USERS directory is that it makes backup much easier. If you want to back up all the user files for instance, just back up the entire USERS tree. This approach gets all users directories at one time. Using this structure also makes restoring directories easier.

5.4.2 Home Directory

The Home directory is the default directory for users when they log in. Administrators should create standard drive letters for all users' home directo-

Table 5.2 NT Default System Directories

Top Level Directory	Subdirectory	Description
WINNT35		This is the default directory for the NT system. If you have upgraded from a Windows 3.x system, the NT directory will most likely be WINDOWS.
	REPAIR	Repairs files for the Registry.
	SYSTEM	Same as SYSTEM for Windows 3.x. Contains font and some system files. If you installed over Windows 3.x, this directory is shared with Windows 3.x.
	SYSTEM32	This is the Windows NT directory for its system files.
	\DRIVERS	The \DRIVERS subdirectory tree contains the NT drivers. This includes not only NT system drivers but also third-party drivers that have been added to the system.
	\DRIVERS\ETC	The \ETC subdirectory contains several TCP/IP configuration files.
	\CONFIG	The \CONFIG subdirectory contains the NT Registry files.
	\DHCP	DHCP log, tmp, and database files.
	\RAS	Remote Access Service files.
	\REPL	Export and Import directories for the Replicator service.
	\SPOOL	Printer drivers and other files.
	\WINS	WINS files.
USERS		The USERS directory is the NT default directory for users' home directories. The actual home directory is \USERS\DEFAULT unless you change it with User Manager. User home directories that are created via User Manager are placed under this directory.
	DEFAULT	The \USERS\DEFAULT directory is the default home directory for users.

ries such as M: for Mine. During the logon process the M: drive should automatically be connected to this directory and made the default drive.

The Home directory is very important to users because it is the directory they should use for their personal files. This directory should be protected from other users via the NT file permissions. This setup allows you to tailor the permissions to a particular user for his or her directory only. You could also use permissions to grant others access to a particular subtree. For instance, you could grant a manager access to his or her files and the files of everyone else in the department. I suggest that you give the Domain Admins group full control access to all users' home directories if possible. This access gives you the ability to manage setup files and other important user files easily.

5.4.3 Data Directories

The user directory concept of a master directory and separate subdirectories for data can be used for shared data directories for applications such as word processors and spreadsheets. You can also use the same concept for database files. I generally create a directory called DATA that contains the subdirectories for different types of data. Table 5.3 shows some samples of the subdirectories I usually place under DATA and their descriptions.

So far we have discussed only one data directory on one disk. What happens when you have two or more disk drives and you want to spread the data over all the drives? The solution is to create a data directory off the root of each drive. This directory becomes the backup point for both drives and allows you to have a common structure for each drive. Spreading the data over multiple drives also improves the performance of your system if you have the drives on separate controllers or the controller handling both drives can perform simultaneous access to each drive.

5.4.4 Executable Programs

I have found the best way to handle executable programs is to separate them by application in their own directory. Most applications such as Word or Excel insist on having their own directory anyway. Place these directories on your server in an area that can be shared for groups of applications. For instance,

Table 5.3 Suggested Data Subdirectories

Subdirectory	Description
DataBase	Contains all the database files for the server. This may include application-specific directory names for different projects.
Clients	Contains a separate subdirectory for each client my firm deals with. This allows us to track correspondence and spreadsheet files for this client. Under the Clients subdirectory I have other subdirectories for general items and specific projects.
Vendors	Same as the Clients subdirectory except it contains a subdirectory for each vendor.
Projects	Allows me to track project-related items that are not related to a vendor or client. This could be programming projects or a manufacturing project for a new product.
Other	Takes into account any other type of information that your users may track. For instance, under my DATA directory there is a directory for Articles, another for Books, and so forth. I also have a directory called Products for information on products that my firm carries.

you can create a directory called MSOFFICE and install all Microsoft Office applications under this directory. Then you can share the MSOFFICE directory and users will have access to all MSOFFICE applications.

What about utilities and in-house programs? Create a directory called U site specific on the server. Place all utilities that are used by everyone on the server U subdirectory. Share this directory as SiteSys$ or something similar. Then make sure that all users connect to this share at startup and place the directory in their path. This connection gives them access to all files in the U directory or the SiteSys$ share. I also place DLLs for programs such as Visual Basic, third-party controls (VBX, OCX, and DLL), and other support programs on the U directory where all workstations will find them because U is located close to the front of the PATH.

You may want to create other directories under the SiteSys$ share for different applications.

NT treats programs with the following extensions as executable files: COM, EXE, BAT, and CMD. Other files with the extension DLL, VBX, or something else may contain code libraries (such as DLLs or VBX files). The search order for a program is specific to the program that launches the program. For instance, all programs that use the NT API function CreateProcess look for an EXE file if the extension is not specified. Programs that use other methods to execute a file must create their own order of precedence for executing a program if the order is important.

Most executable programs are found by NT, and all versions of Windows and DOS occur if they are located in a directory on the PATH or if the program is in the current directory when the attempt to execute the program occurs.

5.4.5 Sharing Directories

Establishing shared directories under NT is simplicity itself. The same process is used for both NT and NT Server. The same or a similar process is also shared by Windows for Workgroups and to some extent Windows 95. The heart of the share process is File Manager.

Sharing a Directory with File Manager

1. Start File Manager.
2. Select the directory you wish to share.
3. Click the Share As icon or select Share Directory As from the Disk menu.
4. Enter the share name.

You can assign security permissions to the share when it is created or after its creation.

Sharing a Directory from the Command Prompt

1. Start a Command Prompt session.
2. Enter the following command:

```
NET SHARE sharename=path
```

Net Share has four different uses.

☞ Create a new share:

```
NET SHARE sharename=path /users /unlimited /remark
```

sharename   Name for the new share.

path   Path for the directory to share.

/users:n   Specifies the maximum number of users as n (/users=10).

/unlimited   Specifies an unlimited number of users.

/remark   Specifies a description for the share (/remark "Kens share").

☞ Display current shares:

```
NET SHARE
```

☞ Change parameters of a share:

```
NET SHARE /users /unlimited /remark
```

☞ Removing a share:

```
NET SHARE sharename /delete
```

/delete   Removes a share definition.

The following example shows how to create a share for the directory DATA on the D: drive:

```
NET SHARE MyData=D:\DATA
```

The next example shows how to obtain a listing of all shares on a server with Net Share:

```
NET SHARE

    Share Name Resource          Remark
    -------------------------------------------------------------
    ADMIN$     C:\WINNT35         Remote Admin
    C$         C:\                Default share
    IPC$       Remote IPC
    mirror     C:\OCTOPUS\mirror
    NETLOGON   C:\WINNT35\System32\repl\imp... Logon server share
    The command completed successfully.
```

NET SHARE is most useful in batch files or other automated operations. A batch file can be created very quickly with several NET SHARE commands. This is a useful trick for setting up a new server.

What happens when you wish to share a directory on a remote system? This can be a frequent occurrence when you have several NT systems on a network, especially if they are located across a WAN and are not readily accessible.

Fortunately, there are two options for remotely creating shares:

☞ Use Server Manager.

☞ Use RMTSHARE.EXE from the NT Resource Kit.

Creating a Share with Server Manager

1. Start Server Manager.
2. Select the server on which to create the share from the list.
3. Select Shared Directories from the Computer menu.
4. Click the New Share button.
5. Enter the share name.
6. Enter the full path (UNC name) for the share.
7. Enter a comment for the share.
8. Set the concurrent user limit.
9. Optionally add permissions for the share.
10. Click OK.

Another handy way to create a share is with the RMTSHARE command from the NT Resource Kit. This command is useful in a batch program when you wish to create a number of shares at once.

Creating a Share with RMTSHARE.EXE (NT Resource Kit)

1. Execute the following command:

```
rmtshare \\name /users /unlimited /remark /delete
```

\\name	UNC Name for the share and the directory specification for the share. The following example illustrates the format to share the C:\TEMP\KEN directory on the server named SERVER1 \\Server1\ThisShare =c:\TEMP\KEN.
/users:n	Specifies the maximum number (n) of users for the share.
/unlimited	Allows an unlimited number of users to simultaneously access the share.
/remark:text	Specifies the comments (in "quotes") for the share.
/delete	Used with only the share name.

5.4.6 Connecting to NT Server Resources

Users can connect to NT Server resources using several methods. Windows for Workgroups and NT systems can use either File Manager or the NET USE command to connect to resources. Workgroup Add-On for MS-DOS clients must use the pop-up interface or the NET USE command. Windows 95 users can connect to shared resources using Explorer, File Manager, the NET USE command, and many other applications that support the connect functions.

5.4.6.1 File Manager   The steps to connect to a shared resource with File Manager are the same for both NT and Windows for Workgroups systems.

Connecting to a Shared Resource (File Manager)

1. Start File Manager.
2. Click the Connect button or select Connect Network Drive option on the Disk menu.
3. Select the drive letter to connect to the resource.
4. Enter the path to the service in the Path box or select the path from the browse list.
5. Click OK. You can also double-click the share name in the browse box.

Checking the Reconnect at Startup box or Reconnect at Logon box (Windows 95) causes Windows for Workgroups, Windows 95, or NT to reconnect to the resource when Windows restarts. This is the default configuration.

If the resource you select requires a password, a dialog box appears requesting the password unless you have connected to this resource before and used a valid password. NT and Windows for Workgroups can remember passwords for resources by user name and automatically supply them when you connect to the resource.

You must explicitly enter the share name when you connect to a hidden share because the share will not be displayed in the browse list. The following steps should work well. Remember that you can also use the NET USE command to connect to hidden shares.

Connecting to a Hidden Shared Resource (File Manager)

1. Start File Manager.
2. Click the Connect button or select Connect Network Drive option on the Disk menu.
3. Select the drive letter to connect to the resource.
4. Enter the path to the service in the Path box.
5. Click OK.

5.4.6.2 NET USE   NT, Workgroup Add-On for MS-DOS, Windows 95, and Windows for Workgroups clients can use the NET USE command from the command prompt to connect to shared resources. This command is useful because it can be used in batch programs or accessed from icons in Program Manager or the Windows 95 desktop. The command is also useful in logon scripts (see page 177) to connect to various resources during logon via a batch program.

The format for NET USE is

```
NET USE drv \\srvr\share /USER:Domain\UserName -PWD
```

drv   Drive letter for the connected drive.

srvr   Server name of the NT Server.

share   Share name of the shared resource.

Domain   Domain name for the desired domain.

UserName   Account name for the user.

PWD   Password for the user account.

/Y   Carries out the command with no prompting.

The following command connects the P: drive letter to the FILES resource on server CTI-NT SERVER. The domain name is CTI.

```
NET USE P: \\CTI-NT SERVER\files /USER:CTI \ken
```

The USER option is used to pass the domain name to the NT server. This is necessary only when the NT system is not logged in to the domain but is logged in to an NT workgroup. Normally NT passes the domain name to the NT Server except when the machine is not logged in to the domain.

NET USE has an undocumented switch (*) that allows you to use the next available drive letter to connect to a resource. For instance, the following command connects the next free drive letter to the resource KEN:

```
NET USE * \\CTI-NT SERVER\files /USER:DOM-KEN\ken
```

You can also use the * in place of the password.

5.5 CONVERTING FILE SYSTEMS

HPFS and FAT file systems can be converted to NTFS by using the Convert command. You can also convert a file system to NTFS during the installation of NT.

Once a file system is converted to NTFS, you cannot convert the system back to FAT or HPFS without backing up the partition, reformatting the partition, and restoring the files.

The syntax for Convert is

```
Convert /NTFS C:
```

/NTFS   Convert the file system to NTFS.

C: Drive to convert.

If Convert cannot lock the file system, it will ask if you wish to convert at the next boot. Answer **Y** and reboot the system at your convenience.

5.6 MANAGING FILE SYSTEMS

5.6.1 Compressing Files and Directories (3.51)

NT 3.51 includes a nice compression feature for NTFS volumes. Both files and directories can be compressed. The compression feature is conveniently integrated into NT and not implemented as separate utilities like DriveSpace in Windows 95 or NS-DOS. For instance, you can compress an entire directory tree with three clicks of the mouse using File Manager (File menu/Compress/Yes). Not only are the current directories and files compressed, but any new files are also compressed added to a compressed directory. Individual files can also be compressed in the same manner—select the files in File Manager and then choose File menu/Compress. You can also compress or uncompress files and directories by selecting the Properties option in File Manager and changing the Compressed check box.

In keeping with the improving graphical nature of many programs, File Manager shows all compressed files and directories in a different color (currently blue). Make sure that you don't set your background to this color or you will not see any compressed files or directories in File Manager.

NT actually places a compress attribute on compressed files and directories. The attribute is visible in the Properties dialog box in File Manager. If you change the Compress attribute on a directory or file, it accomplishes the same thing as using Compress and Uncompress from the File menu.

Uncompressing a File(s)

The COMPACT utility is included to provide access to file compression from the command prompt. COMPACT is very useful for batch file operations where you wish to perform many compression operations on a group of specific files or directories. The next two steps illustrate how to use the command.

Compressing a Directory Using COMPACT

```
COMPACT /C /S
```

This command compresses the current directory and all subdirectories. The compress attribute is also set on the directory and all subdirectories to compress automatically any new files added to one of the directories.

Compress a File Using COMPACT

```
COMPACT /C *.TXT *.DOC
```

This command compresses all *.TXT and *.DOC files in the current directory.

Uncompressing a Directory Using COMPACT

```
COMPACT /U /S D:\DATA
```

This command removes the compress attribute from the D:\DATA directory and all subdirectories. It does not uncompress any files in the directory tree.

Uncompressing a File Using COMPACT

```
COMPACT /U D:\DATA\*.*
```

This command uncompresses all files in the D:\DATA directory.

1. The /F switch can be used to recompress a file that was in the process of being compressed when the system crashed.
2. /A causes COMPACT to also include hidden and system files.
3. The /I option is useful in batch files to cause COMPACT to continue even if errors are encountered.
4. /Q is also useful in batch files to suppress some of the output generated during the compression process.

Checking the Compression Status of a File or Directory

1. Select the file or directory in File Manager.
2. Press Alt+Enter or select Properties from the File menu.

You can also enter **COMPACT** with no parameters to display the compression status for a file or directory.

What happens when you move or copy a compressed file to a noncompressed directory or copy a file from a FAT disk to a compressed directory? The following list illustrates the simple concepts for several actions involving a compressed file or directory:

- *Move a compressed file within an NTFS partition.* All compressed files moved to a target on an NTFS partition retain the file's compressed state and attribute.
- *Copy a compressed file within an NTFS partition.* All compressed files copied to a target on an NTFS partition receive the compression attribute of the target directory and are automatically compressed or uncompressed.
- *Move or copy a compressed file to a non-NTFS partition.* All compressed files moved to a target not on an NTFS partition lose the compression attribute and are uncompressed.
- *Move or copy a file from a non-NTFS partition to a target on an NTFS partition.* All files copied to a target on an NTFS partition receive the compression attribute of the target directory and are automatically compressed or uncompressed.

5.6.2 The Repair Disk

The repair disk created during the installation of NT is both a valuable tool and a potential hazard. The repair disk can be used to correct system problems or to recover configuration information if it is kept up to date. The information stored on the repair disk includes the system configuration and security information.

5.6.2.1 Potential Repair Disk Problems The NT repair disk process is often confusing to new administrators and can lead to problems if it is not handled correctly. If the repair disk is used wisely, it can be a source of help when your system breaks.

One source of trouble that can occur with a repair disk revolves around Primary Domain Controllers and Backup Domain Controllers. If you build a new server and designate it as a PDC at setup time, the repair disk contains the designation for that server as the PDC. If you later make the server a BDC and then use the repair disk to recover the Security Accounts Manager and security files, the server becomes the PDC again.

> *Tip:* If you must use a repair disk to recover the security and SAM files in this type of situation, take the server off the network until it has been rebooted and downgraded to a PDC again.

5.6.2.2 Updating the Repair Disk   RDISK.EXE is a handy utility shipped with NT that allows you to update the repair disk created when NT was installed. You can also copy the repair information to a local or network disk instead of a floppy disk.

The solution to many problems around the repair disk is to use RDISK.EXE utility shipped with NT 3.5x. This utility is located in the SYSTEM32 directory and is most useful if you create an icon for it in Program Manager.

RDISK.EXE can manipulate the NT Registry in several ways. The Emergency Information for a system can be saved to a hard drive/directory and restored later. RDISK stores the information in the REPAIR directory under the WINNT boot directory. After you have updated the repair information with RDISK.EXE, you can rebuild the repair disk for the system.

The best way to run RDISK.EXE is to create an icon for it in Program Manager.

Creating an Icon for RDISK

1. Select the group to contain RDISK.
2. Select New from the File menu.
3. Enter the following information for the command line:

   `C:\WINNT35\SYSTEM32\RDISK.EXE`

4. Enter the following information for the working directory:

   `C:\WINNT35\SYSTEM32`

5. Replace C:\WINNT35 in both lines with the Windows NT root directory for the system you are creating the icon on.

Figure 5.1 shows the simple RDISK form.

RDISK performs two tasks you can access via the command buttons:

☞ Update Repair Info updates the repair information in the REPAIR directory. It can also create a new repair disk.

Fig. 5.1 The Repair Disk Utility (RDISK.EXE) can be used to update the repair information for an NT system and to create a new repair disk.

☞ Create Repair Disk builds a new repair disk from Emergency Information you have previously saved.

Updating the Repair Information

1. Start RDISK.
2. Click the Update Repair Info button.
3. Answer Yes to the prompt.
4. Optionally allow RDISK to build a new repair disk.

Creating a New Repair Disk Only

1. Start RDISK.
2. Click the Create Repair Disk button.
3. Place a floppy disk in the drive and answer Yes.

5.6.2.3 Problems with the Repair Disk and Patches One problem that may occur on your system happens when you have applied patches to NT using either the Microsoft Down Load service, the service packs on TechNet, or patches from another source. Once a patch has been applied, the repair disk is no longer valid for the system. Even if you update the repair disk, the patches are not updated because NT does not have information about the new files in the setup files.

One solution to this problem is to create a list of any patches that have been applied to your system(s). Make sure that the patches are readily available on a network share (that is backed up routinely). If you have to use the repair disk to recover a system, it is easy to reapply the patches by reapplying the patches or restoring a backup of the system files. The latter option is the best if you have performed routine backups of the boot volume.

5.6.3 Duplicate NT System Files

NT installs several files in two places. The exact files and their location depend upon whether or not you installed NT over an existing Windows 3.x system.

All NT-executable files are stored in \WINNT\SYSTEM32 for security purposes. The SYSTEM32 directory is also first on the search path ensuring that files in that directory are the first to be executed even if a file with the same name exists somewhere else on the system. The SYSTEM32 directory is also secured on NTFS partitions.

The duplicate files from SYSTEM32 and their alternate locations are shown in Table 5.4.

Table 5.4 Duplicate NT Files

Executable File	Alternate Directory
NOTEPAD.EXE	\WINNT
TASKMAN.EXE	\WINNT
WRITE.EXE	\WINNT
COMMDLG.DLL	SYSTEM
MMSYSTEM.DLL	SYSTEM
MMTASK.TSK	SYSTEM
OLECLI.DLL	SYSTEM
OLESVR.DLL	SYSTEM
SETUP.INF	SYSTEM

Note: The following files in the SYSTEM directory share the same name as files in SYSTEM32, but the contents of the files are different: SHELL.DLL, SYSTEM, and VER.DLL.

5.6.4 Replacing a System File

There may be time when your system experiences a problem that is traced to a corrupted NT system file or when an existing file must be replaced with a new version. This problem can be corrected if you know the file that is corrupted and can access the system either from that particular machine or from the network.

A likely scenario is when the system is reachable from the network but you cannot log in interactively. In this case you can perform the following steps to fix the problem if it occurs because SHELL32.DLL is corrupt. These steps also work from an interactive NT session if you can successfully log in. Either log in to the machine with an Administrator account or access the machine over the network by connecting with an Administrator account.

There are two possible ways of resolving this problem. The first and most obvious way is to rename the old file and copy the new file to the correct directory. I have used this step to replace the NTFS.SYS file, which controls the NT File System.

Replacing NTFS.SYS or Other Drivers

1. At the Windows NT command line, type the letter of the drive where Windows NT is installed and then change to the Windows NT drivers subdirectory.

   `CD %windir%\SYSTEM32\DRIVERS`

2. Rename NTFS.SYS.

   `REN NTFS.SYS NTFS.001`

3. Copy the new NTFS.SYS from this Update.

   `COPY NTFS.SYS %windir%\SYSTEM32\DRIVERS`

4. Reboot the computer. The new NTFS driver is now in effect.

When this procedure won't work, you may need to resort to fooling NT.

Replacing a System File Normally Locked

1. Copy a new version of the file to the same location on the system with the problem and give the file a new name. For instance, change the last two characters of the file name (not the suffix) (i.e., SHELL32.DLL becomes SHELL-NEW.DLL). Run REDEDT32.EXE and select the machine with the problem.

2. Locate the section HKEY_LOCAL_MACHINE.

   `SYSTEM\CurrentControlSet\Control\SessionManager\KnownDLLs`

   A key under this section points to the affected file. The key should have the same name as the file, and the value for the key is the name of the file.

3. Change the value of the key to point to the new file (i.e., SHELLNEW.DLL).

4. Exit REGEDT32.EXE and reboot the machine with the problem.

5. Log on to the machine as Administrator.

6. Replace the problem file (SHELL32.DLL) by deleting the original file and copying the new file to the original file name (**COPY SHELLNEW.DLL SHELL32.DLL**).

7. Run REDEDT32.EXE on the machine with the problem.

8. Locate the section HKEY_LOCAL_MACHINE.

   `SYSTEM\CurrentControlSet\Control\SessionManager\KnownDLLs`

   A key under this section points to the affected file. The key should have the same name as the file, and the value for the key is the name of the file.

9. Change the value of the key to point to the original file (i.e., SHELL32.DLL).

10. Exit REGEDT32.EXE and reboot the machine with the problem.

11. Delete the new file (SHELLNEW.DLL).

These steps are necessary because NT usually locks its system files when they are in use. If you use this method, you are simply pointing NT to a new file name allowing it to free the affected file the next time it boots. Then you can replace the file and reset the pointer to the file.

5.6.5 Finding Problems with CHKDSK

CHKDSK can be used to find problems on a disk volume. It will check any NT file system and report on any problems it finds. CHKDSK is a DOS prompt command that tests a disk volume for a variety of ills. The /F option causes CHKDSK to also attempt to repair the file system of the disk by turning any mismatched file data (known as cross-linked files) into a group of files with the name FILEXXXX and the extension CHK. The XXXX in the name is replaced with 0001 through 9999, depending upon how many files CHKDSK must create. Once CHKDSK has completed, you can delete these files and recover the space they were using. You may want to browse through the *.CHK files and look for anything that resembles useful data before you delete the files. The files are in ASCII format and can be copied or otherwise manipulated to save the data.

You may encounter a problem with CHKDSK /F for several reasons. One is when CHKDSK is started from the volume you wish to check. This problem most likely generates the message "Cannot lock the current volume." This message may be easily fixed by making another volume current before executing the command. For instance, suppose that you change to the D: volume, run CHKDSK, then receive this error message. Simply enter **C:** and reenter the Chkdsk command with Dial the last parameter. This procedure should allow message to continue.

The second problem occurs when someone has files open on the volume you wish to check. This problem generates the message "Cannot lock the volume for single user." After this message you have two options. If the volume you wish to check does not contain the NT operating system, make sure all files are closed on this volume. If the volume is used for paging, you will have to remove the page file on the volume before continuing or allow NT to run CHKDSK when it reboots.

Another option occurs when the volume to be checked contains NT system files. NT always prompts you when it cannot run CHKDSK and asks if you wish to run CHKDSK /F the next time the system boots. This is the only option for running CHKDSK /F on the volume that contains NT. Simply answer **Y** to the prompt and reboot the system.

Repairing Files with CHKDSK

1. Change to the volume to check.
2. Run the following command:

```
CHKDSK /F
```

3. If any errors are reported, look at all FILE***.CHK files and make sure that they don't contain any valuable data.

4. Delete all *.CHK files.

5.6.6 Defragmenting a Disk

A physical disk becomes less efficient over time because blank spots of different size occur as files are added and removed. This process is called fragmentation because files become fragmented when they are stored on disk and there is not a single block of space large enough to hold the entire file. New files are then "split" over several blank chunks of free space instead of being placed in one contiguous chunk. When a program tries to read the file, the data must be retrieved in several cycles of the disk as the data is read from each chunk and returned to the program.

Fragmentation is a problem because a disk that becomes fragmented continually becomes less efficient over time as the problem becomes worse. Most PC network managers have had to use different utilities from third parties to defragment a disk. Defragmenting a disk is usually a manual process that must be performed from time to time.

Executive Software has recently ported a popular VMS product to NT to solve this problem. Diskeeper for NT is based on a long history of success in the VMS market. Diskeeper is a super product to add to a server because it can be run interactively or automated as a service. Diskeeper can be scheduled to run at certain times and has lots of configuration options for excluding files among other things. You can also defragment multiple disks concurrently.

Client Configuration and Management

6.1 CLIENTS AND CLIENT TOOLS INCLUDED WITH NT SERVER

MS-DOS, Remote Access Server (RAS), LAN Manager 2.2, and LAN Manager OS/2 network clients are now included in the NT Server distribution. The complete Windows for Workgroups distribution is also included and I expect Windows 95 to be included also. Also included in the same directory structure are the new TCP/IP software for Windows for Workgroups, RAS for MS-DOS, and network administration tools for Windows 3.x.

The client packages may be installed using a special boot disk that connects the client to the network and performs the installation or using an installation disk set for some clients (except for Windows for Workgroups). Some of the kits can be installed over the network by creating a special share and performing the installation using the share.

> *Note:* NT Server does not include a client license for Windows for Workgroups or Windows 95. I suggest that you either get an operating system with your client workstations or purchase an MLP (Microsoft License Pack) or MOLP (Microsoft Open License Pack) for your total projected number of clients. The MLP or MOLP lowers your client cost drastically.

6.1.1 Using the Client Tools

If you plan to use the client installation kits, you should copy the installation sets to the server or share the clients directory on the NT server CD-ROM. If you are going to use the client installations infrequently, you can share a CD-

ROM on the server and run the installation from that device. Keeping the NTCD loaded in a drive is a great idea if you house an extra CD online. You may wish to copy only certain clients to the server or to copy the entire set of files then remove the ones you don't need.

The Network Client Administrator in the program Manager Network Administration group is used to perform most of the tasks related to the client kits and utilities. Figure 6.1 shows the main window for the Network Client Administrator.

Copying the Client Tools to the Server with the Network Client Administrator

1. Start the Network Client Administrator.
2. Select Copy Client-based Network Administration Tools.
3. Follow the instructions on the next dialog box.
4. Start File Manager and delete all subdirectories that you will not use. Do not delete the \CLIENTS\MSCLIENT\NETSETUP directory or you will not be able to install Windows for Workgroups or the Microsoft Network Client for MS-DOS.

The other option for installing the files on a server is to use File Manager (or DOS) to copy the files. I like using File Manager because it gives me more control over the process.

Copying the Client Tools to the Server with the File Manager

1. Start File Manager.
2. Select the directory tree to copy (Clients or subtree).
3. Drag and drop the directory tree onto the destination hard drive or select the File/Copy command and enter the target drive and directory.
4. Start File Manager and delete all subdirectories that you will not use. Do not delete the \CLIENTS\MSCLIENT\NETSETUP directory or you will not be able to install Windows for Workgroups or the Microsoft Network Client for MS-DOS.

Fig. 6.1 The Network Client Administrator presents a simple interface for assisting in installing client tools.

6.1.2 Sharing the Client Directory

You should share the clients directory to provide network access to all the installation files.

Sharing the Clients Directory

1. Select the Clients directory in File Manager.
2. Use the Share As command from the toolbar or Disk menu to complete the share.
3. Add a $ to the end of the share name to force the share to be hidden from all browse lists.
4. Set permissions on the share to allow only the appropriate accounts (Administrator or such) to access the accounts.

6.1.3 Making an Installation Boot Disk

One of the best things included with NT Server 3.5x is the ability to make an installation boot disk for a new client system. This process is really cool because it automates the client installation process. You need to perform this procedure once for each client or use another little installation trick. The following steps show how to create the boot disk for Windows for Workgroups 3.11.

Creating a Windows for Workgroups 3.11 Installation Boot Disk

1. Start the Network Client Administrator.
2. Select Make Network Installation Startup Disk.
3. Select the type of system to install and the network adapter card on the Target Workstation Configuration dialog box.
4. On the Network Startup Disk Configuration dialog box (shown in Figure 6.2) enter the following criteria:

    Computer name for the new system

    User name for the installation process

    Domain name for the target domain

    Network protocol to use for the installation

    Other parameters as necessary (i.e., TCP/IP)

5. Click OK.
6. Click OK on the next dialog box to begin building the disk.

The easiest way to use this technique is to assign a unique computer name for the client installation process and then to use this disk only for installations. This technique allows you to create the disk one time and to use it over and over.

Fig. 6.2 The Network Disk Configuration dialog box is used to enter the parameters for the installation startup disk.

6.1.4 Using the Installation Boot Disk

The boot disk built by the Network Client Administrator is just a DOS boot disk that automatically connects to the network using the MSClient for DOS and runs the appropriate setup program. The AUTOEXEC.BAT from a sample Windows for Workgroups 3.11 startup disk follows:

```
path=a:\net
a:\net\net initialize
a:\net\netbind.com
a:\net\umb.com
a:\net\tcptsr.exe
a:\net\tinyrfc.exe
a:\net\nmtsr.exe
a:\net\emsbfr.exe
a:\net\net start
net use z: \\FPMASTER\CLIENTS
echo Running Setup...

z:\wfw\netsetup\setup.exe /#
```

The installation boot disk uses the MS-DOS client software to boot and make the connection. Notice how the connection to the CLIENTS directory is made with the NET USE command? It is pretty simple. The /# switch on the Setup command is not documented when you run SETUP /? but causes Setup to start a network installation of the software.

Place the disk in the boot drive of the new system and reboot. Follow the prompts on the screen to complete the installation. The new system retains the computer name from the installation diskette. After the installation is complete, change the computer name and other related items (user name, comment, TCP/IP parameters) and reboot the system.

You can also use the /H:filename switch to initiate a total batch mode installation. The /H switch allows you to specify the installation parameters in a file. Setup processes the file and answers the questions with no interaction. You can leave out options that vary from the setup file, and Setup uses defaults where possible and performs automatic detection of hardware devices such as mice and hard disks. The setup file should have an SHH extension. The Windows 3.1 Resource Kit contains complete descriptions of the options for the /H switch.

6.1.5 Installing Server Tools

The server tools can be installed by connecting to the CLIENTS share and running the appropriate setup program. The server tools are located in the SRV-TOOLS directory. \Clients\Srvtools\Windows contains the Win32s versions for Windows 3.x, whereas \Clients\Srvtools\WINNT contains the NT version.

Installing Server Management Tools on a Client

1. Connect to the Clients share.
2. Start SETUP.EXE in the appropriate directory (..\Windows or ..\WINNT).
3. Complete the instructions displayed by Setup.

If you are installing the tools on a Windows for Workgroups workstation, a new redirector is installed, and you must reboot the workstation before using the tools. Setup installs Win32s if it is not already installed for Windows or Windows for Workgroups workstations.

6.2 CONFIGURING CLIENT WORKSTATIONS

NT Server supports many different types of client workstations. You can build a network with DOS, Windows 3.x, Windows 95, Windows NT, and Macintosh machines for clients. Client and servers can be mixed and matched to improve network availability and performance. Even within these systems there are several different methods of connecting to the NT server.

DOS machines can use LAN Manager client software, MS Client, and the Microsoft Workgroup Add-On for MS-DOS to connect to an NT server. The Microsoft Workgroup Add-On for MS-DOS provides the most advanced features and is identical to the MS Client included with NT Server in most respects. You can also use almost any old LAN Manager client, including Digital Pathworks as an NT Server client. Make sure that you are using a supported protocol when using a non-Microsoft client. For instance, you can't connect to NT Server over DECnet if NT Server is running only NetBEUI or TCP/IP. Load TCP/IP on both the client and server, and, voila, it works.

Windows for Workgroups can connect to NT Server out of the box. If you answer the network, user name, and work group/domain questions correctly when you install Windows for Workgroups, the workstation connects to NT Server with minor changes to the startup parameters in Control Panel. I suggest that you upgrade to Windows for Workgroups 3.11 for all client workstations. The 3.11 version adds special features for NT Server networks and works much more nicely in the NT Server environment than the 3.1 version. The preferred clients in an NT or other LAN environment are NT Workstation 3.51 or later, Windows for Workgroups 3.11 or later and Windows 95 or later. Other clients work fine but may not provide as many features as the preferred clients. Windows 95 adds many network and management features and places it as the future client operating system for most LANs. The next section has a detailed discussion on configuring Windows for Workgroups 3.11 and Windows 95 for use with NT Server.

The references in this chapter to Windows for Workgroups refer to version 3.11 unless another version is specifically stated. Some of the information in this section repeats information from the Windows for Workgroups manual or accompanying documentation and is included here for completeness for those people who may not have Windows for Workgroups or who may have an earlier version (3.1). This information also is useful for others because it is contained in a single source with the other client information. Windows 95 should be available in 1995 and shares many features with Windows for Workgroups 3.11. I suggest upgrading your Windows client workstations to Windows 95 as soon as it ships.

NT desktop systems can connect to an NT server and/or domain with very little trouble. If you install NT and answer the network-related questions correctly, it works just about like Windows for Workgroups clients. The main exception is the support for NTFS on the workstation and the advanced security for the workstation. NT workstations can also use the enhanced preference management of NT and NT Server.

Macintosh systems also work well in an NT Server environment because of NT Server's Macintosh support using Services for Macintosh. Macintosh systems all support AppleTalk and can use this protocol to communicate with NT Server. For information on configuring NT Server for use with SFM, see Chapter 7 (see page 241).

This section covers the most common methods and how to configure each client system.

6.2.1 Common Features for Clients

The following features are common for Windows 95, Windows for Workgroups, NT, and NT Server systems. Small variations may exist between the same tools. For instance, the connect dialog box in Windows for Workgroups may look slightly different from the Connect dialog box in NT, while the connect box in Windows 95 takes on an entirely new look. New versions of NT (specifically 3.51) inherit many of the user interface features of Windows 95 and begin the migration toward making the two interfaces consistent. In mid-1995 Microsoft made available a Windows 95 interface for NT. This beta should be available in production by late 1995.

The workgroup and computer names identify the computer workstation, whereas the user name and password identify the user of the workstation. NT and Windows 95 use the user name and password of the server for validating all actions (if user level security is set on Windows 95).

6.2.1.1 Workgroup Name   The workgroup name can be up to 15 characters long and can include all characters except:

    ! # $ % ( ) - . @ ^ _ ' ~

If the workgroup name is the same as the Domain Name, the workstation shows up under the domain in the browse list. Figure 6.3 shows the Connect Network Drive dialog box from Windows for Workgroups.

The workgroup name should be set to a separate workgroup name which does not conflict with a domain name. If the workgroup name is different from the domain name, the workgroup can access systems in the domain but will appear in its own workgroup for browsing purposes. I suggest breaking the workgroups into groups of 20 to 25 workstations to improve browsing performance. See Chapter 3 (page 85) for more information on browsing.

6.2.1.2 Computer Name   A computer name should clearly identify the computer on the network. How you identify the machines is dependent upon how you structure and name the systems in your network. You may use the user's name for the computer name or possibly use a code that is linked to another aspect of the network, such as a node address. If you use something other than the user's name, you should use a comment to identify the user or the location of the system.

One nice feature of using a node address for the computer name and the comment for the user name is the ease with which you can move a system or upgrade a system after someone has left the company. If you have used a node address or other unique identifier for the computer name, you must change only

Fig. 6.3 The Connect Network Drive dialog box shows a system with a Domain (DOM-KEN) and a Workgroup (CTI). Setting up your network with your servers in a domain and your workstations in different workgroups segregates your systems whenever you browse the network. This improves response time and makes it easier to find systems.

the comment on the workstation when the user changes. This is especially important if you have built programs that depend upon certain computer names on the network. This approach also works well with SMS because the computer name along with almost every other detail of the workstation is stored in the SMS database.

The comment for a computer name may be up to 48 characters long and may contain all characters except a comma (,). The Comment is displayed by the NT, Windows 95, and Windows for Workgroups browse command whenever a user attempts to connect to a resource from within File Manager, Print Manager, or any other program that uses the Windows API (such as WinPopUp) to show available resources. Figure 6.4 shows the connect to network resource dialog box from File Manager.

6.2.1.3 User Name and Password User names and passwords are discussed in Chapter 4 (see page 163). A user name and password is the key to a user's access to NT Server resources and also unlocks access to the domain for the user.

6.2.2 NT Workstations

NT workstations and NT Server systems are by far the easiest and most secure workstations, to add to an NT Server domain. Any NT system contains the same security, network, and file features as NT Server except for domains and some disk fault tolerance features. Because of its common base with NT Server,

Fig. 6.4 The Connect Network Drive dialog box is used to connect to a shared file resource. Notice how the comment shows up on the TRI-STAR system, whereas the other two systems in the list do not show a comment.

NT workstations are a natural for your network. NT workstations also work well with other types of clients on the network including the sharing of resources. In fact, an NT workstation can serve as a high-powered print server right out of the box, as long as you do not need more than ten connections to its resources.

6.2.3 Windows 95

Windows 95 is the best client operating system along with NT workstations for using on an NT Server network. Windows 95 was designed from the start as a networked workstation with extensible management features. Windows 95 is built on top of Win32 and uses a Registry that is somewhat similar to the NT Registry.

Windows 95 can also use the NT Domain security system for pass-through security. Pass-through security validates everything on the client against the master security database (Domain). For instance, setting permissions on a share using Windows 95 allows you to set permissions for users in the Domain database. Every logon and security check also validates against the Domain database. This integrated security management from a single Domain database is an incredible benefit for the systems manager.

Windows 95 supports sophisticated features such as policies and profiles to simplify management tasks. These features are similar to the ones by the same name in NT but are implemented in a different manner to provide easier management for client systems. Remote Procedure Call (RPC) is supported by Windows 95, providing a mechanism for running programs on remote systems and allowing most Windows 95 management tools to access any Windows 95 system on the network.

6.2.3.1 The Registry
The Windows 95 Registry is composed of two files: USER.DAT and SYSTEM.DAT. Both of these files are stored by default in the Windows directory. The Registry replaces the myriad of INI files that are found with Windows 3.x and, like those INI files, is extensible by application programs.

The Registry is managed by many Windows applications such as Control Panel and Setup. REGEDIT.EXE can also be used to manage the Registry directly. RegEdit can take advantage of RPC to manage the Registry on another Windows 95 system remotely. As with the NT Registry, changing the Windows 95 Registry can be hazardous to your health if you make an incorrect change.

As with NT, the Windows 95 Registry not only stores software settings but also is the complete database for system hardware, software, configuration, and user information. Placing all this information in one database makes it easy to manage and provides much greater security control for controlling access to system and user configuration options.

6.2.3.2 Agents
Agents are basically a snap-in component that provides some level of capabilities. For instance, many systems (including NT) use an agent to provide Simple Network Management Protocol (SNMP) data to management systems. Windows 95 includes built-in agents for several tasks:

☞ Backup agents for Arcada and Cheyenne backup products provide the ability to centrally back up client systems.

☞ An SNMP agent provides SNMP capabilities for the myriad of tools that support the SNMP standard.

6.2.3.3 User Profiles   User profiles track preferences for user settings such as colors and desktop appearance for each user of a Windows 95 system. A user profile also tracks settings such as the desktop configuration, network settings, and application specific settings.

User profiles can be maintained on a server to allow a user to log on to the network from any Windows 95 system and obtain the exact same configuration, including icons on a toolbar. User profiles are a powerful tool for customizing the Windows 95 interface as users log on. Windows 95 processes the user's profile as the logon occurs and sets the desktop and everything else in the profile for the user automatically.

The best way to use profiles is to store them on a network server in the user's home directory. This way Windows 95 finds the profile during logon and makes the correct changes.

6.2.4 Windows for Workgroups

6.2.4.1 Installation   Windows for Workgroups is the next easiest system to add to a domain after Windows 95. The steps for installing Windows for Workgroups are very similar to installing NT and normal Windows. Windows for Workgroups has several switches that can be used with the Setup program. Each switch is documented in Table 6.1.

Table 6.1 Windows for Workgroups Setup Switches

Switch	Description
/A	Copies and expands all Windows for Workgroups files to the specified location. This switch is normally used to place the entire distribution on a network drive for later access and automated installation.
/B	Forces Setup to use monochrome display attributes.
/H:filename	Forces Setup to operate in batch mode. The file name of the driver file for the setup is specified after /H:.
/I	Turns off automatic hardware detection.
/O:filename	Use this option to specify the location and name of the INF file used for the installation.
/S:filename	Allows you to specify the location of the Windows for Workgroups installation files.
/T	Forces a check for known software that is incompatible with Windows.

Creating a Windows for Workgroups Server Installation

1. Create a directory on the server for Windows for Workgroups (I use \WFW311, the default).

2. Share the directory using File Manager or the NET SHARE command.

3. Install Windows for Workgroups to the directory. Select the CD-ROM directory containing Windows for Workgroups and run the command SETUP /A. When Setup asks for the location of the installation directory, enter the directory created in the first step. This command copies all the Windows for Workgroups files into the directory just created.

Installing Windows for Workgroups from the Shared Directory (WFW311)

1. From the new client, connect to the share for the Windows for Workgroups installation (WFW311). The connection can be from a prior version of Windows for Workgroups, a LAN Manager client, Workgroup Add-On for MS-DOS, or other client software.

2. Change to the Windows for Workgroups shared directory.

3. Run Setup by

   `F:\WFW311>SETUP`

4. Answer the prompts and reboot the workstation.

You can also install Windows for Workgroups directly from the CD-ROM containing NT Server 3.5x or from the network location where you placed the files. This process is the one I use most often. It saves space on the server and does not require using SETUP /A to expand the files to the network.

Installing from the NT Server CD-ROM or the Server

1. From the new client, connect to the share for the clients directory for Windows for Workgroups. This may be the CLIENTS directory on the CD-ROM or the location of the files on the server if you copied them to a network drive. The connection can be from a prior version of Windows for Workgroups, a LAN Manager client, Workgroup Add-On for MS-DOS, or other client software.

2. Run Setup by

   `F:\WFW311>SETUP`

3. Answer the prompts and reboot the workstation

6.2.4.2 Configuring a Workstation Setting up a workstation requires careful planning for your system. Minor things such as comments and network names can be extremely helpful if you make the right choice or cause you lots of grief if you don't.

Comments indicating the full name of a workstation and information on the workstation's location are very useful. The computer name, comment, and other network-related information are stored in the SYSTEM.INI file on each Windows for Workgroups workstation. The [Network] section of the file contains entries for the computer name, workgroup, user name, and comment. Notice that there are a number of other options in this section as well. A typical [network] section from SYSTEM.INI follows:

```
[Network]
winnet=wfwnet/00025100
multinet=nonet
FileSharing=Yes
PrintSharing=Yes
LogonDisconnected=Yes
EnableSharing=Yes
UserName=KEN
Workgroup=CTI
ComputerName=TRI-STARWFW
Comment=Ken Spencer
logonvalidated=yes
MaintainServerList=NO
SlowLanas=3
SessTimeout=600
reconnect=yes
reshare=yes
cachethispassword=yes
LogonDomain=DOM-KEN
AutoLogon=Yes
StartMessaging=Yes
LoadNetDDE=Yes
LMLogon=1
```

Table 6.2 lists the options for the [Network] section of SYSTEM.INI that I consider relevant for using on an enterprise network. Table 6.2 does not list specific settings for Windows for Workgroups that are useful only for a Windows for Workgroups workstation or a workgroup network. Most of these options can be set via the Control Panel Network applet, while a few must be manually changed.

Table 6.2 Options for Enterprise Network Settings in Windows for Workgroups

Parameter	Default	Description
AutoLogon	Yes	AutoLogon causes Windows for Workgroups to log you into the network automatically when the system is booted. If you have set a nonblank password for your user name, the logon dialog box is displayed. Changed in the Network applet.
Comment	None	Comment is used for a comment (maximum 48 characters and cannot contain commas) for the workstation. This comment appears next to the ComputerName in browse boxes. Changed in the Network applet.

Table 6.2 Options for Enterprise Network Settings in Windows for Workgroups (Continued)

Parameter	Default	Description
ComputerName	None	ComputerName contains the name for the workstation (maximum 15 characters, consisting of all but !#$%()-.@{}~). It is set during the installation of Windows for Workgroups and can be changed with the Network applet of Control Panel. Changed in the Network applet.
EnableSharing	Yes	Setting this parameter to Yes enables sharing of resources, whereas a setting of No disables sharing. Changed in the Network applet.
FileSharing	Yes	A Yes for this parameter turns on file sharing. Changed in the Network applet.
KeepConn	600	This entry controls the time in seconds that Windows for Workgroups 3.11 waits before disconnecting an implicit network connection. It is useful for applications that are slow or heavily used, namely pipes. It must be changed manually.
LMAnnounce	No	This entry controls whether a system announces its presence to LAN Manager systems on the network. The default of No disables this feature. To enable the feature, edit the SYSTEM.INI file and change the value to Yes. *Note:* Network traffic and workstation overhead increases slightly when this value is Yes.
LMLogon	1	LMLogon determines whether you automatically log on (1) to an LM Domain when Windows for Workgroups starts. It is set to 1 by checking the Logon to Windows NT or LAN Manager Domain check box on the Startup Settings dialog box in the Network applet. Setting LMLogon to No (0) causes Windows for Workgroups to not log you in to the domain at startup. For proper interaction between Windows for Workgroups and domains, this value must be set to Yes (1) unless you are using a product like NTLogon. Changed in the Network applet by clicking the Logon to Windows NT or LAN Manager Domain box.
LoadHigh	Yes	A setting of Yes tries to load all conventional network drivers loaded by Windows for Workgroups into the upper memory area (UMA). Setting LoadHigh to No turns off this feature.
LoadNetDDE	Yes	Turns on NetDDE. Set by checking the Enable NetDDE box in the Network applet of Control Panel.
LogonDisconnected	No	A setting of Yes allows Windows to boot without connecting to previous network services. This option is set by checking the Ghosted Connections box in the Network applet from Control Panel.

Table 6.2 Options for Enterprise Network Settings in Windows for Workgroups (Continued)

Parameter	Default	Description
LogonDomain	Workgroup Name	LogonDomain contains the domain name for the domain that you wish to log in to from Windows for Workgroups. Changed in the Network applet Enterprise Startup dialog box.
LogonValidated	No	This parameter is not user-maintainable. It is used to ensure that you are correctly logged off of the domain if the LMLogon parameter is set to 1. It is set each time you successfully log on to a domain.
MaintainServerList	Auto	This entry specifies whether your system can ever maintain the list of servers in your workgroup. If the setting is Auto, Windows for Workgroups decides when to use your system as the browsemaster. A setting of Yes gives the system a higher priority as the browsemaster, whereas a No means that the system will never be the browsemaster. Each workgroup needs at least one Windows for Workgroups system with a setting of Auto or Yes.
MultiNet	(blank)	This value specifies any secondary networks that are installed for Windows for Workgroups.
NumBigBuf	No Entry	This value contains the number of cache buffers used for the 32-bit redirector. Each cache buffer is 4096 bytes in size and is enabled by choosing 32-Bit File Access in the 386 Enhanced applet in Control Panel. The default memory used for the cache is one eighth of the available physical memory at the time the cache is loaded. It can be manually edited to a larger value to improve performance.
PrintSharing	Yes	A Yes for this parameter turns on printer sharing. Changed in the Network applet.
Priority	80	Sets the priority for sharing resources over local usage. The higher the number, the greater the priority. Changed using the Performance Priority slider in the Network applet in Control Panel.
SlowLanas	none	Specifies which LANA numbers are used for slow network connections. This option typically identifies the RAS LANA and any other slow-speed network adapter. Among other things, it prevents the Windows for Workgroups system from being a browsemaster for systems across a slow speed connection. Set manually or by installing a slow service.
StartMessaging	No	A setting of Yes turns on the WinPopUp application for sending and receiving messages. It is set using the Network applet in Control Panel. When messaging is enabled, Print Manager automatically sends messages on completed print jobs. Changed in the Network applet.

Table 6.2 Options for Enterprise Network Settings in Windows for Workgroups (Continued)

Parameter	Default	Description
UserName	Computer Name	The UserName (maximum of 20 characters) is set to the Computer Name until your first logon to Windows for Workgroups and then reflects the last user name used during a successful logon.
WinNet	wfwnet	Defines the primary Windows network driver. The primary network driver can be changed using the Network Setup program.
Workgroup	Workgroup Name from Setup	This parameter (maximum of 15 characters) contains the Workgroup name for the Windows for Workgroups workgroup. It also sets the default LogonDomain parameter when Windows for Workgroups is installed. Changed in the Network applet.

The SYSTEM.INI file also has information for shares and password lists in the section titled [Password Lists]. A sample of this section (Windows For Workgroups 3.11) follows:

```
[Password Lists]
*Shares=C:\Windows\Shares.PWL
TRI-STAR=C:\Windows\TRI-STAR.PWL
KEN=C:\WINDOWS\KEN.PWL
```

The PWL files contain the passwords and associated shares that Windows for Workgroups uses when it connects to a network resource. If you delete the PWL files, be sure to remove the entries for them under the [Password Lists] header in SYSTEM.INI.

Figure 6.5 shows the dialog box from Control Panel Network applet. This dialog box allows you to configure the network setup for the workstation and provides access to the event log for the workstation.

Clicking the Startup button brings up the Startup Settings dialog box shown in Figure 6.6.

The key parameter in the Startup Settings dialog box is contained in the Options for Enterprise Networking frame. The Logon to Windows NT or LAN Manager Domain check box must be checked to access resources on a domain properly. The Domain Name box is enabled by clicking the Logon to Windows NT or LAN Manager Domain check box. The default Domain Name is the Workgroup name for the system.

You may also want to check the box below the Domain Name box. Checking this box prevents the Successful Logon message from displaying each time the Windows for Workgroups user logs in.

I like to check the other parameters in the Startup Options box. These options turn on logon at startup to display the logon dialog box when Windows for Workgroups boots, turn on messaging (WinPopUp), enable NetDDE, and set up ghosted connections, which bring up network connections unconnected but allows them to connect when they are first used.

Fig. 6.5 The Windows for Workgroups 3.11 Control Panel Network applet is the starting place for most network-related configuration options. This includes setting the workstation name, workgroup, comment, domain, and password.

Fig. 6.6 Most of the options discussed in SYSTEM.INI are set by the Control Panel Network applet. The Startup configuration dialog box is used to set or change the options.

The Set Password button allows users to change their domain passwords. Clicking the button brings up a dialog box asking the user for both the old password and the new password and to confirm the new password.

Windows for Workgroups has another configuration file that is very important: WFWSYS.CFG. This file is created the first time Windows for Workgroups starts and contains settings for resource sharing and password maintenance (see the following discussion of ADMINCFG.EXE). This file is encrypted and is uniquely identified to the workstation that creates the file. The Workgroup Add-On for MS-DOS from Microsoft also uses the WFWSYS.CFG file.

Browsing Functions for Workgroups. The workgroup name should be different from all domain names. Each group of 20–25 workstations should have its own workgroup to segment the browsing functions of the network. This grouping improves browsing performance of both the workgroups and the domains by reducing the number of workstations in each workgroup and domain.

You can set the value **MaintainServerList = no** in the SYSTEM.INI for all Windows for Workgroups workstations that you wish to protect from the performance impact of serving as a browsemaster. This setting forces the Windows for Workgroups system to not act as a browsemaster for the network. At least one NT, Windows for Workgroups, or Windows 95 machine must be running in the network and be available to be a browsemaster at all times to support browsing for a workgroup.

6.2.4.3 32-Bit File Access
Windows for Workgroups 3.11 includes 32-bit disk and file access modes that can drastically improve the performance of a Windows for Workgroups system. Of special interest in this section on clients is the 32-bit file access mode.

Enabling 32-bit file access not only improves local disk performance but enables a fast 32-bit cache. This cache is used by both the file access routines and the protected-mode redirector (VREDIR.386).

The cache is a read-ahead routine that reads ahead by file and not by sector, as most caches do. Reading ahead in this way makes the cache much more effective in reading the information most likely to be requested next.

The 386 Enhanced applet in Control Panel turns on the 32-bit File Access. Figure 6.7 shows the Virtual Memory dialog box.

Fig. 6.7 Turn on both 32-bit Disk Access and 32-bit File Access if your system supports them; 32-bit File Access enables the new 32-bit cache used by both the disk system and the protected-mode redirector.

Configuring 32-bit File Access

1. Start Control Panel.
2. Double-click the 386 Enhanced applets icon.
3. Click the Virtual memory button.
4. Click the Change>> button.
5. Check the 32-Bit File Access box.
6. Answer **Yes** to the question: "Change Virtual Memory?"
7. Restart Windows.

6.2.4.4 Administration Configuration Program (ADMINCFG.EXE) Windows for Workgroups 3.11 introduced a new program for managing Windows for Workgroups clients: ADMINCFG.EXE. This program is located on the last diskette of your Windows for Workgroups distribution disk set and it is not installed by default. The following items are controlled by ADMINCFG:

☞ *Disable Resource Sharing (File, Print, and Net DDE).* These options allow you to selectively disable either File, Print, or Net DDE sharing from a workstation. The workstation still can access shared resources from other servers.

☞ *Extended Password Management.* The password management options of ADMINCFG allow you to tailor how a workstation's passwords are managed. This control includes both options for the local workstation and one option that affects how the workstation interacts with an NT Server or LAN Manager domain.

☞ *Administrative Options.* ADMINCFG has some powerful options for controlling client workstations from your server. These options include creating groups of workstations that share common features and having the workstation configuration file (WFWSYS.CFG) updated from the server each time the workstation is booted.

ADMINCFG must be manually installed either on a workstation or onto the server. I personally like to install the program and then copy it onto a secure area of a server that will be available across the network.

Installing ADMINCFG

1. Load the last disk from your Windows for Workgroups disks into a local drive or make sure that you have access to the Windows for Workgroups distribution over the network.
2. Change your current directory to the directory you wish to install the program into (usually the Windows directory).
3. Install the program with the EXPAND utility:

```
EXPAND A:EXPAND ADMINCFG.EXE
```

Expand can be run either from the DOS prompt or from File/Run within Program Manager or File Manager.

After installing the program, create a Program Manager icon by selecting File/New or drag ADMINCFG.EXE to a Program Manager group from File Manager. Next double-click the icon, and you are ready to roll.

ADMINCFG is very simple to use and has a very simple layout (see Figure 6.8).

This chapter focuses on how to use ADMINCFG and configure your workstations for optimum management ease while saving yourself lots of future hassles.

Managing the WFWSYS.CFG File. Before we jump off into the options of ADMINCFG and you start rushing around configuring a multitude of Windows for Workgroups workstations, let's look at how you can configure your Windows for Workgroups workstation with ADMINCFG and save yourself some headaches.

The first concern for the configuration file is choosing how to create the initial file. This is not a concern for networks that already have Windows for Workgroups installed because the file already is installed on the workstation. You can create a preconfigured WFWSYS.CFG file and place it in the directory with the Windows for Workgroups distribution. The Setup program then copies this file to each Windows for Workgroups system as part of the installation process. The workstation automatically associates the file with that particular workstation the first time it boots. This is the preferred option for systems that do not have Windows for Workgroups clients in place already.

The Windows for Workgroups documentation mentions that the WFWSYS.CFG file can be updated from the workstation if the settings do not change very often or from a server if you expect the settings to change frequently. I suggest using the server option regardless of how often you think they will change. Setting up a remote update when you install or configure the workstation means that you can update all your machines at once as new options become available or when the need arises. Remember that Windows 95 expands upon the configuration options of Windows for Workgroups. Another nice feature of Windows for Workgroups and the Workgroup Add-On for MS-DOS is that they can both use the same network location and configuration to update from.

Remote configuration works this way: each time Windows for Workgroups boots on a workstation configured for remote configuration, Windows for Work-

Fig. 6.8 The Security Settings dialog box allows you to change the sharing settings for a workstation immediately. You can also access the administrative and password dialog boxes from the buttons on the right.

groups opens the configuration file from the server and updates (if necessary) the settings of the local file. This update ensures that the workstation's file is updated to match the server's file each time the workstation boots.

The only caveat to this feature is to make sure that your users do not have access to ADMINCFG.EXE. Smart users who have access to this file can change their settings file. You can and should set a password on your configuration files to make sure that the files cannot be updated except by the proper people.

The update process is also very flexible because of its support for exceptions to standard remote updates. When Windows for Workgroups starts, it looks for a directory on the configuration share that has the same name as the workstation. This procedure allows you to build a standard configuration for all users and then allow certain workstations to be treated differently by name. The Windows for Workgroups manual also suggests creating groups of workstations that have different configuration shares with different settings. To be honest, the limited settings available in WFWSYS.CFG probably do not require grouping workstations in most installations.

Remote updating of the configuration file is enabled by selecting the Admin option from ADMINCFG, which displays the Administrator Settings dialog box (shown in the following list).

Enabling Remote Updating of the Security File

1. Start ADMINCFG.
2. Click the Update Security Configuration from Server box.
3. Enter the network path to the configuration share. This can be a drive letter and path (G:\CONFIG) or a UNC name (\\ADMINSRV\CONFIG). Click the Use Root Directory Only box to force the update from the master configuration even if a subdirectory for the workstation exists.

The following directory structure is an example of a configuration file system that treats all users as the same except for the workstation named TRI-STAR:

```
WFWCFG
    TRI-STAR
```

Other directories contain a copy of WFWSYS.CFG, which is configured for the appropriate user. All users except for the workstation TRI-STAR get the standard configuration file from WFWCFG. TRI-STAR picks up the file from the TRI-STAR directory. The WFWCFG directory should be shared read-only to give all workstations access to the directory.

You may want to set two other configuration options with ADMINCFG: The Display Error Messages box and the Require Validated Logon to Windows NT or LAN Manager Domain. The first option causes Windows for Workgroups to display an error message on the workstation if it is not able to update the security settings remotely. Reasons for Windows for Workgroups to not update the settings could be a network problem or a server that is down. You may or may not want your users to be aware that the settings were not updated. Unless you have recently changed the settings, it will not matter that they were not updated because they should already be the same as the ones on the server.

The other option is used to force Windows for Workgroups to validate your logon with a Windows NT or LAN Manager domain. If the logon is not successful, the user is denied access to network resources, which include resources on the domain and other Windows for Workgroups systems.

6.2.5 Workgroup Add-On for MS-DOS and MS Client

The Workgroup Add-On for MS-DOS is a neat little package for systems that are still running MS-DOS. It allows the MS-DOS workstations to connect and participate in a LAN with both Windows for Workgroups and/or NT Server systems. It is also useful for Windows systems to participate in the network without upgrading to Windows for Workgroups. The retail price for the package is $49.95, but the product can probably be obtained for less from retail sources.

The MS Client included on the NT Server kit is similar to the Workgroup Add-On for MS-DOS except that it cannot be used to share file or print services. Both products are used and installed the same, and they function identically other than the sharing restriction.

Commands for the Workgroup Add-On for MS-DOS and the MS Client can be abbreviated to the shortest length that does not conflict with other commands. This section does not cover every option for the package but hits the most important ones.

6.2.5.1 Installing the Workgroup Add-On for MS-DOS and the MS Client
Both the Workgroup Add-On for MS-DOS and the MS Client included with NT Server 3.5x are installed with the SETUP.EXE program.

6.2.5.2 Starting the Client Software   Most of Microsoft's PC networks now start using the NET START command in AUTOEXEC.BAT. This is true for the Workgroup Add-On for MS-DOS, the MS Client, and Windows for Workgroups 3.11 when running in real mode.

The syntax for Net Start is

```
NET START
```

The full redirector can be started by using

```
NET START FULL
```

There are several other qualifiers that you can use for NET START to control its operation. Enter /? after the command for a description.

6.2.5.3 Using the Workgroup Add-On for MS-DOS
Logging On.   The NET LOGON command is used to log on to the network. It is similar to other logon commands or methods in that it requires you to

provide the domain name, user name, and password if you are accessing an NT domain. Along with logging you on to the domain, Net Logon also restores your persistent connections just like Windows for Workgroups.

The format for the command is

```
NET LOGON [user name [password | ?]] [/domain:domainname /
    savepw:no -
/disconnected]
```

NET LOGON prompts for your user name and password if you enter the command with no options. The ? causes NET LOGON to prompt for the password and echos the password with * in place of the characters.

The domain name must be entered if you are logging on to an NT Server domain. The following example shows the command syntax for accessing the server DOM-KEN:

```
NET LOGON kens ? /domain:dom-ken
```

NET LOGON can save your passwords in a password list file. The password file is named with your user name and a PWL extension: KENS.PWL. Each user of a Workgroup Add-On for MS-DOS has a password list file unless they have always logged on and answered **No** to the create password list prompt or have used the following syntax for NET LOGON:

```
NET LOGON kens ? /domain:dom-ken /savepw:no
```

The password list file is protected by your password. The file is encrypted and can be accessed only by your user name and password through the Workgroup Add-On for MS-DOS utilities. The file holds the UNC definitions and passwords for remote connections you have made in the past. This cache allows the connections to be restored automatically when you log on. The only problem with persistent connections is that they can cause the logon process to take a long time if you have many connections. The /disconnected option can be specified as in the next example to log on and restore the connections in a disconnected state. This process makes the logon proceed very quickly. The connections are connected automatically the first time they are accessed. After the first access the connection remains just like a normal connection.

```
NET LOGON kens ? /domain:dom-ken /disconnected
```

Logging Off.   NET LOGOFF performs the opposite of NET LOGON and disconnects you from the remote systems you are connected to. The next command logs off the current system and prompts you to confirm the process.

```
NET LOGOFF

    You have these connections:
        G: \\KEN\SYS
        Z: \\KEN\APPS
    Continuing will cancel the connections.
    Do you want to continue this operation? (Y/N) [N]
```

The /yes option can be used to force the command to log off immediately without prompting:

```
NET LOGOFF /y
```

```
You have these connections:
   G:  \\KEN\SYS
   Z:  \\KEN\APPS
Continuing will cancel the connections.
KENS was logged off successfully.
```

6.2.5.4 Changing Your Domain Password   The Workgroup Add-On for MS-DOS allows you to change your domain password with the NET PASSWORD command. NET PASSWORD allows you to change both your local Workgroup Add-On for MS-DOS password, which controls your password file and your domain password. The syntax for changing your password for the password file is

```
NET PASSWORD [oldpassword [newpassword]]
```

Entering the command with no parameters causes NET PASSWORD to prompt for both passwords. You can enter the old password with the command and NET PASSWORD prompts only for the new password.

The following syntax shows the Net Password syntax for changing your domain password:

```
NET PASSWORD \\computer | domain:domainname [user oldpassword
   [newpassword]]
```

Notice that NET PASSWORD allows you to change your password on a domain or a single system in the NT or LAN Manager server on your network. Specifying the following syntax allows you to change your password on the server named KEN:

```
NET PASSWORD \\KEN kens junk
```

This command causes NET PASSWORD to prompt for the new password because the user name and old password are specified on the command line. If you do not specify the user name or either password, the command prompts for all three.

The following command changes the password on the domain DOM-KEN:

```
NET PASSWORD domain:DOM-KEN kens junk
```

Other Useful Commands.   Table 6.3 lists several other commands that should prove useful in a network environment. Consult your documentation for more information.

Printing.   What about setting up a cheap print server or controlling print jobs on the current workstation or a remote system? The Workgroup Add-On for MS-DOS can handle both situations. NET USE is the command for connecting to or disconnecting from a remote printer. NET PRINT is used to manage print jobs

Table 6.3 Useful Network Commands

Command	Description
NET	Loads the pop-up interface into memory.
NET CONFIG	Displays configuration information for the workstation. The display includes the user name, computer name, and software versions.
NET DIAGNOSTICS	Displays information about the status of your workstation and can be used to test the connection between two workstations.
NET FILE	Displays the files from your system that other users have open. The command shows the file path, how many systems have the file open, and the number of locks on the file.
NET HELP	Displays information about specific Workgroup Add-On for MS-DOS commands and error messages.
NET INITIALIZE	Used to load the protocol and network adapter drivers into memory without binding them to the Protocol Manager. This command is primarily used when third-party network protocols are used.
NET SESSION	Allows you to monitor connections to your system and optionally disconnect sessions.
NET SHARE	Displays information about current shared resources on your system and is used to connect to shared resources.
NET VER	Displays the current version of the redirector. See the NET CONFIG command.

on a local workstation and remote systems, and NET SHARE is used to share a local printer as a network resource.

I have not done extensive testing with the Workgroup Add-On for MS-DOS and shared printers, but it should be adequate for a print server for most low-end dot matrix printers. It may also work well as a print server for laser printers. You should expect a degradation in performance if you are attempting to share a printer and use the system as a workstation at the same time. Chapter 8 contains more information on using the Workgroup Add-On for MS-DOS as a print server and on using NET PRINT in general.

6.2.5.5 Stopping the Client Software   NET STOP shuts down the network client components and removes them from memory.

6.2.5.6 Net Time   NET TIME displays the time on the client system. It can also be used to set the time on the client from an NT, LAN Manager, or Windows for Workgroups system.

6.2.5.7 Connecting to Network Resources   The NET USE command is used to connect to remote shared resources. This is the same command used by all Microsoft network products including the Windows and DOS versions. See page 200 for more information on its use and format.

6.2.5.8 Sharing Resources   The NET SHARE command is useful for sharing printers for other users. The format follows:

```
Net Share sharename=portname [/remark:"text"]
      [/saveshare:no] - [/full:password]
```

sharename   Name of the shared printer.

portname   Printer port to which the printer to share is attached.

/remark   Comment for the share.

/saveshare   **No** specifies that the share will not be saved. **Yes** causes the share to be restored automatically.

6.2.5.9 Viewing Network Resources   NET VIEW displays a list of shared resources on other systems.

6.3 REMOTE BOOT OPTION FOR CLIENTS

MS-DOS clients can use the Remote Program Load (RPL) protocol to allow the systems to boot over the network. This protocol provides support for diskless systems that remote boot and obtain all services from an NT Server.

Remote boot is not covered in detail in this book because I had many bad experiences with remote boot client systems many years ago. Local boot workstations with adequate disk space always outperform remote boot systems. I prefer to spend more time on getting the clients up to current technology such as DOS 6.22 and Windows for Workgroups 3.11 or Windows 95 than on working on management techniques that allow me to effectively use those systems and upgrade them remotely. Windows 95 and DOS 6.2 both come with remote setup facilities designed for networks. See the information throughout this book on tools such as Systems Management Server that make the task of managing remote systems much easier.

6.4 ADDING NT WORKSTATIONS TO A DOMAIN

Before an NT workstation or server can be used in the domain or access resources on domains with trust relationships, it must be added to the domain.

Systems can be added to a domain by any one of three methods:

☞ by using Server Manager,
☞ during the installation process of an NT or NT Server system, or
☞ by using the Networks applet in Control Panel on the NT workstation.

The following procedure must be used from an NT server in the domain or from an NT or Windows for Workgroups system running Server Manager. You must log on with an account that has Administrator privileges to perform this process.

Adding a Workstation to a Domain with Server Manager

1. Start Server Manager from the Administrative Tools group.
2. Choose Add To Domain from the Computer menu.
3. Select either the server or workstation option to add the system to the domain.
4. Enter the system's computer name in the Computer Name field and click Add. After Add has completed, click Close.
5. Verify that the system has been added correctly by running Networks applet in Control Panel on the system you added and verify that the list of domains includes the domain you added the system to.

Another option that is slightly easier is to add the system to the domain at the time of installation. This step can be performed only if your system has a connection to the domain network during the installation. This option not only simplifies the process of adding the system to the domain, but it also prevents the system from installing an initial user account on the system.

Adding a Workstation to a Domain During Installation

1. Enter the domain name when prompted during the installation process for a BDC. This system should not be configured as the PDC during installation unless the domain does not exist.
2. If an account for the system you are adding is not already in the domain, select an administrator name and password.
3. NT displays a message confirming that the system has been added to the domain.

The following steps add an NT workstation to the domain and must be performed from the workstation.

Adding a Workstation to a Domain with Control Panel

1. Start the Networks applet in Control Panel.
2. Click Add to add the system to a domain.
3. If an account for the system you are adding is not already in the domain, select an administrator name and password.
4. NT displays a message confirming that the system has been added to the domain.

6.5 LOGGING ON TO A DOMAIN

One of the more interesting problems you may encounter is how to log in to your NT server from workstations running different operating systems.

6.5.1 NT Workstation

The easiest workstation to use in a domain is another NT system. Logging on or off of your domain is the same as logging on or off the workstation, except that you specify the domain name in the list box on the Logon dialog box. When you log on from an NT workstation, the logon server in the domain sets your preferences from your profile (if a profile is specified) and then downloads your logon script to the workstation (if a logon script is specified).

After you have logged in, you are set. You can connect to any resources in the domain that you have access to or perform any other tasks that have been authorized for your account.

You must select the domain name in the From list box on the Welcome dialog box. If you select your local machine (which shows up in the list), you are logged in to the local machine if your user name and password match. When you log in to a local machine instead of a domain, your domain logon script (if any) is not run and you are not logged in to the domain. You can however still connect to resources in the domain even though you are not logged in.

6.5.2 Windows for Workgroups

Logging in from Windows for Workgroups is slightly more challenging than from an NT workstation. Windows for Workgroups is the preferred 16-bit client for an NT network, and version 3.11 is the preferred Windows for Workgroups version.

Windows for Workgroups 3.11 introduced a logon/logoff utility in the Network group (LOGONOFF.EXE). Version 3.11 also has an enhanced Control Panel Network applet that understands the difference between domains and workgroups. Figure 6.9 shows the successful Logon dialog box.

You must log on to the Windows for Workgroups machine with a user name and password that is recognized by the domain before you can gain access to any network resources. Figure 6.10 shows the Domain Logon dialog box.

6.5.3 Windows 95

Windows 95 presents the user with a logon dialog box similar to that for Windows for Workgroups, except for the Domain text box at the bottom. This dialog box allows you to log on to the same domain as last time (the last domain

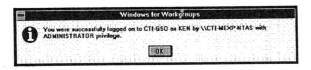

Fig. 6.9 This dialog box results from Windows for Workgroups 3.11 when you have successfully logged on to a domain. Notice that the logon information includes the domain name (DOM-KEN), user account (KEN), and privileges granted (Administrator). The dialog box also shows which server (CTI-MEXP-NT SERVER) in the domain logged you in. You can turn this off in the Control Panel Networks applet.

```
┌──────────────────────────────────────────────────────┐
│ ▬            │         Domain Logon                    │
├──────────────────────────────────────────────────────┤
│  Logon Name:      KEN                ┌──────────────┐  │
│                                      │     OK       │  │
│  Password:     ┌──────────────────┐  └──────────────┘  │
│                │ ········┤        │  ┌──────────────┐  │
│                └──────────────────┘  │   Cancel     │  │
│  Domain:       ┌──────────────┐ ┌─┐  └──────────────┘  │
│                │ CTI-GSO      │ │▼│  ┌──────────────┐  │
│                └──────────────┘ └─┘  │    Help      │  │
│    ☒ Save this Password in Your Password List          │
│                                      ┌──────────────┐  │
│                                      │  Browse...   │  │
│                                      └──────────────┘  │
└──────────────────────────────────────────────────────┘
```

Fig. 6.10 The Domain Logon dialog box is presented the first time you log on to a domain from Windows for Workgroups 3.11 with a new user name or one that does not have a password list. Checking Save this Password in Your Password List causes Windows for Workgroups to retain the password in the password list file for future logons and stops this dialog box from displaying upon subsequent logons with the same user name from that workstation.

name is filled in by default) or enter a different domain. With Windows for Workgroups, you were forced to change the domain in Control Panel or come up with another work-around to easily change domains each time you log in.

Logging Off from Windows 95

1. Click the Start button.
2. Select the Shutdown option.
3. Highlight the Close all programs and log on as a different user? option.
4. Click Yes.

You may have noticed that Windows 95 will shut down all programs during the logoff process. This feature eliminates many support calls for programs that are running when a logoff occurs and the program can no longer find its network connection.

Logging On from Windows 95

1. Click the Start button.
2. Select the Shutdown option.
3. Highlight the Close all programs and log on as a different user? option.
4. Click Yes.
5. Enter your user name (if different from the default).
6. Enter your password.
7. Enter your domain name (if different from the default).
8. Click OK.

6.6 LOGON SCRIPTS

Chapter 4 (see page 177) provides details and examples of logon scripts for DOS, Windows, and NT clients.

6.7 TRACKING NETWORK EVENTS ON CLIENTS

6.7.1 Windows for Workgroups 3.11

Windows for Workgroups 3.11 is the first DOS version of Windows to implement any type of network event-logging for client workstations. The event-logging capabilities are configured in the Control Panel Network applet. The Event Log button brings up the Event Log Settings dialog box shown in Figure 6.11.

The events tracked in the event log follow:

Connect to Server
Unsuccessful Connect Attempt
Server Startup
Server Shutdown
Pause Print Job
Resume Print Job
Delete Print Job
Complete Print Job

Note that all these events are triggered by things that happen on the Windows for Workgroups system as a server and not an NT server on the domain that the workstation may be using resources on.

6.7.2 Windows 95

Windows 95 includes many tools for monitoring the client system and network components. Most of these tools were changing or unstable as this book was completed. The following list points out several items you should look at for your Windows 95 clients.

☞ System Monitor (SYSMON.EXE) provides a tool that is slightly similar to Performance Monitor under NT. System Monitor provides a nice graphical interface, remote monitoring capabilities, an extensible monitoring system using counters like Performance Monitor, and the standard Windows 95 look and feel.

Fig. 6.11 Use this dialog box to configure the event log and determine which events are tracked.

Fig. 6.12 System Monitor lets you see everything in one or two mouse clicks and performance information is displayed graphically.

☞ An SNMP agent ships with Windows 95 providing hooks into most SNMP management systems.

☞ The System Policy Editor (POLEDIT.EXE) provides control over users and computers. You can use this tool to set access privileges by user, group, or computer name. The policy file (*.POL) can be placed on a domain controller and automatically downloaded when a user logs in.

Figure 6.13 shows the Policy Editor. Notice the icons and tree list format common to Windows 95.

Fig. 6.13 The System Policy Editor controls the type of access and control that a user has over a system. This is the Properties dialog box for a user (SDH). Notice how the Network Control Panel features are disabled.

Services for Macintosh

7.1 OVERVIEW

Services for Macintosh (SFM) is the NT feature that smoothly integrates Macintosh services with an NT network. The NT Server administrator needs to manage only one set of users and groups for all NT users, regardless of whether they log on from a PC or Macintosh. The same NT Server security system treats all access of the domain the same..

Services for Macintosh can convert LAN Manager Services for Macintosh 1.0 to NT Server Services for Macintosh.

Macintosh clients must be running System 6.0.8 or later. Users on DOS, Windows, or NT systems can share files with Macintosh users and let NT handle the duties of translating the files. NT Server is also a high-performance file and print server for Macintosh clients. Macintosh clients can use NT printers as if they were LaserWriters and other clients can use Macintosh printers.

7.1.1 Services for Macintosh Network Topologies

LocalTalk (Phase 2), Ethernet, Token Ring, and FDDI are supported by SFM. Ethernet and Token Ring are the most popular topologies for PC networks when integrating SFM. FDDI is typically used for a network backbone or other high-speed interface.

Suffice it to say that LocalTalk networks are by far slower than any of the others. If you are using LocalTalk, I recommend that you upgrade to Ethernet or

Token Ring to improve the performance of your network. You can do this over time because Services for Macintosh can use LocalTalk as well as the other topologies. You can use a router or a LocalTalk card in your NT server to allow the LocalTalk machines to participate in the network until they are upgraded to a faster network.

For more details on setting up networks for use with SFM, you should consult the SFM documentation that comes with NT Server. This documentation has lots of details, including information on Macintosh networks, routing, and seeding routers.

7.1.2 Components of Services for Macintosh

Services for Macintosh has two major components that you will see running as Services.

☞ File Server for Macintosh is the service that handles file sharing for all Macintosh users.

☞ Print Server for Macintosh is another service that handles the printing for Macintosh users and handles printing for PC users that are printing to Apple LaserWriters on the Macintosh network.

7.1.3 Requirements for Services for Macintosh

Services for Macintosh does not require many additional resources on your system. The official Microsoft guidelines are

2MB of free disk

NTFS partition for Macintosh volumes

I suggest adding more memory to your server to support the extra overhead that SFM will add unless your server has lots of free RAM. NT is always happier when you add extra memory as your system grows.

You can easily create an NTFS volume from a FAT volume by using the CONVERT command. This command converts the directory structure from HPFS or FAT to NTFS. The format for the command is:

```
CONVERT /FS:NTFS E:
```

CONVERT converts only a partition to NTFS, it will not go back the other way. The only way to get back from an NTFS partition is to back up the entire file structure to another disk or tape, reformat the partition, and copy the files back.

If you are starting with a unformatted partition for a Macintosh volume, you can use the FORMAT command. FORMAT creates an NTFS volume from scratch. The syntax is:

```
FORMAT /FS:NTFS E:
```

Notice that the syntax is exactly the same as CONVERT. Remember that FORMAT cannot be used on an existing drive because it will destroy the con-

tents of the drive. If you are adding a new disk for use with SFM, you must use
Disk Administrator to partition the disk before you use the FORMAT command.

7.1.4 Requirements for Macintosh Systems Connecting to Services for Macintosh

Macintosh workstations must be able to use AppleShare in order to connect
to a Services for Macintosh server. The Microsoft SFM manual states that all
Macintosh systems except the Macintosh XL and Macintosh 128K can use SFM.
Macintosh workstations must be running System 6.0.8 or higher.

7.1.5 Security

Services for Macintosh uses the same security system as the standard NT
Server, including the user accounts and other security features of NT Server.
Services for Macintosh introduces some peculiarities because of the way the
Macintosh operating system handles security versus the way NT Server and
Windows do.

7.1.5.1 Logon Methods for Macintosh Users Macintosh users can log on
using a user name and password or via a guest logon. The guest logon must be
enabled through SFM. Guest logons are enabled by choosing the Guest account
in User Manager and clearing the Account Disabled check box on the User Properties dialog box.

Guest logons provide the lowest level of security but also provide the least
hassle for your users because they allow users to access services on the server
without having to remember a password.

Using passwords allows SFM to function just like NT Server in the way it
handles other clients when validating user accounts. The Macintosh compli-
cates the issue slightly because it normally uses what are called Cleartext
passwords. A Cleartext password is nothing more than the text representation
of the password being sent over the network. This can cause problems in a
secure environment where someone may have access to a protocol sniffer such
as Network Monitor or other device that can capture network information.
Capturing information in this manner is more difficult than it sounds because
the snooping user must capture several pieces of information to gain any useful
information.

The Macintosh Cleartext password presents one problem: the password is
limited to 8 characters in length. This can be a problem for users of both PC and
Macintosh workstations who use the same account for both workstations
because the NT Server passwords can be 14 characters in length.

One way to solve both of these password problems is to install the Microsoft
UAM that comes with NT Server. The installation of the UAM is covered in
Chapter 7 on page 246.

The Microsoft UAM allows the user to use passwords up to 14 characters in
length. It also encrypts the passwords at the Macintosh workstation before they

are sent over the network. You can also set SFM to force Macintosh users to use the Microsoft UAM when they log on to the SFM server.

The UAM also allows the user to specify another domain than the current domain the NT Server running SFM is a member of. The domain the user wishes to log on to must be a trusted domain of the current NT Server domain. The syntax for logging on to another domain is

```
Domainname\Username
```

The Domainname\Username should be entered in the Name text box.

7.1.5.2 Groups   Each SFM user must be assigned to a global group. This group becomes the default SFM group when assigning permissions under SFM. If you do not have a global group assigned, you will get the error: "This operation is not allowed on this special group. ID 2234."

Each time a Macintosh user creates a new folder, the primary group is the group associated with the folder. The files owner or a system administrator can change the primary group.

7.1.6 File Server Access from Macintosh Clients

SFM allows you to use an NT Server to provide file and print services to both PC and Macintosh clients. NT Server allows up to 255 Macintosh clients to connect to a single server at one time. The Macintosh users see the NT file system as an AppleShare volume. PC users can connect to the same server and share files with Macintosh users. SFM proves the mechanism to share most files transparently between PC and Macintosh users.

Some tricks are necessary when sharing files simultaneously between a PC and Macintosh user. For instance, when a PC user has a file open in Excel and a Macintosh user tries to open the file, the Macintosh user will get an "access denied" message. The problem can be solved on the Macintosh by clicking the Read-only button on the File Open dialog box. This problem occurs because the Macintosh defaults to read-write access when opening a file and encounters an error when the Macintosh user tries to open the file.

The interface between the PC and Macintosh works well because NT Server manages the differences in the file systems behind the scenes. The PC user sees the file as a DOS file, whereas a Macintosh user sees the file as a Mac icon complete with the appropriate icon image. NT Server can also launch Macintosh applications that are stored on the server and associated with a file.

AppleShare volumes can be located only on an NTFS volume. NTFS supports storing the resource fork and Finder information directly in the file. NTFS also supports 31-character file names that are compatible with the Mac file system. File names are automatically translated between different client types.

The system administrator can require Macintosh users to use Windows NT Encryption when they log in to a server, to provide enhanced password and network security. See the section on the Microsoft User Authentication Method in this chapter for more information.

Services for Macintosh allows you to create AppleShare volumes on NT or NT Server from both File Manager and Control Panel.

NT Server automatically translates NT file and directory permissions to and from Macintosh permissions.

7.2 INSTALLING AND REMOVING SERVICES FOR MACINTOSH

7.2.1 Installing Services for Macintosh

SFM can be installed during the installation of NT Server. This section focuses on installing SFM after you have installed NT Server. You must log in as a member of the Administrators group to perform the installation. The installation steps are very simple and can be completed in 10–20 minutes, assuming everything works as planned and there are no problems with your server.

Installing Services for Macintosh

1. Start Control Panel and select the Network applet.
2. Select the Add Software button.
3. Select Services for Macintosh from the Network Software List and select the Continue button.
4. Enter the path to the NT Server distribution files. This dialog box usually defaults to the path originally used to install NT Server. Setup copies the SFM files to the server and configures the Registry for SFM.
5. Select OK on the Network Settings dialog box. Setup completes the setup process and starts the SFM service.
6. The Services for Macintosh Configuration dialog box will be displayed. You can continue by selecting OK or take the time to configure SFM now. You can select a Zone from the Zone list and access the AppleTalk Routing configuration dialog box by checking the Enable Routing box and selecting the Advanced button.
7. Select OK on the next information dialog box and another Network Settings dialog box will appear, asking you to reboot the system. Select Yes to reboot now or No to reboot later. You must reboot to use SFM.

7.2.2 Installing the Services for Macintosh Workstation Programs

You can easily install the Microsoft user authentication software on each Macintosh workstation. The workstation software is installed on the NT Server in a volume called Microsoft UAM Volume. This makes the UAM software accessible to all Macintosh workstations on the network.

The first step in this process is to require workstations using the NT Server to use the Microsoft UAM. This step forces all System 7 or later Macintosh workstations to use the Microsoft UAM and not the AppleShare UAM to log on to the NT domain.

Turning on Forced Authentication

1. Run Server Manager on the NT Server.
2. Select Properties from the MacFile menu.
3. Select the Attributes button.
4. Click the check box for Require Microsoft Authentication.

The UAM must be installed on each Macintosh client before it can be used.

Installing the UAM Software on a Macintosh Workstation

1. Select the Chooser from the Apple menu.
2. Select the AppleShare icon.
3. Select the zone that the NT Server running SFM resides in.
4. Select the NT Server from the list of servers.
5. Log in to the NT Server when the sign-in dialog box appears.
6. Select the Microsoft UAM Volume from the list of volumes on the server.
7. Close the Chooser.
8. Double-click the Microsoft UAM Volume.
9. Double-click the System Folder within the Microsoft UAM Volume.
10. Drag the MS UAM file and drop it into the System Folder for the Macintosh.
11. Disable the Cleartext and guest password options on the server. System 7 or later Macintosh clients are forced to use the Microsoft UAM software.

Once you have installed the UAM, the user will have the option of using the standard Macintosh authentication or the Microsoft UAM when he or she logs on to the SFM server, unless you have performed the first set of steps in this section to force users through the Microsoft UAM.

If your system requires that you use the UAM to provide extended security services for Macintosh clients, you should protect the UAM from the users. Leaving the UAM unprotected allows users to move the UAM or delete it from the Macintosh client.

Microsoft suggests two methods for protecting the UAM from users. You can use one or both of these methods. Using both methods provides the greatest security but still does not keep a sophisticated user from creating problems with the UAM.

Protecting the UAM

Method 1

1. Set the AppleShare folder in the Macintosh's System Folder to invisible using ResEdit or a similar program.

Method 2

1. Select the UAM file in the AppleShare Folder using Finder.
2. Choose Get Info from the File menu.
3. Select the Locked check box.

7.2.3 Removing Services for Macintosh

SFM can be removed very easily. This process takes only a few minutes. As with other administrative-type tasks, you must be logged in as a member of the Administrators group to perform these tasks.

Removing Services for Macintosh

1. Start Control Panel.
2. Select the Devices applet.
3. Select the AppleTalk Protocol from the list and click the Stop button. Click OK when the Stopping dialog box appears. This step stops the AppleTalk protocol and related services.
4. Close the Devices application and select the Network applet.
5. Select Services for Macintosh in the Installed Network Software box.
6. Select the Remove button and answer Yes to the prompt to confirm the removal.
7. Select OK to complete the process.

All SFM files are deleted from this process. Any directories used as Macintosh volumes will become unavailable to Macintosh users although the files will not be deleted.

7.3 ADMINISTRATION OF SERVICES FOR MACINTOSH

SFM adds a number of tools for administering Macintosh services. Most of these tools are integrated into normal NT Server programs by the addition of a Mac-File menu or option. Other SFM features may show up as standard NT options. This section reviews the various management options for Services for Macintosh and how they are integrated into the standard NT options.

7.3.1 Configuring the AppleTalk Protocol

Several features of the AppleTalk protocol can be configured using the Network applet in Control Panel. You can select which network adapter to use for the default, which zone the NT Server should be in, enable NT Server as a router for the Macintosh network, and configure the routing features of SFM.

Choosing a Network

1. Select the Network icon in Control Panel.
2. Select Services for Macintosh from the list of services.
3. Select the network for the default from the Network list.
4. Click OK.

Choosing, Removing, and Selecting a Default Zone

1. Select the Network icon in Control Panel.
2. Select Services for Macintosh from the list of services.
3. Select the desired zone from the list.
4. Click OK.

Zones can also be removed using the same dialog box. Simply select a zone and click Remove or click Remove All to clear all zones.

The default zone can be set by selecting a zone and clicking the default button.

The AppleTalk protocol must be restarted for the change to be visible to other users on the network.

Stopping the AppleTalk Protocol

1. Start Control Panel.
2. Select the Devices applet.
3. Select the AppleTalk Protocol from the list.
4. Click the Stop button. Click OK when the Stopping dialog box appears. This step stops the AppleTalk protocol and related services.

Starting the AppleTalk Protocol

1. Start Control Panel.
2. Select the Devices applet.
3. Select the AppleTalk Protocol from the list and click the Start button. This step starts the AppleTalk protocol and related services.

7.3.1.1 Routing Parameters   You can enable NT Server as a Macintosh router by using the Network applet. Care must be used when setting up routing services because, if you configure the router seeding incorrectly, the other routers on the network may fail.

Setting Up Your Server as an AppleTalk Router

1. Select the Network icon in Control Panel.
2. Select Services for Macintosh from the list of services.
3. Click the check box beside Enable Routing.

To allow the server to be a seed router, select the Advanced button in the AppleTalk Routing box.

To enable the server as a seed router, click the Seed this Network check box. You should make sure that the network you wish to seed is specified in the Networks list box. This list contains all the adapters that the AppleTalk protocol is bound to. If the correct adapter is not shown, select the correct adapter from the list.

After you have checked the See this Network box you can select the network range and add or remove any zones to the current list. When you enter network ranges or zones on this dialog box, remember that you are actually changing the settings for the network.

The Zone Information and Network Range along with the Seed This Network check box all apply to the network shown in the list box. Once you have made your chances, click OK to complete the process.

7.3.2 Administering Macintosh Users

The primary tool for administering Macintosh users is the MacFile applet in Control Panel. Luckily Microsoft was looking out for managers and made this applet almost identical to Server Manager.

MacFile allows you to monitor users, volumes, files, and Services for Macintosh attributes. Figure 7.1 shows the interface for MacFile.

MacFile works the same as Server Manager as well. Click the appropriate button, and the attributes are displayed. You can perform most actions with one or two clicks of the mouse.

Displaying the Users on a Services for Macintosh Server

1. Start the MacFile applet in Control Panel.
2. Click the Users button.

Disconnecting a User on a Services for Macintosh Server

1. Start the MacFile applet in Control Panel.
2. Click the Users button.
3. Select the user to disconnect.
4. Click the Disconnect button. You can disconnect all users by clicking Disconnect All.

Fig. 7.1 The MacFile Properties dialog box is similar to Server Manager.

Sending a Message to Services for Macintosh Users

1. Start the MacFile applet in Control Panel.
2. Click the Users button.
3. Select the user(s) to send the message to.
4. Click the Send Message button.
5. Enter the text of the message and follow the prompts.

Displaying the Volumes in Use on a Services for Macintosh Server

1. Start the MacFile applet in Control Panel.
2. Click the Volumes button.

Breaking a Connection to a Volume on a Services for Macintosh Server

1. Start the MacFile applet in Control Panel.
2. Click the Volumes button.
3. Select the user to disconnect.
4. Click the Disconnect button. You can disconnect users from a volume by clicking Disconnect All with a volume selected.

Figure 7.2 shows the Macintosh-Accessible Volumes window.

Displaying the Files in Use on a Services for Macintosh Server

1. Start the MacFile applet in Control Panel.
2. Click the Files button.

Closing a File in Use on a Services for Macintosh Server

1. Start the MacFile applet in Control Panel.

Fig. 7.2 Notice how closely this dialog box matches the corresponding dialog box for shares in Server Manager. It takes only two clicks of the mouse to disconnect a user from a volume using this tool.

2. Select the file to close.

3. Click the Close Fork button. You can close all Macintosh files on the selected server by clicking Close All Forks.

The attributes option of MacFile is a little more involved than point and click. This tool changes the settings for the SFM server and can cause you problems if you do not handle it with care and plan your changes carefully. The following options can be changed:

☞ Server name as seen by AppleTalk workstations. I suggest leaving this set to the same name as the server name to avoid confusion with having two names for the same server: one for Macintosh users and one for all others. Besides, it is nice for users who use both systems to be able to identify the server with the same name.

☞ The Logon message seen by Macintosh users.

☞ Security settings change the personality of the server. Secure environments want to turn off the first two options and turn on the last option:

   Allow Guests to Logon allows user to log in to the server via guest accounts.

   Allow Workstations to Save Password allows the user to save his/her password locally.

   Require Microsoft Authentication requires the more secure logon authenticator (see page 246 for more information).

☞ The Sessions box allows you to limit the number of concurrent sessions on the SFM server. The default is unlimited.

Changing the Attributes (Settings) for Services for Macintosh

1. Start the MacFile applet in Control Panel.

2. Change the option(s) desired. You must click the Change button to be able to change the server name.

3. Click OK.

Figure 7.3 shows the MacFile Attributes dialog box.

7.4 POTENTIAL PROBLEMS WITH SERVICES FOR MACINTOSH

7.4.1 Macintosh Path Lengths

NT cannot handle path names longer than 260 characters, whereas Macintosh can. You should not create directory names longer than 260 characters because of this problem. This is a potential problem area because NT cannot access files in directory paths longer than 260 characters, causing problems for backup operations and other operations that must access files in these directories.

Fig. 7.3 The MacFile Attributes dialog box provides access to a number of server parameters.

Macintosh file names are allowed to contain a trailing space, although NT does not support this for NT and DOS users. You will most likely receive a message from NT stating that it cannot find the file when you try to access the file. The only resolution to this problem is to rename the file from the Macintosh and remove the trailing space.

Macintosh file names are mapped to UNICODE as files are created on an NTFS volume. File Manager cannot access files that use UNICODE characters that do not have a corresponding ANSI character. The UNICODE characters problem shows up when you try to access the files in NT from either File Manager, the NT Backup program, or the command prompt. The files can be accessed from a Macintosh with no problems.

7.5 FILE SYSTEM ISSUES FOR SERVICES FOR MACINTOSH

7.5.1 Making Shared Directories Available to Macintosh Users

An administrator must designate a directory as a Macintosh-accessible volume before it can be accessed by Macintosh users. The Macintosh user sees the directory as a Macintosh volume, whereas PC users see the directory as a standard shared directory. Macintosh users see the volume and its files as if it were a standard Macintosh volume, whereas PC users see the directory structure and its files as a normal DOS directory tree.

For starters, all Macintosh volumes must be created on an NTFS volume. HPFS and FAT volumes do not support the extended features required for the Macintosh file system.

You can create only one Macintosh volume in a subdirectory tree. This means that one and only one Macintosh volume can exist down any one directory path. For instance, if you make a top-level directory a Macintosh volume, no other subdirectory in that tree can be a Macintosh volume. If you make a subdirectory a Macintosh volume you can make other subdirectories at the same level a Macintosh volume.

Volume names can be from 1 to 27 characters in length. The AppleTalk protocol places a limit on the number of Macintosh volume names that can be displayed to Macintosh users. This limitation is based on the length of the volume names and the number of volumes. The exact formula is

(Number of Volumes) * (Average Length of Volume Names + 2) <= 4624

7.5.2 Disappearing Icons

You may occasionally copy a Macintosh file on a PC and notice that the icon for the new file disappears when the file is accessed from a Macintosh. This error usually occurs when the file has a custom icon. Custom icons are stored as hidden files and cannot be copied correctly if the file name has a UNICODE character in the name. When you lose an icon, File Manager has used the short name to copy the file, resulting in a lost association to the icon. There is currently no work-around to this problem.

7.5.3 Drop Folders

Drop folders are a handy tool that allows users to "drop" files that cannot be changed after they are dropped. A drop folder is created by making a directory that gives the dropping users only Make Changes permission. NT Server supports drop folder permissions only for the immediate contents of the folder.

You should manually add drop folder permissions to all subdirectories under the main drop folder. Use the MacFile menu from File Manager and select Directory Permissions or use the Sharing dialog box on a Macintosh client. You must manually update these permissions if you add a directory to the main drop folder.

7.5.4 Macintosh Files

Macintosh files are bound by the same restrictions as they would be on a normal Macintosh system with a few additional restrictions. The restrictions occur because it is possible for a user to create a file with a file name that contains illegal NTFS characters. SFM checks each file name as it is created and changes any invalid characters to NTFS characters. Macintosh users see the unaltered name as they entered it, whereas other users see the name with the replaced characters.

File names that are too long for FAT names will have a short name created using the same process as any other NTFS name. Macintosh file names can have up to 31 characters, whereas NTFS file names can be up to 255 characters.

The diversity in file names does make for some potential confusion for systems with mixed DOS, NT, and Macintosh users. The problem comes about because of the diversity in file name lengths, as shown in Table 7.1.

Table 7.1 File Name Lengths

File System	Characteristics
FAT	8.3 (eight characters + . + 3 characters), 255 on Windows 95 or NT
NTFS	255
Macintosh	31

What does this mean to us as users? Any file that is over 8.3 characters in length will look different to users on different Macintosh and Windows 3.x or DOS systems. For instance, any file over 8.3 and up to 31 characters will look fine to Macintosh users and NT users but not DOS users because DOS users will see only the short 8.3 name created by NTFS or SFM. Any file longer than 31 characters will look okay to NTFS users but not Macintosh or DOS users, both of whom will see the short 8.3 name. For more information on file systems in general and how the NTFS short name is created, see Chapter 5 (page 192).

7.5.5 File and Folder Permissions

NT Server and SFM resolve the differences in the way the Macintosh and NTFS handle permissions on files, and directories/folders. Even though NTFS provides the ability to fine-tune the permissions on a file and/or directory, the Macintosh operating system provides only four types of permissions for a folder. SFM automatically translates between the Macintosh and NTFS permissions on the fly. Table 7.2 shows the Macintosh permissions and the corresponding NTFS permission.

The Macintosh permissions are much more restrictive than NTFS permissions. Permissions cannot be assigned to multiple users or groups as in NTFS. The Macintosh allows permissions to be assigned to the owner of the folder, a single user or group, and a special classification called Everyone, which includes all users on the system.

Comparing the security features of Macintosh versus this or that system is like comparing Ethernet to Token Ring—it's a religious war. The practical side of the limitations on the Macintosh for permissions means that you must

Table 7.2 Macintosh and NTFS Permissions

Macintosh	NTFS	Description
Cannot move, rename, or delete	N/A	User cannot move, rename, or delete the folder.
Make Changes	Write, Delete	User can perform any action on files within the folder.
See Files	Read	User can see folders contained within the folder.
See Folders	Read	User can see and read files within the folder.

create more groups on the server if you have security requirements that involve intricate sharing of files or folders. For more information on how the Macintosh deals with permissions, see the SFM documentation or your Macintosh documentation.

The SFM manual points out one interesting caveat regarding the translating of NTFS and Macintosh permissions: permissions assigned to Everyone on the Macintosh overrides any other rights assigned to the Owner or a group. Permissions set to the group Everyone on NTFS do not override any other permissions for users or groups.

NTFS also has file permissions that can be applied directly to any file on the system. The Macintosh has no corresponding file permissions, only folder permissions. What SFM does when it encounters file permissions is to give the appropriate access to the Macintosh user transparently. The Macintosh user never sees the permission but is affected by the permission. For instance, if a file has read-only access for a user, no Macintosh permission on the parent folder can override the specific file permission. In this instance, the user could read the file but not modify or delete the file.

7.5.5.1 Setting Folder Permissions Setting permissions on folders applies to almost the same restrictions that NTFS uses for NTFS files and directories. Only a file's owner or an administrator can change the permissions on the folder. A Macintosh, a PC, or an NT can be used to change the permissions. File Manager can actually set Macintosh-type permissions using the MacFile menu.

7.5.5.2 Volume Passwords Volume passwords are case-sensitive and can be assigned to a volume when it is created. These passwords apply only to access to the volume from a Macintosh and not from a DOS or NT system. Macintosh users must always supply the password when mounting the volume.

A volume with a password cannot be automatically mounted because of a limitation with System 6 and System 7.

7.5.6 Mac and NTFS File and Directory Properties

NTFS and the Macintosh file system both use different attributes for files and directories (folders on the Mac). As you can imagine, there must be some mechanism for Services for Macintosh to map NTFS attributes to Macintosh attributes. Table 7.3 shows how this is done. If an attribute from one system is not listed, it does not have an equivalent on the other platform and is not mapped.

Table 7.3 Macintosh and NTFS File Attributes

Macintosh Attribute	Windows NT Server Attribute
File Locked	Read Only
Invisible	Hidden

7.5.7 Copying a Macintosh File to a FAT Volume

Users must be careful when copying a file from an SFM volume to a DOS floppy disk. A Macintosh file has two parts: a data fork and a resource fork. NTFS tracks both of these forks, which allows the file to reside in its native format on the NTFS volume by using an extended attribute to track the resource fork.

Most systems that copy Macintosh files to a FAT disk split the file into two different pieces representing the data and resource forks. When the file is copied back to a Macintosh the two pieces are put back together. These two parts are not required with SFM because NTFS treats the two parts as a single unit just like the Macintosh.

Copying a Macintosh file to a FAT diskette results in the loss of the extended attribute that represents the resource fork. When an application needs the resource fork, the operation fails because the attribute is not present.

7.6 PRINTING WITH SERVICES FOR MACINTOSH

SFM provides printing services for both Macintosh and PC users on the same printers. Macintosh users can use both PostScript and many non-PostScript printers, while PC users can print to a LaserWriter that is connected to the Macintosh network.

NT Server supports all printers through its printing system. This support makes management easy because each printer can be managed by Print Manager. The spooling system improves printing for Macintosh users by allowing Macintosh users to print a document and return quickly to their applications, whereas NT Server spools the print job to the printer. The spooling takes place on the server and does not use disk space on the Macintosh client.

SFM has an integrated PostScript-compatible print engine that allows a Macintosh user to print to almost any printer connected to the NT network as if that printer were a LaserWriter. The print engine translates the PostScript file to the appropriate format for the target printer, allowing your Macintosh and PC users to share easily the printer investment on your network.

7.6.1 Captured Printers

SFM has the ability to capture a Macintosh printer such as a LaserWriter that is connected to the Macintosh network and not directly to the NT server. Capturing allows SFM to maintain complete control over the printer and not allow the printer to accept print jobs from any other source but the SFM server.

Failing to capture a printer may cause interference between the printer and the SFM server. When another system tries to print, either that system or NT sees the printer as busy.

Another good reason to capture a printer is to avoid the LaserPrep wars that can occur when Macintosh workstations have different versions of the LaserPrep file. The LaserPrep file is used to reset PostScript printers. The SFM manual goes into more detail on the subject of LaserPrep wars. Let's just say that when you capture a printer with SFM you can guarantee that LaserPrep wars will be avoided.

Printer Use and Management

Windows NT introduces a new printing system to the Windows and LAN environments. This system works with and looks like the printing system in Windows 3.x, but is a very different and powerful animal. The significant thing about this new printing system is that it is designed to work with future systems and is able to work with existing systems until and after these newer systems come along.

8.1 ARCHITECTURE

The NT printing architecture is a giant step into new technology for managing printers and printer resources. NT's printing architecture is modular and supports an easy management scheme for printers. For instance, you do not need to install a printer driver on every NT system that will use a printer. The driver needs to be resident only on the server that every NT workstation or server has access to. This is a far cry from Windows 3.x when you have many different printer drivers spread over your workstations. Storing only one copy of all your drivers on a server makes managing updates much easier than having a copy on each workstation, although having a locally stored copy improves performance slightly. There is more on drivers later.

NT uses several special terms that relate to printers. Some of these terms are new, some are used differently than on other systems, and the rest are generic terms for the industry. Table 8.1 lists the most important terms for NT's printer systems.

Table 8.1 Vocabulary for NT's Printer Subsystems

Term	Description
Print Device	The physical printer such as a LaserJet IV.
Printer	The printer name and the software that controls the printer. This is what users see as the printer name in browse lists and other places.
Queue	The software that users see as the printer. The term *printer* in NT refers to the same thing as a queue in other systems.
Network-Interface Printer	A printer that interfaces directly to the network.
Dots Per Inch	DPI. The most frequent term used for printer resolution. DPI refers to the number of dots per inch that are used to make up the characters and graphics on a printer. The higher the DPI, the better the print quality.
Pixel	The resolution of a screen. Pixels are similar to DPI.
Graphical Device Interface	GDI. The command set that applications output defining the print job. The GDI output contains both content and formatting information for the print job. The GDI is the boundary between the application and the graphics engine.
Graphics Engine	The print processor that takes the GDI output from an application.
Device Driver Interface	DDI. The interface between the graphics engine and the print processor and print driver.
Journal File	Files that contain the commands and data to print. Journal files are very precise and are tuned to the target printer.
Halftoning	A method of providing higher-quality output and improved color accuracy on a print device or monitor. Halftoning support is provided by the graphics engine.
Print Processor	A DLL that interprets data types passed from the spooler. NT comes with two print processors: • WINPRINT.DLL interprets journal files and raw files. • SFMSPRT.DLL supports Macintosh clients printing PostScript files. The Print Processor sends the document back to the spooler when it has completed its tasks.
WYSIWYG	What You See Is What You Get. This term is used to describe an application such as Word for Windows that displays a document as it will look when printed.
Print Router	Device that passes printer information from a workstation to the print server. The print router is used only if the workstation is printing to a remote printer. The Print Router is made up of several files: • Print Servers: SPOOLSS.EXE, SPOOLSS.DLL, and WINSPOOL.DLL.

Table 8.1 Vocabulary for NT's Printer Subsystems (Continued)

Term	Description
Print Router (continued)	• Client: WINSPOOL.DRV. The print router manages tracking local printers that have been connected to a remote printer and provides support for downloading the drivers from a server to the local workstation.
GDI Server	Graphics Device Interface server.
Printer Driver	A file or set of files that provide some type of print services for a particular printer. Printer drivers are also used by NT to provide WYSIWYG support for applications. Printer drivers can be stored on the NT print server and are not needed on each NT workstation or server that uses the remote printer. Printer drivers are composed of three files: • Graphics driver such as PSCRIPT.DLL • Printer interface driver such as PSCRPTUI.DLL • Configuration file or minidriver
Configuration File	A file used as part of the printer driver such as Adobe PostScript (PPD) file.
Printer Graphics Driver	The portion of the printer driver that handles rendering the print output and managing the process. It is called from GDI Server.
Printer Interface Driver	The portion of the printer driver that contains the user interface and manages configuration of the printer. It is called from the client side of the printer router.
Minidriver	Usually contains printer information and not code, except in some instances. PostScript minidrivers are Adobe PostScript (PPD) files.
Remote Printer	A printer on another system on the LAN or WAN. You must connect to a remote printer before you can use it on your local system.
Spooler	Runs on each NT system (both client and server) and manages the entire printing process. Client and server spoolers communicate directly with each other in the background. The spooler works with the print system components such as drivers and the router and with the physical printer.
Print Monitor	Found on each printer device to manage it. NT includes the following print monitors: • LOCALMON.DLL supports LPT and COM ports, remote print shares, and named pipes. • HPMON.DLL supports HP laserjets that connect through network interfaces. • SFMON.DLL is included with NT Server and provides support for AppleTalk clients. Developers and others can write their own print monitor for managing specific printers. The print monitor provides the direct interface to a printer. It opens and closes the port, monitors the status, and writes the data

Table 8.1 Vocabulary for NT's Printer Subsystems (Continued)

Term	Description
Print Monitor (continued)	to the port. It can also provide real status information because it does not report that a job is complete until the printer actually finishes printing.
Printer Port	A physical port that is used for a printer, such as COM1:, LPT2: or logical port (\\Server\Printer).
Forms Database	Database that contains information on all forms used by the printers on a server. The database is managed by the spooler.
Print Provider	Another software component that NT uses between the spooler and the print device. NT includes several print providers: • LOACALSPL.DLL • WIN32SPL.DLL • LMSPOOL.DLL

Print Manager is used to create and manage NT printers. You must specify a printer port and a printer driver for each new printer. The entire process of creating a new printer usually takes about 2 minutes to complete. You also use Print Manager to create printers for print devices that are connected to the network and managed by an NT Server. Print Manager can also connect a printer to a network queue on another system.

A printer can be used as soon as it is created and the print device is available. The printer name is the most visible part of the printing process that will be seen by the end user. Printer names show up in applications, Print Manager, and the NET USE command.

You can link multiple print devices to a single printer. This feature is useful for setting up pools of printers that have the same capabilities. You can also point multiple printers to one print device. This is useful when you need to control certain aspects of a print device where some users have access to certain features and other users have full access. There is more on both of these options later in the section on printer pools and multiple printers (see page 268).

8.2 PRINT MANAGER

Print Manager is the heart of the user interface to the NT printing system. Print Manager is an enhanced version of the program we have grown to know and love in Windows 3.x.

The NT version of Print Manager provides tools for viewing printers, managing documents, installing and removing printers, and setting security on printers. Print Manager also provides the tools to connect to network printers, share printers over the network, to disconnect network printers, and to cancel shares on printers.

The layout of Print Manager is convenient. It has a menu bar for providing quick access to often-used functions, a menu bar to provide access to all functions, and a nice MDI layout of the windows Print Manager uses. Each printer has its own window for its status and the documents that are currently scheduled to print on the printer. When you minimize the window of a printer, it becomes an icon at the bottom of the Print Manager window. For each printer the minimized icons show you the type of printer, the name, and whether it is shared or not. Icons also represent servers that you have remotely attached to for administration purposes. There is also a separate window that shows all printers connected to the server. Figure 8.1 shows Print Manager with several icons and windows. Notice how quickly you can get to any printer or server by clicking a window or double-clicking an icon.

The balance of this chapter focuses on a number of different tasks that relate to printing and NT. All these tasks involve Print Manager in one form or another. You can find more information on Print Manager in the NT or NT Server documentation and in the NT Resource Kit.

8.3 PRINTER SECURITY

NT allows you to assign security permissions to printers to control many different aspects of printer operation and maintenance. Security for printing may not sound like a big deal until you consider printers like check or invoice printers that stay loaded with a particular form. Setting permissions on these printers is a handy way to control access to this type of printer.

The security features are also nice for controlling who can manage a printer and the documents that have been sent to the printer.

Fig. 8.1 The layout of Print Manager allows quick access to all of its functions.

Table 8.2 lists special categories of access for printer users and administrators that are controlled through Print Manager.

By default, a user must be a member of either the Administrators, Print Operators, or Server Operators group to create a printer. Users must also have write access to the DRIVERS directory if they are printing from an NT system and the printer requires a new driver to download to the system.

NT allows you to audit your printers in the same manner as other objects. You can track the following events:

☞ Printing documents
☞ Changing job settings for documents
☞ Moving, pausing, restarting, and deleting documents
☞ Sharing a printer
☞ Changing printer properties
☞ Deleting a printer
☞ Changing printer permissions
☞ Taking ownership

Auditing must be enabled for a given printer in Print Manager. Before you enable auditing for a printer, you must turn on auditing in User Manager. The following steps walk you through setting up an audit on a printer.

Configuring Auditing a Printer

1. Start Print Manager.
2. Select the printer to audit.
3. Select Auditing from the Security menu.
4. Choose the auditing properties for the groups and users you wish to audit and set the appropriate audit events.

Table 8.3 lists the events that can be audited and the possible actions reported by the events.

Table 8.2 Categories of Access Through Print Manager

Permission	Description
Full Control	Gives a user complete control and access to a printer. Administrators, power users, server operators, and print operators have full control permission by default. (NT Server does not have a Power User group.)
Manage Documents	Provides a user the ability to change anything related to all documents for a Printer. The creator owner of a printer has Manage Documents permission by default.
Print	Allows a user to submit jobs to a printer. The Everyone group has Print permission.
No Access	Prohibits all access to a printer. This permission must be explicitly assigned to a user or group.

Table 8.3 Printer Events That Can Be Audited

Event	Actions Reported
Print	Printing of documents to the printer
Full Control	Changing job settings, pausing, restarting, moving, and deleting documents, sharing a printer, and changing printer properties
Delete	Deleting a printer
Change Permissions	Changing permissions for a printer
Take Ownership	Taking ownership of a printer

All audited events are trapped in the Security event log. Event Viewer is used to review the audited events and event details (see page 61).

8.4 INSTALLING AND CONFIGURING PRINTERS

Print Manager is used to create a new printer or modify an existing printer. As mentioned in the Architecture section of this chapter (see page 257), you do not need to install a remote printer on NT if it is managed by another NT system. You can simply connect to the printer using Print Manager, and NT will use the driver on the server.

The installation process is as simple as it is in Windows 3.x systems. The following outline covers the basic steps for installing a printer. Other sections in the chapter discuss how to configure various aspects of the printer such as sharing the printer after it is installed or configuring the ports that a printer uses.

Installing a Printer

1. Select Create Printer from the Printer menu. Enter a name for the printer. The printer name will show up everywhere the printer is shown, so make sure it is descriptive. You may want to use a name such as Accounting Laserjet IV or Laserjet IV—Accounting instead of just the department name. The name can be from 1 to 32 characters.

2. Select a driver for the printer. You may have to use a generic driver for your printer if it is not listed (such as an HP Laserjet driver for HP compatibles) or use a driver supplied from another source.

3. Enter a description for the printer. This description appears when network users browse the printers on the network. You can use the description to provide additional information about the printer.

4. Select a destination for the printer in the Print to: box. You can select a local port (i.e., LPT1: or COM2:), a file, or a network address or enter a local port that is not listed. If you are installing a network interface printer, see the section on network printers (see page 269) later in this chapter.

5. Share the printer if necessary. You can click the Share This Printer on the

Network box and share the printer as part of the installation process. Simply click the box and enter a share name and optionally a location for the printer. The Location information shows up in the Connect to Printer dialog box whenever a user browses printers on the network.

6. Enter the location of the NT distribution files if necessary. This step is required only if NT needs to install a driver that is not already installed on the system.

7. Assign any special features for the printer.

As soon as the printer is created, you can use it either on the local system or share it over the network.

8.5 CHANGING PRINTER PROPERTIES

8.5.1 Installing and Changing Drivers

Printer drivers are only one of the properties that you may wish to install or change for a printer. You may purchase an updated driver for your printer or possibly install a second driver for a printer if your system has mixed RISC and x86 NT systems.

RISC systems must have a driver installed for each type of RISC system installed on the network. Each different RISC system such as an DEC Alpha or MIPS system has a different binary architecture and requires a separate driver. If your network has different RISC systems, then you must have the correct driver for each RISC system loaded either on the RISC system or on the server. Placing multiple drivers on the server is the best way to handle them because you will have a central place to maintain all your drivers.

When you install the drivers on the server, each system downloads the appropriate driver for its processor.

Installing Printer Drivers

1. Start Print Manager and select the printer you wish to modify.

2. Select Properties from the toolbar or the Printer menu.

3. Select Other in the Driver box.

4. Specify the location for the driver. This should be the location of the driver and the PRINTER.INF file. You may have different locations for these files on your network if you have different types of systems installed.

5. Select the new driver from the list.

Once you have completed these steps, Print Manager installs the driver on your system.

8.5.2 Other Properties

You can change many other properties besides the printer driver with the Printer Properties command. Printer properties can be accessed from the toolbar and the Printer menu. You must be logged on as an administrator, server operator, or print operator to change a printer's properties.

The Printer Properties dialog box is the same dialog box you saw in the Install Printer process. Using this dialog box, you can change any of the properties that were set during installation. This section focuses on changing properties that are specific to the Printer Properties dialog box. For properties such as sharing a printer, see the next section in this chapter.

The Printer Properties dialog box provides access to a number of other functions, which are listed in Table 8.4.

8.6 SHARING AND UNSHARING A PRINTER

You can share a printer when it is installed by clicking the Share This Printer on the Network check box during the installation process. This check box is located on the Printer Properties dialog box and can be accessed after installation by selecting the Printer Properties command from the toolbar or the Printer menu.

After you have clicked the check box, simply fill in the Share Name and optionally the location. You may also want to change the description because this field will be displayed in the Connect to Printer dialog box in the Printer Information area. The Location field also shows up in the Connect to Printer dialog box along with the printer name and the name of the driver.

NT systems and Windows for Workgroups workstations use the printer name to connect to printers on NT systems. The printer name can be up to 32 characters in length.

Use care in choosing the Share Name if you have any DOS-based clients on your network. They can only see and connect to a share name that is 12 characters within the 8.3 file name format. The default Share Name is the name of the printer. A default share name is automatically constructed by Print Manager and truncated to a format that DOS systems can recognize.

Table 8.4 Buttons on the Printer Properties Dialog Box

Button	Description
Setup	The Setup button displays a Printer Setup dialog box that is specific to your particular printer. This dialog box usually looks somewhat similar to the Windows 3.x Printer Setup dialog boxes for the same printer.
Details	The Details button displays the Printer Details dialog box for the selected printer. This dialog box allows you to set available hours, separator file to be used, additional ports for the printer, priority, and other configuration options. It also provides access to the Job Defaults dialog box for choosing default orientation, forms, and other options.
Settings	The Settings button provides access to particular hardware settings for the port used by the printer.

Sharing a Printer (Print Manager)

1. Start Print Manager.
2. Select the printer to share.
3. Select Properties from the Printer menu.
4. Click the Share check box.
5. Change other properties as needed.
6. Close the dialog box.

8.7 DELETING PRINTERS

You can delete a printer with either Print Manager or RegEdit. Notice how much shorter the steps are by using Print Manager. Print Manager is also much less hazardous to the health of your NT system than RegEdit.

The easiest way to delete a printer is by using Print Manager.

Deleting a Printer (Print Manager)

1. Select the printer you wish to delete.
2. Select the remove command from the toolbar or from the Printer menu.
3. Answer Yes to the confirmation question. The Printer is gone.

Changes to printers and print shares are normally made with Print Manager, but there may be a time when you may need to delete a printer or print share manually when you are troubleshooting your system. The following procedure uses RegEdit to accomplish this task.

Deleting a Printer (RegEdit32)

1. Search for all references to the printer or print share in the Registry under the following keys: HKEY_CURRENT_USER, HKEY_LOCAL_MACHINE, HKEY_USERS.
2. Delete every reference to the printer or print share except the ones in the ControlSets other than CurrentControlSet.

These changes will not take effect until you log out and back in.

8.8 CONNECTING AND DISCONNECTING TO PRINTERS

Using a printer that is connected to or managed by another system requires you to connect to the printer over the network. Print Manager can be used for this task, as well as a number of other applications. Many applications have a Network button located on the printer setup dialog box that allows you to perform the same connect operation as Print Manager. You can also call the WNetAddConnection and WNetCancelConnection API functions from a programming language such as C or VB. This chapter focuses on only the options provided by the standard NT and client tools (such as Print Manager and the NET commands), although the same techniques work in many applications.

The process of connecting to a remote printer in Print Manager is identical to connecting to a remote file service in File Manager.

Connecting to a Remote Printer (Print Manager)

1. Start Print Manager.
2. Select the Connect To Printer command from the toolbar or the Print menu. This command displays the Connect To Printer dialog box that lists most of the workgroups, servers, and printers on your network. If you have servers on your network that do not support browsing, they are not listed. For instance, if you are running Pathworks for NT and have a Pathworks 4.2 or earlier server, you can connect to the printers managed by the Pathworks server, but the servers and printers do not show up in the browse list unless the Pathworks Naming service is installed.
3. Select a printer from the list. You may need to double-click a network or server to display the servers/printers in that group. The servers, printers, and networks each have their own icon. A plus sign (+) is displayed to the left of any item in the list that may be expanded.
4. Click OK.

A neat feature of the Connect To Printer dialog box is the information box at the bottom. This little box shows the description of the printer, the status, and the number of documents waiting for the printer. Let's use an example to describe how this information can be used:

> It's four thirty on Friday and you need to print a 100-page proposal before you leave. Your department has two laser printers and the department next door has four, one of which is a 16-ppm (page per minute) printer. Which printer should you send your document to? The easiest way to find out is to bring up the Connect to Printer dialog box and check its Print Information box. Simply click on each printer one at a time and note the printer's status and the number of documents waiting on that printer. Pick the one with 0 documents or the shortest list and the fastest output. You can send the job to the printer and then walk over in 6 minutes to make sure it has plenty of paper.

If you are connecting to a printer that is not shown on your list because its server cannot be browsed or you know the server and printer name, you can enter the printer information directly. In the Printer box at the top of the dialog box, enter the server and printer name in the following format:

`\\Server\PrinterName`

Once you have entered the server name and printer names, click OK.

You can disconnect from the remote printer by selecting the Disconnect Printer command from the toolbar or the Printer menu Remove Printer command. You can also remove a network printer you have connected to by using the Remove Printer command when the printer is selected.

When you connect to a printer served by a non-NT system NT will tell you that the server does not have a suitable printer driver available. You will be asked if you would like to pick one for your system to use; I call this a "polite user interface." Simply choose the correct printer from the list and click OK. If the server is an NT system, you will not go through this step because NT simply uses the printer driver on the server, unless the server does not have a suitable driver.

8.9 Using Multiple Printers Connected to One Print Device

You can create numerous printers and point them to one print device, which allows you to set different criteria on each printer such as access times or priorities. The printers can be located on the same machine as the physical print device or on other NT workstations or servers.

Multiple printers are really handy when you use a print device that can switch between PostScript and non-PostScript jobs. For these types of print devices, you should create one printer using a PostScript driver and another that uses the generic driver for the print device. This procedure allows you to send both types of jobs to the printer without the need to reconfigure it.

8.10 Printer Pools

A printer pool is a handy way to improve the throughput of your printing operations drastically. With the price of printers continuing to drop as the performance goes up, you can take three or four laser printers and attach them to an NT server and have one heck of a fast printer pool.

When you configure printers in a pool, the total throughput for the pool is the sum of the throughput for each printer. For instance, if you have three 8-ppm printers, your pool output should be approximately 24 ppm.

I use the term *approximately* because several factors have an impact on the performance of the pool. If you routinely send very long documents to a pool, your performance may be down. This decrease in performance would occur because each document would be sent to a specific printer. If you have four printers and only send three long documents to the pool, three of the printers will print the documents while the fourth will be idle. If, on the other hand, you send 20 five- or ten-page documents, all the printers will fire up, and the load will be spread across them all.

Another thing that has an impact on the performance of your pool is the servers that manage the printers. If you use a Pentium with only 16MB of memory to handle several very fast (16-ppm) printers, you may bog down the server and slow the throughput to the printers. If, on the other hand, you put 32MB on the server, the printers should fly. NT is very sensitive to the amount of memory in the system, the more the better.

Creating a Printer Pool

1. Physically attach all the printers to the server or the network. The printers can be attached to a single server, to multiple servers with shared connections, or as network devices.

2. Use Print Manager to create a single printer that points to all three printers.

3. Using Print Manager, point the printer to all the printer ports that will be used. Use Print Manager and select Printer Details. Then select the Print to Additional Ports option to select the ports that the print devices are attached to.

There are several things to keep in mind for printer pools:

☞ Make sure all print devices are of exactly the same type or capability. For instance, you could have LaserJet IVsi and LaserJet IV printers mixed in a pool, but not LaserJet IV and Epson printers.

☞ Any action on the printer takes effect on all print devices. These actions include changing properties and pausing the printer.

☞ Jobs are sent to the print devices in the order of how the print devices were added to the pool. Make sure that you add the fastest printer first because it will be the most heavily used printer in the pool.

☞ You can mix the types of ports used for the print devices in a pool. For instance, you can have two locally attached print devices (LPT or COM) and two network print devices.

☞ All the print devices in the pool should be in close physical proximity. This arrangement reduces the leg work required to find out where your document printed.

Figure 8.2 illustrates a printer pool with three identical laser printers.

8.11 CONSIDERATIONS FOR SPECIAL PRINTERS

8.11.1 Direct Network Interface Printers

Network interfaces for printers are a handy way to free up resources on your server and improve your printing performance at the same time. Network interfaces generally plug into the special video port of HP Laserjet printers or into the parallel printer port using a special network print server such as NetQue from Emulex. The difference in network printers normally is their support for different protocols. For instance, the HP printer interfaces use DLC, whereas many others such as those from Emulex and Goldkey support TCP/IP, LAT, and other popular protocols.

Network interfaces reduce the need for special cables and ports because they can attach to the network just like a workstation or server. They also allow NT to manage the printer just as if it were directly attached to the NT server.

Fig. 8.2 A printer named LaserPool that consists of three physical laser printers. Users see only one printer named LaserPool.

Most network interfaces also improve the performance of your printer if it is a fast laser printer like the HP LaserjetIV si.

Another nice benefit of the network interface is the ability to manage the printer remotely if your printer and network interface support remote management. This feature should be coming to more and more printers in the future. Remote management usually means you can access the printer over the network and check its status and issue commands to change its configuration.

8.11.2 DLC Printers

The network printer options from HP typically use DLC to talk to the printer. DLC is directly supported by NT and must be installed before you can configure a printer using this type of interface (see page 101 for more information).

Configuring a Laserjet with a DLC Network Interface

1. Decide which NT system will be the print server for the printer.
2. Install the DLC protocol in the Control Panel Network applet. Choose Add Software.
3. Use Print Manager to create a printer for the new device.

4. Select Network Port from the list and then HP or Other Network Port.

5. Configure the network address for the printer and name the port.

6. Share the printer with a descriptive name. No other computer needs to have DLC installed to use the printer over the network.

8.11.3 TCP/IP Printers

The TCP/IP printing support of NT Server 3.5 is another one of those features that should make using printers on a network much easier. NT Server can manage a TCP/IP printer using the TCP/IP protocol on only the server that is used to control the printer. Other NT-compatible systems on the network can print on the printer using the same protocol they use for connecting to the NT server. Before installing a printer using TCP/IP, you must make sure that the TCP/IP printer support is installed (see page 106).

Creating a TCP/IP Printer

1. Make sure that the Microsoft TCP/IP printing service is running.

2. Create the printer using Print Manager.

3. In the Print To box choose Other.

4. Choose LPR Port.

5. Enter the host address or name of the system providing the lpd (line printer daemon) service.

6. Enter the name of the printer on the system providing the lpd service. For instance on Emulex printer servers, the default is PASSTHRU, whereas Goldkey print servers use HP_PRINTER.

Notice that step 5 can use the host IP address or the host name to define the printer destination. Using the actual name makes much more sense because it readily identifies the printer destination when you view the list. I carry this one step farther and make the host name and the printer name almost the same. I simply prefix the host name with NJ for NetJet or something similar for your printer server. This step uniquely links the destination printer and print server name and eliminates many potential mistakes with mismatched printer destinations (IP address) and printers (printer name). Make sure that you can PING (see page 110) a printer with its name before defining the printer. The print server IP address and name must be defined in the HOSTS file (see page 94), WINS (see page 95), or another method of name resolution.

8.11.4 PostScript Printer Characteristics

PostScript print devices require only slightly more care and feeding than generic print devices. PostScript print devices process print jobs that consist of the PostScript language format in the print job. PostScript jobs are usually sent as ASCII files that are processed by the print device. PostScript print devices are normally much slower than other printers, taking what seems to be an eternity to print a file.

PostScript print devices also cause problems when you try to print non-PostScript files on them. These problems usually occur when you try to print an ASCII file from the NT DOS prompt, resulting in no printer output or an error on the printer. Likewise, when you send a PostScript file to a non-PostScript print device, you get a real mess. The print device usually starts printing lots of strange-looking codes on the device, prompting users to scream.

You should make sure that PostScript-specific drivers and configuration files are used for all PostScript printers. For instance, if you need a separator page, you must use the PSCRIPT.SEP file instead of the generic files.

8.12 SEPARATOR PAGES

Separator pages are files that NT uses to separate documents that print on a printer. The files can contain codes that cause NT to print various types of information on the separator page identifying the user, file, print time, and so forth.

Each separator file uses a series of codes to determine the actions and text that is printed each time a document prints, as shown in Table 8.5.

NT comes with several default separator files:

☞ PCL.SEP causes a printer to use switch to PCL mode.
☞ PSCRIPT.SEP causes a printer to use PostScript mode.
☞ PSLANMAN.SEP ejects a page before each document that prints.

You can specify only one separator page at a time per printer. The current separator page can be changed at any time. The Printer Details dialog box in Print Manager is used to change the current separator page. You can access Printer Details by first selecting Properties from the Printer menu and then clicking the Details button.

Simply enter the name of the separator page file in the Separator File box and click OK. You can also select a separator page file by using the ... button next to the box. Separator pages are normally stored in the \WINNT35\SYSTEM32 directory.

Be sure to test the separator page after you have made the preceding changes by printing any file on the printer.

The best approach to building separator page files is to copy the standard NT file that most closely matches the printer you will use. For instance, for a Laserjet using PCL, choose the PCL.SEP page file and copy it to a new name. Change the file using Notepad or some other ASCII editor and test.

8.13 PRINTER MESSAGES

NT automatically sends a message to the user who submitted a print job notifying him or her of the status of a print job when it completes. This feature is handy for network users who are normally located at some distance from the physical print device. Figure 8.3 shows what a typical message looks like.

Table 8.5 Separator Page Codes

Code	Description
/	Defines escape character for the file. Must be on the first line in the file. Make sure that this character does not conflict with other characters such as the \ used in file path names.
/B/M	Turns on printing double-width block characters. Turned off by a /U code.
/B/S	Turns on printing single-width block characters. Turned off by a /U code.
/D	Prints the print date for the job.
/E	Causes the printer to eject a page before printing the file. This is usually the last line in a separator file.
/Fpathname	Causes Print Manager to print the file pointed to by path name. Handy way to change the contents of the separator page simply by changing this file.
/Hnn	Sends a hex code to the printer. The PCL.SEP file included with NT shows an example of using this code to send commands directly to the printer.
/I	Prints the job number for the print job.
/L*****	Prints the characters following /L until a new escape code is encountered.
/n	Skips the number of lines specified by n.
/N	Prints the user name of the user submitting the print job.
/T	Prints the time the job printed. Useful with /D.
/U	Turns off printing block characters.
/W	Allows you to change the separator page width. The default is 80 with a maximum of 256.

This message can be displayed on systems that pick up messages from the NT Messenger service. NT systems do this automatically, but Windows for Workgroups may not. The solution is to start WinPopUp in tne Windows for Workgroups client.

Starting WinPopUp on Windows for Workgroups Clients

1. Start Control Panel on the Windows for Workgroups client.
2. Start the Network applet.
3. Click the Startup button.
4. Click the Enable WinPopUp check box.
5. Click OK.

WinPopUp starts the next time Windows restarts. You can also start Win-

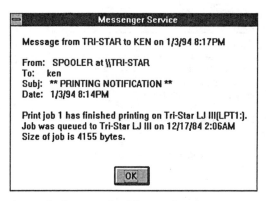

Fig. 8.3 A message triggered when a print job completed.

PopUp directly by starting WINPOPUP.EXE in the Windows directory. Make sure that you do not close WinPopUp or you will disable messaging.

You can install WinPopUp over the network for remote users. Simply edit the WIN.INI file and place WinPopUp in the Load= line:

```
Load=Winpopup.exe
```

Specifying WINPOPUP.EXE on the Load= line starts WinPopUp as an icon each time Windows starts. You could automate the task by using SMS or another tool to update the user's WIN.INI file automatically the next time the user logs on.

8.14 PRINTING FROM AN NT SYSTEM TO A REMOTE NT PRINTER

NT clients printing on remote printers controlled by other NT systems is a dream environment. An NT system does not normally need a driver installed for a remote printer as long as that printer is managed by another NT system.

When a user connects to a remote printer from an NT workstation or server, the spooler determines which printer driver is needed and then copies the driver to the DRIVERS directory of the user's system. If the spooler determines that the driver already exists but is an older version than the one on the server, it automatically updates the driver with the new version. The user must have write permission to the DRIVERS directory if he or she is using a remote printer.

The exception to this rule is when the driver already exists on the NT system that the user is trying to connect from. In this case the connect operation works even if the spooler is not able to replace the driver because there already is a compatible driver installed. NT in this instance automatically uses the driver on the system managing the printer by downloading it into memory on the local system for the duration of the printing requirements.

One problem you may run into is with NT clients printing to printers that are managed by NT systems running on different architectures. For instance an Intel client prints to a printer managed by an Alpha NT Server. In this scenario, the NT system managing the printer must have drivers for both systems available for the client to be able to use the driver.

Installing a Nonnative Print Driver on a Server

1. From a remote system (not the system managing the printer), log on to the domain with an Administrative account.
2. Start Print Manager.
3. Choose Server Viewer from the Printer menu.
4. Select the server that manages the printer you wish to install the driver for.
5. Select the first printer you need to install a driver for.
6. Choose Properties from the Printer menu.
7. Enter the location for the printer drivers.
8. Repeat steps 5 and 6 for each printer that needs drivers for the architecture of the system you are currently logged on from.

8.15 PRINTERS ON NON-NT SYSTEMS

Printing on non-NT print devices is slightly different than using an NT print device. A non-NT print device in this discussion is considered any printer that is attached to another system such as Windows for Workgroups or UNIX and is managed by that system. NT cannot use the printer driver from a non-NT system and must have a locally installed NT driver for the printer. NT prompts you to install on your system a driver that matches the target Printer.

This process works in the same fashion as printing on a Windows 3.x system. The printer you install on NT is simply connected to the print queue on the target system. You must be a member of the Administrators group to install a printer because the driver must be into the Windows NT directory tree.

8.16 USING PRINTERS FROM NETWORK CLIENTS

Microsoft network clients share the same basic printer connection interface via the NET commands. Windows systems add another interface via Print Manager or Windows 95.

8.16.1 Workgroup Add-On for MS-DOS and MS Client

The NET USE command is used to connect to printers from MS-DOS systems using the Workgroup Add-On for MS-DOS. The syntax is

```
NET USE port \\computername\sharename [password]
```

The following command illustrates how to use this command to attach to the LAS printer on the KENS server:

```
NET USE LPT1: \\KENS\LAS
```

Once this command is complete the user can access this printer as LPT1. To disconnect from the printer on LPT1:

```
NET USE LPT1: /delete
```

The print server section in this chapter (see page 278) contains information on other printer commands for the Workgroup Add-On for MS-DOS.

8.16.2 Windows for Workgroups

Windows for Workgroups users can connect to printers on the domain quickly. Print Manager makes the connections in much the same way that File Manager makes file resource connections. The Printer applet in Control Panel can also be used to connect printers, as well as the Network button found on many Printer dialogs in applications.

Connecting to Network Printers with Print Manager

1. Start Print Manager.
2. Select the printer you wish to connect.
3. Click the Connect button.
4. Choose the correct port from the device list.
5. Choose the network printer from the browse box or enter the UNC name in the Path box.
6. Click OK.

Connecting to Network Printers with Control Panel

1. Start Control Panel.
2. Double-click the Printers applet icon.
3. Select the printer you wish to connect.
4. Click the Connect button.
5. Select the port to connect from the list.
6. If the port is not already connected to the appropriate network printer, click the Network button.
7. Choose the correct port from the device list.
8. Choose the network printer from the browse box or enter the UNC name in the Path box.
9. Click OK.
10. Click OK on the Connect box.
11. Click Close.

Connecting to Network Printers Using NET USE

You can use the same command prompt approach as the Work Group Add-On for MS-DOS and MS Client.

1. Enter the proper NET USE command at the command prompt. The following example shows the successful completion of this command.

```
net use lpt2: \\ntas-tri-star\hp_lj_ii
```

The command completed successfully.

Newer applications also provide the ability to connect to network printers in the Printer Setup dialog box. This is usually indicated by a Network button on the dialog box. Click the button and it should display the standard browse dialog box for connecting to printers.

8.16.3 Windows 95

Windows 95 incorporates a totally new printing system compared to Windows for Workgroups. The Printers folder (accessed from the Start menu, Settings option) contains icons for all the printers for a client and the Add Printer application. Add Printer is a wizard that walks you through the configuration of a printer. The Printers folder is shown in Figure 8.4.

The Printers folder is accessed from the Start menu and can optionally be placed on the desktop. You can also place any printer icon or the Add Printer application directly on the desktop.

Adding a Network Printer with Windows 95

1. Open the Printers folder and start the Add Printer application.
2. Follow the prompts of the wizard.
3. Specify Network Printer instead of Local Printer by highlighting the Network Printer button.
4. Enter the queue name (UNC) or click the Browse button to select the printer. Drill down with the mouse to select the printer from the browse list.
5. Answer the remaining prompts to complete the installation.

Fig. 8.4 A sample Printer folder with only one printer and Microsoft Fax connection. Printers are created with the Add Printer application.

You can change a local printer to a network printer by using the Printer application for that printer and accessing the printer's properties. Windows 95 also lets you create printer ports, which are simply connections to network printers. A printer port does not require that a printer exist or be connected to the port when it is created. This is a big change over other versions of Windows, which required a specific printer be attached to a network port. Figure 8.5 illustrates the new interface for a printer in Windows 95.

Connecting to a Network Printer with Windows 95

1. Start the Printer application for the printer you wish to connect to the network resource. Select the Properties option from the Printer menu. You can optionally simply right-click on the icon for the printer and select properties.
2. Click the Details tab.
3. Choose the port to use for the printer from the drop-down list. You can easily add a new connection by clicking the Add Port button and choosing Browse.
4. Click OK.

The Properties dialog box is shown in Figure 8.6.
The NET commands also work with Windows 95.

8.17 NON-NT PRINT SERVERS

8.17.1 Windows for Workgroups

Windows 95 and Windows for Workgroups 3.11 are the preferred choice for non-NT computer-based print servers.

Windows for Workgroups handles printers well with Print Manager and third-party tools such as the laser printer upgrades from LaserMaster Corporation.

The main drawback to using Windows 95 or Windows for Workgroups or any other system (except for NT) as a print server is that the operating system

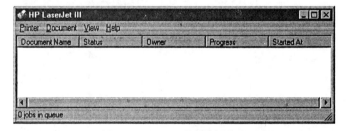

Fig. 8.5 The new Printer application has a nice clean interface. The Printer menu contains the Properties option for access to the detailed setup for the printer, including network connections.

Fig. 8.6 The Properties dialog box contains the network settings for a printer and most other printer-related settings. The network information is contained under the Details tab.

does not automatically share the printer drivers with NT. Windows for Workgroups uses a printer driver just like all Windows 3.x systems in that the driver must be installed and configured on the workstation before you can connect to and use a printer.

The steps for creating your Windows for Workgroups print server are deceptively simple.

Creating a Windows for Workgroups Print Server

1. Connect the printer and configure Windows for Workgroups with the proper driver.

2. Share the printer with Print Manager.

3. Connect to the printer from remote workstations.

8.17.2 Workgroup Add-On for MS-DOS

The Workgroup Add-On for MS-DOS can be used as a low-cost print server on low-end DOS systems. I suggest using Workgroup Add-On for MS-DOS only for systems that do not run Windows well such as 386/25 or slower systems or systems with less than 4MB of memory. Systems that run Windows adequately should use Windows for Workgroups or Windows 95 as a print server.

The steps for creating your Workgroup Add-On for MS-DOS print server are easy and are almost exactly the same as the steps for Windows for Workgroups.

Creating a Workgroup Add-On for MS-DOS Print Server

1. Connect the printer and configure Workgroup Add-On for MS-DOS with the proper driver.

2. Share the printer with NET SHARE.

3. Connect to the printer from remote workstations.

Once you have shared the printer, you can manage print jobs from the Workgroup Add-On from MS-DOS workstation. The command used for managing printers and displaying information about current print jobs is NET PRINT.

NET PRINT works with the current system and other systems. The syntax for displaying information about print jobs is

```
NET PRINT \\computername[\printername] | port
```

Entering NET PRINT with no options displays all printers on the current system and the respective print jobs for each. You can display the print queue for a remote system by entering

```
NET PRINT \\DOSPRT
```

This command displays all the print queues and associated print jobs for the system named DOSPRT. You can refine the output by entering the printer name after the computer name as in the following example:

```
NET PRINT \\DOSPRT\PRTR1
```

The other option for displaying information is to use the port name for a local printer to display the associated print queue and print jobs. The following command displays the printers on LPT2:

```
NET PRINT LPT2:
```

The output of the command displays the name of the queue and the details of the print jobs. The details include both totals for all jobs for a queue and the individual job name, status, and size. The following command shows the command format and the resulting output:

```
NET PRINT LPT1:

    Printer queues
    Name           Job #      Size        Status
    --------------------------------------------------------------
    KENS Queue     2 Jobs                 * Queue Active *
                   102        231         Printing
                   105        1022        Waiting
```

NET PRINT can also be used to manage your print queues. The syntax for the management options is

```
NET PRINT \\computername[\printername] | port job# /pause -
    | /resume | /delete
```

The options for this command (/pause, /resume, and /delete) cannot be used at the same time. Table 8.6 explains these options.

The job number is entered after the printer specification. The next command shows how to delete job number 102 on the current system:

```
NET PRINT lpt1: 102 /delete
```

You can also specify a computer name if you wish to delete a print job on a remote system. The following command deletes job 102 on KENS:

```
NET PRINT \\KENS 102 /delete
```

Did you notice that print job numbers are unique for a given system even if the system has multiple printers? These numbers allow you to specify only the computer name in a command related to print jobs.

```
NET PRINT \\DOSPRT\PRTR1
NET SHARE sharename=portname [/remark:"text"] [/saveshare:no]
    [/full:password]
```

The syntax looks much more complex than it is. The following command shares the printer attached to LPT2: as DOTPRT and adds a comment:

```
NET SHARE DOTPRT=LPT2: /remark:"Kens office"
```

The following example performs the same share except that it assigns the password MINE to the printer:

```
NET SHARE DOTPRT=LPT2: /remark:"Kens office" /full:MINE
```

Adding a share password allows you to restrict the printer to users who know the share password.

NET SHARE is also used to delete existing shares. The following command deletes the printer DOTPRT:

```
NET SHARE DOTPRT/delete
```

8.17.3 NetWare Printers

Did I say that correctly? What are NetWare printers doing in a chapter on NT Server printers? The NWLINK and NetWare Compatible Gateway provide

Table 8.6 Net Print Options

Option	Description
/Pause	Suspends the print job specified with the command until /Resume or /Delete is entered.
/Resume	Causes a paused print job to continue.
/Delete	Deletes the specified print job.

access to both file and print services on NetWare servers. Chapter 3 has information on installing the gateway and sharing print and file resources on a NetWare server. The section also includes information on sharing NetWare printers to NT Server clients.

CHAPTER 9

Disaster Preparedness and Management

NT provides many different options for disaster preparedness. The most obvious are tape backup and some type of on-line backup for disk drives such as mirrored or duplexed drives. More sophisticated systems use RAID 5 to provide faster access to disk storage and fault tolerance.

What happens when a critical component such as a CPU or a memory chip goes out? This type of problem usually brings down a server regardless of what type of backup you have for the drives. Octopus Technologies provides a product called Octopus that provides real-time backup of selected files or directories to another server. Digital Equipment Corporation and AT&T are currently (as of Spring 1995) working on clustering technology for NT. Clustering should allow NT to have two or more servers in a cluster providing improved performance and hot-swapover if a server goes down.

Other aspects of disaster preparedness are the mundane but critical things such as backup schedules and off-site storage of backup media. These items are often left over and fall by the wayside but can be the most critical part of the plan. Remember that the job is not complete until the paperwork is done.

9.1 MAINTAINING TAPE DEVICES

NT supports a variety of different tape devices for backup. Before you start a backup on an NT tape device, you must install the tape device in the system and configure NT. Once this is completed, you can use the device with the NT Backup program.

NT supports several different tape devices out of the box. Hardware vendors that offer new products should also provide drivers if the current drivers don't work with their products. You may be able to use the generic option "4 millimeter DAT drive" for different drives of this type. I have successfully used this option with drives from Conner (MS2000DAT) and Digital Equipment (TLZ06).

DAT and DLT drives are my favorite option because of their high capacity and fast performance over older drives. The new DLT drives from some vendors offer extremely high capacity in a small package.

Adding a Tape Device

1. Start the NT setup program.
2. Select Add/Remove Tape Devices from the Options menu.
3. Select your drive from the list or select the Other (Requires a disk from a hardware manufacturer) option, which allows you to load a driver that is not listed.
4. Once you have selected your tape device from the list, click the Install button to complete loading the driver.
5. Once the tape device is loaded, you must restart NT before the change takes effect.

Another option for maintaining tape devices is to use the Tape Devices applet from the NT Resource Kit in Control Panel. This applet is designed to perform one task only and that is to make life easier for managing tape devices under NT. It is very useful for many tasks. For instance, I had removed a Colorado Memory Systems floppy tape from an NT system and all of a sudden the SCSI tape drive quit working. I tried to reinstall using Setup and checked the devices on the system, among other things, but to no avail. Then I fired up the Tape Devices applet, selected the tape drive, and clicked Setup. Tape Devices informed me that as soon as I started the 4-mm dat service the device would be ready. When I clicked the Start button, the drive was ready.

Tape devices can also be used to check the status of your tape device. Figures 9.1 through 9.3 illustrate the interface of the applet and show off its features. The following steps show how to use the applet.

Fig. 9.1 Tape Devices dialog box showing one tape drive loaded.

Fig. 9.2 Tape Device Detail dialog box showing the current status of the device, the SCSI port used for the device, and details for the controller the device is attached to.

Fig. 9.3 Tape Device Setup dialog box is used to add or remove a driver for a tape drive. You can also start and stop the drive from this dialog box.

Tape Devices is a handy tool to have around for managing tape devices.

Adding a Tape Drive with Tape Devices

1. Start the Tape Device applet in Control Panel.
2. Select the tape drive to install. If the correct drive is not listed, make sure it is attached to the system and turned on, and then click the Rescan button.
3. Click the Setup button.
4. Click the Add button to display the list of available drivers.
5. Select the correct driver from the list.
6. Complete the prompts for installing the new driver. You will probably have to reboot the system to recognize the new driver.

Removing a Tape Drive with Tape Devices

1. Start the Tape Device applet in Control Panel.
2. Select the tape drive to remove.

3. Click the Setup button.

4. Click the Remove button.

5. Complete the prompts to remove the driver.

Stopping a Tape Drive with Tape Devices

1. Start the Tape Device applet in Control Panel.

2. Select the tape drive to stop.

3. Click the Setup button.

4. Select the driver to stop and click the Stop button.

After NT is restarted, the new tape device will be visible to NT. Using the Backup program, you can select Hardware Setup from the Operations menu to verify that the new device is loaded. Selecting Hardware Setup displays a dialog box that should list the new drive. If the drive is not visible as the current selection in the list, drop the list by clicking on the down arrow and you should see the new drive. If not, there was most likely a problem in configuring the new device with Setup.

9.2 TAPE BACKUP PROGRAMS

9.2.1 NT's Backup Program

NT's backup program works okay but it is not my favorite. Either the graphical interface or command prompt method is very slow when used with a floppy interface tape (such as those from Colorado Memory Systems), and I do mean slow. Neither of the programs uses any compression on the tape so the backup tapes are limited in how much they can back up.

The capability of the NT Backup program is also somewhat limited. Backup does not have the ability to store catalogs or predefined backup sets. Other parts of the interface are also rather rudimentary compared to the Central Point or Norton backup programs for Windows 3.x. Arcada Software (formerly Conner Systems) developed the program for Microsoft and markets a more powerful backup program named Backup Exec. More information on Backup Exec is provided after the NT backup programs.

Other companies are working on 32-bit versions of their backup programs that should work well with NT. More applications for NT will be available as Windows 95 moves into the market because both systems use the WIN32 API. Be careful when using non-NT-specific programs and make sure that they support backing up the NT system files such as the Registry before depending upon them for your backup needs.

You should also note that Windows 95 includes backup agents for Backup EXEC but not for the standard backup program. Windows 95 also includes an agent for the Cheyenne backup program for NT.

9.2.1.1 NT Backup (Graphical Method) The NT backup program is easy to use for casual backups and for restoring files. Make sure that your tape device is installed and configured for NT as detailed in the Adding a Tape Device section (page 284) in this chapter.

I suggest running a test of the tape device to make sure that it works correctly before proceeding too far. Perform a backup of just a few directories to the device and make sure that you have Verify After Backup checked.

The backup program is composed of three windows and a menu across the top. Table 9.1 provides the definitions of the various windows.

Backup creates a separate save set for each volume that is backed up.

The requirement to use a formatted tape poses a potential problem when you perform a backup that spans several tapes and you don't happen to have a formatted tape around. Backup rejects the new tape until it has been formatted and you can't format it until the backup is complete. The only solution is to use a formatted tape or abort the backup and restart it after you have formatted the tape.

You will be forced to erase a tape before using it when you use a tape for the first time with backup.

Erasing a Tape (Backup—Graphical Method)

1. Place the tape to be erased in the drive.
2. Select the Erase Tape option on the Operations menu.

Performing a Backup (Backup—Graphical Method)

1. Select the files to back up.
2. Place a tape in the tape drive.
3. Select the Backup option either from the Operations menu or the Backup icon.
4. Complete the Backup Information dialog box and click OK.

Backup takes over and performs its tasks without interruption.

The Backup Information dialog box appears after you have instructed backup to begin the Backup operation. The backup occurs when you click the

Table 9.1 Backup Program Windows

Window	Description
File	Contains a list of the directories and files on the currently selected drive. The directories and/or files selected for backup have the check box to the left of the name checked.
Drives	Shows the drives on the local system and any current network connections.
Tapes	Is normally minimized when you start backup and shows the current tape in the tape drive. The tape and creation date are shown on the left, and the drive and other information are shown on the right.

Backup icon or select Backup from the Operations menu. Table 9.2 contains the options and parameters displayed on the Backup Information dialog box.

Table 9.2 Backup Information Dialog Box Options

Option	Description
Current Tape	Displays the current tape name, if the tape has been used before.
Creation Date	Displays the date the original backup set was created or the date when it was last replaced.
Owner	The owner of the tape, which will be the user account name of the individual making the first backup to the tape.
Tape Name	Contains the name of the tape. The name can be 1 to 32 characters in length.
Append or Replace	The Operation box contains two options. Append instructs NT Backup to append the save set(s) to the tape. Replace instructs NT Backup to overwrite the contents of the tape. When Replace is specified and more than one backup set is required (for instance for multiple path names), NT Backup overwrites the tape with the first save set and then appends the balance of the save sets to the tape.
Verify	Causes NT Backup to verify the contents of the backup sets created. The verification process is performed in a second pass through the tape after the backup files are created.
Backup Local Registry	Causes NT Backup to back up the Registry information on the system running NT Backup. See the section on using RDisk on page 204 for more information on protecting the Registry backups on multiple systems.
Restrict Access to Owner or Administrator	Restricts access to the owner of the tape and a user with administrator privileges.
Drive Name	Displays the name of the drive backed up on the current save set.
Description	Allows you to add a description to your backup save set. Specifies the description text in the appropriate box.
Backup Type	Specifies the type of backup operation. Allowable options are:
	Normal — Specifies that a normal (full) backup be performed and that each file be marked as backed up.
	Copy — Performs a normal backup but will not mark the files as backed up.
	Incremental — Backs up all files that are marked as modified on the path specified. Files processed are marked as backed up.
	Differential — Performs an incremental backup but does not mark the files.
	Daily — Causes all files modified today to be backed up. The files processed will not be backed up.

Table 9.2 Backup Information Dialog Box Options (Continued)

Option	Description
Log File	Specifies the file name for the log file. The ... button beside the Log File box can be clicked to display a dialog box to select an existing log file.
Full Detail	Instructs Backup to write the full details of each operation to the log file, including the file names and directories processed in the backup.
Summary Only	Can be used to cause the log file to contain only exceptions and major operations, drastically reducing the size of the file and making it much easier to spot errors in the backup process.
Don't Log	Instructs Backup to not log any information.

9.2.1.2 NT Backup (Command Prompt)

The problem with the graphical Backup program is its lack of automation. The NTBackup program can be also accessed from the command prompt. Running NTBackup from the command line is better than the graphical method for setting up automated operations from a batch file. NTBackup is also useful in conjunction with the NT Scheduler's AT command.

NTBackup's command-line options provide many of the same features as the graphical format but are much more useful for backup operations because NTBackup can be used to automate the operations.

NTBackup solves this somewhat by using the familiar command-line interface and a variety of switches to control its operation. The syntax for the command follows. Note that BACKUP is the operation name and is the only valid operation.

```
NTBACKUP BACKUP [pathname(s) options]
```

pathname(s)   Describes the path(s) that the command will back up. The pathname is specified by listing the path(s) separated by spaces after the word BACKUP.

options   Specifies exactly how the backup operation will be performed. The options allowed are the same as the ones for the graphical backup command but use switches to select the option.

Table 9.3 lists each option. For full details on the options, see the section in this chapter (page 287) on the graphical NT Backup program.

Now that we have covered the gory details of syntax for this command, let's see how this command can be used to our advantage.

```
NTBACKUP BACKUP C:\ /D "Backup Number 1" /B /L -
"c:\BackupLog" /E /T NORMAL
```

Note that this command is continued on two lines for clarity only. The entire command must be on a single line whether executed at the DOS prompt or in a batch program.

Table 9.3 NT Backup Command Line Options

Option	Description
blank or /A	The mode option uses a blank or /A. /A instructs NTBackup to append the save set(s) to the tape. If /A is not specified, NTBackup overwrites the contents of the tape. When /A is not specified and more than one backup set is required (for instance for multiple path names), NTBackup overwrites the tape with the first save set and then appends the balance of the save sets to the tape.
/V	The verify option is specified with /V and causes NTBackup to verify the contents of the backup sets created. The verification process is performed in a second pass through the tape after the backup files are created.
/R	Restricts access to the owner of the resources backed up and a user with administrator privileges.
/D "text"	Allows you to add a description to your backup save set. Specifies the description text after the /D and a space. The text should be enclosed in quotes.
/B	Causes NT Backup to back up the Registry information on the system running NTBackup. See the section on using RDisk on page 204 for more information on protecting the Registry backups on multiple systems.
/T option	Specifies the type of backup operation. Allowable options are
	Normal Specifies that a normal (full) backup be performed and that each file be marked as backed up.
	Copy Performs a normal backup but does not mark the files as backed up.
	Incremental Backs up all files that are marked as modified on the path specified. Files processed are marked as backed up.
	Differential Performs an Incremental backup but does not mark the files.
	Daily Causes all files modified today to be backed up. The files processed are not backed up.
/L "filename"	/L is used to specify the file name for the log file. Place the file name in quotes and insert a space between /L and the name.
/E	/E can be used to cause the log file to contain only exceptions and major operations.

9.2.2 Using NTBackup with the NT Scheduler

The NT Scheduler service is powerful and easy to use. Chapter 2 has details on configuring the Scheduler service. One important distinction for the service is important when it is used to drive the NT Backup command. Remember the NT permissions and how all resources are affected? If the Scheduler is used with NT

Backup, then the account used by the Scheduler must be a member of the Backup Operators group.

This change can be made by running User Manager and placing the account for the Scheduler in the Backup Operators group. Make sure that you also provide for the account to be used on all servers in the domain.

I recommend using a batch program to contain the actual NT Backup command(s) that is used by the Scheduler. Using a batch program makes it easy to manage the command syntax and properly debug the process. You can even include the entire syntax for the Scheduler and the backup process in the batch program. You may want to create a Visual Basic program that sets up the entire process each time NT boots. Let's look at each of these options.

Using the Scheduler with a Backup Batch Program

1. Create a batch program with your backup commands (BACKUPNORM is used in this example).
2. Place the batch program in a directory that is on the path in order for it to be located by NT.
3. Set up the schedule by executing the AT command as in the next example:

```
AT 03:00 /every:M,T,W,TH,F BACKUPNORM
```

9.2.3 Other Backup Options

The backup program included in NT is somewhat limited in its capabilities. For instance, Backup can't save different backup configurations. What happens if you want to back up several different directory structures from one disk and then back up several other directories from another disk except that for the second disk you want to skip several subdirectories under one directory while still backing up other directories under the same main directory? This type of scenario is easy to define with the graphical backup program, but you can't save the settings. To accomplish the same thing with the NT backup command, you need to develop several different commands and place them in a batch file.

Let's take a quick look at another backup option that adds more capabilities to the backup process and makes it a lot easier.

9.2.3.1 Arcada Backup Exec Server   Arcada Software is the company that developed the NT backup program. Arcada is the same company that used to be called Maynard then Conner Systems. Backup Exec is an enhanced version of the NT Backup program and fills in many of the holes.

This product packs lots of features that are a must for network managers. Backup Exec allows you to create backup selections that specify the disk and/or directories to back up. Selections can contain both local and network selections. Once a selection has been created, you can use it interactively or within a backup job. You can create jobs for different backup types or days, then schedule the jobs to run at predefined times using the graphical scheduler that comes with Backup Exec. It takes only a matter of minutes to set up a new selection and schedule a job to run it every day or only on certain days. Backup Exec also works with Microsoft Mail to send notification of completed backups automatically.

There are many other options that allow you to tweak and configure the operation of Backup Exec and your backup jobs.

There is an optional module (AutoLoader) that works with many different tape drives with loaders. I have used this tool with a Digital Equipment TLZ06 tape drive with a 12-tape loader. Installing both Backup Exec and AutoLoader took only a few minutes. Configuring the AutoLoader module took a little longer but was still accomplished in less than 1 hour.

Backup Exec also comes with an easy-to-use Scheduler that makes setting up routine backups painless. You can schedule one-at-a-time backups or routine backups that occur on certain days of the week. It is also easy to set up named backup jobs that back up certain files and systems that are run on different schedules. Figure 9.4 shows the Job Launcher for Backup Exec.

9.2.4 Picking the Files to Back Up

9.2.4.1 Data Files Data files are the most critical items on a network to back up. Your directory structure can play a critical part in making this task very simple or very difficult. I like to have only one or two directories off the root directory of a drive that actually hold the data directories and files. This approach allows me to pick only one directory tree to back up. The top level directories I use are

DATA

USERS

The backup process is simple because backing up these two directory trees gets all the data on the system. This structure also works well because you may also have a database manager such as SQL Server or other types of files that cannot be directly backed up.

Systems that are running a database such as SQL Server most likely have

Fig. 9.4 Backup Exec Job Launcher with a daily backup ready to run at 11:00 p.m.

a separate directory for the database backup files. Backups for high performance databases such as SQL Server typically use a special backup function of the database to perform an on-line backup to disk. The backup files placed on disk are the ones backed up with the normal backup program. You must make sure that the database backup completes before the scheduled backup of the system starts because open files are not backed up.

9.2.4.2 Registry   The Registry can pose an interesting problem for backups because it contains all the configuration information for the NT system. Backup programs that are designed specifically for NT should be able to back up the Registry with no problems. Some programs have a check box that must be checked for the Registry files to participate in the backup.

REGBACK and REGREST (NT Resource Kit).   Another way to back up only the Registry files is to use the REBACK.EXE program to back up the Registry on all your systems to a common server. This approach is handy because with the Registry files for all systems on a server, you can update a system very quickly if you have a problem. It also makes sure that all your Registry information is backed up as long as the REGBACK program is run every day.

REGBACK can back up all the Registry hives or only certain hives. It also works when the hives are open and, in fact, only backs up Registry hives that are open. Other hives that are closed must be copied using File Manager or XCOPY. The account used to run REGBACK must have SetBackupPrivilege to execute this program.

You should always use REGBACK to back up the Registry to a hard disk directory. Running REGBACK targeted to a floppy disk is a recipe for disaster because the program fails if the floppy disk runs out of space. REGBACK also does not overwrite existing files, so make sure that you have deleted any backup files from the target directory.

The DOS Errorlevel variable is set to 0 if REGBACK does not encounter any errors. Errorlevel is set to 1 if the program encounters a hive that must be manually backed up and 2 for any other errors.

The format for REGBACK is

```
REGBACK [directory]
```

directory   Directory name to place backup in.

The following command backs up all open Registry hives:

```
REGBACK K:\BACKUP\CONFIG\THISERV
```

This command backs up the Registry to the K:\BACKUP\CONFIG\THIS-ERV directory. Replace the last directory entry (THISERV) with a unique ID for the server you are backing up. Note that you can use the full server name for the file name if you are using NTFS or have extended names turned on for FAT drives.

REGREST is used to restore a backup made with REGBACK. This command works just like REGBACK in reverse:

`REGREST backupfile savefile`

backupfile   Specifies the file name of the Registry backup to restore.

savefile   Specifies the name of a file to save the current Registry file in before the replacement is made.

9.2.5 Other Files

There may be other files that you have missed in planning your backup strategy, unless you are backing up the entire drive each night. The following list covers several types of files that could be important. Review this list and research what other files or directories should be added to the list.

☞ WINS and DHCP database files

☞ WINNT35 and all subdirectories

☞ HOSTS, LMHOSTS, and other similar files if used

☞ Batch program directory or directories

☞ Directory containing user profiles

☞ NETLOGON shared directory

☞ SMS data directories

9.2.6 Backup Tapes

NT backups can span multiple tapes, creating a possible problem with tape management. The tapes in a backup set must always be in numbered order and in the sequence they are used. A backup set should always be kept together. Most managers also create a unique number for each tape set, allowing a set to be reconstructed if it is mixed up with other tapes.

One handy feature of some newly affordable technology provides us with auto loader tape drives. Many auto loaders use inexpensive magazines (less than $100) to hold the tapes. These magazines make a great caddie for storing the backup tapes and for automatically keeping them in order. Simply use a different magazine for each day's backup and label the magazine for the day. The tapes within the magazine should be labeled as to their position within the magazine. Using this technique, you might have a total of 20 magazines (5 each week of the month) or more. Even with this many magazines, this is a cost-effective and practical solution.

It is possible to restore and list files from a backup set that has a missing tape by using the /MISSINGTAPE switch to start the backup program.

9.2.7 Restoring the System Files (Registry)

You can restore the NT boot volume if you have a backup copy. This process may be a pain because it usually requires that NT first be reinstalled and then booted before you can access the backup tapes.

Restoring the NT System Files from Tape

1. Boot the system with NT. You may have to install a new copy of NT to accomplish this.
2. Restore the SYSTEM32\CONFIG directory and all Registry files. If you are using a third-party backup product, you will probably have to reinstall the backup product before you can restore anything from the backup tapes.
3. Reboot the system.
4. Restore the entire backup of the NT volume except for the Registry files.
5. Reboot the system.

The system information should now be completely restored and operable. At this point, you can restore the remaining files from the backup tapes.

You can do things to minimize the pain of reinstalling NT during a backup. One technique is to use a mirrored disk or duplexed disk for the system and boot volume(s). This disk prevents the system disk from failing and causing a reinstall of NT. The other step is to keep an automated installation setup handy on more than one server. This backup allows you to reinstall very quickly over the network if there is a need. Using the SETUPMGR program from the NT Resource Kit, you can build automated answer files for each server, which saves lots of time in an emergency (see page 15). You can always reinstall from CD, but this process takes longer as you answer all the prompts of a generic installation.

Restoring the NT System Files from Disk

1. Boot the system with NT. You may have to install a new copy of NT to accomplish this.
2. Restore the SYSTEM32\CONFIG directory and all Registry files using REGREST. If you used a utility such as File Manager or Xcopy to back up any non-open files, you should reverse the procedure to reinstall these files.
3. Reboot the system.
4. Restore the entire backup of the NT volume except for the Registry files.
5. Reboot the system.

The system information should now be completely restored and operable. At this point, you can restore the remaining files from the backup tapes.

9.3 BACKING UP NETWORK SYSTEMS

You can back up resources on other systems from an NT workstation or server. These other systems can include any resource that is accessible from the NT system. For instance, if you have Pathworks for Windows NT installed, you can back up resources on a Pathworks server during your NT backup session. Similarly, if you have access to Windows 95, Windows for Workgroups, or NetWare resources, they can be included in the backup as well.

9.4 REAL-TIME BACKUP OF SERVER

9.4.1 Octopus

Octopus from Octopus Technologies provides real-time backup to any data on your NT server. Candidates for Octopus backup are user data files, database files, mail system files, and any other critical files that change routinely. The following list covers the most important features of Octopus:

- operates in real-time, capturing file I/O as it happens;
- mirrors actual file operations, without full file compares or copies;
- mirrors files and directories, rather than entire disks, partitions, or volume sets;
- uses store-and-forward, with no absolute requirements for connectivity or timing;
- recovers from lost connections or blocked files;
- mirrors over the network to anywhere NetBIOS can connect;
- permits mirroring to multiple sites;
- protects files on-line;
- processes automatically, with no manual intervention;
- stores in the file system, with no special format;
- is efficient for CPU, disk, and network resources;
- does not hold up application processing for its operations; and
- is transparent to the applications and to the users.

This list is basically a hit list from the vendor, but it does justice to the product.

9.4.1.1 Problems with Tape Backup   Tape backup is a great tool but has one major problem: Every tape backup system that I have used requires that all files backed up are closed. This presents problems for several types of files:

- Many database files are usually open 24 hours a day for production operations.
- Most mail systems also run 24 hours a day.
- Users almost never exit all applications before leaving the office. You can force users to log off by using the logon time feature of NT and automatically logging users off. What happens to users who must work during the backup period?

These types of systems are prime candidates for Octopus because it performs the backup as the file activity occurs and does not require the files to be closed.

9.4.1.2 Off-Site Backup with Octopus   Octopus can also be used to back up files to an off-site location. This feature is useful if you have a high-speed connection to the off-site location that is not highly used during normal operations. This situation is the ideal one in which to deploy Octopus because it provides hot off-site backup, providing almost total disaster preparedness.

You may be in a better position to use the off-site backup than you think. If your system has separate buildings that are connected by a WAN, you may be able to run a separate segment that can be used for backup. The new segment provides high throughput for the backup operation and can serve as a backup segment for disaster recovery.

9.4.2 Real-Time Fault Tolerance with Clusters

As mentioned earlier, Digital, AT&T, and other vendors are working on clustering or other fault tolerance software for NT Server. A true clustering system allows you to group several servers that are seen as one by the network. Generally a cluster is known by an "alias" that relates to the entire cluster. For instance, if your cluster is known by the alias MYCLUSTER, you could connect to a shared directory using the UNC name:

`\\MYCLUSTER\sharename`

The cluster shares access to the drives, so that any server in the cluster can provide access to the resource to satisfy a request, providing load balancing and fault tolerance.

The best example of clustering with legacy systems is Digital's VMS cluster software. A VMS cluster is fault-tolerant and spreads the load across the cluster. The drawback to a VMS cluster is the large amount of overhead associated with running the cluster.

Digital has developed cluster software for NT that is based on its long track record with successful cluster systems on VMS. Digital Clusters for Windows NT should be released in late 1995. The first release of the product should include fault tolerance and load-balancing features for most applications except for client/server databases. Cluster management for a client/server database requires more sophisticated software in the cluster system and will most likely not be available until the second release in 1996. Watch DEC Professional and other publications for further developments on Clusters for Windows NT.

9.5 POWER BACKUP AND MONITORING SYSTEMS

Uninterruptable Power Supply (UPS) devices are viewed by many LAN managers as a necessity. I consider myself one of that group due to the benefits they provide in reducing not only hardware problems or lost data but also in the improvement in up-time of network servers. A UPS is the most viable type of power backup (its name implies that it is uninterruptable when power goes off).

Choosing a UPS can be a difficult proposition because of the many options available. This decision process is best considered like many other system decisions—consider all other related options during the process. By this I mean that you should consider which UPS monitoring programs are available for the system you choose and what other devices and features are supported by the system. You should consider if the UPS is expandable and if it can be shared by several servers with smart connections to each server in case of a power problem.

9.5.1 APC Power Chute

American Power Conversion (APC) has many years of experience in power systems and has developed its hardware and software accordingly. The integrated nature of its products provides the system manager with a complete suite of power management tools. Adding products such as Measure-UPS and Share-UPS to a system running the Power Chute Plus monitoring software gives you the unique ability to monitor many different events that impact the environment your system is running in from both a local or remote location. The ability to monitor power quality as well as the UPS temperature with the standard Power Chute Plus software is especially nice.

APC codeveloped the original UPS monitoring with Microsoft for the LAN Manager UPS program. Simple UPS monitoring has made its way into the NT product via the UPS applet in Control Panel. Power Chute Plus is a software product from APC that adds a new level of UPS power management and control for system administrators. APC has a number of other products that augment Power Chute Plus in controlling and monitoring the environment our systems run in. These products run on NT, VMS, NetWare, and other systems.

The most important features of Power Chute Plus and its UPS interface follow:

- ☞ There is a safe system shutdown in case of extended power failures.
- ☞ UPS Testing and status checks run at every UPS startup and can be scheduled to run at different times automatically.
- ☞ Remote UPS management allows a manager to log on to a server from anywhere and check the UPS. An additional product called Call-UPS II allows remote out-of-band management.
- ☞ Another product called Measure-UPS allows you to add on to the standard power monitoring features of Power Chute Plus and monitor environmental things such as temperature, humidity, smoke alarms, and fire alarms.
- ☞ FlexEvents is new to version 4.2 of Power Chute Plus and allows a manager to choose different actions for certain types of power events. For instance, Power Chute can run a program or send electronic mail when a certain event is triggered.

Power Chute Plus on NT includes not only the standard UPS information we are used to but also some nice graphics depicting the status of the UPS and the incoming power. Tools are available under the Diagnostics menu for setting up regular UPS testing and performing on the spot tests.

Share-UPS is a small hardware box that allows up to eight servers to be connected to one UPS. One server becomes the UPS manager running Power Chute Plus and attaching to the Share-UPS with the black cable, whereas the other servers all have a connection to the Share-UPS box using the standard NT UPS applet and the gray cable.

Using this technique, you can manage the UPS from one server or the network and effectively control all your systems attached to it. No longer do you need one UPS for each server or maybe two servers. The Share-UPS also has a serial port for out-of-band management from either a PC, terminal, or modem connection.

Tuning NT Servers and Networks

10.1 Tuning Overview

NT performs many tuning operations during normal operations. It normally tunes itself sufficiently except when it runs out of hardware resources such as disk, memory, or processor. NT cannot tune itself for how you wish to use the system or for particular applications. NT also has no way of determining when specific users are overloading the system, when a bad application has gone haywire, or when some particular subsystem such as the network is causing problems.

Performance tuning is part art and part science. NT provides a number of tools both for monitoring performance in both the NT Server box and the NT Resource Kit. This chapter focuses on a number of these tools and how to use them with NT and NT Server systems. This chapter goes into more detail on tuning than most NT Workstation books (including my NT book from Cardinal Business Monitors) because I am assuming that you will be placing a much higher demand on the system by using it as a server. After all, that is why you are reading this book, right?

Along with the tools included with NT and the NT Resource Kit, this chapter also touches briefly on Systems Management Server and a little bit of Simple Network Management Protocol using a couple of different tools.

10.2 NT Performance Monitoring System

The primary NT tool used for tuning is the Performance Monitoring System (PMS). The PMS (the acronym is mine) includes the NT Performance Monitor and the various parts of NT and other systems that maintain the objects and counters used for tuning.

The PMS provides a nice view of many parts of the NT system and was built to extend this support to NT applications. The NT Resource Kit also includes a program that can be used to add your own objects to the PMS database (LODCTR).

10.2.1 Objects and Counters

The PMS system uses objects and counters to track the performance of particular parts of the system. The term *object* refers to any distinguishable entity in the system. A good example of PMS objects are the objects associated with the physical disks in your system.

Along with the objects, NT maintains counters for each part of an object that is tracked. The counters are usually broken down into percentages, discrete counts, or readings over time to provide useful information to system managers.

The Physical Disk object contains counters that relate to the total physical disk. If you have a disk that is partitioned into two logical disks, when you look at the Physical Disk object you will see the activity for the disk as a whole, which includes both logical disks. If you look at the Logical Disk object you will see the counters for a specific logical disk partition. You will find both types of counters useful in managing your system.

Instances are used to track multiple occurrences of a type of object. For example, you may have a system with two disk drives. When you look at the Physical Disk counters you will see two copies of the counters, one for instance 0 and one for instance 1. You will also see multiple instances for processors with systems that use two or more CPUs.

Objects may be added to a system by any program that is installed on the system. Systems that ship with NT Server may also include additional counters for specific processors (such as the DEC Alpha or Intel Pentium chips). You may also install new hardware that has new counters that are loaded when you install the driver for the device. Table 10.1 lists the core objects that are included on all NT systems.

Some instances have a parent instance that is used to identify the aggregate information for all instances. Examples of objects with parents are the Logical Disk (Physical Disk) object and the Thread Object (Process).

Objects are referenced by first specifying the object and then the counter:

`Object:Counter`

Multiple instances are expressed as you would an index to an array in a programming language:

`Object:Counter[instance name]`

Some instances are mortal because they exist only during the time the entity they report on exists. For instance, a process instance exists only when the process is actually running on the system. Mortal instances can be added to a chart

Table 10.1 NT System Core Performance Object

Object	Tracks
Cache	File system cache.
Logical Disk	Counters related to the logical disk systems, such as partitions and space usage.
Memory	System memory (RAM).
Objects	Certain parts of system software.
Paging File	Virtual memory paging files.
Physical Disk	Counters related to the physical disk systems.
Process	Running programs.
Processor	System processor (CPU).
Redirector	File system redirector used to redirect file system requests to other systems.
System	Common counters to all system hardware and software.
Thread	Running threads.

only during the time they exist. Performance Monitor records data for the instance every time it is checked while the instance is alive once the instance has been added to a chart. Whenever the mortal instance dies, the counter drops to 0 and picks up counting when the instance starts again.

10.2.2 Producing a List of Performance Monitor Counters

CTRLIST (NT Resource Kit) is used to produce a text file containing the Performance Monitor objects and counters. The information in the file includes the Explain text for each item. The file is useful for reviewing the objects and counters for a better understanding and for searching with a text editor like Notepad. You could also easily import the resulting file into an Access database for ease of use. The syntax for its use follows:

```
ctrlist > counters.txt
```

10.2.3 Performance Monitor

Performance Monitor is one tool you should become very familiar with. It is great for tracking system performance and for sending alerts to a particular user and/or computer when a particular condition occurs.

As shown in Table 10.2, Performance Monitor has four different views.

For more information on the details of using Performance Monitor, consult your NT documentation, my book *A Practical Guide to Windows NT*, or Marshall Brain's book *Using Windows NT*.

Table 10.2 Performance Monitor Views

Display Name	Description
Chart	Provides a nice graphical display. You can select between a line graph or histogram.
Report	Displays the counters in a simple report format. The values are displayed separately for each server.
Log	Displays the objects that are tracked in the log. You can also use the Add to Log dialog box from this view to add objects to the log.
Alert	Displays the current alerts. The Add dialog box can be used in this view to add new alerts.

Performance Monitor can monitor only one instance of a program at a time. If you need to monitor multiple instances of the same program, you should make a copy of the EXE file with a different name and execute both programs. Performance Monitor also cannot track multiple instances of a 16-bit Windows program in the 3.1 release of NT and NTAS because all 16-bit Windows programs run in a single NT Virtual DOS Machine (NTVDM).

Performance Monitor can monitor objects from one or more computers at a time. Each item you place on a chart or report for instance can be from a different system. You must have the Access This Computer From The Network to place objects from other systems on a Performance Monitor display.

You should be conscious of the performance hit that occurs when Performance Monitor is used to monitor lots of data from remote systems. The overhead on the monitored machine will be very low, but the network traffic and the load on the monitoring machine will be higher. The NT Resource Kit points out that you can actually measure the added Performance Monitor overhead by running another copy of Performance Monitor and watching the load on the monitoring system.

While Performance Monitor can monitor multiple systems at the same time, the data retrieved from the different systems will never be completely synchronized. This lack of synchronization occurs because of the differences in timing from the different systems and the varying network traffic when the counters are reported. Most of the time the synchronization is not crucial because you are looking at representative numbers as far as timing is concerned.

Before using Performance Monitor to monitor disk performance, you must enable disk performance measurement. Disk measurement is disabled by default because it consumes some amount of overhead. The following statement turns on disk performance monitoring:

```
DISKPERF -Y
```

Before the disk counters show up, the system must be rebooted. You can also run this command on a remote system by specifying the system name after the command:

```
DISKPERF -Y \\SYSNAME
```

Turning on disk counters places a performance penalty on your system, but it is minor on all but the slowest systems. Pentium and faster systems with good performing disk systems should not see a hit by leaving disk counters enabled all the time.

The Processor Queue counter is another important counter that has a hidden secret. Before the Processor Queue counter is activated, you must select at least one thread for monitoring. Once the Performance Monitor is collecting data for the thread, the Processor Queue shows the length of the queue by counting the number of threads waiting to execute.

> *Tip:* Another little trick to use with Performance Monitor is to create different settings files and then create icons that start Performance Monitor with the settings file. This is accomplished by placing the settings file name on the command line after the command to start Performance Monitor. You can also start Performance Monitor with the AT command in this manner.

The NT Resource Kit gives several options for measuring remote statistics:

☞ collect data at less frequent intervals,

☞ reduce the number of objects that are monitored,

☞ carefully choose which objects to monitor (The Thread object is the most expensive, with the Process object ranking second), and

☞ run multiple copies of Performance Monitor that each monitor only one type of object.

10.2.4 General Performance Monitor Tips

Performance Monitor is a powerful and easy-to-use tool. Figure 10.1 shows Performance Monitor and the Chart view. Notice how the far left button on the toolbar is depressed. The other buttons are for Alerts, Log file, and Reports. The

Fig. 10.1 The Chart view is the default when Performance Monitor starts.

other buttons on the toolbar are Add to dialog, Modify Counter Parameters, Remove Counter from View, Update Counters Now, Add Bookmark to Log, and Display View Parameters for the Current View.

The Add to dialog box is used to add a counter to the current Performance Monitor view. The Add to button on the toolbar displays the Add to dialog box. This dialog box is specific to the particular view you are currently using. Figure 10.2 shows the Add to Alert dialog box.

The Add dialog boxes allow you to select a different computer for each counter you add. Click the ... button next to the computer name to display the Select Computer dialog box shown in Figure 10.3.

10.2.5 Setting Alerts with Performance Monitor

You should use Alerts to provide an on-going pro-active check on your system(s). Performance Monitor is used for setting Alerts via the Alert view. Alerts

Fig. 10.2 The Add dialog box is used to add a counter to a view. The dialog box is basically the same for all views, except for specific view options, such as the Run Program on Alert box shown here. Other dialog boxes have additional options or fewer options.

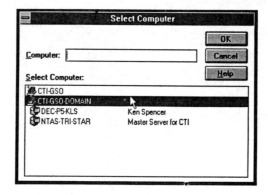

Fig. 10.3 The Select Computer dialog box provides a quick method of selecting another system for a counter. Click on the system to monitor and then click OK or double-click the computer name.

are very useful because they can send a network message to a user or computer and/or run a program when an Alert occurs.

Alerts must be chosen carefully because they can generate a lot of overhead and can be a pain to the users and managers who receive the alerts. I usually use the 80/20 rule for choosing alerts. This rule states that you can get approximately 80% of the benefits from monitoring only 20% of the values. I also like to start by selecting the values to catch only the worst offenders and then tighten the alerts as performance improves.

I also suggest monitoring certain values over longer periods of time. You may want to have several copies of Performance Monitor running with different settings files for different types of alerts. For instance, certain things such as disk space can probably be done once a day. Others such as paging rate or disk I/O must be monitored on a more frequent basis when the load is occurring on the system.

You should be aware of a couple of items when sending alert messages over the network. If the user who is to receive the alert message is logged in to multiple systems with the same account, the alert messages are received only by one system that the user logged in on. Alerts can also be irritating if you have a large number of alerts that send messages to users each time they are triggered.

Alerts can also be sent to an arbitrary name across the network. You can create the name by using the NET NAME command on any NT system. This command creates an arbitrary name on the computer that allows the computer to receive any messages sent to the name. The format for using the command is

    NET NAME newname

Another intriguing thing about the Performance Monitor alert view is its ability to run a program when an alert occurs. This alert can be useful for triggering many different actions. What happens when your system periodically fills a disk with many temporary files. You can create an alert on disk space so that when it hits a certain percentage the alert runs a program to delete or move some of the temporary files. Another possible candidate for this type of action is triggering an alert on a database to archive information when the database reaches a certain size. Figure 10.4 shows the Performance Monitor Alert View.

Performance Monitor can also run an alert only when a specific alert occurs. This is quite handy when you wish to monitor a specific counter and trigger a program when a certain condition occurs. The First Time button can be used to run the program on the first alert and ignore the program on subsequent alerts.

Running a Program on a Specific Alert with Performance Monitor

1. Click the Add or Modify button on the toolbar.
2. Choose the object to monitor.
3. Enter the alert condition in the text box.
4. Enter the name of the program to run when the alert occurs. Be sure to include the full path to the program.

Fig. 10.4 Performance Monitor dialog box with the Alert view showing. Notice how many alerts have been triggered on a shortage of drive space.

5. Click the First Time to run the program only the first time the alert occurs or click the Every Time button to run the program each time the alert occurs.

6. Close the dialog box.

See the section on the DATALOG program from the NT Resource Kit on page 309 for information on running Alert functions as a service.

10.2.6 NT Resource Kit

In addition to Performance Monitor shipped with NT, the NT Resource Kit contains several tools for monitoring the performance of your system. Table 10.3 shows these tools.

Table 10.3 NT Resource Kit Tools for Monitoring Performance

Program	Description
DATALOG	A service version of Performance Monitor, implementing the Alert and Logging functions.
PERFMTR	Monitors systems performance numbers during the execution of a program. Different presentation views are selectable when PERFMTR starts.
PMON	Useful for monitoring a large number of memory statistics. Displays the same data available in Performance Monitor, but in a tailored form.
PVIEWER	Nice tool for reviewing processes. Similar to PMON in that most of the data are available in Performance Monitor but presented in a different manner.
WPERF	Another tool that is similar to Performance Monitor but displays its information in a different format.
TLIST	Used to display a list of all running processes and their process ID.

10.2.7 Automating Performance Monitor with DataLog (NT Resource Kit)

The NT Resource Kit is the new DataLog service version of Performance Monitor. DataLog provides support for the alert and logging features of Performance Monitor. Also included with DataLog is the Monitor utility to control the DATALOG service. You can start DataLog on the current NT system or on any other NT system over the network.

This is a great utility for monitoring performance. The best way to use this utility is to plan the items you wish to monitor, create a settings file with Performance Monitor, and then automatically start DataLog to perform the tasks. DataLog runs as a service and does not have a user interface. DataLog places the results of any log activity in the log file specified by the settings file.

Configuring DataLog

1. Copy DATALOG.EXE to the system root directory (\WINNT35 \SYSTEM32). The settings file does not have to be in the system root directory.

2. Install DataLog using the Monitor command:

```
monitor [servername] SETUP
```

   Replace [servername] with the name of the server to run DataLog. If you are installing DataLog on the current system, leave this blank.

3. Create a workspace settings file using Performance Monitor. Set the Alert and Log settings (include the Log name), but do not start the log. Save the settings file using the Save Workspace option on the File menu.

4. Specify the settings file for DataLog to use:

```
monitor [servername] filename
```

   Replace [servername] with the name of the server to run DataLog. If you are installing DataLog on the current system, leave this blank.

   Replace filename with the name of the settings file (i.e., PHYS-DISK.PMW or OVERVIEW.PMW). If you are specifying the settings file on a remote system, make sure the settings file is on that system and specify the full path to the file.

Starting DataLog

1. Start DataLog with the command:

```
monitor [servername] START
```

Stopping Datalog

1. Stop DataLog with the command:

```
monitor [servername] STOP
```

Once DataLog has created a log file, you can use Performance Monitor to review and manipulate the file. Simply open the file as you would any log file and use the normal Performance Monitor features from there.

You can automate DataLog using the AT command to drive the scheduler service. Review the DATALOG.TXT file included with the NT Resource Kit for more information.

Warning: You can create some very large log files in a hurry with DataLog and Performance Monitor. You should use care when setting up these tools for logging and consider placing log files on a disk with lots of space. You should also consider setting up an automated routine to check for log files and delete them after a period or to alert you to large and old files.

10.2.8 Automating GUI Operations

Microsoft Test is a neat product for automating operations. This product can automate the tasks that you must perform when using a GUI tool such as Performance Monitor or Event Viewer. MS Test can record and play back keystrokes to any application. This capability makes MS Test a useful tool for automating tasks such as starting Performance Monitor at certain times and performing a series of tasks such as starting and stopping logging and switching settings files and others.

10.3 Monitoring Performance

10.3.1 Bottlenecks and Other Problems

You may run into a vast number of problems using a network operating system such as NT Server. Bottlenecks in one portion of the system, problems with applications, or user problems are just a small taste of the fun that awaits you.

A bottleneck typically occurs when your system begins to run out of a particular hardware or software resource. For instance, the system may swap a lot of data from RAM to the disk causing the system to slow down for everyone using the system. When the amount of data swapped to disk becomes very high, the only resolution is to add more physical memory to the system, which will alleviate the bottleneck.

You also may experience a sort of bottleneck from an application program. A good example of a bad program is the EXTERNAL program for Microsoft Mail version 3.0 to 3.2. This program causes NT to experience a drastic drop in performance when EXTERNAL is running even when the program is supposedly not doing anything. I suspect that this occurs because EXTERNAL expects to be running on a DOS system, which is by nature not multitasking. Under DOS, the only way for EXTERNAL to monitor the system is to continually loop. Performance Monitor is a great tool to use to look for exactly this kind of problem.

Note: If you are using Microsoft Mail, get the NT version of External [called the Multitasking Transfer Agent (MTA)], and you will not experience these problems.

You should use care when monitoring your system's performance and making judgments on what to upgrade. I try to approach every problem using the Systems approach. This approach dictates that you must consider the entire system in any decision, not just the problem at hand. For instance, if the CPU is 100% utilized, your first guess is to move some of the load to another system or just add another processor. The proper response is to continue the investigation until we find out what is causing the 100% utilization. It could be a problem program or a particular piece of hardware that is creating the load.

10.3.2 Creating an Overview Performance Monitor Settings File

The Resource Kit suggests creating an overview settings file that provides a good glimpse of how your system is performing. This file should be called OVER-VIEW.PMW or some such representative name and will save all the settings for your system overview. The objects and counters in Table 10.4 are good candidates for this file.

Table 10.4 Objects and Counters for Overview Setting File

Object	Counter	Description
Processor	Percent Processor Time	Tracks percent of time that the processor is busy. This counter should go up as the load on the system increases and performance decreases unless some other factor besides the processor is causing the bottleneck.
	Percent Total Processor Time	The same as Percent Processor Time except that it combines the values for all processors in a multiprocessor.
	Processor Queue Length	Measures the backlog for your processor. This counter gives you a clue when a process(s) is hogging the processor.
Memory	Pages/second	Tracks the number of pages swapped to disk per second by the virtual memory system. When this counter gets consistently very high, your system is most likely running out of RAM.
Physical Disk	Percent Disk Time	Shows how busy the disk drive is. A separate instance should be monitored for each disk in the system. When this counter gets very high, it is an indicator that something such as paging or other high-disk usage is occurring.
NetBEUI	Bytes Total/second	Tracks the number of bytes per second sent and received over the NetBEUI interface and indicates when network traffic is high.
TCP/IP	Bytes Total/second	The same as the last one except it is for the TCP/IP interface.
Server	Bytes Total/second	Tracks the total bytes per second for the server.

10.3.3 Steps for Tuning

NT automatically adjusts its configuration due to workload changes. Some manual steps to augment this are discussed in this section. One major step that should be taken before any drastic tuning is to establish a benchmark of the system before the tuning takes place. The benchmark allows you to compare the performance of the system accurately after the tuning to the performance before the tuning.

Benchmarking a System Before Making Changes

1. Record the current state of system with Performance Monitor.
2. Make changes.
3. Record the state of revised system with Performance Monitor under same load conditions.

Suggestions for Improving Server Performance

☞ Add lots of memory to NT servers. NT loves memory, especially when it gets busy. High-usage servers are a prime candidate for more RAM.

☞ Use SMP servers in particular situations. Database servers running SQL Server or another similar client/server system improve substantially on an SMP platform. File and print services usually do not see the same measure of performance improvement using SMP.

☞ Distribute the server load in your network around using several servers instead of one or two big ones. Many functions can be segregated to separate servers to provide a big performance improvement and some degree of fault tolerance. The following list contains several potential candidates:

> SMS
>
> Database Servers (i.e., SQL Server)
>
> Primary Domain Controllers
>
> File and print servers
>
> Application servers
>
> WINS servers
>
> DNS servers
>
> DHCP servers

☞ Use the fastest CPU feasible. Incremental prices between different processor speeds are usually not extremely large these days.

☞ Create multiple-page files on different drives and controllers. Multiple files are more efficient because each disk and controller can simultaneously process requests for information from the page files. Placing each page file on a different disk also shares the paging load rather than one file on a single disk carrying all the load.

☞ Analyze the paging requirements for your system before you create the page files. NT expands page files as needed, but this is inefficient and can cause disk fragmentation. Creating a page file of the proper size performs much better.

☞ Place the page file(s) on separate disks from the NT boot partition.

☞ Make sure the boot partition has plenty of free disk space (50MB or more). I have seen NT servers act very strange when disk space begins to disappear (less than 10MB free). Connections would disappear, and the system would quit synchronizing with other BDCs, or the PDC, depending upon its role.

☞ Use high-performance disk drives. Drives that are 1GB or larger often have much higher performance rates than smaller drives.

☞ Use multiple high-performance disk controllers.

☞ Use only PCI and EISA bus systems for disk controllers.

☞ Create stripe sets with parity over multiple disks.

☞ Do not use any disks or controllers that would use the default ATDISK driver.

☞ Continuously analyze disk requirements and capacity.

☞ Continuously analyze memory requirements and capacity.

☞ Manage memory settings for the server.

☞ Match the network card bus (PCI, EISA, ISA) to the servers bus.

☞ Use high-performance network cards in the server.

☞ Spread the network load over multiple network adapters. Be sure to group the networks on an adapter logically to make sure workstations can communicate with other workstations in the group.

☞ Use only the NetBEUI protocol if possible.

☞ Use high-speed network components such as 100BaseT, FDDI, and Ethernet switches.

☞ Select Maximize Throughput and Connections for the server and NetBEUI protocol. This option allows unlimited network connections and improves network performance. Be aware that network applications such as Net-BEUI and the Server use nonpaged memory. This makes less nonpaged memory available to application programs.

10.3.4 Monitoring and Controlling Server Usage

NT creates a session between a workstation and the server each time a user successfully connects to the server. The session validates the user's permissions and sets up the performance statistics for the session. You can track session usage statistics from any NT system and LAN Manager 2.x servers. Windows 95 also provides session statistics.

There are several ways to get a handle on server usage. One of the tools to use for this is the Server applet. Server shows you a current picture of the server; it does not store statistics over time. Even though it doesn't store statistics, it is a very good tool for checking the current status of your system and determining where the excessive load is coming from. For instance, maybe several users are copying their C drives to the server at the same time.

Quickly Checking on What Users Are Hitting Your System

1. Start Server Manager.
2. Click the Users button.
3. Review the Connected users on your system. Note how many opens the users have and the idle time for the user. The idle time will be very low (as in 0 or close to 0) if the user is actively using a resource. Select the user with the most opens and active time close to 0 and note the resources accessed by the user.

Now that you know who is using a resource you can use Performance Monitor to look at that particular resource or maybe you used Performance Monitor and have determined which resource has the highest load first.

What happens if you know that a particular resource is heavily used? How do you determine who is using it? The next set of steps assume that you know a particular drive is heavily used and you are trying to find out why.

Quickly Determining Who Is Using a Particular Resource

1. Start Server Manager.
2. Click the Shares button.
3. Select the resource in question.
4. Review the bottom window, which will show all users connected to the resource. Pay attention to the In Use column. In Use indicates when a user has a file open on the resource (Yes). A No value indicates that the user has a connection to the resource but is not actively using the resource. A quick look down this list should show what users are placing the load on the resource.

Quickly Checking Only Open Resources

The In Use button displays the Open Resources dialog box (shown in Figure 10.5), which is a quick way to check for users of currently open resources.

1. Start Server Manager.
2. Click the In Use button.
3. Review the list for resources and users in question.

Click the Refresh button once in a while to update the display to current information.

Sometimes you will want to disconnect a user from a share or disconnect all users for a particular share. You can do this with the In Use button, but this would be time-consuming and would show only what files are in use. The easiest

Fig. 10.5 The Open Resources dialog box from Server Manager allows you to see who is using what resources and to close a resource. This dialog box is displayed by clicking the In Use button from the Server Properties dialog box.

way to disconnect a user from a share is with the Shares button, which displays the dialog box in Figure 10.6.

Closing a Resource or Disconnecting a Share

1. Start Server Manager.
2. Click the Shares button.
3. Select the share to close.
4. Click the Disconnect button or click Disconnect All to disconnect all users from the share.

Another tool for monitoring shared resources is Net Watch, which is described on page 119. This tool is included in the NT Resource Kit and provides a nice graphical interface for monitoring shares. Server Manager is a more

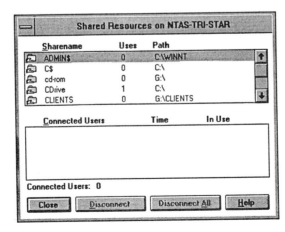

Fig. 10.6 The Shared Rescues dialog box shows the actual share name and the number of connections to that share. It also includes the path for the share.

generic tool, providing access to numerous other options such as users on the system and files in use.

You can also use the Users dialog box to close a resource. This dialog box displays the users logged on to the server and the shares they are connected to.

Disconnecting a User with Server Manager

1. Start Server Manager.
2. Click the In Use button.
3. Select the user to disconnect.
4. Click the Disconnect button or click Disconnect All to disconnect all users.

There are several times that a systems manager must determine who is using a file. They usually occur when maintenance must be performed or for some reason there is a problem with a file. The following steps show how to determine whether there is a problem quickly using File Manager. This feature is a great way to access this information because you may well be using File Manager to perform the research regarding the file.

Quickly Determining Who Is Using a Particular File

1. Start File Manager.
2. Click the file in question.
3. Press Alt+Enter or select File/Properties to display the Properties dialog box.
4. Click the Open By button.

Server Manager can also show you who is using a file although this will take a little longer if you have lots of files in use as you must browse through the list to find the file.

Determine Who Is Using a Particular File (Another Way)

1. Start Server Manager.
2. Click the In Use button.
3. Review the list for resources and users in question until you find the file you are looking for.

Make sure that you have notified all users of a resource or the user you are going to disconnect before taking action to close the connection or resource. Failure to do so may cause loss of data or worse. Under severe circumstances you may have to take a close or disconnect action before a user is notified, but try to keep this to a minimum.

File use is also a good candidate for auditing. Auditing a file can show who is using the file and how often the file is opened and used. The DUMPEL program from the NT Resource Kit can be used in a batch file to dump the Event Log and summarize information on audited resources.

10.3.5 Collecting Statistics with NET STATISTICS

Performance Monitor, the Server applet, Server Manager, Event Viewer, and several other programs display or collect statistics on NT. One command that is useful for reviewing server statistics is the NET STATISTICS command. NET STATISTICS (NET STATS) displays statistics that were captured over time. Tables 10.5 and 10.6 show items that are output by this command and provide a short explanation on the item.

Several pieces of information from NET STATISTICS are useful in managing your system. Notice that at a glance you can determine how many files have been accessed on the server or how many jobs have been spooled to the printer. Maybe you want to know how many sessions were accepted on the server versus

Table 10.5 Server Statistics

Item	Description
Server Statistics for \\NTAS-TRI-STAR	Indicates that this set of statistics is for a server and the server name is \\NTAS-TRI-STAR.
Statistics since 4/1/94 5:47PM	Provides the starting date for the statistics.
Sessions accepted	Number of sessions that connected to the server.
Sessions timed-out	Number of sessions that timed-out and were automatically disconnected.
Sessions errored-out	Number of sessions that were disconnected because of an error.
Kilobytes sent	Number of kilobytes sent.
Kilobytes received	Number of kilobytes received.
Mean response time (msec)	The average server response time for responding to requests.
System errors	Number of system errors.
Permission violations	Number of times that a violation of some type of permission occurred.
Password violations	Number of times that a password violation occurred.
Files accessed	Number of files accessed.
Communication devices accessed	Number of times all communications devices were accessed.
Print jobs spooled	Number of print jobs spooled.
Times buffers exhausted	
Big buffers	Number of times that big memory buffers were exhausted.
Request buffers	Number of times that request buffers were exhausted.

Table 10.6 Workstation Statistics

Item	Description
Workstation Statistics for \\NTAS-TRI-STAR	Indicates that this set of statistics is for a workstation and that the workstation name is \\NTAS-TRI-STAR.
Statistics since 4/1/94 5:47PM	Provides the starting date for the statistics.
Server Message Blocks (SMBs) received	Number of SMBs received.
Bytes transmitted	Number of bytes transmitted.
Server Message Blocks (SMBs) transmitted	Number of SMBs received.
Read operations	Number of successful read operations.
Write operations	Number of successful write operations.
Raw reads denied	Number of failed read operations.
Raw writes denied	Number of failed write operations.
Connections made	Number of successful connections that were made from the workstation.
Reconnections made	Number of times reconnections were made from the workstation.
Server disconnects	Number of times the server disconnected resources connected by the workstation.
Hung sessions	Number sessions from the workstation were hung.
Failed sessions	Number of session connect attempts that failed.
Failed operations	Number of operations from the workstation to the server that failed.
Use count	Use count is related to the number of connections to a network resource. Each time you successfully connect this counter increments, although not necessarily by one. Tests showed the counter changing from 3 to 5 for each new connection.
Failed use count	Shows the number of failed connections to a network resource.

how many were disconnected from time-outs or errors. The output also gives you a quick indication of the average response time.

Sample output from a lightly loaded system:

```
NET STATS SERVER

    Server Statistics for \\NTAS-TRI-STAR
    Statistics since 4/1/94 5:47PM
```

```
Sessions accepted                      1
Sessions timed-out                     0
Sessions errored-out                   3

Kilobytes sent                         83352
Kilobytes received                     41272
Mean response time (msec)              0

System errors                          0
Permission violations                  0
Password violations                    0

Files accessed                         1714
Communication devices accessed         0
Print jobs spooled                     0

Times buffers exhausted

  Big buffers                          0
  Request buffers                      0

The command completed successfully.
```

10.3.6 Domains

10.3.6.1 Domain Monitor (DOMMON.EXE) (NT Resource Kit) Domain Monitor is a tool for monitoring the status of NT domains. It shows the status of a domain and its trusted domains, the PDC for each domain, and other useful information. Domain Monitor also allows you to disconnect and reconnect the connection to a trusted domain. Figure 10.7 shows the main Domain Monitor window.

Domain Monitor can provide details on the servers in a domain via the properties window. Double-click a domain name or select Properties from the Domain menu to display the window in Figure 10.8. Notice the status of CTI01

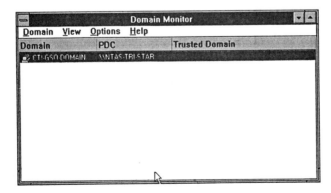

Fig. 10.7 Main window for Domain Monitor with one domain displayed. Notice that there is no trusted domain for CTI-GSO-DOMAIN at this time.

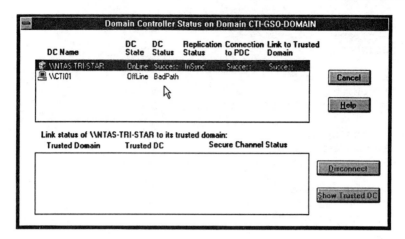

Fig. 10.8 Properties window for Domain Monitor. Notice that Domain Monitor cannot find server CTI01.

which is a Backup Domain Controller that happens to be off-line (because it is turned off).

Domain Monitor is also useful for checking the status of file replication between servers.

See the RKTOOLS.HLP file or Domain Monitor help for more information.

10.3.7 Processes

Both NT and the NT Resource Kit provide tools for monitoring the status of a process. The NT Resource Kit tools are the most advanced outside of Performance Monitor and provide lots of detail on a process and its threads, as well as some control over them.

10.3.7.1 PERFMTR (NT Resource Kit)   PERFMTR.EXE (Performance Meter) displays a simple text screen with performance information related to various topics. Table 10.7 lists the options for Performance Meter and contains a short description of the statistics for the option.

The display for Performance Meter is simply a header followed by one line of information for each read. Performance Meter refreshes approximately every 5 seconds. You can set the H option to redisplay the header when it scrolls off.

PERFMTR.EXE is executed from the command prompt or an icon with the following syntax:

```
perfmtr
```

This routine is text-based and provides a simple menu of options. Its nicest feature is one key selection of the various options.

Table 10.7 Performance Meter Options

Option	Description of Display
C	CPU usage via a short graph (using *) and cache, pool, and other miscellaneous statistics.
F	File cache usage statistics.
H	Redisplays the header for the current statistics.
I	I/O usage.
L	Statistics on the LPC subsystem.
P	Memory pool usage.
R	Cache manager reads and writes.
S	Server statistics.
V	Virtual memory usage.
X	x86 VDM usage.
Q	Quit Performance Meter.

10.3.7.2 PMON (NT Resource Kit) PMON.EXE displays resource usage by process. This information includes things like the amount of CPU used, page faults, and thread count. The format for executing PMON is

```
pmon
```

If you have very many processes running on your system, the information quickly scrolls off the display. I usually run PMON with the following command:

```
pmon > PMONRUN.TXT
```

This command runs PMON and redirects the output to the specified text file. Pressing Ctrl+C aborts PMON and returns you to the command prompt. You can also run PMON like this from an icon and use the task list to abort the command when it has collected enough information. Use caution with this approach because a run of 30 seconds or so can generate a 32K file.

The output from PMON looks like Figure 10.9.

10.3.7.3 PVIEWER (NT Resource Kit) Process Viewer (PVIEWER.EXE) is a cool little utility for checking out the processes on your system. PVIEW can not only view information on the various processes but can kill a process once you've determined who the hog is. PVIEWER can also look at a process running on another NT system over the network. The syntax for executing the command is

```
pviewer
```

The Pviewer interface is pure simplicity as shown in Figure 10.10.

```
                   Command Prompt
          Mem  Mem   Page  Flts Commit   Usage    Pri Thd  Image
%CPU CpuTime Usage Diff Faults Diff Charge NonP Page  Cnt Name
             1944    0 345277    0              0       0   0  1 File Cache
100 17:44:38   16    0      0    0      0     0    0   0   1 Idle Process
  0  3:53:46   20    0   4942    0     32     0    1   8  27 System
  0  0:00:00    0    0    882    0    168     0    0  11   6 smss.exe
  0 391:04:54 3428   0 398685    0   4028     8   15  13  26 csrss.exe
  0  0:00:55   20    0  28098    0    400     9    6  13   3 winlogon.exe
  0  0:02:49  664    0 288177    0   1212   155   11   9  15 services.exe
  0  0:01:10  120    0 223193    0    784    18    6   9  13 lsass.exe
  0  0:05:53  280    0 256055    0    992   700    7   9   8 spoolss.exe
  0  0:00:00   20    0   2283    0    248     1    5  13   1 nddeagnt.exe
  0  0:01:18  268    0 127169    0   1028  2108    7   7  19 OCTO_SRV.EXE
  0  0:00:00    0    0    260    0    308    17    5   7   5 LOCATOR.EXE
  0  0:02:18  156    0  56010    0    396    33    6   7   3 snmp.exe
  0  0:01:32  120    0  11740    0    580  1795    6   7  11 FG_RECU.exe
  0  0:00:00    0    0    346    0    320   161    5   7   1 FG_RTR.exe
  0  0:00:07   64    0  52950    0    528   108    6   7  10 RPCSS.EXE
  0  0:00:56  308    0  12996    0    592     2    7  13   2 progman.exe
  0  1:30:28  304    0  61799    0   3424     3  138   7   5 ntvdm.exe
  0  0:00:00    0    0    283    0    220     1    4   7   1 CMD.exe
  0  0:00:00    0    0    647    0    668     2   70   7   3 OS2.exe
  0  2:10:54  120    0    490    0    512    10    8  24   6 OS2SRV.EXE
  0  0:00:00    0    0     60    0     88     0    0   8   1 os2ss.exe
  0 32:49:09  788    0 74827107  2    832     3   71   7   7 OS2.exe
  0  0:00:00    0    0    655    0    300     1    5   7   3 scm.exe
  0  0:00:00    0    0    491    0    300     1    4   8   4 psxss.exe
  0  0:01:31 1416    0  15437    0    624     2    7   7   3 WINFILE.EXE
  0  0:00:00   20    0   1224    0    276     9    4   7   4 AtSvc.Exe
  0  0:00:01  120    0    569    0    328     1    5   7   5 PRINTMAN.EXE
  0  0:00:00  844    0    233    0    224     1    5   9   1 CMD.exe
  0  0:00:27 1400    0    664    0    888     1   10   9   3 ntvdm.exe
  0  0:00:00  336   24    170   16    272     0    4  13   1 PMON.EXE
```

Fig. 10.9 PMON's output provides a glimpse of the resource usage at any point in time.

Fig. 10.10 Pviewer has a simple interface. Processes are shown in the top window and the threads for the selected process are shown in the lower window. Click on a new process to display its threads.

Killing a Process with Pview

1. Start Pviewer.
2. Select the process to kill from the top list box.
3. Click the Kill Process button.
4. Clicking the Memory button will provide lots of detail on the memory usage of the selected process.

Due to its simplicity, the syntax of PVIEWER is straightforward. If you have any questions, see the RKTOOLS.HLP file in the NT Resource Kit directory.

10.3.7.4 QSlice (NT Resource Kit)   Qslice is another of those magical tools included with the NT Resource Kit. Qslice takes a quick slice of the processes at very short intervals and displays the results using a handy bar graph. This tool looks like magic as the performance of your system unfolds before your eyes. Figure 10.11 shows the simple interface for QSlice.

This tool allows you to get a quick handle on your systems performance when you suspect a process is going nuts or taking over. Double-click a process and Qslice displays details on the threads for the process. What a great little tool!

10.3.8 SNMP Management

10.3.8.1 HP OpenView (Hewlett Packard)   HP OpenView is available in both Windows and UNIX versions. OpenView provides network diagramming capabilities and, most important, SNMP management tools. The Windows version does suffer the resource blues when running on Windows 3.x or Windows for Workgroups 3.x or lower. Running it on NT or Windows 95 should provide no resource problems.

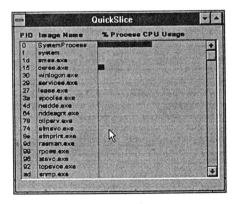

Fig. 10.11 Notice how the System Process stands out in this example. This screen shot was taken when the system was idle with almost no load.

The nicest feature of a tool like OpenView is the SNMP capability. SNMP gives you access to information about many different components on your network, including everything from NT Server to network devices such as routers and repeaters.

Add-on tools for many products allow you to actually manage the devices from OpenView. ChipCom has a product called On-Demand that integrates with OpenView and provides access directly to the ChipCom device. Using On-Demand, you can not only monitor devices but also set features on the device such as disabling a port.

10.3.9 Network Monitor (Microsoft)

How about a no-cost sniffer for your network? If you purchased either Microsoft Systems Management Server or Microsoft Back Office you have a neat one called Network Monitor.

Network Monitor performs a number of different tasks:

☞ Captures frames (packets) from the network.

☞ Captures frames remotely from an NT system and displays them on the local system.

☞ Displays and searches captured frames.

☞ Performs network loading by sending captured frames over the network.

☞ Displays summary statistics of network performance.

☞ Determines how many copies of Network Monitor are currently running.

☞ Sets filters to determine which nodes and types of frames are monitored.

☞ Sets display-only filters to restrict the display of captured data.

Figure 10.12 shows the main window of Network monitor.

Network Monitor must be used on a system that supports "promiscuous mode." Promiscuous mode is a state in which a network card detects all packets flowing over the network the card is attached to. This is what allows Network Monitor to capture frames from all systems on the network. Check the documentation for your network card if you are not sure if promiscuous mode is supported. The Network Monitor Capture window is shown in Figure 10.13.

This overview of Network Monitor is not meant to be an in-depth review but rather a glimpse of the product and how it can be used effectively in your network environment.

Network Monitor is useful if you spend the time to understand what normally happens on your network. This means understanding what type of traffic is normal, what a normal utilization looks like, and so forth. It is also useful to understand a little about what type of traffic is generated during certain operations.

For instance, if you know what happens when a Windows for Workgroups client performs a browse operation, you can quickly determine if a user is having a problem by looking for those types of packets from that workstation.

The Network Monitor Capture Summary window is shown in Figure 10.14.

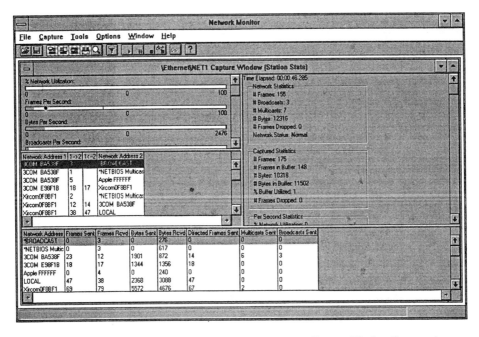

Fig. 10.12 Network Monitor from Systems Management Server. Notice the great overview provided by the main form.

Fig. 10.13 The Capture form shows all the frames captured by the Network Monitor.

Fig. 10.14 Capture form with the detail panes open. You can open the detail panes any time by double-clicking a frame. The detail panes are synchronized with the selected frame.

We have successfully used Network Monitor for a number of tasks in the first few months after installing it:

☞ Comparing the output of a home-grown SNMP monitor to that of OpenView for debugging.

☞ Monitoring network utilization during moves from VMS to client/server systems.

☞ Monitoring a PC that we thought had died while running a big task. Network Monitor showed us the I/O that was going on over the network proving the system was alive and well.

☞ Performing research on exactly what happens to Windows for Workgroups and NT during normal and simulated operations like browsing and logon.

10.3.9.1 Address Database Before you use Network Monitor very much, you should build an address database that allows Network Monitor to display the name used to identify the system instead of the hexadecimal address associated with a frame. Network Monitor can store the names in a database for later use.

Building an Address Database

1. Start Network Monitor.

2. Choose Start from the Capture menu. Allow Network Monitor to run for some time (5 minutes or more for example) to collect frames.

3. Choose Stop from the Capture menu.

4. Choose Find Friendly Names from the Capture menu.

5. Click the OK button.

6. Choose the Addresses option from the Capture menu.

7. Click the Save button to save the names.

This database can be loaded later when you build a capture filter. Figure 10.15 shows a filtered view of captured packets.

10.3.9.2 Using Network Monitor   The easiest way to use Network Monitor when you have a problem is to fire it from SMS. SMS can provide many different displays of workstation information including various queries sorted by user.

Starting Network Monitor to Trace a Single Workstation or Server

1. Start SMS Administrator.

2. Find the workstation or server you wish to monitor in a query or any displayed list.

3. Double-click the workstation or server to display Properties window.

4. Scroll down the Properties list until you come to the Network Monitor icon.

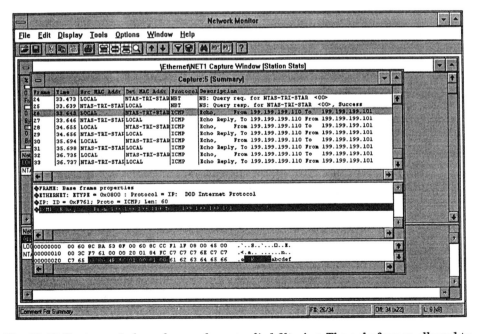

Fig. 10.15 Capture window when we have applied filtering. The only frames allowed to show must use the IP, TCP/IP, or SNMP protocols.

5. Click the Network Monitor icon.

6. Click Start Network Monitor.

7. Click the Start Capture button once Network Monitor starts.

Performing these steps allows you to quickly pin-point the traffic from a particular system. You can also start Network Monitor by itself and set the filter options manually. Setting the options manually provides the ability to monitor a selected group of systems at one time.

Network Monitor also adds two objects to the Performance Monitor database: Network Segment and Network Interface. These two objects contain a number of counters that provide detailed network statistics on various aspects of network performance. You should not use these counters for long periods of time on a server because when activated they place the network card into promiscuous mode. Promiscuous mode is not shut down until Performance Monitor exits resulting in reduced performance over the network card. Always use these counters from an NT workstation or a noncritical server.

10.4 TUNING SPECIFIC NT SUBSYSTEMS

10.4.1 Virtual Memory System

The NT Virtual Memory (VM) system uses a paging file(s) (PAGE-FILE.SYS) to augment the physical memory of a system. The paging file in effect extends the memory of the system by allowing NT to move objects from memory to disk when it requires the memory for other tasks. The paging system is very effective, but it is much slower than physical memory (RAM). The counters for the Memory object in Table 10.8 are useful for monitoring the paging system within NT.

Table 10.9 lists several objects for the Paging File object that are useful to monitor.

You should be able to improve the performance of an NT system by splitting your paging files over multiple disk drives. This is accomplished by creating multiple page files on different disks. This is a good option if your system has different disks attached to separate controllers or if the controller is able to process requests to each disk concurrently. Changes to the paging system are made in the Control Panel System applet.

Changing the Page File(s)

1. Start Control Panel.

2. Start the System applet.

3. Click the Virtual Memory button.

4. Choose the drive to create a paging file on.

5. Enter the size.

Table 10.8 Performance Monitor Memory Output Counters

Counter	Description
Commit Limit	Roughly the size of the physical memory of the system plus the paging file. The total is slightly less than the combination of these two because NT reserves a small amount of memory for itself.
Committed Bytes	The total amount of virtual memory committed at any point in time. When Committed Bytes approaches the Commit Limit, the system is running out of virtual memory and the paging file must be extended.
Pool Non-paged Bytes	Measures the amount of nonpaged memory in the system. When this value is greater than the physical memory of the system (4MB), the system will start thrashing, swapping memory back and forth to disk at a very fast rate. The only resolution to this problem is to add more physical memory to the system.
Pages Per Second	Measures the rate at which NT swaps memory to disk. The normal rate for this value is less than 5 pages per second. If the system begins to sustain a value of 10 or greater the system is thrashing. You can lower the paging rate by adding physical memory to the system.

Table 10.9 Performance Monitor Paging File Objects

Counter	Description
Percent Usage	Shows the current percentage of a page file in use. If this counter nears 100%, the system is running out of paging space, and the page file should be expanded. The page file should not be allowed to expand because it will become fragmented, and performance will really suffer.
Percent Peak Usage	Shows the peak percentage of a page files usage. If this counter nears 100%, the system is running out of paging space, and the page file should be expanded.

6. Click the Set button.

7. Repeat the process for each page file.

10.4.2 System Memory (RAM)

The shortest resource on most systems is RAM. This resource probably causes more grief than any other except for maybe disks. You should equip your servers with plenty of memory (32MB or more). In 1995 prices you can add 32MB to your system for approximately $800. This is a small price to pay for the benefits it will bring in performance. I suggest that any server with more than ten users should have 32MB or more of RAM.

You should be aware of one quirk with some Intel systems. Some systems use the memory above 16MB for caching parts of system ROM to improve performance. For instance, my Tri-Star system caches the ROM BIOS in the memory above 16MB. To install more than 16MB you may need to disable caching of certain parts of the ROM in your system. Consult the technical manual for your system and/or the technical support department of your hardware vendor to determine how your system is set up.

ROM and BIOS caching should be turned off on all NT systems. NT does not use the BIOS for disk and screen operations like DOS. Turning off caching will free up memory that NT can use.

You can use WINMSD.EXE to monitor memory usage. The Memory display contains several bits of summary information on both physical memory, paged memory, and the paging files. It also includes the Memory Load Index in the status bar at the bottom of the Memory window. The Memory Load Index provides an indication of memory utilization: 0 is no memory use and 100 is full memory use.

Many servers that I have been implementing since late 1994 have used from 64MB to 640MB of RAM. This increase in RAM makes lots of sense because of its low cost and greatly improves the performance of the system. Table 10.10 shows two useful memory counters. Notice that the second counter is only for SQL servers.

You can come up with a fair approximation of additional memory requirements by using the Paging File: % Usage Max counter. This counter shows the amount of expansion the page file has incurred. The following formula uses this counter to determine how much memory to add to satisfy the memory demands to date.

New Memory = "Paging File: % Usage MAX * Page File Size

For example,

"Paging File: % Usage MAX = 20

Page File Size = 200MB

New Memory = 200 * 20

This example shows that we should add 40MB of memory to this server.

This very general approach should be used only as a starting point. Consider how application uses memory, when during the day memory is used (if only one application runs at 2:00 p.m. each day and consumes all the memory, move it to after hours), and any other parameters that may affect memory usage.

Table 10.10 Performance Monitor Counters for Selected Memory Options

Counter	Description
Memory: Available Bytes	Displays the amount of free physical memory. A reading that stays less than 1MB on NT Server indicates paging is occurring.
SQL Server: CacheHit Ratio	Displays how well the SQL Server cache is performing. If this counter is less than 80–90%, then adding more memory may improve the performance of SQL Server.

You should also consider increasing the secondary cache size any time that you add memory. Adding memory without increasing the secondary cache size could degrade processor performance because the hit rate from secondary cache would go down with more memory and the processor would be busier. This is a good example of why it is important to consider other factors instead of the most obvious before making drastic changes.

10.4.3 Balancing the System Loading

The performance of the system should be balanced between network resources and responsiveness of the system for interactive users. I would suggest setting the Tasking property to Foreground and Background Applications Equally Responsive for most NT Server systems because the heaviest use of the system probably comes from network resource usage, which will be running as background tasks.

You can access the Tasking box dialog from the System applet in Control Panel, as shown in Figure 10.16.

Configuring Priority Settings

1. Start the Systems applet in Control Panel.
2. Click the Tasking button.
3. Click the Tasking option for your system.
4. Click OK.

The second step in balancing the system loading is to determine how your system is used. Table 10.11 shows the settings for the Memory Optimization dialog box for the Server in Network applet.

Configuring Server Memory Usage

1. Start the Network applet in Control Panel.
2. Double-click the Server in the Network Software and Adapter Cards box.
3. Click the Optimization option for your system.
4. Click OK.

Fig. 10.16 The Tasking dialog box controls how NT sets priority for different types of applications.

Table 10.11 Memory Optimization Dialog Box Settings

Setting	Type of Server Usage
Minimize Memory Used	Interactive with minor file and print server usage (up to 10 network users).
Balance	General usage with some file and print server usage (up to 64 network users).
Maximize Throughput for File Sharing	File and print server (greater than 64 network users). This is the default setting for NT Server.
Maximize Throughput for Network Applications	Primary Application Server and some File and Print server usage (64 or more network users). Application access to memory has priority over file cache access. Use this option for systems primarily running SQL Server, Systems Management Server, and Exchange Server.

10.4.4 Network Performance

When your system seems to be experiencing performance problems, you can take several steps. The NT network system provides quite a number of counters that track various aspects of performance. It is always important to remember when tuning or troubleshooting a network that not only the network counters must be monitored but also the counters involving the server because the two are inseparable. Table 10.12 contains a set of objects that are good candidates for a network settings file. These objects track both network settings and several settings for the server that impact the network. Use Performance Monitor and/or Network Monitor to check the areas shown in Table 10.12.

Table 10.12 Potential Problem Areas

Area to Check	Suggest Solution
Server workload	If the server workload is different on multiple servers, consider redistributing the load over all the servers.
Paging	If a system is paging at a high rate, it is probably running out of physical memory. The only solution is to change the load on the system or to add more memory.
Disk saturation	Disk saturation can result from many causes including adding too many users or intensive applications reading and writing to an already heavily used disk. The normal resolution to this problem is to get a faster disk/controller or spread the application over several disks. Implementing a RAID 5 disk subsystem is an ideal candidate for this type of environment.
Network saturation	Network saturation occurs when your system has reached the capacity of the network or network card(s) in the system. The solution is to switch to a faster card or network system or to split the network. Splitting the network involves creating several physical networks with routers or adding additional network cards to the system and splitting the network across the additional cards.

There are a tremendous number of counters available for network-related functions. Table 10.13 lists several counters that you should monitor.

There are a number of ways that you can improve network performance. Many of these are covered in other parts of this book but are mentioned briefly here for completeness.

☞ Match network controllers to the fastest bus on your system. Use PCI or EISA controllers instead of ISA. This should improve a high interrupt/second reading.

☞ Add memory to relieve Pool Paged Failures and Pool Nonpaged Failures.

☞ Use faster network cards in the server. New technologies such as the 3Com Parallel Tasking controller tend to off-load the CPU in servers.

Table 10.13 Performance Monitor Counters for Network-Related Functions

Object Name	Short Description	Description
NetBEUI: Bytes Total/second	Number of bytes per second sent and received over the NetBEUI interface.	This counter indicates when network traffic is high. This counter includes only data bytes that were sent or received. Overhead for the protocol is not counted.
TCP/IP: Bytes Total/second		This counter is the same as the last one except that it is for the TCP/IP interface.
Server: Bytes Total/second	Total bytes per second for the server.	A steadily increasing value indicates an increasing load on the server.
Work Item Shortages	How many shortages of work item storage space is occurring.	An increasing value indicates that the server is overloaded and does not have enough SMB storage space, indicating a bottleneck at the server service.
Context Block Queue Time	How long a server request must wait in the server before it is processed.	This counter is one of the best parameters to use to detect a busy server. Watch for this value to increase as client load increases. If it averages greater than 50 (msec), it indicates the server service is the bottleneck.
Context Blocks Queued/second	Rate at which context blocks must be placed on the queue.	It should increase as more client traffic changes and the context block queue time goes up.
Pool Paged Failures and Pool Nonpaged Failures	How often NT ran out of page and nonpaged memory.	Any value greater than 0 normally indicates a shortage of physical memory.
System: Total Interrupts/second	Total number of interrupts that occurred on the processor per second.	When this value is high for a given system, the processor may be heading toward saturation.

☞ Faster networks such as 100BaseT and FDDI can relieve network bottle-
    necks. Make sure that you match your network segments to use fast net-
    work technologies on the same segment.

☞ Network switches can provide high performance on the same network by
    providing dedicated segments to users and servers.

☞ If transport (NetBEUI, TCP/IP): Bytes Total/second approaches the maxi-
    mum transfer rate for your network, it indicates a saturation of that net-
    work segment. The saturation point is usually much less than the rated
    throughput for the network. Ethernet is reputed to max out at around
    1.2MB/sec, even though Ethernet is rated at 10MB/sec. When you think
    that the network is approaching the saturation point, you can segment the
    network using a router, multiple network cards in the server, or a network
    switch. You can also combine some of these methods.

Network Monitor (included with SMS) provides a number of additional statistics for Performance Monitor and lots of additional features from its own interface. Network monitor is described more fully on page 324. Let's look at some
things we may want to do with the results of inquiries with Network Monitor.

☞ Sort the Network Monitor Broadcasts Multicasts column in the Station
    Statistics pane (the bottom pane) to find the source of a broadcast storm.
    Rates of over 100 per second should be investigated. If the source is a PC,
    replace the network card. If the source is a router, check out the features
    for tuning the router.

☞ Monitor % Network Utilization for increasing trends. When this counter
    starts approaching 40% or higher, the network will most likely start slow-
    ing down significantly. Using faster media (cable), network cards,
    switches, and combining routers can improve network performance dra-
    matically.

10.4.5 CPU

The question is "How do you tune a system to improve CPU performance?"
This question traditionally has been the all-time question for networks. Most
networks do not place a tremendous load on the CPU because they are offering
mainly file and print services. NT can place much more stress on the CPU
because of the wide variety of tasks NT can perform.

Most of the tuning options for improving or removing a CPU bottleneck
require some investigation and a common sense approach. If you have developed
your network with solid and upgradeable servers, used multiple servers to
spread the network load, and have some control over your applications, you are
in good shape for this type of approach. Table 10.14 contains notes on several
counters that should be monitored to try to determine what is causing the load
on the CPU.

After checking these counters, you can do a number of things to improve the
CPU utilization of your system.

Table 10.14 Performance Monitor Counters for Determining CPU Loads

Object Name	Short Description	Description
Processor: % Processor Time	% of time that a processor is performing useful work.	When this counter approaches 100%, you may be experiencing a processor bottleneck. The next step is to determine "what" or "who" is causing the problem.
Processor: Interrupts/second	Number of device interrupts per second.	When this counter hits 1000 or over, you should check the efficiency of hardware I/O devices (disk controllers, network cards, any other system devices).
System: System Calls/second	Number of calls to NT system service routines per second.	If Processor: Interrupts/second is greater than System: Calls/second, a hardware device may be triggering the excessive interrupts.

☞ If a hardware device is generating excessive interrupts, upgrade the device, use a PCI network or disk controller instead of an ISA device, or use an intelligent communications controller.

☞ Add an additional processor to the system with the bottleneck. This option is especially helpful for application servers or any system that has multiple threads contributing to the bottleneck.

☞ Upgrade the secondary cache.

☞ Use PVIEW to lower the priority of a process. Use the START command to execute an application and add one of the priority options: /low, /normal, or /high.

10.4.6 Disk Subsystems

The disk subsystems in network servers have traditionally presented a bottleneck at one point or another. Faster systems and faster disk devices have alleviated this problem to some degree, but the disk system is still one of the most important elements of any server.

The Physical Disk object is the primary indicator for monitoring disk activity. Table 10.15 contains several counters and notes that should be routinely evaluated on all servers.

Table 10.15 Performance Monitor Counters for Routine Evaluation

Object Name	Short Description	Description
Physical Disk: % Disk Time	% of time the disk is busy.	A reading near 100% indicates a physical disk as the bottleneck.
Physical Disk: Disk Queue Length	Number of pending disk I/O requests.	A number greater than 2 indicates that requests for disk services are backing up.

You can do quite a number of things to improve disk performance:

☞ Spread the disk load over multiple disks. Place the NT boot partition and the paging file(s) on different disks. Place user data on separate disks or a stripe set.

☞ Use NTFS instead of FAT or HPFS.

☞ Choose new disk drives with the lowest possible seek time.

☞ Match disk controllers to the fastest bus on your system. Use PCI or EISA controllers instead of ISA.

☞ Use a defragmentation utility (such as Disk Keeper) to reduce disk fragmentation.

☞ Disable short-file-name generation on NTFS partitions.

☞ Use a RAID 5 hardware controller for data disks. The more drives the better.

☞ Use mirrored or duplexed disks if you are not using the ATDISK driver and your disk controller can perform asynchronous I/O. NT performs alternating reads on mirrored and duplexed disks to improve performance.

☞ Add memory to improve cache performance.

☞ Upgrade to a faster controller. Fast SCSI-2 (10MB/sec throughput), SCSI-2 (5MB/sec), ESDI (3MB/sec), IDE (2.5MB/sec).

Security

11.1 SECURITY CONCEPTS

NT security was designed into the system from the beginning. The target for the NT security system was to obtain a C-2 rating. The security system is very thorough and applies to all objects in the system. The security controls of NT even carry to objects such as accessing pixels on the screen during a screen copy.

This chapter delves into the NT security system and related matters and provides some useful suggestions on how to use the security system in a manner appropriate for your network. What is appropriate depends entirely upon your environment and requirements. Most networks require use of only the standard NT user account and password system in combination with setting permissions on certain objects. This type of network is the focus of this chapter. If your system requires very strict security requirements such as a C-2 rating, you should take the concepts from this chapter, thoroughly read and understand the NT Resource Kit for version 3.5 sections on security (Chapter 2), and consult other information resources on how to apply your knowledge to your network.

11.2 OVERVIEW

11.2.1 Validation of Logons

A logon process validates every logon request from a user to an NT server. The local logon process manages interactive logons through the system console, including display of the initial logon dialog box.

A remote logon process similarly handles validation of users that request a logon over the network.

Once a user is logged on, if any logon script is specified for the user, it is executed.

Users can access resources on an NT server when they are not logged into a domain. This logon is accomplished by simply connecting to the server resource from File Manager or another application and specifying a correct user name and password when prompted. Any logon script that is assigned to an account *is not executed* when connections are made in this manner. Standard NT permissions still apply to all access to an NT resource and prevent access to a resource from an unauthorized user.

11.2.2 Security Account Manager

The Security Account Manager maintains the user accounts database. This database contains all information for user accounts and groups. The database is stored in the SAM and SAM.LOG files in the \WINNT35\SYSTEM32\CONFIG directory.

SAM not only maintains the user accounts database, but it also provides user validation services when requested by the Local Security Authority.

11.2.3 Security and RAS

The primary way to dial into an NT Server or NT network is to use the Remote Access Service. RAS is covered in detail in Chapter 3 (see page 144). The security impact of RAS access to the network is consistent with the general security of NT.

Before a user gets access to the network with RAS, the user must be validated. All user passwords and the authentication procedure are encrypted before they are sent over a phone line. This protects access to the network from snooping without a proper validation of the user account and password.

Once the user has accessed RAS server, their access can be further managed using standard NT tools and RAS tools. Table 11.1 lists several ways to control RAS access and provides a short description and the tools necessary to perform the task.

11.2.4 Access to Server Administrative Functions

For starters, only NT systems can fully administrate other NT or NT Server systems. Some applications and application environments are exceptions to this rule. SQL Server for instance comes with utilities for administrating the SQL Server system from MS-DOS systems. NT Server also includes 16-bit tools mentioned earlier for managing certain parts of NT.

You should consider removing utilities such as RegEdt32 from NT systems that are not authorized to maintain NT servers and workstations. You can also prevent access to the utilities if they are located on an NTFS volume by denying access to all users except administrators.

Table 11.1 Remote Access Server Security Access Controls

Type of Access	Tool	Description
Network	Network Applet	Network access can be enabled or restricted by binding the protocols that allow access to the network to the appropriate adapter. For instance, if TCP/IP is bound to an adapter, the RAS users can access all services that can be accessed through TCP/IP. This setting is global for all users.
All Access	RAS Administrator	You can disable or enable access through RAS by starting the RAS Administrator and choosing the proper option from the Computer menu. To temporarily stop RAS, select Pause from the Computer menu.
Callback	RAS Administrator	Setting the callback parameters for a user triggers RAS to dial the user back after the user has been authenticated. The callback number can be set by the administrator or the user can be prompted to enter the callback phone number. The default is no callback.
User Access	RAS Administrator	Access for each user must be set using the RAS Administrator program. This program allows you to enable or disable access by account and configure callback for a particular account.

11.2.5 Permissions

Permissions are used by NT to control everything from file and print services to entries in the NT Registry. Permissions are activated in the application that controls the object. For instance, permissions that control access to files are set in File Manager. Print Manager sets permissions for print services, and RegEdt32 sets permissions for Registry entries.

NT sets permissions on files and directories for NTFS volumes only. FAT and HPFS file systems do not support the NT security scheme for files and directories. You can, however, set permissions on shares for these file systems, as well as NTFS file systems. SFM supports security because you must use NTFS for Macintosh volumes.

The NTFS file system uses a concept called an Access Control List (ACL) to manage permissions on an object. The ACL is attached to an object when you first define a permission on the object. Each time you change or add a new permission on the object, an entry called an Access Control Entry (ACE) is added in the ACL for the object. The ACE identifies the type of permission and the user or group ID assigned the permission.

When a user tries to access an object, NT reads the ACL for the object to determine the user's access. NT makes only one pass through the list and stops when it reaches the end of the list or reads an ACE with "deny access" as the permission. Deny access overrides all other permissions on an object. All other NTFS permissions are cumulative for access to an object. For instance, if a user has certain permissions granted directly and other permissions granted through a group the user belongs to, the permissions accumulate giving the user the total of his individual and group permissions. The only exception is "deny access," which overrides all other permissions, denying the user access to the object.

Files are "owned" by users. The user who owns a file can grant or deny access to the object as he/she pleases. Permissions can be placed on an NTFS object by the owner of the object. A user with administrator rights can take ownership of an object and then give others rights to the object, but an audit trail is created for all changes if auditing is turned on for the object.

You can also protect system functions on an NT system such as setting the system time, shutting down the system, and formatting the hard disk using User Rights.

11.2.6 Securing NT System Files

Because NT supports permissions only on NTFS volumes, you should create your boot partition on an NTFS volume. Using an NTFS volume for the boot partition means that you can use the NT security system to protect important files such as those in the Registry. An NTFS boot partition also means no one can boot the system with a DOS floppy disk and gain access to any NT files. You should review the Server Management section (see page 23) for concerns on providing backups and alternate boot methods for NT systems using an NTFS partition for the boot drive because you will not be able to access the NT system files from DOS if the system fails to boot NT.

RISC systems are a bit of a problem because you can't make the boot partition anything but a FAT partition. This problem is somewhat simplified because you can't boot a RISC system from a floppy DOS drive and the only way you can get to a FAT partition on the RISC system is from NT or possibly from a DOS emulator running under UNIX. You can and should make the FAT partition around 6MB and place the NT system files on an NTFS disk drive.

11.2.7 Securing Floppy Disk Drives on a Server

If your NT system is not locked inside a room, you may need to use Floppy Lock from the NT Resource Kit to restrict access. This program allows you to lock the floppy drive to prevent someone other than an administrator from using it.

When you install the Floppy Lock service on a system, make sure the path name on the INSTSRV command includes the complete path to the file including the file name.

Installing Floppy Lock

1. Copy the Floppy Lock program (FLOPLOCK.EXE) to a hard disk.
2. Execute the following command:

```
INSTSRV FloppyLocker D:\RESKIT35\FLOPLOCK.EXE
```

You can change the name FloppyLocker to any descriptive name of your choosing, as long as it is a legal name for a service.

Once Floppy Lock is installed, you must configure the service to start automatically.

Configuring the Floppy Lock Service

1. Start the Services applet in Control Panel.
2. Select the FloppyLocker service and click Configure.
3. Enter the account name for the service to use (such as an account in the Administrator group) and the password for the account.
4. Reboot the system.

Once you have performed the installation and configuration steps, the floppy drive(s) on the server are locked to everyone except for an administrator. Note that this procedure works only as long as NT is running. If your system can be rebooted with another operating system (DOS or UNIX), someone may be able to obtain access to the system. A user gaining access in this manner will still not be able to access any files if you are using NTFS. The user could conceivably reinstall NT and gain access to the files unless the files are protected using NTFS security.

Floppy Lock can be disabled by stopping the service with Server Manager or Control Panel. Once Floppy Lock is disabled, the floppy drives work normally until the system reboots. To remove Floppy Lock permanently, set the Floppy Lock service to disabled.

11.2.8 File Deletions

NT does not support recovering deleted files on any of its disk partitions (NTFS, FAT, and HPFS). This restriction is a direct result of the C2 security features of NT because under C2 the ability to recover a deleted file is considered a security breach. Third-party utilities and other tools are also restricted from recovering files.

11.2.9 Computer Accounts

NT and NT Server systems that belong to a domain must have an account for the computer on the domain. Computer accounts are usually created automatically by NT or NT Server during the installation process. Server Manager can be used to view, add, or delete a computer account.

Passwords for the computer accounts are changed regularly by the Net Logon service. The password change occurs on both the PDC and a workstation or server at the same time to keep the passwords in sync. The passwords must match on the domain and the workstation to allow a successful logon into the domain from the workstation.

Before reinstalling NT Server or Workstation, delete the computer account for the domain using Server Manager before beginning the reinstallation.

11.3 DOMAINS AND TRUST ACCOUNTS

Domains can ensure that users have only one account to log on from anywhere in the enterprise. The trusted domain concept facilitates managing the accounts because a user from one domain can access resources on another. This concept can also cause security problems because an administrator of a domain can give anyone access to a trusting domain by adding the user to a group that has permission to access resources on the trusting domain. The permissions can be granted explicitly to the group or the group can be added to a local group, either of which has the same effect of opening up access to the domain.

11.4 GUEST ACCOUNTS

NT Workstation systems have a default Guest account enabled at installation. NT Server installs a Guest account but flags the account as disabled by default. Enabling the account allows unrestricted access to resources available to the account unless the account is protected with a password. Guest accounts should be used with care as many hackers normally look for Guest accounts on target systems. Leaving the Guest account disabled prevents any access through the account.

Integrating NT with some other networks such as Pathworks 5.x may require the use of a Guest account. In these environments make sure that you tightly control the services accessible through the account.

11.5 AUDITING

NT can audit certain resources, events, and users. The auditing facility provides a powerful tool for monitoring and administering a system. This tool is especially useful on systems that have tight security requirements or have problem users who tinker where they shouldn't. Auditing is also useful when used judiciously to monitor your system and make sure that the things you have put in place are working as they should. For instance, you may want to monitor system startup and shutdown requests to make sure that no one but administrators are performing this task.

Auditing is turned on in User Manager. Specific resources are set to be audited using either File Manager or Print Manager.

11.6 RIGHTS

User rights are one of the ultimate controlling mechanisms of NT. User rights work by giving the user the right or ability to perform a task. For instance, accessing a system over the network is a right that is by default assigned to the groups Administrators and Everyone, allowing all users to access the system over the network. Conversely, the right to log on to the server locally (via the system console) is given only to the Account Operators, Administrators, Backup Operators, Print Operators, and Server Operators groups, preventing everyone who is not in one of these groups from logging on from the system console. These two examples of user rights illustrate how powerful the concept can be for controlling the system. This example also illustrates how NT automatically sets the defaults for rights to certain groups, thus setting up standard account control from a standard installation.

User rights are divided into two categories:

☞ normal user rights such as logging on over the network or performing backups and

☞ advanced user rights such as allowing a user to act as part of the operating system or debug programs.

Modifying User Rights

1. Start User Manager.
2. Select the User Rights option from the Policies menu
3. Select the Right to modify from the drop-down list. Click the Show Advanced User Rights check box to add advanced user rights to the list.
4. Add or remove users to the right by clicking the Add or Remove button.
5. Close the dialog box by clicking OK.

You may have guessed by now that user rights are a powerful tool. Table 11.2 provides a quick list of some rights that you may want to change to restrict access to a specific server.

Careful management of your user rights can ease your security management task.

11.7 SNMP AND SECURITY

Simple Network Management Protocol opens up access to certain parameters of NT to any system that can talk using the SNMP protocol, including almost any system that runs TCP/IP because of the widespread availability of SNMP tools and management systems.

You can control access to NT over SNMP by shutting off access to certain group names called Communities. NT can also restrict access over SNMP by IP address, effectively shutting down SNMP management except from certain host systems.

Controlling SNMP Access

1. Start the Network applet in Control Panel.
2. Double-click SNMP service in the Installed Network Software list.
3. Click the Security button.

Table 11.2 Useful Rights to Change to Restrict Access

Type of Restriction	User Right to Modify and Default Group(s)
Prevent access to a system over the network	**Access this computer from network.** Granted to administrators and everyone by default.
Perform backups	**Back up files and directories right.** Granted to administrators, backup operators, and server operators by default.
Perform restores of files and directories	**Restore files and directories.** Granted to administrators, backup operators, and server operators by default.
Boost process priorities	**Increase scheduling priority.** Granted to administrators by default.
Perform a remote shutdown	**Force shutdown from a remote system.** Granted to administrators and server operators by default.
Log on as a service	**Log on as a service.** Granted to none by default. This SMS service is granted this right during installation.
Traverse directory trees	**Bypass traverse checking.** Granted to everyone by default. This right allows a user to move around in directory trees and is granted by default to everyone. Denying this right to a user stops a user from moving from the current directory.
Prevent manipulation of the Audit and Security log	**Manage auditing and security log.** Granted to administrators by default.
Take ownership of files and objects	**Take ownership of files or other objects.** Granted to administrators by default.

4. Enter any community names to restrict access from in the top box. Enter the allowable IP addresses in the lower box. Be sure to delete the Public community name as this is the default used by most systems.

5. Close the Network applet.

11.8 PASSWORDS

NT Server and NT Workstation store both an NT and LAN Manager version of a password for user accounts. The LAN Manager passwords are not case-sensitive, whereas the NT passwords are. Both SFM and RAS always use the LAN Manager version of the password.

NT's Password validation is case-sensitive with a couple of exceptions. Case-sensitivity works as long as the machine you are trying to access and the one you are accessing from are both NT machines. If the machine you are accessing from is not running NT, then passwords become case-insensitive.

This validation is further complicated if you use a non-NT machine to change your password with the NET PASSWORD command. Once the password has been changed from the non-NT system, the password is treated as case-insensitive from that point on.

11.8.1 Password Tips

Passwords are trouble. Have you ever noticed how many passwords the average user has to contend with today? One or more for their bank account, one for the garage door, one for the security system, one for the network, another for the mini-computer or mainframe, and another for the mail system. Is it any wonder that users complain when system managers ask them to have another password or two or maybe three.

Passwords are best used like many other things in life: Keep them simple. Many systems today use passwords that change every 30 or 90 days and must be of a certain length. Many systems also allow you to force the user to use a password he or she hasn't used in the last X months. NT works with all of these schemes, but using them may complicate the users' lives to the point that they blow your whole security scheme by writing down their passwords or coming up with a scheme that is easy to figure out.

A user can change to a blank password at any time even if password history is turned on and he or she used a blank password before. This occurs because NT does not store blank passwords in the history file. You can work around this by specifying a minimum password length of one or more characters in the Password Policy.

NT does not cache passwords for persistent connections to share-level services as Windows for Workgroups does. This means that NT prompts you for each password-protected connection to a share-level service when you log on.

Windows for Workgroups clients and their cousins such as the Workgroup Add-On for MS-DOS and the MS Client share a potential hole into the network. When a user enters a blank password for a password list and that user is the default user for the system, the user is logged on when the system boots. This approach is convenient, but problem-laden. If the user has logged in to a domain and the password for the domain account is cached in the password list (PWL), the user will be logged in next time with no prompting. This is a useful feature for systems such as a DOS box used to run EXTERNAL for Microsoft Mail, but it can be a real headache for any other type of interactive account. Make sure that you use the configuration utility for Windows for Workgroups (ADMINCFG, page 228) to prevent blank passwords.

11.8.2 Changing Passwords

There are several ways to change passwords on a domain. You can accomplish this from Windows for Workgroups by using the network applet in Control

Panel, clicking the Startup button, and then clicking the Password button to display the dialog box in Figure 11.1.

Changing your password via the password button on the initial dialog box of the Network applet changes only the password for the password list for your user name, not the domain.

I have created a change password program for Windows for Workgroups in Visual Basic that calls both the Windows for Workgroups and domain password dialog boxes. The program uses these two API calls:

```
i = I_ChangePassword(Me.hWnd)
i = I_ChangeCachePassword(Me.hWnd)
```

I_ChangePassword changes the domain password, whereas I_ChangeCachePassword changes the Windows for Workgroups password list (.PWL) password. Of course you must use the Declare statement to define the calls before they can be used. These two functions and lots of others are defined in the Windows for Workgroups Software Development Kit (SDK). The NT and Windows 95 SDKs define Win32 functions within the Windows 32 API.

Passwords can be changed using tools within NT when you log on interactively or use one of the NT tools over the network. User Manager can be used to change your own or anyone else's password. Simply select the user and access the Properties dialog box.

The Windows NT Security dialog box provides a Change Password button that can also be used. Simply press Ctrl+Alt+Del and then click the Change Password button.

11.9 LOGON RESTRICTIONS

11.9.1 Warning Messages at Logon

You can create a special caption and notice for a special dialog box that is displayed before users log on after they press the Crtl+Alt+Del key sequence. These values are entered via RegEdit32 in LegalNoticeCaption and LegalNoticeText located under the key:

```
SOFTWARE\MicrosoftWindow NT\Currnet version\Winlogon
```

Fig. 11.1 Change Domain Password dialog box from the Network applet in Windows for Workgroups 3.11, simplifying access for users to change their password on the domain.

11.9.2 Restricting Access to Certain Programs

You should restrict access to programs on both the servers and workstations on your network that you do not want users to have access to. User Manager is a good example of such a program. A user who can access User Manager but is not a power user or administrator can still create a mess on the network by entering new local groups and user accounts. Even though the user could not add any permissions to the user accounts, they would still clutter up the account database and cause confusion for your managers.

The easiest way to restrict a user's access is by not letting them know the program is there. Place programs that everyone should not have in Personal Program Manager groups for administrators or lock up access to the servers. Remember also to protect the Windows 3.x versions, although these programs are not quite as destructive because they require the user to enter the administrator password as the program runs.

11.10 AUTOMATIC NT LOGOFF

The NT Resource Kit includes the WINEXIT.SCR program, which is an automatic logoff screen saver. When the time-out period expires and the screen saver starts, the user has a limited number of seconds to prevent the system from logging them off.

WinExit is a handy tool for secure environments or anytime you need a little extra caution for NT workstation or server systems. Servers that are not in locked rooms or sensitive users' NT workstations are good examples of places where this tool is handy.

Installing the Logoff (WinExit) Screen Saver

1. Copy the WINEXIT.SCR file from the resource kit directory to the \WINNT35\SYSTEM32 directory.
2. Start the Desktop applet in Control Panel.
3. In the Screen Saver list, choose the Logoff Screen Saver option. The NT Resource Kit documentation incorrectly shows the name as Windows Exit. In future versions, either the name or the documentation could change.
4. Set the delay time value in the delay box.
5. Click the Setup button.
6. Force Logoff setting: Checking this box causes the screen saver to shut down all applications without giving the user the opportunity to save any unsaved data. This box must be set to cause a totally unrestricted logoff, but it can cause a loss of data if users do not save frequently. Use caution.
7. Enter the delay time before the user is logged off in the Time To Logoff box. This is the actual amount of time in seconds the user has to cancel a logoff when the screen saver starts. Values can be between 0 and 999 seconds.
8. Enter the message to display for the Logoff dialog box in the Logoff Message box. The message can be up to 255 characters.

9. Test the screen saver

This is another of those little tools that brings mainframe power to the desktop and server. Remember the time function on most larger systems that forces a user out after a certain period of inactivity?

When the Logoff screen saver activates, it will beep and display its Logoff dialog box with the countdown timer until the value reaches 0. When the timer reaches 0, the logoff process is initiated.

The user can abort the logoff by moving the mouse over the dialog box or pressing any key.

11.11 USING PROFILES FOR RESTRICTING USERS

User profiles are handy for restricting users that log on from NT systems. A profile can restrict users to certain groups and not others, disable commands in Program Manager, and set other privileges for the user. Profiles can be established as defaults for new users and can be specified on a per user or group basis. For instance, everyone in a certain department could have one profile while another department would have another profile. Chapter 4 (see page 174) contains more information on how to set up and manage profiles.

You should also explore the use of profiles with Windows 95. The profiles allow you to easily control access to workstation features for different users regardless of where they log on.

11.12 STARTING A SCREEN SAVER BEFORE LOGON

NT can start a screen saver before a user logs in. This feature hides the logon prompt but can be used for amusement. You can also use it to show the name of the server in the banner of the screen saver. Displaying the server name on the screen saver is nice if you have a bank of servers or use a switch to move the monitor/keyboard/mouse across systems. In this way, whenever the switch changes systems, the monitor displays the server name using the screen server whether or not a user is logged on.

Configuring NT to Start a Screen Saver Before a User Logs On

1. Run RegEdit32.

2. Select HKEY_USERS.

3. Select the key \DEFAULT\Control Panel\Desktop.

4. Select ScreenSaveActive.

5. Choose String from the Edit menu.

6. Enter the value 1 and click OK.

7. Select SCRNSAVE.EXE from the parameter list.

8. Choose String from the Edit menu.

9. Enter the name of the desired screen saver (BLACK16.SCR, LOGON.SCR, SS3DFO.SCR, SSBEZIER.SCR, SSMYST.SCR, SSMARQUE.SCR, SSPIPES.SCR, OR SSTARS.SCR).

10. Select ScreenSaveTimeOut from the parameter list.

11. Choose String from the Edit menu.

12. Enter the time-out value before the screen saver starts.

These changes take effect the next time you reboot NT. When a user fails to log on within the time-out of the screen saver, the screen saver starts.

11.13 FILE AND PRINT RESOURCE PERMISSIONS

11.13.1 Finding a User's Permissions with PERMS.EXE (ResKit)

There should be a way to check on the permissions assigned to an individual or group for a directory or file. Thankfully there are a couple of ways to accomplish this using File Manager or PERMS (included with the NT Resource Kit). File Manager is the easiest to use for normal operations because of the standard point-and-click interface. PERMS is useful when you wish to execute a command from the command line or a batch file. It is also useful to capture the permissions to a file for later use. For instance, you could create a batch file that checked permissions on a number of directories or files and collect them in a file.

PERMS.EXE can be used to display a user's access permissions for one or more files. PERMS.EXE can be used on the local system or against a remote system. You can also specify wildcards for the path. PERMS has the following format:

```
PERMS [domainname\|computername\]username path [/i] [/s]
```

domain	Specifies the domain to check. Defaults to the current domain if a domain name is not specified.
computername	Specifies the computer name for a remote system. Defaults to the current system if no computer name is specified.
username	Specifies the user name to check.
path	The wildcard characters * and ? are supported.
/i	Assumes that the specified user is logged on locally at the system the check is to be performed on. /I causes PERMS to treat the user as a member of the Interactive group, not the Network group, which is the default.
/s	This switch displays permissions on files within all subdirectories. The /s switch is useful for displaying the permissions for an entire directory tree.

The PERMS command is ideal for a maintenance utility to check security for all users. Using the NET USER, you can obtain a list of all users. Using VB or another programming language, you could read the output of NET USERS and then construct a batch file to run PERMS selectively for each user, looking at the root directory and all subdirectories of each disk on the server. Taking the output of all the PERMS commands and combining them into one file gives you a list of all permissions on all directories for all users. Sort the file in different manners, and you have a nice security database for research.

11.14 HIDDEN SHARES

NT systems automatically create a hidden administrative share for every drive on an NT system. The share name is the drive letter plus a $, such as C$. These shares can be connected to only by users with administrative access or backup operator access.

You can use a dollar sign ($) as the last character in the share name to create a hidden share. Users can connect to the share but will not see the share name using the browse features of any system browsing the network. This technique works on Windows for Workgroups, Windows 95, NT, NT Server, and the Workgroup Add-On for MS-DOS systems. As you may have guessed, any Microsoft network that can share resources can hide them from browsing by adding a $ to the end of the name. Don't forget that you can create a hidden share for a printer such as the one loaded with invoices or checks.

11.15 CLIENT SECURITY ISSUES

11.15.1 Windows for Workgroups

11.15.1.1 NTLogon (by CTI) and AdminCFG   Security on Windows for Workgroups clients can be tightened up with the NTLogon program from Computer Technologies, Inc. NTLogon (see page 180) adds more security to Windows for Workgroups systems by taking control of a workstation when Windows starts. This tool locks up the Windows for Workgroups system by displaying only the Logon dialog box when the system boots or a user logs out. The user must successfully log on to the network before he or she can gain access to the network. This precaution prevents the user from accessing the workstation without a valid username/password. NTLogon also works with FloatBar (also from CTI) to control the user's access to programs such as Program Manager, Print Manager, Control Panel, and virtually anything else. Programs can be controlled on a user-by-user basis, making systems management much easier.

The logon routine also kills all persistent shares and connects the user explicitly to shares specified for the user by a USER.INI file on their network account (personal share). More information is available on page 180.

ADMINCFG is another tool that can tighten security on a Windows for Workgroups system. ADMINCFG can set parameters for passwords and control shares. This program uses a security file that cannot be manipulated by the user.

Support is also provided for maintaining the file on a network share. See page 228 for more details.

11.15.2 Windows 95

Windows 95 is the second secure desktop system of the WOSA family, following NT Workstation. Windows 95 includes pass-through security, which takes the user name and password information from the client logon process and performs the validation on the network server. With pass-through security, the user is trapped at the Logon dialog box until he or she successfully logs on to the network. This type of security denies them access to any system resources on either the desktop, network, or server.

Pass-through security has another big benefit because it uses the server user name and password. When pass-through security is used with user-level security, access to your local shares on a Windows 95 system are also validated using the network user names and passwords. This centralization of the security database is a great management enhancement for network managers.

Pass-through security is automatically enabled when you choose to participate in either a Windows NT or NetWare network during installation.

Windows 95 also includes user-level security, which provides the controls for a systems manager to make sure that unauthorized users do not have access to a system or make changes to setup information. Managers can also control resources available to specific users from a server. User-level security can also work in conjunction with pass-through security. User-level security must be explicitly enabled because share-level security is enabled by default during installation.

Windows 95 includes a Registry database that is similar to the NT Registry. The Registry houses most of the information that we normally have seen in INI and other setup files on Windows 3.x networks. The Registry provides a secure storage center that cannot be accessed with a simple editor.

Windows 95 includes a version of RegEdit (REGEDIT.EXE) that must be used to manually change the Registry. RegEdit can access the local Registry or the Registry of a remote system.

Listing of Products and Companies Mentioned

A.1 AMERICAN POWER CONVERSION

American Power Conversion (APC) produces a wide variety of products for managing and monitoring power issues and computer systems. The following are a few of their current products:

>Power Chute Plus software for NT
>Measure-UPS
>Call-UPS
>Share-UPS
>Smart-UPS
>Back-UPS
>Matrix-UPS
>APC can be reached at
>>132 Fairgrounds Road
>>P.O. Box 278
>>West Kingston, RI 02892
>>800-800-4APC
>>401-789-3180 fax

A.2 ARCADA SYSTEMS

Arcada produces Backup Exec and AutoLoader for Backup Exec. These tools are designed to automate backup tasks in an NT environment.

Arcada can be reached at
Arcada Software
37 Skyline Drive, Suite 1101
Lake Mary, FL 32746
1-800-3ARCADA

A.3 CARDINAL BUSINESS MEDIA

Cardinal Business Media (CBM) publishes a wide range of books on computer systems and topics. This includes Ken Spencer's books:

The Complete Guide to Pathworks

A Practical Guide to Windows NT

Windows 95 — due in late 1994/early 1995

CBM can be reached at 215-643-8000.

A.4 COMPUTER TECHNOLOGIES, INC.

Computer Technologies, Inc. (CTI) is a Microsoft solutions provider and Digital Equipment reseller that specializes in enterprise systems, client/server development, and Windows platforms (NT, NT Server, Windows 3.x, 4.x, WinPad, and Visual Basic/Visual C++). CTI also provides design, implementation, and support for NT network and systems.

CTI has also developed numerous tools that are used during a migration/downsizing project. For instance, we can automatically move an Rdb database structure to Access/SQL Server, or take a PowerHouse data dictionary and move it to Access/SQL Server.

Ken Spencer is a principal of CTI.

CTI also produces the following products:

FloatBar is a toolbar for Windows 3.x and Windows 95, including network hooks for administrators.

CTIWatch monitors resources usage on Windows 3.x.

CTIInfo displays information on various system options on Windows 3.x and Windows 95.

NTLogon is the automatic logon and security control program for Windows for Workgroups 3.11.

CTI can be reached at
> P.O. Box 8927
> Greensboro, NC 27419-0927
> 910-547-1407

A.5 DigiBoard

DigiBoard produces a wide line of fast serial and other communication products. You can reach them at 800-344-4273.

A.6 Consensys Corporation

Consensys makes the ChiliPorts high-speed communication products for NT and the new SMTP Mail product for NT and Microsoft Mail. You can reach them at 905-940-2900.

A.7 Black Box

Black Box provides all types of cable and network products, including switching products for multiple servers using one CRT/keyboard/mouse.
> Black Box can be reached at
> P.O. Box 12800
> Pittsburgh, PA 15241
> 412-746-5500

A.8 Digital Equipment Corporation

Digital has a number of products for NT:

Pathworks for NT

X-Windows products

Alpha servers

Digital can be reached at 800-DIGITAL.

A.9 Executive Software

Executive Software markets several NT products, including Diskeeper for NT and Diskeeper for NT Server.
> Executive Software can be reached at 800-829-4357.

A.10 INTERGRAPH

Intergraph has released a number of NT products, including products for

> NFS connectivity
>
> X-Windows
>
> Workstations and servers
>
> Intergraph can be reached at 205-730-6112.

A.11 MICROSOFT

Microsoft provides Windows NT, Windows for Workgroups, Windows 95, Systems Management Server, and so forth.
> Microsoft can be reached at 800-426-9400.

A.12 NETMANAGE

NetManage has released NFS products for NT.

> NetManage can be reached at 408-973-7171.

A.13 NETWORK TECHNOLOGIES

Network Technologies provides a number of switching and network products. They make great switches for RGB-type monitors such as those used on Alpha and other RISC systems.
> Network Technologies can be reached at 800-RGB-TECH.

A.14 OCTOPUS TECHNOLOGIES

Octopus for Windows NT provides System Fault Tolerance (SFT) to NT systems.
> Octopus Technologies can be reached at 215-822-8075.

A.15 PRENTICE HALL TECHNICAL REFERENCE

Prentice Hall Technical Reference (PTR) is a division of Prentice Hall and is the publisher of the Managing the Enterprise with Microsoft BackOffice series which includes:

> *NT Server: Management and Control* (this book)
>
> *Systems Management Server*

SQL Server

Exchange Server

Prentice Hall can be reached at
   Prentice Hall—PTR
   Upper Saddle River, NJ 07458

Glossary of Terms and Definitions

Account Domain	A domain that exists for the purpose of managing the user account and security database for a number of other domains. See Chapter 3.
API	Application Programming Interface. An API is provided by many vendors for an interface into applications. NT and Windows 95 support the Win32 API, while Windows 3.1 and 3.11 support the Win16 API. Other APIs such as MAPI are available for products such as mail or various applications.
ARC menu	Menu system used on RISC systems to change system parameters.
BDC	Backup Domain Controller. A BDC is used for an NT server that maintains a copy of the account and security database.
Cairo	Code name used for NT 4.0, NT 96, or something close.
Chicago	Code name used for Windows 95.
Complete Trust Domain	A domain model that specifies how domains are managed. See Chapter 3.
Daytona	Code name used for NT 3.5.

DCD	Data Carrier Detect. A DCD is used to indicate when a line condition exists between a modem or other serial device and the computer.
DCE	Data Communications Equipment (modems, etc.).
DHCP	Dynamic Host Configuration Protocol. DHCP is an RFC (1533, 1534, 1541, 1542) for a TCP/IP management protocol. Microsoft has included tools for managing both TCP/IP clients and servers in Windows 95, NT, and the Windows for Workgroups (via the new TCP/IP drivers).
Directory	A container for other directories or files.
DLC	Data Link Control. DLC is a protocol used to communicate with IBM mainframes and printers such as the Laserjet 4si that attach directly to the network.
DMI	Desktop Management Interface. DMI is the proposed management interface from the Desktop Management Task Force.
DNS	Domain Name Service. A DNS translates computer names to IP addresses for TCP/IP networks.
Domain	A grouping of NT servers and other servers in a network.
Domain Database	The user account and security database for a domain.
DTE	Data Terminal Equipment.
DTR	Data Terminal Ready. A DTR indicates when a line condition exists between a modem or other serial device and the computer. The DTR line is used to signal a particular condition such as the telephone line has been hung up.
EISA	Extended Industry Standard Architecture. An EISA defines the successor bus for the PC to replace the original ISA bus.
Environment Variable	A named memory location that is accessible from programs or DOS batch programs. A typical example is TEMP, which usually contains the location for temporary files.
Folder	A directory that is accessible from Macintosh clients in Services for Macintosh.
FTP	File Transfer Protocol. An FTP provides a method to transfer files from one system to another. NT includes an FTP program.

Gateway	A system (computer or dedicated device) that moves data from one network to another.
Global Group	A group that is accessible across domains. Global groups can be included in local groups.
Home Directory	A directory that serves as the users default logon directory and primary location for the users files.
Host	A network node in the UNIX or TCP/IP world. For instance, a PC and a server are both considered a host.
Internet	The virtual network of interconnected systems around the world. An internet is also a network segment on a TCP/IP network.
IP Address	An address used to uniquely identify every TCP/IP network and node.
IPC	Inter-Process Communication. IPC defines a communication process between two processes.
IPX/SPX	The Internetwork Packet Exchange protocol, which is standard on Novell NetWare networks.
ISDN	Integrated Services Digital Network. ISDN is a newer telephone technology that has been slowly growing in popularity since the mid-1980s. It can provide speed and access advantages as it becomes available in more locations.
JBOD	Just a bunch of disks. Traditional disk configuration.
Local Group	Local groups are the groups created on an NT or NT Server. Local groups cannot be used by trusted domains (see Global Groups).
LPC	Local Procedure Call. LPC is a localized method of RPC used by NT in many of its programs. It is at its simplest one program calling routines in another program in the same system.
LSAPI	Licensing Services API. LSAPI provides routines for controlling software licensing.
MAPI	Messaging Application Programming Interface. MAPI is the Microsoft interface into its messaging and mail systems.
Master Domain	A domain model that specifies how domains are managed. See Chapter 3.
MDI	Multiple Document Interface. MDI provides the ability for an application to have multiple windows contained within a master parent window. When the child windows are minimized, they become icons at the bottom of the parent.

Multiple Master Domain	A domain model that specifies how domains are managed. See Chapter 3.
MUP	Multiple UNC Provider. MUP is a component of the NT network subsystem.
Named Pipes	A system interface that programs use to communicate between different systems.
Name Server	A computer running DNS.
NBF	NetBEUI protocol driver for NT.
NBT	NetBIOS over TCP/IP. This module provides NetBIOS naming over TCP/IP for interpretability with systems and applications using NetBIOS.
NCP	NetWare Core Protocol. NetWare uses NCP. It runs over NWLINK in an NT environment.
NDIS	Network Device Interface Specification.
NetBEUI	NetBIOS Extended User Interface. NetBEUI is the transport protocol used by Microsoft and other networks.
NetBIOS	Network Basic Input Output System. NetBIOS has been in use by many networks for quite a while. See NetBEUI and NBF.
NIC	Network Interface Card.
NT	Short name for Windows NT.
NTFS	NT File System. The NTFS is new with NT and NT Server. It includes support for long file names, transaction logging, directory and file security, and other new features.
NTS	Short name for NT Server.
NWCS	NetWare Compatible Service. NWCS runs over NWLINK and provides NT workstations and servers with NetWare client functionality for attaching to NetWare servers.
NWLINK	The NetWare Link transport protocol is Microsoft's NDIS compliant version of IPX/SPX.
Object	Anything that can be thought of as a single entity such as a file, printer, or Registry entry.
OpenView	A network management package from Hewlett-Packard.
PCI	Peripheral Component Interconnect. PCI defines a new bus architecture for systems. It was developed by Intel.
PDC	Primary Domain Controller. PDC is the NT Server that maintains the master copy of the account and security database.

PPP	Point to Point Protocol. PPP is used to transmit packets over serial lines.
Profile	A profile tracks the personal configuration information for a particular user. The profile editor can be used to create profiles for single users or groups of users and control the user changes to configuration data and other options.
Protocol	A protocol defines the rules of how a network device such as a server or workstation will communicate with other network devices. Examples are TCP/IP and IPX/SPX.
RAID	Redundant Array of Inexpensive Disk. RAID defines a range of disk management and striping techniques.
RAS	Remote Access Server. RAS provides remote access to NT networks.
Registry	The NT database that holds configuration, user, and security information for the system. The Registry files are normally located in the \WINNT35 \SYSTEM32\CONFIG directory.
Router	A system (computer or dedicated device) that moves traffic from network to another. A router is an intelligent device that can make decisions about what packets it moves from one network to another.
RPC	Remote Process Communication between two or more processes and Remote Procedure Call of subprograms. RPC is mainly used when a program on one system calls a subroutine in a program on another system over the network.
SAM	Security Accounts Manager. SAM is the manager of all the security stuff in NT and NT Server.
Server	Any system in a network that provides (serves) services to other systems on the network. This can be an NT Server or an NT desktop system that shares files or simply a print server that manages a few printers.
SID	Security ID. SID is a unique ID created by NT for every user account that logs on to an NT system.
SFM	Services for Macintosh that run under NT Server.
SFT	System Fault Tolerance. SFT is a technique for shadowing a server, thus making the server immune to a single point of failure. SFT is not supported under NT—yet.
SLED	Single Large Expensive Disk.

SLIP	Serial Line Internet Protocol. SLIP is used to transmit packets over serial lines.
SMB	Server Message Block. SMB is a high-level protocol used when two Microsoft systems communicate over a network. SMB commands are imbedded in transport protocols such as TCP/IP or NetBEUI.
SMS	Systems Management Server. SMS is the network management software from Microsoft.
SNMP	System Network Management Protocol. SNMP was defined by OSF and is part of the broad ranging management system for both servers, workstations, and active network components like routers and bridges.
Sockets	A method of network communications that are more portable than Named Pipes or Mail Slots. NT supports them over TCP/IP only.
SQL	Structured Query Language. SQL is a standard tool for accessing a relational database.
TCP/IP	Transmission Control Protocol/Internet Protocol. TCP/IP is a transport protocol that was developed by the Defense Advanced Research Projects Agency in the 1970s.
TDI	Transport Device Interface. The TDI is used by the LAN Manager service to talk to the network protocols.
Trusted Domain	A domain that is allowed by another domain to access resources on that domain.
Trusting Domain	A domain that allows another domain to access resources on its network.
UNC	Universal Naming Convention or Uniform Naming Convention. UNC defines the format for a consistent network connection to a shared resource.
User Account	A users access to NT. Each user account is assigned a unique user name and user ID.
User Profiles	Profiles that store information and restrictions about user accounts.
Volume	A disk volume (partition) in Services for Macintosh.
Volume Password	A password that is assigned to a Macintosh volume when it is created.
WFWSYS.CFG	Security configuration file for Windows for Workgroups 3.11.
WINMSD	The Windows NT version of the Microsoft Diagnostic utility.

WINS	Windows Internetwork Naming Service. WINS maintains the name database for a Windows NT TCP/IP network.
WinSockets	A network programming interface that allows systems to communicate with other systems.
WNet	Windows Network Interface functions stored in the MRP.DLL.
WOSA	Windows Open Services Architecture. The WOSA, which is from Microsoft, defines how operating systems, networks, databases, electronic mail, and applications interface.

Contacting the Author

I can be contacted at Computer Technologies, Inc., via the following address:

Computer Technologies, Inc.
P.O. Box 8927
Greensboro, NC 27419–0927
910–547–1407
910–632–8924 FAX
71551,2724 CompuServe

A

B

C